LIBRARIES AND INFORMATION IN THE ARAB WORLD

**Recent Titles in
Bibliographies and Indexes in Library and Information Science**

English-Language Dictionaries, 1604–1900
Robert Keating O'Neill, compiler

Government Information: Education and Research, 1928–1986
John Richardson, Jr.

Library and Information Science in China: An Annotated Bibliography
Karen T. Wei, compiler

Children's Services in the American Public Library: A Selected Bibliography
Fannette H. Thomas, compiler

Research Guide to Libraries and Archives in the Low Countries
Martha L. Brogan, compiler

Catalog of Dictionaries, Word Books, and Philological Texts, 1440-1900: Inventory of the Cordell Collection, Indiana State University
David E. Vancil, compiler

Guides to Archives and Manuscript Collections in the United States: An Annotated Bibliography
Donald L. DeWitt, compiler

The Academic Library of the 90s: An Annotated Bibliography
Rashelle S. Karp

The Internet and Library Information Services: Issues, Trends, and Annotated Bibliography, 1994–1995
Lewis-Guodo Liu

Articles Describing Archives and Manuscript Collections in the United States: An Annotated Bibliography
Donald L. DeWitt, compiler

LIBRARIES AND INFORMATION IN THE ARAB WORLD

An Annotated Bibliography

Compiled by
Lokman I. Meho and Mona A. Nsouli

Bibliographies and Indexes in Library
and Information Science, Number 12

GREENWOOD PRESS
Westport, Connecticut • London

Library of Congress Cataloging-in-Publication Data

Meho, Lokman I., 1968–
  Libraries and information in the Arab world : an annotated bibliography / compiled by Lokman I. Meho and Mona A. Nsouli.
    p.   cm.—(Bibliographies and indexes in library and information science, ISSN 0742–6879 ; no. 12)
  Includes indexes.
  ISBN 0–313–31098–X (alk. paper)
  1. Library science—Arab countries—Bibliography.   I. Nsouli, Mona A.   II. Title.   III. Series.
Z666.M44   1999
016.020′917′4927—dc21   99–10850

British Library Cataloguing in Publication Data is available.

Copyright © 1999 by Lokman I. Meho and Mona A. Nsouli

All rights reserved. No portion of this book may be reproduced, by any process or technique, without the express written consent of the publisher.

Library of Congress Catalog Card Number: 99–10850
ISBN: 0–313–31098–X
ISSN: 0742–6879

First published in 1999

Greenwood Press, 88 Post Road West, Westport, CT 06881
An imprint of Greenwood Publishing Group, Inc.
www.greenwood.com

Printed in the United States of America

The paper used in this book complies with the Permanent Paper Standard issued by the National Information Standards Organization (Z39.48–1984).

10 9 8 7 6 5 4 3 2 1

To our families and special friends

CONTENTS

PREFACE	ix
INTRODUCTION - Mona A. Nsouli	1
THE BIBLIOGRAPHY	9
General Works	9
Arabian Gulf	83
Algeria	93
Bahrain	99
Djibouti	103
Egypt	105
Iraq	127
Jordan	135
Kuwait	157
Lebanon	169
Libya	173
Mauritania	177
Morocco	179
Oman	187

Palestine	**191**
Qatar	**197**
Saudi Arabia	**201**
Somalia	**257**
Sudan	**261**
Syria	**269**
Tunisia	**275**
United Arab Emirates	**283**
Yemen	**287**
AUTHOR INDEX	**289**
TITLE INDEX	**299**
SUBJECT INDEX	**331**

PREFACE

The idea behind this bibliography developed out of a search for materials on libraries in Palestine and on national libraries in the Arab world. While looking for information on these two topics, several problems ensued, including lack of comprehensive and current specialized bibliographies, lack of comprehensive and specialized regional indexing and abstracting services, ill-coverage of Arab-related Library and Information Science (LIS) literature in international LIS databases, and the necessity to use many databases and various search strategies to ensure a comprehensive coverage of the published material. Needless to say, not all researchers have access to a wide variety of databases nor many of them have enough time and resources or even knowledge to locate their scattered information. It is hoped that this bibliography will greatly assist these researchers in their seeking for needed information and make their search process less frustrating and cheaper.

This comprehensive bibliography aims to fill a major gap in the coverage of world librarianship and library and information science. It is intended as a comprehensive guide to published works on libraries and information centers of all types in the Arab world.[1] Librarians, information specialists, library and information science students, educators and researchers, government information policy makers, and many others will find this bibliography as an indispensable guide for any research in the field. Over 1,000 items are included in this bibliography ranging from books, scholarly and professional journal articles, and chapters in books to doctoral dissertations, conference papers, and expert reports. Items included are mainly in Arabic, English, and French, but a few German, Swedish, Danish, Finnish, and Italian items are included too, all covering the period between 1977 and 1998. The year 1977 was selected as a start date in order to continue earlier works and avoid

---

[1] The countries covered include: Algeria, Bahrain, Djibouti, Egypt, Iraq, Jordan, Kuwait, Lebanon, Libya, Mauritania, Morocco, Oman, Qatar, Palestine, Saudi Arabia, Somalia, Sudan, Syria, Tunisia, United Arab Emirates, and Yemen.

duplicating them.[2] Researchers who wish to locate sources published before 1977 should consult these earlier works, as well as the bibliographies listed in this present work. Users of the present bibliography may find some topics (e.g., copyright issues and ethics) or countries (e.g., Djibouti, Mauritania, Somalia, and Yemen) underrepresented. This was beyond the compilers' control; fewer studies have been published on these topics and countries.

Non-Arabic titles have been gleaned from many sources, including all the major LIS and LIS-related databases (e.g., *Library and Information Science Abstracts*, *Library Literature*, *ERIC*, *Information Science Abstracts*, and *INSPEC*), *Dissertations Abstracts International*, and *Social Sciences Citation Index*, along with the Library of Congress catalog. Arabic titles were derived from browsing several major Arabic LIS periodicals[3] and from searching the available Arabic general periodical indexes (e.g., *al-Fihrist*), as well as library catalogs. For both Arabic and non-Arabic materials, the reference collections of several libraries were manually browsed and the bibliographies of many items included in the present bibliography, particularly doctoral dissertations and research papers, were scanned to locate additional sources. The majority of the items included in this work were located at the library of the School of Information and Library Science at the University of North Carolina at Chapel Hill, the library of the Institute for Palestine Studies (Beirut, Lebanon), and Jafet Library of the American University of Beirut (Lebanon). The libraries of the School of Library and Information Science at North Carolina Central University and Duke University libraries were also used.

To make the bibliography easier to use, the items included are divided into sections. After a general section and one on Arabian Gulf region, a section was included for each country. In addition, items within each section are classified according to broad subject headings and arranged alphabetically by author name. Because many titles cover more than one country or topic, users are encouraged to consult the more comprehensive subject index provided at the end of the bibliography. More specific topics could be located through this index. Also provided, is an author index, a title index, and a brief chapter introducing the history and development of libraries and information technology in the Arab world from the earliest times to the present.

The annotations of the items are primarily 50-250 words long and come from various sources. When an original abstract is provided by an item, the abstract was taken as is or summarized and adopted for our records; these are referenced as 'A' for author. It was believed that the authors of the items are the

---

[2] Mohammed Fathi Abdel-Hadi, *al-Dalil al-Bibliyughrafi lil-Intaj al-Fikri al-'Arabi fi Majal al-Ma'lumat, 1976-1980* (Tunis: Jami'at al-Duwal al-'Arabiyah, al-Munazzamah al-'Arabiyah lil-Tarbiyah wa al-Thaqafah wa al-'Ulum, Idarat al-Tawthiq wa al-Ma'lumat, 1983); Veronica S. Pantelidis, *The Arab World: Libraries and Librarianship, 1960-1976: A Bibliography* (London: Mansell, 1979).

[3] For example, *'Alam al-Kitab*, *'Alam al-Kutub*, *al-Jadid fi 'Alam al-Kutub wa al-Maktabat*, *al-Majallah al-'Arabiyah lil-Ma'lumat*, *Maktabat al-Idarah*, *AL-Mustaqbal al-'Arabi*, *Risalat al-Maktabah*.

PREFACE

best candidates to excellently describe their own works. Items that did not have abstracts were read and eventually got summarized. Items that we could not get our hands on were kept without annotations. A few annotations were taken from *Library and Information Science Abstracts*; these are referenced as 'LISA'.

While compiling this bibliography, we received plenty of moral support from our families and special friends. We owe them a debt of gratitude which we feel honored to acknowledge. We also wish to thank the institutions which offered us the opportunity to use their resources to bring this project into its current state. These institutions include the School of Information and Library Science at the University of North Carolina at Chapel Hill, the Institute for Palestine Studies, the School of Library and Information Science at North Carolina Central University, the American University of Beirut, and Duke University.

LIBRARIES AND INFORMATION IN THE ARAB WORLD

INTRODUCTION

Mona A. Nsouli

Books and libraries have been accorded the greatest interest in the Islamic world. With the rise of Islam in the late sixth century, libraries began to flourish and contribute to the development of world civilization. In the early Muslim era, the library consisted only of one book: *The Koran*. Eventually, mosques became meeting places for discussion and the center of religious and educational life: People used to gather in the mosques, after the prayers, to listen to parts of the Koran and ask questions, while scholars ('Ulamas) stayed in the mosques to explain the message of the Koran. In the first century after Muhammad's death, accounts of the prophet and the wars he fought were kept by memorization. The necessity was felt to collect these records and write them down. The first publications were Ibn Ishaq's (d. 768) *Sirah* (Life of Muhammad) and Ibn Hisham's (d. 834) *Sirat Rasul Allah* (Life of Muhammad). As more books were published, the need to establish institutions to collect, arrange, and preserve these valuable historical accounts was greatly felt. As a result, many libraries were built, particularly in the mosques or as appendages to the mosques. The development of mosque libraries was a major phenomenon of Islamic civilization. Scholars, caliphs, and sultans donated their private libraries to the mosques of their cities to make their books accessible to the public. Authors too, donated copies of their works.

Muslim caliphs gave considerable attention to books and libraries. In the late 7th century and first half of the 8th century, some princes of the Umayyad dynasty collected, copied, and translated many Greek manuscripts into Arabic. Both these literary activities and the introduction of paper had great impacts on the intellectual activity of the Islamic peoples. Tens of libraries were built (e.g., the public library founded in Damascus by prince Khalid Ibn Yazid—ca 700). In addition, the largest cities of the Islam—Damascus first, and then Baghdad, Cairo, Tunis and Fez—became the centers of learning and housed great collections of manuscripts and books covering the Islamic disciplines, jurisprudence, history, astronomy, grammar, biography, medicine, law, and literature.

During the Abbasid dynasty (8th to 12th century), Baghdad became the center of intellectual activities in the Islamic world. In this period, Arab libraries reached what is described as its golden age. Baghdad, for example, was abounded with private and public libraries. The most famous public library in it, *Bait al-Hikma*, was founded by the Abbasid Caliph, al-Ma'mun, in the 9th century. It survived under different names until the 12th century when it was overshadowed by the *Nizamiyah* college (founded in the 11th century). During the 11th and 12th centuries, Egypt took on more prominence and became the second center of intellectual activities in the Islamic world. The first library in Cairo was founded in 988 A.D. by the Fatimid Caliph, al-Aziz Billah and was attached to *al-Azhar* Mosque. In 1004, another important institution was established: *Bait al-Hikmah*, which was attached by *Dar al-'Ilm*, the greatest public library in the Islamic world then.

Private libraries were also predominant in early Islam. They were owned by *sultans*, *wazirs*, and scholars and had rich collections of books in all branches of knowledge which they opened to the public. Specialized libraries were also found in the mosques and other information centers, with collections of medical books, books on astronomy, mathematics, and so on. In Tunisia, for instance, Ibn al-Jazzar was reported to have owned a private medical library in al-Qairawan. Among the finest private libraries, one can name that of al-Baiqani, in Baghdad (1033 AD), whose collection consisted of rare manuscripts.

With the establishment of educational centers in the mid-Abbasid era, mosque libraries of the early Muslim period began to develop into *Madaris* (plural of *Madrasah*—Islamic seminary college) and university libraries. Al-Qadi al-Fadhil, one of Salah al-Din's *wazirs*, founded the Fadiliyah Madrasah in Egypt (late twelfth century) with a library attached to it. The Nizamiyah college, a theological *madrasah*, was established in Baghdad (1064) with a very valuable library. The Mustansiriyah college was built in Baghdad in 1228 and its library possessed rare and valuable works in various subjects.

Under the Ottomans (15-20th centuries), mosque-universities continued to prosper and develop into important learning centers (e.g., al-Aqsa, al-Azhar, al-Zaytuna, al-Qarawiyin, and the mosques of Mecca and Medina) and almost every Ottoman sultan established new *madrasah* with libraries attached to them. Libraries with rare collections of manuscripts were established too, like *al-Khizana al-Mahmadiya*, endowed by Sultan Mahmud II (18th century).

With the French occupation of Egypt between 1798 and 1801, a new era in the history and development of modern libraries in the Middle East started. The French expedition by Bonaparte had a great impact in the establishment of many educational institutions beginning with the French themselves and then by other Western societies. To mention a few, the French founded Institut d'Egypte, which existed for a brief time; the Roman Catholic orders in Cairo and Damascus founded important institutes with their libraries covering a wide range of knowledge; and the American Protestant denominations founded Robert College in Istanbul (1863) and the Syrian Protestant College in Beirut (1866). The missionaries established the Université Saint-Joseph in Beirut (1881), the Gordon Memorial College in Khartoum (1902) and the American

University of Cairo (1919). All of these institutions had important libraries attached to them let alone the separate public libraries that were established here and there in Alexandria, Baghdad, Beirut, Cairo, Damascus, Jerusalem and Tunis.

During the same time, many Arab universities were also founded and Arab notables established numerous valuable public and family libraries. Palestinian, Ragheb al-Khalidi, and Egyptian, Ahmad Taymur Pasha, were known for striving to preserve the culture of their own countries through the collection of manuscripts. The creation of the first national libraries in the 19th century marked the development of modern librarianship in the area. Algeria's national library, Bibliothèque nationale d'Alger, was established in 1835 on the initiative of the civil administrator of the Regency of Algiers, Genty de Bussy. Egypt's national library (formerly the Khedieval Library) was established in 1870 and was integrated in 1971 to the National Archives and the National Publishing House to form the General Egyptian Book Organization. In Syria, and as a result of the Arab national movement, the Medical Bureau—which became later on the University of Damascus Library—was established in 1903. Lebanon's National Library was opened in 1922 as a result of the personal initiative of Viscount Philippe de Tarazi. Morocco's National Library was established in 1926. Handwritten books and religious collections formed the first nucleus of the national libraries' collections. Besides local efforts, the major powers also established outstanding libraries and information centers in a great number of Arab countries; for example, British Council libraries were opened in Cairo (1938), Aden (1941), Jerusalem (1944), Beirut (1945), and Damascus (1948), and the first United States Information Service library was opened in Beirut in 1946.

With the development of the printing presses in the 1950s, the preservation of the national culture became one of the main concerns of Arab countries. The importance of education was stressed and the number of schools, universities, and libraries of all types—school, academic, public, special and national—began to develop. True, the development of libraries in the North African countries did not take place until after their independence in the 1960s, and it is still in its early stages of development in certain countries (e.g., Djibouti, Somalia, Mauritania)' the library system in Arab countries, in general, has been steadily improving and greater attention has been given to raise the standard of library services there. Nowadays, the major Arab libraries are located in Egypt, Iraq, Jordan, Lebanon, and Saudi Arabia.

Very few countries have public libraries with adequate collections, services, or physical facilities. However, although they leave much to be desired, public libraries are still the most popular type of libraries in the Arab world because they serve all citizens and are located all over the country. Among the most important public libraries, one can cite the Amman Public Library which houses a special collection for the blind, the Abdel-Hamid Shouman Public Library and Information Center in Amman which makes an extensive use of modern information technologies, and the King Abdul Aziz Public Library in Riyadh. Bookmobile services are also provided to remote villages and nomadic tribes, especially in Egypt, Jordan, and Syria in an attempt to reduce illiteracy.

Academic libraries are considered as the most developed among all types of libraries in the Arab world in terms of their collection, buildings, staff, equipment, and services, especially those located in Iraq, Jordan, Lebanon, Saudi Arabia, and Tunisia. Some of these libraries, however, suffer from some kind of duplication of work because they have one central library and separate library facilities for men and women (e.g., Saudi Arabia). Other libraries suffer from inadequate budgets and lack of coordination between librarians, faculty, and administration. Library collections vary in size and most of them are deficient in up-to-date scholarly literature.

National libraries—also called *al-Maktaba Wataniya*, or *Dar al-Kutub al-Wataniya*, or *al-Khizana al-Wataniya*—are still inexistant in some countries like Palestine, Djibouti and Oman. In Kuwait, Libya, Sudan, and Yemen, other libraries perform the functions of the national library, while the national libraries of Abu Dhabi, Bahrain, Egypt, Mauritania, Morocco, Qatar, Saudi Arabia, Syria, and the United Arab Emirates act also as public libraries. In Lebanon and Somalia, the national libraries are not functioning. Not all national libraries compile a regular bibliography which is essential to keep a complete record of the intellectual heritage of a nation. Indeed, published national bibliographies suffer from inadequacy in coverage and irregularity in publication. This is mainly due to a lack of an efficient method in compiling the bibliographies. Important and serious attempts have been undertaken in some countries. In Lebanon, for example, MERS (Middle East for Research & Studies), a specialized institution in the field of information technology, documentation, indexing and automation, published the 1995 Lebanese National Bibliography and a comprehensive list of dissertations on CD-ROM. However, the project was discontinued later on because of lack of funds.

There is minimal attempt to develop union catalogues, though important progress has been made, especially in the Gulf countries. In 1976, the National Scientific and Technical Information Center (NSTIC) of the Kuwait Institute for Scientific Research developed a project for the publication of a union list of scientific and technical periodicals in Kuwait covering 13 universities. Later, NSTIC included periodical holdings from major libraries in the Gulf and a regional union list was published. In 1983, the regional union list was published in a COM format (computer output on microfilm). The invasion of Kuwait interrupted the whole project. The King Abdul Aziz City of Science and Technology has developed an automated database of science and technology literature pertaining to Saudi Arabia or produced by Saudi nationals. Important achievements are also reported in Tunis and Morocco. None of the national libraries can claim to fully implement the legal deposit law of their own countries, and, generally speaking, the collection of material pertaining to their country is not a comprehensive one.

In general, the condition of school libraries is lamentable. They are underdeveloped and neglected. A great number of schools do not have library services at all or the services there are severly ineffective. Most libraries are managed by school teachers, the collections are outdated, and no clear policy for developing the collections is available. Unlike school libraries, the number of children's libraries is very restricted but are well developed, have good collections, and offer many activities for children, especially in Iraq and Jordan.

INTRODUCTION

As for special libraries, almost every ministry, governmental agency, firm, bank, and institution in the Arab world has established its own library or documentation center to serve the needs of its clientèle. Some of them provide services of a high standard which represent a modern thinking in special librarianship and information services. Among these services are indexing and abstracting, special bibliographies, current awareness services, etc. A brief list would include the libraries of the Institute of Public Administration (Egypt), The Royal Scientific Society (Jordan), The Documentation and Information Section of the Kuwait Insitute of Scientific Research (Kuwait), The Institute for Palestine Studies (Lebanon), The King Abdul Aziz City for Science and Technology (Saudi Arabia), The Tunisian National Documentation Centre, and the Agricultural National Documentation Center (Tunisia). The control of Arabic medical literature and the publication of specialist bibliographies (e.g. The Saudi Medical Bibliography) are developments that should be emphasized.

Library associations are very effective in Egypt, Iraq and Jordan where they play leading roles in their country's national movement, whether in terms of training librarians and information specialists, or in terms of developing systems, libraries, and publishing.

Library automation is a recent development in the Arab world. Today, international communication networks are available in many regional libraries and more and more computers are used in the libraries and information centers there. While library softwares are mainly imported, some countries have developed in-house packages. A large number of libraries in Egypt, Iraq, Jordan, Morocco, Palestine, Sudan, Saudi Arabia, and Tunisia have found the MINISIS software to be sufficient for their present needs. A member of the ISIS (Individual Service Information System), the MINISIS and its micro version CDS/ISIS were arabized by the Arab League Documentation Centre (ALDOC) in the late 1980s. They were made available to developing countries through the financial support of UNESCO and the UNDP. MINISIS is known for supporting Arabic scripts material.

Major libraries in the Gulf countries have acquired sophisticated systems. The King Fahd University of Petroleum and Minerals is working for the installment of an Arabic version of the Dobis-Libis in an integrated form. The Main Library of the Sultan Qaboos University is fully automated using the Dobis-Libis integrated system. In Lebanon, the Library of the Institute for Palestine Studies and the libraries at the American University of Beirut have automated their libraries very recently using the OLIB system.

In the mid-1980s, ALDOC, founded by the UNDP through UNESCO, attempted to establish an Arab information network, ARISNET (Arab Information System Network) to promote and support the development of information systems as a basis for technical cooperation and development among the Arab countries. This attempt failed along with the plan for the exchange of bibliographic and non-bibliographic information via ARABSAT (Arab Satellite Communications Organization). Many countries in the region are involved in networking and important developments have been achieved, especially in the Gulf Region and North Africa (Tunisia and Algeria). The Gulfnet, an online information database, is just one example.

Recently, many libraries in the Arab world have acquired databases on CD-ROM. Direct online access to databases (such as MEDLINE, DIALOG, etc.) is available in a number of libraries–especially those specializing in science, technology and medicine. The first online connection from a country in the Arab world to an international network was made in 1975 by the National Documentation Centre at Rabat which was linked to ESANET. It was followed in 1978 by the National Information Centre for Science and Technology of the Kuwait Institute for Scientific Research which was linked to DIALOG. These attempts were followed by Egypt (DIALOG) and Lebanon (Medline). However, the use of information networks is still facing problems because of high costs of linking, expensive rates for searching via international networks, and lack of technical support.

Both ALDOC and UNESCO have provided many countries of the Arab world with expert advice in many areas of library science. They have both promoted library, documentation, and information services between Arab countries, offering training courses and expert meetings in order to strengthen the development and coordination of libraries at a regional level. The UNESCO book coupons have facilitated the acquisition of books and periodicals from hard currency sources which was otherwise difficult due to problems of transferring currency.

Despite all attempts, libraries in the Arab world are still facing serious problems. The most important ones could be summarized as follows: lack of a national information policy in most countries, lack of funds, inexistant library legislation, minimal interlibrary loans, inadequate premises, shortage of skilled staff, lack of cooperation and coordination, absence of active and professional library organizations, and restricted access to information. In Palestine, for instance, libraries suffer from censorship on books and periodicals imposed by the Israeli authorities. In many countries, foreign literature is severely underrepresented in the collections.

The wars in different Arab countries (Lebanon, Iran, Iraq, Kuwait, etc.) have greatly affected the development of librarianship. Not only the wars prevented library cooperation and resource sharing, but also it did not spare the libraries themselves: some library buildings were severely damaged and collections were either stolen or destroyed. Libraries also suffered from a shortage of librarians as a result of emigration, budget cuts, and closure of foreign libraries.

Even though the situation of library and librarianship in the Arab world seems gloomy, the future of libraries in this region could be promising. Joint efforts should be undertaken to improve the present situation, and develop a serious and increasing awareness and appreciation of the role of libraries and their contribution to the economic, social and cultural development of the region. There is a wealth of material in the Arab world that should be accessible. Besides funds, support, and library legislation, the improvement of library science education, research and training programs is needed as well as the implementation of a national information policy for all Arab countries. Such a policy would lead to a better coordination of information resources and would help in the establishment of an information network. Library networking, cooperative processing and resource sharing are essential. Efforts should continue in order to standardize the application of the Dewey Decimal Classification system, the Anglo-American cataloging rules, and the entry rules for Arabic names. Finally, the emergence of new modern libraries (Bibliotheca Alexandrina in Egypt, the King Fahd National Library in Saudi Arabia, and the Library of the American University of Sharjah) are positive signs that show interest in the role of libraries and in library development in the Arab world.

CHAPTER 1

GENERAL WORKS

GENERAL

1   el-Akhras, Mahmud. *Maqalat fi 'Ulum al-Maktabat wa-al-Tawthiq wa-al-Ma'lumat*. 2nd ed. al-Zarqa', Jordan: Maktabat al-Manar, 1985. 304 p.

2   'Alami, Ahmad. *Fi al-Maktabah al-'Arabiyah wa-al-Ma'ajim*. al-Quds: al-Wakalah al-Filastiniyah, 1984. 150 p.

3   Alqudsi-Ghabra, Taghreed M. "Librarianship in the Arab world." *International Library Review* 20, no. 2 (April 1988): 233-245.

This article describes the main characteristics of librarianship in developing countries in general and discusses the status of librarianship in the Arab countries in particular. It identifies problems, lists issues in the literature needing more attention, and discusses future prospects issues in the literature needing more attention, and discusses future prospects.

4   Aman, Mohammed M. "Arab countries." In *International Handbook of Contemporary Developments in Librarianship*. Edited by Miles M. Jackson, pp. 119-134. Westport, Conn.: Greenwood Press, 1981.

Gives a general overview of the national, public, school, university, and special libraries in Egypt, Iraq, Jordan, Kuwait, Lebanon, and Saudi Arabia. Library education in these countries is also discussed.

5   Aman, Mohammed M. "Libraries in the Middle East: an overview." In *Information and Libraries in the Arab World*. Compiled and edited by Michael Wise and Anthony Olden, pp. 1-11. London: Library Association

Publishing, 1994. [Information and libraries in the developing world, vol. 3]

An article included in a collection of papers presenting a comparative review of librarianship and library practices in Arab countries. Reviews the state of libraries in the 21 countries making up the Arab World, focusing on: readership, status of librarians, library and information science education, national information policies, library laws, finance, preservation, and computerization. Although there are many negative signs of overall library development in Arab countries, the author implies that there are also some hopeful signs that modern library and information systems are emerging.

6   Aman, Mohammed M., and Sha'ban 'Abd al-'Aziz Khalifa. "Library and information services in Arab countries." In *Librarianship in the Muslim World 1984: Volume-2*. Edited by Anis Khurshid and Malahat Kaleem Sherwani, pp. 3-45. Karachi, Pakistan: Islamic Library Information Centre, Library and Information Science Department, University Karachi, 1985.

7   Arab Symposium on Information (7th : 1996 : Amman, Jordan). *Waqa'i' al-Nadwah al-'Arabiyah al-Sabi'ah lil-Ma'lumat: al-Nashr wa-al-Dabt al-Bibliyughrafi lil-Nitaj al-Fikri al-'Arabi: 'Amman, 20-23 Jumadi al-Akhir 1417 H/2-6 Tishrin al-Thani 1996 M*. 'Amman, al-Urdun: Amanat 'Amman al-Kubrá, 1997. 552 p. : ill. Includes bibliographical references.

8   Arfaoui, Hassan, Salima Boukris, Radhie Dziri, Ali Hamouda, and Odile Kerouani. *Repertoire des bibliotheques et des organismes de documentation sur le monde Arabe*. Paris: Institut du Monde Arabe, 1986. 474 p.

An exhaustive guide to archives, libraries, and research centers in each country. It includes names and addresses of people in charge of these institutions, access conditions, the number of library holdings and areas of study.

9   Atiyeh, George N. (ed.). *The Book in the Islamic World: The Written Word and Communication in the Middle East*. Albany: State University of New York Press, 1995. xviii, 305 p. Includes bibliographical references (p. 273-281) and index.

Consists of papers presented at a conference held at the Library of Congress, Washington, D.C., November 8-9, 1990. See items 69, 158, 333, 335, 341, 672.

10 Badr, 'Adil Fahmi. *Bunuk al-Ma'lumat wa-Atharuha 'ala al-Tanmiyah al-Shamilah*. 'Amman, Jordan: al-Munazzamah al-'Arabiyah lil-'Ulum al-Idariyah, Idarat al-Buhuth wa-al-Dirasat, 1986. 255 p.

GENERAL WORKS

11 Badr, Ahmad Mahumud. "Mashru' al-bahth wa masadir al-ma'lumat fi 'alam al-maktabat wa-al-ma'lumat." *'Alam al-Kutub* 6, no. 1 (April 1985): 32-41.

12 Badr, Ahmad Mahmud. "Tahlil al-intaj al-fikri fi majal manahij al-bahth fi 'ilm al-maktabat wa-al-ma'lumat." *'Alam al-Kutub* 6, no. 3 (September 1985): 298-309.

Discusses research methods applied or used in library and information sciences.

13 Badr, Ahmad Mahmud. "al-Bahth al-tajribi fi al-maktabat wa-al-ma'-lumat." *Maktabat al-Idarah* 14, no. 1 (September-October 1986): 5-24.

14 Benhawy, Mohamed Amin. *'Alam al-Kutub wa-al-Qira'ah wa-al-Maktabat*. Jaddah: Dar al-Shuruq, 1980.

The main elements of this book are: the importance of books, the book publishers, problems of publishing, the library and general education, the information age and the library schools.

15 Bezirgan, Basima. "Near East since 1920." In *Encyclopedia of Library History*. Edited by Wayne A. Wiegand and Donald G. Davis, Jr., pp. 460-463. New York: Garland Publishing, Inc., 1994.

Provides a brief summary of the history of libraries in the Arab world since 1920.

16 Buchanan, Elizabeth Anne. "Cultural heritage, social values, and information in the Arab world." *Journal of Education for Library and Information Science* 38, no. 2 (Summer 1997): 215-220.

Examines the forces of cultural value and specificity in relation to information in the Arab world.

17 Camarero, C. G. "Aproximacion a la situation de los paises arabes en materia de informacion y documentacion." [The situation of the Arab countries in information and documentation subjects.] *Revista Espanola de Documentacion Cientifica* 16, no. 1 (January-March 1993): 9-18. [In Spanish.]

Reports on the tremendous efforts made by Arabic countries to develop scientific and technical information systems in recognition of the importance of these systems in the economic, social and cultural development of their countries. [LISA]

18 Faris, Basim Muhammad. "al-Maktabah wa-al-tilifizyun wa dawrihima al-i'lami fi al-'alam al-'Arabi." *Risalat al-Maktabah* 31, no. 3 (September 1996): 24-46.

Discusses the role of libraries and television in mass media. Also discusses the audio-visual library services.

19 Francis, Simon. *Libraries and Information in the Middle East*. London: British Library, British Library Research and Development Department, 1993. 125 p. [British Library Research Review, 16.]

Provides a survey of the current state of libraries and information in the Middle East. Briefly describes the economic, political, historical and education position of each country in the region. Describes the important national, public, academic and specialist libraries concentrating on developments since 1980. Draws attention to common features and contrasts between the countries.

20 Francis, Simon. *Libraries and Information in the Near East and Central Asia*. London: British Library, 1995. 94 p. [Library and Information Research Report, 106.]

Reports results of a survey, based largely on published sources but supplemented by visits to certain countries, of the current state of libraries and information services in the Near East and Central Asia. Armenia, Azerbaijan, Bulgaria, Cyprus, Georgia, Israel, Kazakhstan, Kyrgyzstan, Lebanon, Syria, Tajikstan, Turkey, Turkmenistan, Uzbekistan, West Bank and Gaza were included in the survey. The report begins with a country survey, devoted to the historical, political, economic and educational background of each country, and a description of the major national libraries, academic libraries, special libraries and public libraries in each country, concentrating on development since the mid-1980s. This is followed by an analysis and review of some common features of the libraries and contrasts between the countries or groups of countries. Particular attention is paid to CD-ROM and document delivery services, bibliographic record formats, conservation of library materials and national library and information policies.

21 Green, Arnold H. "The history of libraries in the Arab world: a diffusionist model." *Libraries & Culture* 23, no. 4 (Fall 1988): 454-473.

Library history in Arab societies is linked to interaction among civilizations. Adapting their Hellenized subjects' institutions, from about 700 A.D., the Arabs produced mosque and palace libraries. Sophisticated research libraries materialized when Arab-Islamic civilization acquired more of the Hellenistic legacy and via global trade routes acquired techniques like paper-manufacturing. Subsequently, while *madrasa* libraries flourished, library development stalled as cultural interaction ebbed from classical levels. Arab societies have recently interacted with modern Europe. While colonialism entailed strategic constraints on Europeans' willingness to lead and psychological constraints on nationalist Arabs' inclination to borrow, through travelers, notables, Western-trained Arab librarians and library education have been among the institutions diffused from Europe to the Arab world during the last 2 centuries. As an explanatory model for library history, diffusion may well apply to other societies having traditions of interaction with neighboring high cultures and/or with modern European powers. [A]

22 al-Hajrasi, Sa'd Muhammad. "Aqsam al-maktabat fi al-bilad al-'Arabiyah: tahlil manhaji li mutatallibat al-insha' wa-al-tatwir (1)." *Maktabat al-Idarah* 14, no. 2 (January 1987): 5-35.

23 al-Hajrasi, Sa'd Muhammad. "Aqsam al-maktabat fi al-bilad al-'Arabiyah: tahlil manhaji li mutatallibat al-insha' wa-al-tatwir (2)." *Maktabat al-Idarah* 14, no. 3 (April-May 1987): 5-62.

24 al-Hajrasi, Sa'd Muhammad. "Takhassus al-maktabat wa-al-ma'lumat fi al-kharitah al-akadimiyah." *Maktabat al-Idarah* 15, no. 3 (April-May 1988): 9-92.

25 al-Hajrasi, Sa'd Muhammad. *Hamasat wa-Nida'at fi Afaq al-Qira'ah wa-al-Kutub wa-al-Maktabat*. [Cairo]: al-Hay'ah al-Misriyah al-'Ammah lil-Kitab, 1990. 807 p.

26 al-Hajrasi, Sa'd Muhammad, and Sayyid Hasbullah. *Takhassus al-Maktabat wa-al-Ma'lumat: Madkhal Manhaji Wi'a'i*. al- Riyadh: Dar al-Marrikh lil-Nashr, 1995.

An introduction to library and information sciences. Among other topics, the authors describe the different classification systems, cataloging, abstracting, and bibliographic control tools.

27 al-Hawash, Abu-Bakr Mahmud. "Mustaqbal mihnat al-maktabat wa-al-ma'lumat bayna al-nazariyah wa-al-tatbiq." *al-Majallah al-'Arabiyah lil-Ma'lumat* 13, no. 1 (1992): 92-98.

The author discusses the future of librarianship and information science as a result of the technological developments. He reviews the literature and curricula.

28 Heffening, W. "Maktaba." In *The Encyclopaedia of Islam*. New ed. Vol. 6 (pp. 197-200). Leiden: E. J. Brill, 1987.

This is an excellent overview of the history and development of libraries in the Islamic world. It also discusses the arrangements, administration and use of libraries over the centuries since the early mosque libraries were found. Provides a very long list of sources.

29 Itayem, Mahmoud A. "Libraries: the Arab states." In *World Information Report 1997/98*. Prepared by UNESCO (pp. 47-61). Paris: UNESCO Publishing, 1997.

After a brief introduction, the author provides an excellent overview of the academic, national, public, school and special libraries in the Arab world, as well as the national scientific and technical information centers found there. He also discusses the workforce development both in library and information science schools and in continuing education programs. Finally, he provides a brief discussion on the international organizations found in the region and on the situation of communications and information marketing. He concludes the paper with a list of constraints facing all types of library and information services at all levels. Includes several tables which provide statistical information on the libraries and library education in the region.

30 Khalifa, Sha'ban A. "Middle East." In *International Encyclopedia of Information and Library Science*. Edited by John Feather and Paul Sturges, pp. 297-299. London: Routledge, 1997.

Topics briefly discussed include: national libraries, public libraries, school libraries, university libraries, special libraries, cataloging and classification used in the region, library education, library associations, and professional publications.

31 Khurshid, Anis, and Malahat Kaleem Sherwani (eds.). *Librarianship in the Muslim World 1984: Volume-2*. Karachi, Pakistan: Islamic Library Information Centre, Library and Information Science Department, University Karachi, 1985.

This is the second publication in the series inaugurated in 1974 by the Islamic Library Information Centre (ISLIC) at the Library and Information Science Department of the University of Karachi to synchronize with the Second Islamic Summit Conference held in Lahore on 22-24 February 1974. Includes an opening 47-page publication, Fact Sheet on Libraries in Islamic Countries. The present publication is divided into three parts. The opening section presents an overview of the current issues and trends in Asia including the Middle East. The second section gathers together background and statistical information about 42 countries and the third and last section contains bibliographical data about these countries.

32 Monastra, Yahya. "Libraries." In *The Oxford Encyclopedia of the Modern Islamic World*. Edited by John L. Esposito, vol. 3, pp. 2-4. New York: Oxford University Press, 1995.

The author provides a brief summary of the history of libraries in Islamic countries starting from the early mosque libraries in the 6th and 7th centuries to the present. Also provided is a list of sources some of which are annotated.

33 Qasim, Hishmat Muhammad 'Ali. *al-Maktabah wa-al-Bahth*. 2nd ed. [Beirut]: Maktabat Ghrayyib, 1994.

The book is a reference work describing all kind of libraries, their collections, users, and information sources.

34 Salem, Shawky. "The Arabic literature of library and information science." *Journal of Information Science* 1, no. 4 (October 1979): 231-234.

Arab literature is still weak in the developmental and modern branches of library and information science, with only 18 Arab periodicals in this subject, and 90% of the literature in the form of textbooks and teaching books. Discusses the improvement of the Arab literature by the establishment of Arabic translations for library and information science terms and publications, but is critical of the unplanned increase in literature, and the limited topics covered by the 13 library and information science schools. The summary lists the obstacles and problems which face the Arab library and information literature policy.

35 Salem, Shawky. "Information infrastructure in the Arab countries: an analysis." *Journal of Information Science* 12, no. 5 (1986): 217-230.

Arab planners in the library and information field are faced with lack of statistics, data, and extensive surveys of the field. In an attempt to rectify matters, this paper considers the existing Arab information infrastructure, the characteristics and potential of Arab data banks, the use of foreign networks in the Arab world, and an analysis and conclusions. A range of statistical data is presented, as tables, including a complete listing of library schools in Arab countries.

36 Sliney, Marjory. "Arabia Deserta: the development of libraries in the Middle East." *Library Association Record* 92 (December 1990): 912-914.

Describes the problems hindering progress in the region, particularly in library cooperation, which have been intensified by the conflict in the Gulf.

37 Veenhof, Klaas R. "Libraries and archives." In *The Oxford Encyclopedia of Archaeology in the Near East*. Vol. 3. Edited by Eric M. Meyers, 351-357. New York: Oxford University Press, 1997.

Provides an excellent detailed account on the ancient libraries and archives found in the region, including their history, storage and filing system followed, and their contents. A long list of sources provided at the end of the article could be very helpful for interested researchers.

38 Younis, Abdul Razeq Mustafa, Fadl Klib, and 'Abd al-Jawad al-Lahham. "al-Wasf al-wazifi lil-'amilin fi al-maktabat aw marakiz al-ma'lumat wa-al-tawthiq." *Risalat al-Maktabah* 29, no. 3 (September 1994): 4-22

A job description that specifies the duties associated with each library job. It contains the following elements: Job title, job description, and the educational requirements.

ACADEMIC LIBRARIES

39 Ahmad, Nazir. *University Library Practices in Developing Countries*. London: KPI, 1984. xvi, 207 p.

A survey of university library practices in Jordan, Kuwait, Malaysia, Nigeria, Pakistan, Qatar, Saudi Arabia, and Sudan. The book is divided into chapters based on different aspects of library work: management, reference and information, selection and acqisition, collections and finances, planning and designing library buildings. The book ends with a chapter entitled: "Coordination and mobilisation." Provides important statistical information on academic libraries in these countries.

40 Badr, Ahmad Mahmud. "al-Mustafidun min al-maktabat al-akadimiyah: dirasah li-manhajiyyat bahth mushkilat ta'limihim wa-ittijahatihim wa-naw'iyyatihim." *al-Majallah al-'Arabiyah lil-Ma'lumat* 9, no. 2 (1988): 5-23.

The authors describes the types of library users in academic libraries and some of their problems such as the problem of training users, the availability of reference materials, etc.

41 Dyab, Miftah Muhammad. "University libraries in Arab countries." *International Library Review* 15, no. 1 (January 1983): 15-29.

This paper examines a number of university libraries in Arab countries including those of Tunisia, Libya, Jordan and Syria, Egypt, Lebanon, Algeria, Morocco and Iraq. It discusses their collections, services, strengths and weaknesses and concludes that the situation of library services in most of the countries is not encouraging as they are lacking in many dimensions which hinder their effective performance.

42 al-Ittihad al-'Arabi lil-Maktabat wa-al-Ma'lumat. *al-Maktabah al-Jami'iyah Da'amah lil-Bahth al-'Ilmi: A'mal al-Nadwah al-'Arabiyah al-Thalithah lil-Ma'lumat lil-Ittihad al-'Arabi lil-Maktabat wa-al-Ma'lumat*. Zaghwan, Tunis: Markaz al-Dirasat wa-al-Buhuth al-'Uthmaniyah wa-al-Muriskiyah wa-al-Tawthiq wa-al-Ma'lumat, 1994.

43 Khurshid, Anis. "Academic library resources of the Muslim Asia." In *Librarianship in the Muslim World 1984: Volume-2*. Edited by Anis Khurshid and Malahat Kaleem Sherwani, pp. 46-64. Karachi, Pakistan: Islamic Library Information Centre, Library and Information Science Dept., University Karachi, 1985.

44 al-Mumani, Hasan Ahmad. "al-Maktabat al-jami'iyah wa-tahaddiyat tiknulujyah al-ma'lumat." *Risalat al-Maktabah* 30, no. 2 (June 1995): 4-23.

Discusses databases published on CD-ROMs and their importance for university libraries.

45 al-Nahari, Abdulaziz Mohamed. "al-Maktabat al-wataniyah al-jami'iyah: dirasah tahliliyah." *'Alam al-Kutub* no. 1 (March 1987): 19-25.

46 al-Samirrai, Hafidh S., M. Hassan al-Safadi, and Ahmed E. Zidan. "Automated information system for academic Islamic institutions." In *Proceedings of the 48th ASIS Annual Meeting, Las Vegas, Nevada, October 20-24, 1985*. Edited by Carol A. Parkhurst, pp. 155-160. White Plains, N.Y.: Knowledge Industry Publications Inc. for the American Society for Information Science, 1985.

In a project planned, designed, and conducted by the Islamic Foundation for Science Technology and Development (IFSTAD) and Computer Consultants (CCH), Saudi Arabia, data concerning universities, colleges, and research centers in all Islamic countries were collected, analyzed and automated. The long-term objective is to establish an automated data bank. It comprises information on 986 research centers and 260 universities representing 36 and 39 Islamic nations, respectively. This data have been stored in the computer and in micrographic system. A semi-automated system allows fast micrographic retrieval with the aid of the computer.

ARABIC SCRIPT AND BIBLIOGRAPHIC RECORDS/TOOLS

47 Aliprand, Joan M. "Arabic script on RLIN." *Library Hi Tech* 10, no. 4 (1992): 59-80.

Arabic script is the most recent addition to the scripts available on the Research Libraries Information Network (RLIN). Bibliographic control and retrieval using the authentic writing system are available for titles in Arabic, Persian (Farsi), Urdu, Ottoman Turkish, and other languages written with Arabic script. RLIN is the world's largest bibliographic database for Middle Eastern language material. This paper is a comprehensive description of the Arabic script features of RLIN. It covers Arabic character sets and RLIN's character repertoire for Arabic script; how Arabic characters are input and stored in the RUN database; the equipment needed for Arabic script support; the indexing, retrieval, and presentation of records containing Arabic script; the inclusion of non-Roman data in USMARC bibliographic records; and statistics on the RLIN databases. Sidebars explain features of Arabic writing. The discussion of data storage and presentation of text is relevant to any computer application that involves Arabic script. [A]

48 Aman, Mohammed M. "Use of Arabic in computerized information interchange." *Journal of the American Society for Information Science* 35, no. 4 (July 1984): 204-210.

There is a growing demand in the Arab world for the use of Arabic script in inputting and accessing information systems and the establishment of Arab databases. In all Arab countries, Arabic is the working language in management, business, accounting, education, arts, and literature and to a lesser extent in science, medicine, and engineering. Arab member countries in the International Information System for Agricultural Sciences and Technology (AGRIS), whose carrier language is English, face some difficulties in preparing documents in the Arabic language for AGRIS input. The method of script conversion through transliteration, which is used by AGRIS and the Library of Congress is neither helpful or acceptable to Arab librarians and information specialists. These and similar complaints have prompted information and computer specialists to address the issues of Arabization of computer terminals and input/output procedures. This article addresses the problem of Arabic computerized information exchange and highlights the basic differences between treatment of Arabic and English. It also discusses the various Arab attempts to formulate standards for coding Arabic letters and vowel points and their sorting sequence. Another area that this article explores is the high degree of syntactical flexibility which characterizes the Arabic language and complicates data retrieval, computer aided translation, and human machine interface. A unified standard for the Arab/Latin Computer Code known as CODAR-UFD based on the ASCII Code was adopted in 1982. This article discusses this new code and describes some of the existing terminals that use other codes. [A]

49 Aman, Mohammed M. "Use of Arabic script in computerized information systems." In *Automated Systems for Access to Multilingual and Multis-*

cript Library Materials: Problems and Solutions. Papers from the pre-conference held at Nihon Daigaku Kaikan Tokyo, Japan, August 21-22, 1986. Edited for the Section on Library Services to Multicultural Populations and the Section on Information Technology by Christine Bossmeyer and Stephen W. Massil.Munchen: K.G. Saur, 1987. [IFLA publications, 0344-6891; 38]

50 Branca, Paolo. "Il trattamento informatico della lingua araba." [Complete processing of the Arab language.] *Informatica e Documentazione* 14, no. 4 (October-December 1987): 280-286. [In Italian.]

Arabic writing and the various shapes each letter has depending on its position within the word were the first problems to be solved in designing terminals and printers capable of reproducing Arabic characters in the right sequence and with the right link between letters. Sketches the philological groundwork for approaching the computer processing of Arabic text. [LISA]

51 Khurshid, Zahiruddin. "ARABMARC: a long way to go." *World Libraries* 8, no. 2 (Spring 1998): 60-68.

Notwithstanding the availability of USMARC and UNIMARC as international exchange formats, the need for national formats continues to be felt, especially in countries or regions which use non-Roman scripts. This paper reviews the attempts made in the Arabian Gulf Region to prepare the framework for developing the ARABMARC format during the last thirteen years. It also gives details of the availability of Arabic script support in various automated systems currently in operation, as well as formerly in use, in the Gulf Region, including STAIRS, DOBIS/LIBIS, MINISIS, VTLS, and Horizon. A critical review of the Arabic script support on RLIN is also provided. [A]

52 Srouji, J., and D. Berry. "Arabic formatting with Ditroff/ffortid." *Electronic Publishing* 5, no. 4 (December 1992): 163-208.

Describes an Arabic formatting system that is able to format multilingual scientific documents, containing text in Arabic or Persian, as well as other languages, plus pictures, graphs, formulae, tables, bibliographical citations and bibliographies. The system is an extension of ditroff/ffortid that is already capable of handling Hebrew in the context of multilingual scientific documents. Ditroff/ffortid itself is a collection of pre- and post-processors for the UNIX ditroff (Device Independent Typesetter Run-OFF) formatter. The new system is built without changing itself. The extension consists of a new preprocessor, fonts, and a modified existing post processor. [A]

53 Vernon, Elizabeth. "Hebrew and Arabic scripts materials in the automated library: the United States scene." *Cataloging & Classification Quarterly* 14, no. 1 (1991): 49-67.

The online catalog has revolutionized the library environment, but for materials in Hebrew and Arabic script languages the transition to automation has had serious obstacles due to the particular characteristics of these scripts. Until recently the solution for those libraries wishing to automate their Hebrew and Arabic scripts holdings has been romanization, generally based on the Library of Congress romanization rules. Now advances in computer technology have provided new possibilities for using these scripts within the online record, although the need to romanize has not been eliminated. [A]

54 Vernon, Elizabeth. *Decision-Making for Automation: Hebrew and Arabic Script Materials in the Automated Library*. Champaign, Illinois: Illinois University at Urbana-Champaign, Graduate School of Library and Information Science, July 1996. [Illinois University at Urbana-Champaign, Graduate School of Library and Information Science, Occasional Papers Nos. 205.]

Surveys the computerization options available to libraries with Hebrew and Arabic script collections and examines the library automation decisions that different libraries worldwide have made, with consideration of how these choices relate to the priorities of these institutions. Focuses on academic and research libraries, with reference to other libraries when appropriate. Considers: Romanized cataloging; Non Roman script cataloging; CDS/ISIS and MINISIS; DOBIS-LIBIS; ALEPH; Ameritech Horizon and other non roman script implementations; combination of Romanized and Non Romanized script cataloging; authority control of Hebrew and Arabic materials; name authority control in the Romanized, Non Romanized and combination script cataloging environments; and the Unicode Standard and the future of multiscript library automation.

ARCHIVES

55 Fakhfakh, Moncef. "Archives: the Arab states." In *World Information Report 1997/98*. Prepared by UNESCO (pp. 136-143). Paris: UNESCO Publishing, 1997.

Topics discussed include: legislation and standardization; organization of archival institutions; buildings, equipment, and budgets; holdings, collections and communication of documents; staff and training; records management; professional associations; archives, history, culture and administrative organization; archives and multimedia and; issues specific to the Arab region.

GENERAL WORKS

56 McIlwaine, John. *Writings on African Archives*. With an essay by Anne Thurston and contributions by Pino Akotia & Justus Wamukoya. London: Hans Zell Publishers, 1996. xviii, 279 p.

Provides an important inventory of materials—monographs, articles, reports, conference papers and pathfinders—written about archives and manuscript collections within Africa, as well as about African-related archives located outside Africa. Contains over 2,300 entries, many with brief annotations. The volume is indexed by authors, editors, series titles, and names of individuals and institutions. Includes many entries on all North African Arab countries.

57 Pedersen, Olof. *Archives and Libraries in the City of Assur: A Survey of the Material from the German Excavations*. Uppsala: Uppsala University, 1986.

58 Pedersen, Olof. *Archives and Libraries in the Ancient Near East, 1500-300 B.C*. Bethesda, MD: CDL Press, 1998.

59 Tamimi, 'Abd al-Jalil. *Min ajl al-Takhtit li-Tatwir al-Arshiv bi al-Bilad al-'Arabiyah*. Tunis: al-Ma'had al-A'lah lil-Tawthiq, 1984.

BIBLIOGRAPHIC CONTROL

60 Anwar, Mumtaz A. "Bibliographic control of academic dissertations." In *Building Information Systems in the Islamic World*. Edited by Ziauddin Sardar, pp. 101-106. London: Mansell, 1988.

The author finds that bibliographic control of dissertations, even at the individual university level, is inadequate. He calls for the publication of a comprehensive listing of dissertations produced in Muslim countries--a project he has himself taken up with some zeal. His other suggestion that each university should require its post-graduate candidates to submit abstracts of their dissertations is surely not beyond the capabilities of Muslim universities.

61 Diyab, Hamid Shafi'i. "al-Dabt al-bibliyughrafi lil-intaj al-fikri fi majal al-tufulah." *'Alam al-Kutub* 2, no. 1 (May 1981): 60-65.

62 Husam al-Din, Mustafa. "al-Dabt al-bibliyughrafi al-qawmi lil-intaj al-fikri al-'Arabi." *Shu'un 'Arabiyah*, no. 11 (January 1982): 181-190.

The author explains the meaning of "bibliographic control", discusses the main aims and objectives of a national bibliography, as well as its importance, its present role and future developments.

63 Jirjis, Jasim Muhammad, and Muhammad Hasan Qasim al-Khafaji. "al-Raqm al-duwali al-mi'yari lil-kitab: al-darurah wa-mustalzamat al-tatbiq." *Risalat al-Maktabah* 29, no. 2 (June 1994): 55-64.

The issue of bibliographical control is discussed in this article. Special emphasis is put on the ISBN and its use in the storage and retrieval of machine-readable bibliographic data.

64 al-Tay, Ja'far Ibrahim. "al-Dabt al-bibliyughrafi lil-rasa'il al-jami'iyah fi al-'alam al-'Arabi." *'Alam al-Kutub* 2, no. 2 (August 1981): 191-207.

The author stresses the importance of the theses and dissertations as information sources and lists the different dissertation indexes that are published in the Arab world.

BIBLIOGRAPHIC SYSTEMS

65 Chen, Pah I., and Vladimir T. Borovansky. "A bibliographic system for solar energy information on the Middle East." *Aslib Proceedings* 32, no. 4 (April 1980): 187-198.

Describes a bibliographic system that has been developed at the University of Petroleum and Minerals, Dhahran, Saudi Arabia, for gathering, organizing and disseminating the solar energy information pertaining to the Middle East. Programs covering all phases of the work were developed, the three main categories being data entry, data validation and conversion and processing. Data handling programs have been specifically designed for unskilled users. Tables show number of solar energy publications in the Middle East, major publication areas and a subject/country listing.

66 Clews, John. "Bibliographic systems and Arabisation: an overview." *Sesame Bulletin* 4, no. 4 (Winter 1991): 112-115.

Paper delivered at the MELCOM (Middle East Libraries Committee) Workshop on Arabic Bibliographic Databases, held at the School of Oriental and African Studies, London, July 9, 1991. It examines the special needs that Arabist librarians require from computers focusing on what a library system should do; what sort of records are required and whether the system will provide full Arabic functionality. It suggests a series of questions to ask any potential Arabic database suppliers, maintaining that the development of good Arabic bibliographic databases is perfectly possible and that some are already being developed.

BIBLIOGRAPHIES

67   Abdel-Hadi, Mohammed Fathi. *al-Dalil al-Bibliyughrafi lil-Intaj al-Fikri al-'Arabi fi Majal al-Ma'lumat, 1976-1980*. Tunis: Jami'at al-Duwal al-'Arabiyah, al-Munazzamah al-'Arabiyah lil-Tarbiyah wa-al-Thaqafah wa-al-'Ulum, Idarat al-Tawthiq wa-al-Ma'lumat, 1983. 231 p.

68   Abdel-Hadi, Mohammed Fathi. "al-Intaj al-fikri al-'Arabi fi majal al-maktabat bayna al-kamm wa-al-kayf." *al-Majallah al-'Arabiyah lil-Ma'lumat* 5, no. 2 (1984): 124-159.

Public libraries should organize the appropriate information material in order to facilitate library services to public users. The author analyzes Arab intellectual contribution in the field of public libraries.

69   Albin, Michael W. "The book in the Islamic world: a selective bibliography." In *The Book in the Islamic World: The Written Word and Communication in the Middle East*. Edited by George N. Atiyeh, pp. 273-282. Albany: State University of New York Press, 1995.

70   Ibrahim, Abu al-Sa'ud. "al-Hajah ila markaz bibliyughrafi 'Arabi." *al-Mustaqbal al-'Arabi* 4, no. 27 (May 1981): 57-67.

Discusses the importance of an Arab Bibliographic Center and its prospective role.

71   MacKee, Monique. *A Handbook of Comparative Librarianship*. 3rd ed., rev. and enl. London : Bingley, 1983. xiii, 567 p.

Intended as a research guide. Aims at facilitating the initial identification of the sources available at the international, regional, or national level and at introducing a country's librarianship in its historical, geographical and social perspectives. Includes entries on most Arab countries.

72   Makdisi, John. "Islamic law bibliography." *Law Library Journal* 78, no. 1 (Winter 1986): 103-189.

Presents a survey of the publications of primary sources of Islamic law (in Arabic) and secondary sources (in English and French). The bibliography is preceded by a discussion of the basic sources of the law and schools of legal doctrine and a brief treatment of the development of Islamic law.

73   Pantelidis, Veronica S. *The Arab World Libraries and Librarianship 1960-1976: A Bibliography*. London: Mansell, 1979. xiii, 100 p.

A bibliography listing books, periodicals, conference and working papers, reports, abstracts and audio-cassettes which are accessible to the general user, in libraries or from the publisher, and which relate to libraries and librarianship in the Arab World from 1960-1976.

BIBLIOMETRIC STUDIES

74   'Abd al-Jalil, Muhammad al-Fayturi. "al-Tahlil al-bibliyughrafi wa-imkaniyyat al-istifadah minhu fi al-khadamat al-maktabiyah." *al-Majallah al-'Arabiyah lil-Ma'lumat* 8, no. 1 (1987): 158-166.

Bibliographic citation is discussed, as well as its application to library and information services.

75   Frame, J. D. "Measuring scientific activity in lesser developed countries." *Scientometrics* 2, no. 2 (March 1980): 133-145.

Quantitative indicators of scientific and technological activity are often questionable in terms of validity and reliability. This is particularly true in lesser developed countries where the lack of data gathering skills may result in the development of misleading indicators. A number of manpower, education, expenditure and publication indicators are examined for thirteen Middle Eastern countries. Reliability and validity problems are discussed for each indicator. The indicators are found to correlate with each other in reasonable ways, suggesting that, despite their possible flaws, they measure scientific activity with some consistency. [A]

76   Hamade, Samir N. "Characteristics of the literature used by Arab authors in library and information science: a bibliometric study." *International Information & Library Review* 26, no. 3 (September 1994): 139-50.

This paper attempts to shed some light on the scientific communication behavior of Arab authors in library and information science by studying the characteristics of the literature used by these authors. A bibliometric study by way of citation analysis was conducted on the articles published from 1978 to 1988 in *Maktabat al-Idarah*, a scholarly Arab journal in the field. It was concluded from this study that English language materials are the main source of information for Arab authors in library and information science. They rely on English literature that is between 5 and 15 years of age more than on their own literature and use books more than any other form of publication. They cover almost all areas of the field with special emphasis on technical services as represented by cataloging, classification and acquisitions, library administration and library education. [A]

77   al-Kindilchie, 'Amir Ibrahim, and Iman Fadil al-Samirra'i. "al-Ihsa' al-bibliyughrafi (al-bibliyumatriks) wa-istikhdamatuhu fi al-dirasat al-'Arabiyah." *al-Majallah al-'Arabiyah lil-Ma'lumat* 18, no. 1 (1997): 94-124.

78 al-Maliki, Majbal Lazim Musallam. "al-Qiyas al-bibliyughrafi wa-tatbiqatihi fi majal al-ma'lumat wa-al-maktabat." *Risalat al-Maktabah* 32, no. 2 (June 1997): 21-56.

Reviews the importance of bibliometrics, its objectives, history and basic laws.

79 Uzun, A. "A bibliometric analysis of physics publications from Middle Eastern countries." *Scientometrics* 36, no. 2 (June 1996): 259-269.

Analyzes the publications of physicists from Egypt, Iraq, Iran, Jordan, Saudi Arabia, Syria and Turkey in international journals in the period 1990-1994, in terms of national contributions, main subjects of activity, journal preferences of authors and coauthorship patterns. Results highlighted include: 75 per cent of the total output came from Egypt and Turkey; the highest concentration of papers in a few journals was found in Egypt; condensed matter physics was found to be the among the three most active subject areas for the countries except Iran where astrosciences, nuclear science and technology were preferred; and finally a change in publication patterns towards increased collaboration and decreasing isolation. [A]

80 Yitzhaki, Moshe. "Determining the mutual dependence between two related disciplines by means of citation analysis: the case of biblical studies and ancient Near-East studies." *Libri* 36, no. 3 (September 1986): 211-223.

Describes a study conducted by means of citation analysis to determine if biblical studies scholars make use of Near-East studies materials, and whether Near-East scholars use biblical studies materials in their research. The findings indicate that the extent of mutual use of biblical studies and ancient Near-East studies material has been relatively very low and possible explanations are put forward: the representiveness of the eight samples chosen; variance between subfields; and whether scholars' basic training manifests itself in both a methodological approach and a practical approach.

BIOGRAPHIES

81 Albin, Michael W. "Sarkis, Yusuf Ilyan." In *Encyclopedia of Library and Information Science*. Vol. 39 (pp. 394-396). New York: Marcel Dekker, Inc., 1985.

Provides an account of Yusuf Ilyan Sarkis (1856-1932), an Arab bookman and bibliographer who compiled the *Mu'jam al-Matbu'at al-'Arabiyah wa-al-Mu'arrabah* (1928-1931), which remains an indispensable record of Arabic publishing.

BOOK PUBLISHING

82   Albin, Michael W. "Book publishing." In *The Oxford Encyclopedia of the Modern Islamic World*. Edited by John L. Esposito, vol. 1, pp. 226-229. New York: Oxford University Press, 1995.

Provides a detailed discussion on the history and development of book publishing in Islamic counties.

CATALOGING AND CLASSIFICATION

83   Abdel-Hadi, Mohammed Fathi. *al-Fahrasah al-Mawdu'iyah: Dirasah fi Ru'us al-Mawdu'at al-'Arabiyah*. Tab'ah jadidah wa-Munaqqahah. Jaddah: Dar al-Shuruq, 1981.

84   Abdel-Hadi, Mohammed Fathi. "al-'Amaliyyat al-fanniyah fi marakiz al-tawthiq wa-al-ma'lumat." *al-Majallah al-'Arabiyah lil-Ma'lumat* 4, no. 2 (December 1983): 32-47.

85   Abdel-Shafi, Hasan Muhammad, and Jamal 'Abd al-Hamid Sha'lan. *Muqaddimah fi al-Fahrasah wa-al-Tasnif*. al-Qahira: Maktabat al-Dar al-'Arabiyah, 1994.

The book is intended to help librarians in public and school libraries in the fields of cataloging and classification.

86   Abid, Abdelaziz. "al-Taqnin al-duwali lil-wasf al-bibliyughrafi: tahlil wa taqyim min wijhat nazar 'Arabiyah." *al-Majallah al-'Arabiyah lil-Ma'lumat* 4, no. 1 (1983): 19-50.

Traces the development of the International Standard Bibliographic Description (ISBD), with special reference to the work on variant ISBD's. Evaluates the ISBD system, particularly the problems faced by librarians in Arab countries. Concludes that ISBD has only partly met its objectives and suggests that ALECSO's role should be to help librarians in Arab countries with the practical application of ISBD.

87   Abu-Laban, 'Abd al-Hakim. "al-Nizam al-duwali li-sijil bayanat al-musal-salat (ISDS)." *Risalat al-Maktabah* 25, nos. 2-3 (June-September 1990): 47-52.

A description of the ISDS since its development and its relation to other international information systems.

88   Ahmad, Nazir. "Cataloguing operations in Arab university libraries." *Pakistan Library Bulletin* 15 (March-June 1984): 1-17.

Discusses developments in cataloging practices in the Arab world focusing mainly on university libraries in Saudi Arabia. Also discussed is practical problems faced in automating technical services, criteria for evaluating a library catalog, standardization of cataloging practices, and the cataloging system, DOBIS/LIBIS. Recommendations are provided.

89 el-Akhras, Mahmud. "al-Tasnif wa-anzimatuhu." *al-Majallah al-'Arabiyah lil-Ma'lumat* 2, no. 2 (1980): 40-77.

90 el-Akhras, Mahmud. "al-Jadid fi 'alam al-tiqaniyyat al-duwaliyah lil-wasf al-bibliyughrafi." *al-Majallah al-'Arabiyah lil-Ma'lumat* 4, no. 1 (1984): 11-18.

This paper discusses the Arabic editions of the ISBD, its purpose and use.

91 al-'Amad, Hani. *al-Mu'alajah al-Fanniyah lil-Ma'lumat: al-Fahrasah, al-Tasnif, al-Tawthiq, al-Takshif, al-Arshiv*. 'Amman: Jam'iyyat al-Makatabat al-Urduniyah, 1985.

92 *A'mal Mu'tamar min ajl Tawhid Fahrasat al-Kitab al-'Arabi Maghriban wa-Mashriqan, Tunis, 28 November-1 December 1984*. Tunis: Markaz al-Buhuth fi 'Ulum al-Maktabat wa-al-Ma'lumat, al-Ma'had al-A'la lil-Tawthiq, 1985.

93 Aman, Mohammed M., and Shawky Salem. "The use of the DDC in the Arab world." In *Dewey: An International Perspective: Papers from a Workshop on the Dewey Decimal Classification and DDC 20*. Edited by Robert P. Holley, pp. 32-47. Sponsored by the Section on Classification and Indexing, IFLA and Forest Press. Mèunchen: Saur, 1991.

A paper presented at the General Conference of the International Federation of Library Associations and Institutions (IFLA), August 24, 1989, Paris, France. In 1984 an Arabic translation with appropriate modifications to suit the needs of libraries in Arab countries was published in Kuwait. The edition was the result of a joint collaboration between Forest Press, publisher of the Dewey Decimal Classification, and the Arab League Educational, Cultural, and Scientific Organization. After a brief description of earlier efforts to Arabize the DDC, the authors describe the charcateristics of the authorized Arabic edition, the significance of the changes made to accommodate the subject orientation of collections found in libraries in Arab countries, and the needs and expectations of their users. [A]

94 Ashoor, Mohammad Saleh. "The formation of Muslim names." *International Library Review* 9, no. 4 (October 1977): 491-500.

Discusses the history of Muslim names, the influence of religion and local cultures and languages on them, and their cataloging in theory and practice. A strong devotion to religion has caused Muslims to limit their names to those of God, or the Prophet and his family and followers. The continuous repetition of a few names and the absence of surnames cause serious problems for catalogers: some enter a Muslim author under forename, others under the most common form of name. Calls for a standard authority list, the expansion of Rule 54, 'Names in the Arabic Alphabet', of the Anglo-American Cataloging Rules, and a greater awareness of the cultural differences among Muslim countries and their important effect on names.

95   al-Bakhit, Bakhit Sulayman. "Istikhdam barnamij CDS/ISIS: al-mustafidun wa-wasa'il al-aman." *Risalat al-Maktabah* 26, no. 1 (March 1991): 17-22.

The CDS/ISIS package is discussed as well as the problems of data security and safety.

96   al-Bakhit, Bakhit Sulayman. "I'adat tarqim al-tasjilat fi qawa'id al-bayanat al-mabniyah bi-istikhdam hazmat barmajiyyat CDS/ISIS li-isdar qawa'im biblughrafiyah." *Risalat al-Maktabah* 27, no. 1 (March 1992): 34-45.

The article gives a brief description of the CDS/ISIS package and stresses the need for renumbering the records in the database to produce bibliographies and other lists.

97   Chammou, Eliezer. "Near or Middle East? Choice of name." *Cataloging & Classification Quarterly* 7, no. 3 (Spring 1987): 105-120.

Based on a paper presented at the annual meeting of the Middle East Libraries Association, New Orleans, November 1985. Subject access to information has become increasingly important in recent years, and geographic names play a significant role. Some geographic name headings have been changed by the Library of Congress to comply with common usage, in order to improve access. However, it continues to use the name Near East rather than the name Middle East. By comparing definitions and use of Near East to that of Middle East, and by analyzing data dealing with the use of these names in titles, this study demonstrates that Middle East is more commonly used than Near East. This supports the hypothesis that the name currently in use by the Library of Congress, the Near East, is no longer appropriate. Therefore, users will be better served if Near East is replaced by the more common name, the Middle East. [A]

GENERAL WORKS

98 Chelbi, K. "'*Al Fahrast*', la premiere bibliographie et classification ancienne connue." ['*Al Fahrast*', the first known ancient bibliography and classification.] *L'Ecluse* 7, no. 1 (January-March 1995): 14-16.

Article first published in *Fabadef-Liaison*, 4 (October 1994). '*Al Fahrast*', which means 'bibliography' in Arabic, was produced by an Arab scholar in 10th century Baghdad as a tool for listing all known Arab books from the 8th to the 10th centuries. Only a few copies, printed in Leipzig in 1928, are known to exist. The classification system is divided into 10 main classes: general; grammar and linguistics; history and biography; poetry; mysticism; theology; philosophy and ancient sciences; stories, tales and magic; religions; and chemistry and alchemy.

99 Dahbur, Sidqi. *Tadub (mim, ghayn, kaf): al-Taqnin al-Duwali lil-Wasf al-Bibliyughrafi lil-Mawad Ghayr al-Kutub*. Tunis: Jami'at al-Duwal al-'Arabiyah, al-Munazzamah al-'Arabiyah lil-Tarbiyah wa-al-Thaqafah wa-al-'Ulum, 1983.

The first Arabic edition of the ISBD (NBD): International Standard Bibliographic Description for Non-Book Materials.

100 Gomaa, Nabila. "Application of ISBD(M) to Arabic works." *MELA Notes*, no. 23 (May 1981): 4-8.

Summarizes some of the main problems of applying International Standard Bibliographic Description for Monographs—ISBD(M)—to Arabic works. Discusses the limited success of the application of ISBD(M) in Arab countries, and its application by the Library of Congress. Concludes that the gulf between the national application of ISBD(M) conventions and the non-national applications to the same works is gradually widened by the over-use of European biased conventions which are inherent in it. Argues that if such a process continues without some controlling rules, ISBD(M) could completely lose its international character as far as applications are concerned. Offers some suggestions for revision of the code.

101 Habaili, Hussein. "al-Taqnin al-duwali lil-wasf al-bibliyughrafi wa-qawa'id al-jam'iyah al-faransiyah lil-taqnin." *al-Majallah al-'Arabiyah lil-Ma'alumat* 4, no. 1 (1983): 63-76.

This paper compares the original International Standard Bibliographic Description for Monographs—ISBD(M) in English to the French version published by the Association Francaise de Normalization (AFNOR), which is used in some North African Arab countries such as Tunisia. It urges that the French version of ISBD(M) be adopted in Arab countries for the sake of unified catalogs and bibliographies.

102 Hamshari, 'Umar Ahmad. "al-Nata'ij al-murtabata bi-'amaliyat i'adat al-fahrasah." *Risalat al-Maktabah* 12, no. 1 (March 1977): 19-22.

This paper discusses the consequences of re-cataloging and the procedures to be adopted for organizing successful re-cataloging. It also deals with some problems of Arabic libraries and ISBD. Some recommendations are presented.

103 Hamshari, 'Umar Ahmad. "Fahrasat al-kitab al-'Arabi: mashakil wa-hulul muqtaraha." *Risalat al-Maktabah* 17, no. 1 (March 1982): 11-16.

Cataloging problems in Jordan as well as the other Arab countries are very varied. This article discusses these problems such as the lack of Arabic cataloging code, the problems of Arabic/Muslim names, filing, style of entry, marginal works, government publications and subject headings. Suggests some solutions such as the introduction of centralized cataloging, the cataloging in publication, the compilation and publication of a standard subject heading list in Arabic and the establishment of a standard authority list for the names of Arabic authors.

104 Houissa, Ali. "Arabic personal names: their components and rendering in catalog entries." *Cataloging & Classification Quarterly* 13, no. 2 (1991): 3-22.

Arabic personal names are illustrative of the kind of difficulties emerging from the attempts to establish headings and retrieve material in a non-roman script. The complexity of elements making up these names can be puzzled even to the native speaker. Identifies and discusses the most common elements of Arabic names, both classical and modern in the light of the appropriate rules in various cataloging codes. Places particular emphasis on the order of elements and the choice and formulation of access points in accord with the cataloging rules and practices in US libraries. An updated and more detailed version appears in *Encyclopedia of Library and Information Science*, vol. 52 (pp. 351-366). New York: Marcel Dekker, Inc., 1993, under the title: "Structure and rendering of Arabic proper names for bibliographic purposes."

105 Husam al-Din, Mustafa. "Faharis maktabatina wa-al-lughah al-'Arabiyah: qadiyyah lil-munaqashah." *al-Majallah al-'Arabiyah lil-Ma'lumat* 4, no. 1 (1983): 51-61.

Most library catalogs, national bibliographies, indexing and abstracting services published in the Arab region are divided into two or more sections according to language and/or script. Describes some reasons for this division. Urges the Arab national bibliographic agencies to use Arabic in preparing and arranging bibliographic records. Discusses the obstacles to the use of Arabic in such publications.

106 Itayem, Mahmoud A. *Tadub (kaf): al-Taqnin al-Duwali lil-Wasf al-Bibliyughrafi lil-Kutub*. Tunis: Jami'at al-Duwal al-'Arabiyah, al-Munazzamah al-'Arabiyah lil-Tarbiyah wa-al-Thaqafah wa-al-'Ulum, 1982.

Discusses the Arabization of the ISBD (M): the International Standard Bibliographic Description for Monographic Publications.

107 Itayem, Mahmoud A. "Qawa'id al-fahrasah al-anglu-amirkiyah/al-tab'ah al-thaniyah: al-tab'ah al-'Arabiyah al-ula." *al-Majallah al-'Arabiyah lil-Ma'lumat* 4, no. 1 (1983): 93-104.

An analysis of the Anglo-American Cataloguing Rules–2nd edition, which was translated into Arabic.

108 Itayem, Mahmoud A. *Tadub ('ayn): al-Taqnin al-Duwali al-'Am lil-Wasf al-Bibliyughrafi*. Tunis: Jami'at al-Duwal al-'Arabiyah, al-Munazzamah al-'Arabiyah lil-Tarbiyah wa-al-Thaqafah wa-al-'Ulum, 1984.

Discusses the Arabization of the first standard edition of the ISBD (G) General International Standard Bibliographic Description for Monographic Publications.

109 Itayem, Mahmoud A. *al-Dalil al-'Amali li-I'dad al-Tasjilat al-Bibliyugrafiyah li-Nizam al-Ma'lumat*. Tunis: Jami'at al-Duwal al-'Arabiyah, al-Amanah al-'Ammah, Markaz al-Tawthiq wa-al-Ma'lumat, 1987. 255 p.

110 Itayem, Mahmoud A. *al-Dalil al-'Amali li-Bina' al-Malaf al-Ustaz (Asma' al-Ashkhas, Asma' al-Hay'at, al-Asma' al-Jughurafiyah)*. Tunis: Jami'at al-Duwal al-'Arabiyah, al-Amanah al-'Ammah, Markaz al-Tawthiq wa-al-Ma'lumat, 1990.

111 Itayem, Mahmoud A. "Hal nahnu bi-hajah ila tab'ah 'Arabiyah thaniyah li-qawa'id al-fahrasah al-anglu-amirkiyah al-mu'arrabah?" *Risalat al-Maktabah* 27, no. 1 (March 1992): 4-17.

The need for a revision of the Arabic edition of AACR2 is shown in the article.

112 Itayem, Mahmoud A. "al-Isharat al-bibliyughrafiyah allazimah lil-bahith." *Risalat al-Maktabah* 27, no. 3 (September 1992): 4-20.

This article is based on ISO 690/1997–Documentation-Bibliographic References–Content, Form and Structure. It covers the following types of publications: books, periodicals, parts of books, contributions to books, journal articles and patents. Both essential and optional elements of description are stated with examples.

113 Itayem, Mahmoud A. "Qawa'id al-fahrasah al-anglu-amirkiyah, al-tab'ah al-thaniyah muraja'at 1988." *Risalat al-Maktabah* 30, no. 1 (March 1995): 4-15.

114 Itayem, Mahmoud A. "al-Tab'ah al-hadiyah wa-al-'ishrun min nizam tasnif diwi al-'ishri." *Risalat al-Maktabah* 32, no. 1 (March 1997): 4-12.

Discusses the 21st edition of the Dewey Decimal Classification system and calls for the translation of this edition into Arabic.

115 Jajko, Edward A. "Cataloging of Middle Eastern materials (Arabic, Persian, and Turkish)." *Cataloging & Classification Quarterly* 17, no. 1-2 (1993): 133-147.

Cataloging of materials in Arabic, Turkish, Persian, and related languages presents numerous special difficulties. The author discusses in detail problems presented by the languages and scripts and their romanizations. He also deals with different calendar systems used in the Middle East and with representative problems in Library of Congress classification of Middle Eastern materials. The Middle East cataloger must be aware of and deal with these and other problems on a daily basis. Library administrators, heads of technical services and catalog departments, and other catalogers also need to be aware of the particular difficulties that Middle East catalogers face. [A]

116 Jawadah, Kamal Mas'ud. "Hawla ab'ad wa-masafat al-bitaqah al-'Arabiyah fi al-maktabat." *Maktabat al-Idarah* 13, no. 2 (January-February 1986): 67-78.

117 Khalifa, Sha'ban 'Abd al-'Aziz, and Muhammad 'Awad al-'Ayidi. *Qa'imat Ru'us al-Mawdu'at al-'Arabiyah al-Kubra*. al-Qahirah: al-Maktabah al-Akadimiyah, 1994.

118 al-Kharuf, Yunis Isma'il. "al-Malamih al-jadidah fi al-tab'ah al-jadidah min tasnif diwi al-'ishri." *Risalat al-Maktabah* 26, no. 1 (March 1991): 23-31.

119 al-Kindilchie, 'Amir Ibrahim. "al-Siyar wa-al-tarajim fi tasnif *"al-Fihrist"* li Ibn al-Nadim." *Risalat al-Maktabah* 27, no. 2 (June 1992): 35-48.

Reviews the classification system used by Ibn al-Nadim in *al-Fihrist*, a bibliography of all Arabic books written by Arabs and foreigners before the year 377H.

120 Momeni, Mahvash Keshmiri. *Socio-Cultural Factors Affecting the Adaptations of the Dewey Decimal Classification in the Middle East*. Ph.D., 1982. University of Maryland. 344 p.

This study analyzes the socio-cultural factors that affect the adaptations of the Dewey Decimal Classification (DDC) in its translations from English into other languages, more specifically, into Arabic, Farsi, Hindi, and Turkish. The purpose of the study was to find general and specific guidelines for making the future foreign language editions/translation of DDC more standardized and compatible with each other. The study was performed in three stages: (1) In order to find specific adaptations, each entry in each translation of DDC was compared with the edition of DDC on which it was based. (2) Each class of each translation (except classes 000 Generalities, 500 Pure Science, and 600 Technology) was compared and analyzed with its respective English DDC edition. (3) The adaptations in each class of all four translations of DDC and their English DDC edition were compared and analyzed. Specific attention was paid to the religion of Islam and its effect on the adaptations not only in class 200 Religion, but also in classes 300 Social Sciences, 700 Arts, and 900 History and Geography. The study also included a review of the impact of adaptations in the various translation on the editions of DDC that followed these translations (DDC 15-19, and Abridged DDC 8-10 were considered). The study demonstrated the following: (1) Socio-cultural factors, such as religion, language, customs, history, etc. are the cause of most of the adaptations. (2) Since the translations studied are aimed at serving the countries which share some common socio-cultural features, the same concepts were often adapted by all these translations, but the methods of adaptations and the notations used are not always compatible. (3) Although the DDC options or provisions for local emphasis are useful, they are not always the most suitable ones, and are often ignored by the translations. Finally, the study provides guidelines and instructions for standardization of future foreign language editions of DDC. [DAI 43/06-A: 1734.]

121   Momeni, Mahvash Keshmiri. *Adaptations of DDC in the Middle East*. [Urbana-Champaign]: University of Illinois, Graduate School of Library and Information Science, 1985. 41 p.

122   Mustafa, 'Awdah Mahmud, and Walid 'Atmah. *Qadayah fi Fahrasat al-Matbu' al-'Arabi: al-Qawa'id wa-al-Hulul*. al-Riyadh: Maktabat al-Malik Fahd al-Wataniyah, 1997.

123   Qasim, Nizar Muhammad 'Ali. "Madakhil al-hay'at al-'Arabiyah wa-muqtarahat li-hululiha." *al-Majallah al-'Arabiyah lil-Ma'lumat* 8, no. 1 (1987): 134-157.

According to the author, the Anglo-American cataloging rules have some limitations when applied to Arabic entries. He proposes a solution for entries related to Arabic organizations.

124 Sa'ati, Yahya Mahmud. "Ru'us al-mawdu'at al-'Arabiyah: madkhal li-dirasah." *'Alam al-Kutub* 2, no. 1 (May 1981): 2-9.

The author reviews the literature pertaining to Arabic subject headings, and the lists of subject headings presently used.

125 Salih, G. Khamas. "Ahammiyyat al-'inwan fi fahrasat al-mawad al-thaqafiyah lil-maktabah al-'Arabiyah." *Risalat al-Maktabah* 26, no. 2 (June 1991): 43-63.

The importance of descriptive cataloging, to facilitate accessibility of library materials, is stressed. The problems of Arabic names and the attempts to unify their forms are discussed.

126 Soltani, P. "Translation and expansion of classification systems in the Arab countries and Iran." *International Cataloguing and Bibliographic Control* 25, no. 1 (January-March 1996): 13-15.

This study focuses on the two most commonly used classification systems: the Library of Congress (LC) and the Dewey Decimal Classification (DDC). It discusses the necessity for their expansion and translation in developing countries, and covers translations and expansion of DDC and LC in Arab countries and Iran.

127 al-Suwayna', 'Ali al-Sulayman. "al-Tahlil al-mawdu'i wa-al-takshif." *Maktabat al-Idarah* 15, no. 1 (August 1987): 27-76.

128 Swaydan, Nasser M. "Akhta' al-nashirin al-'Arab wa-in'ikasatiha 'ala al-fahrasah." *Maktabat al-Idarah* 9, no. 2 (February 1982): 23-35.

129 Vassie, Roderic. "A reflection of reality—authority control of Muslim personal names." *International Cataloguing and Bibliographic Control* 19, no. 1 (January-March 1990): 3-6.

Outlines the basic elements and forms involved in Muslim names. It argues that western libraries have difficulty in deciding on the correct entry element, AACR2's guidance is inadequate, and the problem is increased by variations in romanization of Arabic scripts.

130 Yusuf, Qasim. "Ru'us al-mawdu'at al- 'Arabiyah al-maqlubah afdal min al-ru'us al-tabi'iyah." *'Alam al-Kutub* 10, no. 4 (November 1989): 498-504.

CD-ROM DATABASES INFORMATION SERVICES

131 el-Hadidy, Bahaa. "The breakeven point for using CD-ROM versus online: a case-study for database access in a developing country." *Journal*

of the American Society for Information Science 45, no. 4 (May 1994): 273-283.

The introduction of CD-ROM products has offered promise in accelerating the access to computer-based databases in developing countries. CD-ROM has been considered the most appropriate technology to the infrastructure of these countries. This article discusses a case study which seeks answers to two major questions that can impact on the use of CD-ROM by developing countries: (1) the extent to which publicly available CD-ROM databases can satisfy the information needs of a particular information requirement for a particular development situation in a developing country; and (2) the economics of an alternative system of CD-ROM, supplemented by online searching. The relative costs of searching CD-ROM vs. online are investigated, and the breakeven analysis of the costs of CD-ROM vs. online is discussed as a potential approach to a cost-effective system for accessing databases in developing countries. This article discusses the implications of the law of core and scatter on the volume of use of databases and its effects on the economics of searching CD-ROM vs. online. [A]

132 Kanamugire, Athanase B. "Partners in developing CD-ROM services for developing-countries." *Libri* 45, no. 2 (June 1995): 106-112.

This article contends that although CD-ROM is probably the most appropriate media of access to information for developing countries at the moment, the application of the CD-ROM technology in developing countries is fraught with many problems which may be overcome through joint ventures of donor agencies, recipient local institutions and CD-ROM publishers. It is argued that many CD-ROM products do not meet the information needs of the majority of the potential user population. Peasants and workers who constitute the majority of the population are illiterate, or semiliterate, and lack computer literacy. Thus, they cannot effectively use CD-ROM products. Nonetheless, the paper asserts that CD-ROM has many advantages over other media of information storage, distribution and access in developing countries. Some major shortcomings of CD-ROMs within the context of developing countries are discussed. It is contended that donor agencies, national institutions, and publishers can cooperate in producing databases pertinent to the needs of developing countries. This may be accomplished through, among others, inter-donor agency cooperation or cooperation with individual regional information systems. Donor agencies may also cooperate with indigenous information systems or information professionals. [A]

133 Nicholls, Paul, and Shaheen Majid. "The potential for CD-ROM technology in less-developed countries." *Canadian Library Journal* 46, no. 4 (August 1989): 257-263.

The information infrastructure supporting scientific and technical research in less-developed countries is often so inadequate that attempts to transfer certain information technologies, such as online database searching, have proven unsuccessful. This paper explores the role CD-ROMs can play in expanding the physical, communications, documentary and human resources available to the developing world.

134 Salem, Shawky. "Tiqaniyyat al-aqras al-daw'iyah al-madghutah CD-ROM wa-tatbiqatiha al-haliyah wa-al-mustaqbaliyah: dirasah wafiyah li-ihda mazahir sina'at al-ma'lumat al-mutaqaddimah wa-ta'thiratiha 'ala bunyat al-ma'lumat al-'Arabiyah." **al-Majallah al-'Arabiyah lil-Ma'lumat** 10, no. 1 (1989): 5-29.

Reviews the development of CD-ROMs, their application and impact on the Arab information system.

135 al-Shorbaji, Najeeb. "Ma huwa hatha al CD/ROM." **Risalat al-Maktabah** 28, nos. 1-2 (March-June 1993): 53-58.

CHILDREN'S LITERATURE

136 Abu al-Nasr, Julinda. "Tanmiyat adab al-atfal fi al-'alam al-'Arabi." In *al-Atfal al-'Arab wa Mu'awiqat al-Tanshi'ah al-Sawiyah*. 4th annual book, pp. 113-140. Kuwait: Kuwait Society for the Development of Arab Childhood, 1987.

CLIPPINGS

137 Itayem, Mahmoud A. *al-Dalil al-'Amali li-Tasnif al-Malaffat al-Suhufiyah wa-al-Mawad al-Mukammilah Laha*. Tunis: Jami'at al-Duwal al-'Arabiyah, al-Amanah al-'Ammah, Markaz al-Tawthiq wa-al-Ma'lumat, 1987.

138 Jajawi, Hayfa' Ayyub. "Istikhdam al-hasib al-ali fi tanzim al-qisasat al-suhufiyah." **al-Majallah al-'Arabiyah lil-Ma'lumat** 14, no. 1 (1993): 84-96.

COLLECTION DEVELOPMENT/ACQUISITION

139 Albin, Michael W. "Acquisition of conference proceedings from the Arab world." **Library Acquisitions: Practice & Theory** 6, no. 2 (1982): 201-209.

Contribution to an issue devoted to library acquisitions from the Third World. Proceedings of 143 conferences held in the Arab world are examined to: (1) define what a librarian means by conference; (2) delineate the morphology of conference proceedings; and (3) highlight various problems in identifying and acquiring conference proceedings from the Arab Middle East.

140 Atiyeh, George N. "Acquisitions from the Middle East." *Library Acquisitions: Practice & Theory* 6, no. 2 (1982): 185-194.

Despite the growth of Middle Eastern studies in the US and accompanying growth of library collections, in general these lag behind other areas of the world. Efforts to address this problem include the PL-480 acquisitions program and the current effort to compile a Near East Union List. Many of the problems in developing collections lie with the countries of the Middle East. National bibliographies and other bibliographical compilations are, where they are even available, often published only after the books are out of print. Some recent reference bibliographies and serials lists have made a small beginning to correcting this. Part of the problem lies with the publishing industry which is often diffuse, subject to political policies, and directed toward existing limited markets. Similarly, dealers are reluctant to offer blanket order service as currency and export restrictions act as deterrents. The two best approaches are acquisitions trips and exchanges. In general the political volatility of the region precludes generalizations about any aspect of acquisitions, publishing, or distributing. A list of dealers in Middle East materials in Europe, the USA and Middle East is appended. [A]

141 Shahin, Sharif Kamil. "al-Asalib al-mukhtalifah li taqyim al-muqtanayat fi al-maktabat wa-marakiz al-ma'lumat ma' dirasah li-manhaj al-nazrah al-shamilah (conspectus) wa-istikhdamatihah al-mukhtalifah." *al-Majallah al-'Arabiyah lil-Ma'lumat* 15, no. 2 (1994): 30-74.

Reviews the motives, methods, and procedures used in assessing library collections and holdings.

COMPUTERS IN LIBRARIES—USE

142 el-Akhras, Mahmud. "Dawr al-Munazzamah al-'Arabiyah lil-Tarbiyah wa-al-Thaqafah wa-al-'Ulum fi istikhdam al-hasib al-iliktruni fi al-maktabat wa marakiz al-ma'lumat fi al-Watan al-'Arabi." *al-Majallah al-'Arabiyah lil-Ma'lumat* 3, no. 1 (1982): 104-118.

Examines the activities and achievements of the Department of Documentation and Information and the Department of Science attached to ALESCO, and the use of computers for bibliographic services in libraries and documentation centers of the Arab world.

143 Aman, Mohammed M. "al-Hasib al-saghir wa-istikhdamatuhu fi al-maktabat wa-marakiz al-ma'lumat (1)." *al-Majallah al-'Arabiyah lil-Ma'lumat* 5, no. 1 (1984): 103-120.

144 Aman, Mohammed M. "Baramij al-hasibat al-saghirah (al-mikruwiyah) al-mustakhdamah fi al-maktabat wa marakiz al-ma'lumat (2)." *al-Majallah al-'Arabiyah lil-Ma'lumat* 5, no. 2 (1984): 9-64.

Examines microcomputer programs used in libraries and documentation centers.

145 Inayat, Fatin. "Istikhdam al-hasibat al-iliktruniyah fi a'mal al-maktabat wa-al-tawthiq bi al-Watan al-'Arabi." *Risalat al-Maktabah* 13, no. 2 (June 1978): 26-34.

Emphasizes the importance of computerization in library and documentation centers in the Arab world. Main issues discussed at conferences in Cairo in 1973 and in Khartoum in 1975 were: needs of the computer and its uses; requirements and problems in its application; substitutes for the computer in the Arab countries. Concludes that cooperation at both international and national levels is important; arrangements for the necessary funds are being made. Also calls for library training on a larger scale.

146 Itayem, Mahmoud A. "Imkaniyyat istikhdam al-hasib al-iliktruni fi al-khadamat al-bibliyughrafiyah." *al-Majallah al-'Arabiyah lil-Ma'lumat* 3, no. 2 (1982): 28-47.

The author discusses the possibilities of using computers in bibliographical services.

CONSULTANCY AND CONSULTANTS

147 al-Maliki, Majbal Lazim Musallam. "al-Khadamat al-istishariyah fi al-maktabat wa-marakiz al-ma'lumat." *Risalat al-Maktabah* 31, no. 1 (March 1996): 27-45.

Provides a survey of the historical development of library consultants and consulting services, and their roles and functions.

COPYRIGHT/INTELLECTUAL PROPERTY

148 al-Haluji, 'Abd al-Sattar 'Abd al-Haq. "Haq al-mu'allif fi al-qawanin al-'Arabiyah." *'Alam al-Kutub* 2, no. 4 (January- February 1982): 645-652.

149 Kan'an, Nawwaf. "Haq al-mu'allif fi al-ittifaqyiyyat al-duwaliyah." *'Alam al-Kutub* 2, no. 4 (January-February 1982): 597-644.

The author analyzes the copyright laws that are applied internationally, the Arab agreement concerning the intellectual property, and the protection of authors.

150 al-Khawli, Jamal. *Ithbat al-Mulkiyah fi al-Watha'iq al-'Arabiyah*. al-Qahirah: al-Dar al-Misriyah al-Lubnaniyah, 1994.

The author describes different kinds of ownership and how to prove the manusripts' property.

DICTIONARIES/ENCYCLOPEDIAS

151 Barudi, 'Abd Allah 'Umar. *al-Mu'jam al-Mu'arrab lil-Mustalahat al-Maktabiyah: Inkilizi-'Arabi*. Bayrut: 'Alam al-Kutub, 1983. 319 p.

152 Benhawy, Mohamed Amin. *Dictionary of Library Terms, English-Arabic*. 2nd ed., rev., enl., annotated. Cairo: Dar al-Fikr al-Arabi, 1985. 296 p.

153 Dyab, Miftah Muhammad. *al-Mu'jam al-Hadith fi 'Ilm al-Maktabat wa-al-Ma'lumat: Injilizi, 'Arabi* [English, Arabic.] Tarabulus, Libya: al-Hay'ah al-Qawmiyah lil-Bahth al-'Ilmi, 1985. 114 p.

154 Dyab, Miftah Muhammad (comp.). *Mu'jam Mustalahat 'Ilm al-Ma'lumat: Mu'jam Mashruh: Injilizi-'Arabi*. [Tripoli, Libya]: Jami'at al-Fatih, 1985. 135 p.

155 Faduli, Fa'iq (comp.). *Mu'jam al-Mustalahat al-Maktabiyah: 'Arabi-Inkilizi, Inkilizi-'Arabi*. al-Fajjalah [Cairo]: Dar al-Thaqafah lil-Tiba'ah wa-al-Nashr; Kuwayt: Dar al-Nashr wa-al-Matbu'at al-Kuwaytiyah, 1986. 103, 99 p.

156 al-Husayni, 'Abd al-Hasan. *Qamus al-Ma'lumatiyah: 'Arabi, Inkilizi, Faransi*. Bayrut, Lebanon: Dar al-Qalam, 1987. 450 p.

157 Khalil, Jurj, Zuha 'Isa, and Najib al-Nimr, with 'Ali Fa'ur and Muhsin Ibn Fath Allah. *Qamus al-Ma'lumatiyah; Faransi-Inkilizi-'Arabi=Dictionnaire informatique: francais, anglais, arabe*. Bayrut, Lebanon: Sharikat Adunis, 1987. 343 p.

158 al-Qadi, Wadad. "Biographical dictionaries: inner structure and cultural significance." In *The Book in the Islamic World: The Written Word and Communication in the Middle East*. Edited by George N. Atiyeh, pp. 93-122. Albany: State University of New York Press, 1995.

A paper originally presented at a conference held at the Library of Congress, Washington, D.C., November 8-9, 1990. Biographical books are among the earliest and most extensive genres of Arabic literature. The author believes that biographical dictionaries are not only indispensable tools of research, but also a mirror in which are reflected important aspects of the intellectual and cultural development of the Islamic community. A study of the inner structure of biographical dictionaries produced during the first nine centuries of Islam reveals that development.

159   al-Shami, Ahmad Muhammad, and Sayyid Hasabullah. *al-Mu'jam al-Mawsu'i li Mustalahat al-Maktabat* wa-al-*Ma'lumat: Inglizi-'Arabi = Encyclopedic Dictionary of Library and Information Science Terms: English-Arabic*. al-Riyadh: Dar al-Marrikh lil-Nashr, 1988. 1206 p.

160   Sharaf al-Din, 'Abd al-Tawwab. *al-Mawsu'ah al-'Arabiyah fi al-Watha'iq wa-al-Maktabat*. al-Dawhah, Qatar: Dar al-Thaqafah, 1986. 738 p.

161   Sharaf al-Din, 'Abd al-Tawwab, and Abdul Fattah El-Shaer. *Cyclopaedic Glossary of Library, Documentation, and Information Sciences: English, Arabic*. al-Kuwayt: Kadhma Company, 1984. 448 p.

162   al-Sharif, 'Abdullah M. *Dictionary of Library and Information Science Terminology: (English-Arabic)*. 3rd ed. enl. and rev. Tripoli, Libya: General Publication, Distribution and Advertising Co., 1985. 327 p.

DOCUMENTATION

163   Abu-'Izza, 'Abdullah. "Dawr al-arshiv al-watani fi-istratijiyyat al-tawthiq wa-al-ma'lumat fi al-Watan al-'Arabi." *al-Majallah al-'Arabiyah lil-Ma'lumat* 15, no. 1 (1994): 23-40.

164   Abu al-Nur, 'Abd al-Wahhab. *Dirasat fi 'Ulum al-Maktabat wa-al-Tawthiq wa-al-Bibliyughrafiya*. al-Qahirah: 'Alam al-Kutub, 1996.

165   Itayem, Mahmoud A. Mashru' "al-muwasafah al-'Arabiyah: al-ma'lumat wa-al-tawthiq–dalil 'anasir al-bayanat al-bibliyughrafiyah: tatbiqat al-tazwid." *Risalat al-Maktabah* 29, no. 2 (June 1994): 4-54.

A translation of the international standard ISO 8459-2 of 1992 which specifies and describes data elements required in the interchange of data between institutions involved in the acquisition of bibliographic material.

166   Khafagi, Muhammad Tawfiq. "Nazrah shamilah 'ala khadamat al-tawthiq fi al Watan al-'Arabi." *al-Majallah al-'Arabiya lil-Ma'lumat* 4, no. 2 (December 1983): 9-20.

167   Khalifa, Sha'ban 'Abd al-'Aziz. *Awraq al-Rabi' fi al-Maktabat wa-al-Ma'lumat*. [Cairo]: al-'Arabi lil-Nashr wa-al-Tawzi', 1989-. vols. 1-5.

168   Qaddurah, Layla Ghandur. "Ahammiyyat al-tawthiq." *Tarikh al-'Arab wa-al-'Alam* 3, no. 30 (April 1981): 39-41.

169 Razzuqi, Nu'ayma Hasan. "al-Tawthiq li-baramij wa-nuzum al-ma'lumat: dirasah li-mustalzamatihi wa-ma'uqatihi." *al-Majallah al-'Arabiya lil-Ma'lumat* 15, no. 2 (1994): 98-109.

Data processing is facing a number of problems mostly due to poor documentation. The author reviews a number of information and research centers that have developed specialized applications dealing with documentation.

170 Regnier, Jean-Jacques. "Une experience de gestion documentaire integree, l'IREMAN." [An experience of integrated documentation management, IREMAN.] *Documentaliste* 25, no. 2 (March-April 1988): 67-71.

The Institute of Research and Study on the Arab and Muslim World, IREMAN, based at Aix-en-Provence, has developed a computerized documentation management system based on using a standard program for a range of different operations: bibliographic control of books and periodicals, information retrieval, and production of bibliographies etc. Details are given of the hardware and software used, procedures for processing documents and online searching, and the products of the system. The system has now been in operation for three years and modifications are continually being introduced, chiefly to facilitate direct access for end users.

171 Salih, Muhammad Amin. "Manhajiyyat nizam al-ma'lumat: tatbiq fi al-tawthiq." *al-Majallah al-'Arabiyah lil-Ma'lumat* 5, no. 2 (1984): 65-80.

Discusses an information system methodology and its application to documentation.

172 al-Zahhawi, Fari'ah. "Nashat al-tawthiq wa-al-ma'lumat fi Jami'at al-Duwal al-'Arabiyah." *Shu'un 'Arabiyah*, no. 13 (March 1982): 447-452.

ETHICS

173 Hashwah, Butrus. "Akhlaqiyyat al-mihnah lil-maktabiyyin." *Risalat al-Maktabah* 31, no. 2 (June 1996): 19-24.

Provides a discussion of the ethics that should be applied for those who work in the field of information.

GOVERNMENT PUBLICATIONS

174 al-'Askar, Fahd Ibrahim. "Taqyim al-watha'iq al-rasmiyah." *Maktabat al-Idarah* 11, no. 3 (June 1984): 33-51.

175 Nurcombe, Valerie J., and Avril Shields. "Middle East." In *Information Sources in Official Publications*. Edited by Valerie J. Nurcombe, pp. 467-521. London: Bowker-Saur, 1997.

Article included in a practical guide to sources of information on government publications and official documents. Describes libraries, information sources and library materials with particular reference to countries in the Middle East.

INDEXING AND ABSTRACTING SERVICES

176 Bachir, Imad, and Andrew Buxton. "The information content of titles of Arabic periodicals." *Journal of Information Science* 17, no. 1 (1991): 57-63.

Provides a partial answer to the question of whether titles of Arabic periodical articles can be used for keyword indexing techniques. Examines the information content of titles of Arabic research papers in 16 scientific and non-scientific fields by counting the number of their substantive words and comparing the results with those for English periodical articles in the same subject areas. Although significant differences are found between the two samples in some subjects, such as agriculture, philosophy, linguistics, law and library and information science, Arabic titles generally appear to be as informative as English titles. Some practical problems are found in using Arabic titles for indexing, for example, the need to strip prefixes from keywords.

177 Bachir, Imad, and Andrew Buxton. "The use of topic sentences for evaluating the representativeness of Arabic article titles." *Journal of Information Science* 19, no. 6 (1993): 455-465.

This paper provides another partial answer to the question of whether titles of Arabic periodical articles can be used for keyword indexing techniques and for the production of Arabic title-derivative printed indexes. It examines and evaluates the representativeness of Arabic article titles in five different disciplines by comparing the substantive words found in titles to the content of their accompanying topic sentences in the introduction or objectives parts of articles. Although significant differences are found between titles in library and information science and titles in philosophy, Arabic titles appear to provide good representations of their articles. Between 70% and 88% of the substantive words in titles matched substantive words in the corresponding topic sentences. [A]

178 Baydas, Rasha Barghuthi. *Dalil al-Takshif wa-al-Istikhlas*. 'Amman: al-Munazzamah al-'Arabiyah lil-'Ulum al-Idariyah, 1987.

GENERAL WORKS

179 Dahbur, Sidqi. "al-Nashat al-bibliyughrafi fi al-Watan al-'Arabi." *al-Majallah al-'Arabiyah lil-Ma'lumat* 2, no. 1 (1980): 89-100.

An assessment of bibliographic activities that are taking place in the Arab world, generally by individuals.

180 Ghani, Abdul. "Arabic literature: uniterm indexing system for storage and retrieval." *International Library Review* 19, no. 4 (October 1987): 321-333.

The information explosion has created a demand for analyzing, organizing and disseminating information and has popularized the subject approach to information. Mortimer Taub's Uniterm system of coordinate indexing purported to be the most practical and popular form of indexing, is described. The possibilities of using uniterm indexing system for storing information in the Arabic language are examined. Problems encountered are outlined and fields in which standardization is needed are identified.

181 Habaili, Hussein. "al-Mu'alajah al-lughawiyah lil-ma'lumat." *al-Majallah al-'Arabiyah lil-Ma'lumat* 5, no. 2 (1984): 107-123.

The author introduces the different tools and techniques of linguistics used in information processing.

182 Hmeidi, Ismail, Ghassan Kanaan, and Martha W. Evens. "Design and implementation of automatic indexing for information retrieval with Arabic documents." *Journal of the American Society for Information Science* 48 (October 1997): 867-881.

The authors have put together a corpus of 242 abstracts of Arabic documents using the proceedings of the Saudi Arabian National Conferences as a source. Most of these abstracts involve computer science and Information systems. They also designed and built an automatic Information retrieval—from scratch to handle Arabic data. The system was implemented in the C language using the GCC compiler and runs on IBM/PCs and compatible microcomputers. The authors have implemented both automatic and manual indexing techniques for this. A long series of experiments using measures of recall and precision has demonstrated that automatic indexing is at least as effective as manual indexing and more effective in some cases. Since automatic Indexing is both cheaper and faster, their results suggest that one can achieve a wider coverage of the literature with less money and produce as good results as with manual indexing. The authors have also compared the retrieval results using words as index terms versus stems and roots, and confined the results obtained by al-Kharashi and Abu-Salem with smaller corpora that root indexing is more effective than word indexing. [A]

183 Itayem, Mahmoud A. *al-Dalil al-'Amali lil-Tahlil al-Mawdu'i wa-al-Takshif*. Tunis: Jami'at al-Duwal al-'Arabiyah, al-Amanah al-'Ammah, Markaz al-Tawthiq wa-al-Ma'lumat, 1987.

184 Itayem, Mahmoud A. *Qawa'id al-Shabakah al-'Arabiyah lil-Ma'lumat li-Tartib al-Madakhil fi al-Faharis wa-al-Bibliyughrafiyat wa-al-Adillah*. Tunis: Jami'at al-Duwal al-'Arabiyah, Markaz al-Tawthiq wa-al-Ma'lumat, 1989.

185 Jirjis, Jasim Muhammad, and Muhammad Hasan Qasim al-Khafaji. "Kashshafat al-dawriyyat al-'Arabiyah: dirasah hasriyah taqyimiyah." *al-Majallah al-'Arabiyah lil-Ma'lumat* 10, no. 2 (1989): 74-96.

186 al-Kharuf, Yunis Isma'il. "al-Takshif." *Risalat al-Maktabah* 31, no. 3 (September 1996): 4-23.

The author considers "Indexing" as one of the major services offered by libraries and information centers. He discusses the different types, forms and specifications of indexing.

187 Mashali, Huriyyah Ibrahim. "'Ilm al-bibliyughrafiyah: al-nash'ah wa-al-tatawwur." *'Alam al-Kutub* 9, no. 4 (November 1988): 489-499.

188 Qasim, Hishmat Muhammad 'Ali. "Kashshaf al-kalimat al-muftahiyah fi al-siyaq wa-ihtimalatihi fi al-lughah al-'Arabiyah." *'Alam al-Kutub* 5, no. 4 (January 1985): 638-650.

The author discusses the KWIC index concept, the Arabic language in specialist information systems and the linguistic problems that are reported.

INFORMATION CENTERS

189 Ali, Syed Iftekar. "Arab League Educational, Cultural and Scientific Organization (ALECSO) and its contribution to Middle Eastern libraries." *International Library Review* 17, no. 1 (January 1985): 67-75.

After providing a brief historical description of libraries in the Arab countries and of the Arab League, the author provides a detailed account of ALECSO: its history, aims, finance, department of documentation and information, library, library education program, and achievements. A few suggestions for further enhancement of ALECSO's work and popularity are made at the end.

190 Arab League Educational, Cultural and Scientific Organization. *Dalil Marakiz al-Tawthiq wa-al-Ma'lumat fi al-Watan al-'Arabi*. Jami'at al-Duwal al-'Arabiyah, al-Munazzamah al-'Arabiyah lil-Tarbiyah wa-al-

Thaqafah wa-al-'Ulum, Idarat al-Tawthiq wa-al-ma'lumat. al-Qahirah: al-Idarah, 1978. 134 p.

191 Habib, 'Abd al-Halim. "Dawr marakiz al-ma'lumat wa tatbiqatiha al-muqaranah: 'ard wa-talkhis." *al-Idarah* 18, no. 1 (July 1985): 64-70.

192 Khafagi, Muhammad Tawfiq. *Dalil Khidmat al-Tawthiq fi al-Watan al-'Arabi*. Tunis: Jami'at al-Duwal al-'Arabiyah, al-Munazzamah al-'Arabiyah lil-Tarbiyah wa-al-Thaqafah wa-al-'Ulum, Idarat al-Tawthiq wa-al-ma'lumat, 1985. 206 p.

193 Khafagi, Muhammad Tawfiq. "Arab League Educational, Cultural and Scientific Organization." In *World Encyclopedia of Library and Information Services*. 3rd ed. (pp. 53-54). Chicago: American Library Association, 1993.

Discusses the history and development of ALECSO and its main activities. An earlier but more detailed version appears in *IFLA Journal* (vol. 15, no. 3, 1989, pp. 246-250) under the title: "ALECSO and its activities in the field of information." This earlier version reviews the aims and goals of ALECSO, its institutional framework, and its major achievements in the fields of education, culture and science. Also included is the role played by AID (ALECSO Information Department) in the development and promotion of documentation and library services in the Arab world.

194 Salem, Shawky. "FID/NANE adopts AID program for libraries and information centres in its region." *FID News Bulletin* 44, no. 3 (March 1994): 49-50.

The FID Regional organization for North Africa and the Near East (FID/NANE) was established to help libraries and information centers in 21 Arab countries, Mali, Chad and Niger to develop information systems and services, especially an infrastructure of library and information centers in the region. Discusses the background to the creation of an AID program, describes the program and policy devised, and outlines the following acquisitions which might be funded by the program: books, journals, reports, studies, research material, theses, information technology and general equipment.

195 al-Sharif, 'Abdullah M. "al-Bunyah al-asasiyah li-marakiz al-tawthiq wa-al-ma'lumat." *al-Majallah al-'Arabiyah lil-Ma'lumat* 5, no. 1 (1984): 147-161.

196 Tadmuri, 'Umar. *Dar al-'Ilm fi al-Qarn al-Khamis al-Hijri*. Tarabulus [Lebanon]: Dar al-Insha' lil-Sihafah wa-al-Tiba'ah wa-al-Nashr, 1982. 95 p.

197 UNESCO. *Dalil Marakiz al-Buhuth wa-al-Tawthiq fi al-'Ulum al-Ijtima'iyah bi-al-Mintaqah al-'Arabiyah*. al-Qahirah: Yunisku, al-Markaz al-Iqlimi al-'Arabi lil-Buhuth wa-al-Tawthiq fi al-'Ulum al-Ijtima'iyah, 1980. 12, 158 p.

INFORMATION POLICY

198 Imam, Ibrahim, et al. *Qadiyat al-Takhtit al-I'lami fi al-Watan al-'Arabi*. Ijtima' li-Khubara' al-Takhtit al-I'lami fi al-Watan al-'Arabi, Cairo, 1979. al-Qahirah: Jami'at al-Duwal al-'Arabiyah, al-Munazzamah al-'Arabiyah lil-Tarbiyah wa-al-Thaqafah wa-al-'Ulum, 1980. 168 p.

199 Istasi, Cecile Wesley. "National information policies and networks in Morocco, Tunisia, Egypt and Sudan: a comparative study." *Alexandria* 2, no. 3 (December 1990): 23-38.

Compares the development and functions of the National Documentation Center of Morocco, Egypt's National Documentation and Information Center, the National Committee for Documentation in Tunisia, and the National Documentation Center of Sudan.

200 Skreslet, Paula Youngman. "A people of the book: information policy and practice in the Muslim world." *Libri* 47, no. 1 (April 1997): 57-66.

Library and information services are still deficient in many developing countries, and policies to set goals and facilitate planning in support of these activities are often lacking. Explores what information policy may mean for the Moslem world; identifies some of the special strengths that Islamic tradition can bring to information work; and calls attention to the obstacles impeding progress in this area. Discusses the need to consider policy making at the tribal, regional, national and transnational level. A number of misconceptions and anxieties may be preventing an accurate understanding of the situation, and also inhibiting the development of coherent, realistic and original strategies for improvement. [A]

INFORMATION SERVICES

201 Ali, Syed Nazim. "Science and technology information transfer in developing countries: some problems and suggestions." *Journal of Information Science* 15, no. 2 (1989): 81-93.

The importance of science and technology information in technological advancement and research and development is obvious. Likewise, it contributes directly to the economic development of a country. Providing access to information for scientists and technologists working in developing countries is a challenging task. This paper examines various methods practiced in the dissemination of science and technology information in developing countries.

202 Anwar, Mumtaz A. *Information Services in Muslim Countries: An Annotated Bibliography of Expert Studies and Reports on Library, Information and Archive Services*. London: Mansell, 1985. xiv, 146 p.

The author has brought together a list of 338 documents about the then 45 member states of the Organization of the Islamic Conference. He identifies published and unpublished reports on developing library, information and archive services. Most entries are annotated and are provided with subject keywords. The work is introduced by two essays, and separate author, title, and subject indexes are included.

203 Chandler, George. "Recent developments in Muslim, Arab and Egyptian library and information services." *International Library Review* 18, no. 4 (October 1986): 389-397.

This paper reviews four comprehensive publications which are sources of information on Muslim, Arab and Egyptian libraries and information services. It includes a list of selected Arab and Muslim papers, which have appeared in *International Library Review* between 1969 and 1985.

204 Dahbur, Sidqi. "al-Mawad al-sama'iyah wa-al-basariyah fi al-maktabat wa-'ilaqatiha bi al-maktabah al-'Arabiyah." *al-Majallah al-'Arabiyah lil-Ma'lumat* 3, no. 1 (1982): 143-167.

The author presents a historical account of the use of audio-visual materials in libraries in general and in the Arab countries, in particular. He enumerates the obstacles facing the use of these materials in the Arab countries.

205 al-Daly, 'Abd al-Baqi. "Mutatallibat al-nuhud bi-qita' al-ma'lumat." *al-Majallah al-'Arabiyah lil-Ma'lumat* 14, no. 1 (1993): 26-41.

206 Itayem, Mahmoud A. (ed.). *al-Ma'lumat min ajl al-Tanmiyah fi al-Watan al-'Arabi: Mabniyah 'ala al-Awraq allati Quddimat ila al-Multaqa al-Awwal Hawla al-Shabakah al-'Arabiyah lil-Ma'lumat, Tunis, 1987/6/12-8*. Multaqa hawla al-Shabakah al-'Arabiyah lil-Ma'lumat, Tunis, 1987. Tunis: Jami'at al-Duwal al-'Arabiyah, al-Amanah al-'Ammah, Markaz al-Tawthiq wa-al-Ma'lumat, 1988. 2 vols. (1137 p.).

207 Itayem, Mahmoud A. "Itahat al-ma'lumat al-'ilmiyah fi al-Watan al-'Arabi." *al-Majallah al-'Arabiyah lil-Ma'lumat* 14, no. 1 (1993): 42-57.

The author describes the different approaches made by Arab countries to promote access to scientific literature.

208 Khafagi, Muhammad Tawfiq. "Dawr al-maktabat fi al-nuzum al-qutriyah lil-Ma'lumat wa makaniha fi al-buna al-asasiyah." *al-Majallah al-'Arabiyah lil-Ma'lumat* 5, no. 1 (1984): 9-25.

209 Markaz al-Imarat lil-Dirasat wa-al-Buhuth al-Istiratijiyah. *The Information Revolution and the Arab World: Its Impact on State and Society*. Abu Dhabi, United Arab Emirates: Emirates Center for Strategic Studies and Research, 1998. xii, 236 p. Includes bibliographical references (p. 215-229) and index.

The papers contained in this volume were among those presented at the Emirates Center for Strategic Studies and Research (ECSSR) Third Annual Conference, entitled: *The impact of the information and communication revolution on society and state in the Arab world, held in Abu Dhabi, 4-7 January 1997*. Introduction/Jamal S. Al-Suwaidi—The information-communications revolution and the global economy/Lester Thurow—What makes Arabian Gulf satellite TV programs? A comparative analysis of the volume, origin, and type of program/Abdellatif Aloofy—The contribution of public opinion research to an understanding of the information revolution and its impact in North Africa and beyond/Mark Tessler—Mass media and the policy process/David Morgan—Triumph of the image and its aftermath: the Gulf War as media ecology/Hamid Mowlana -- The Arab World and the information age: promises and challenges/Mustapha Masmoudi—Telecommunications trends and policies in the United Arab Emirates and their implications for national development/Muhammad I. Ayish—The impact of the information revolution on society and state in Jordan/Saqer Abdel-Rahim—The age of creation and communication / Michel Saloff- Coste.

210 Mohajir, A. R. "Development of information system in the cultural context of Muslim Ummah." *Pakistan Library Bulletin* 18, no. 1 (March 1987): 19-31.

The Muslim Ummah has to interact through the modern information communication systems and develop an Islamic pattern of life by creating equality of opportunity for its people in intellectual, moral, social, cultural and material fields. Information system development in Muslim Ummah represents a way of achieving ideal development and its benefits are outlined.

211 Muhammad, Yunis 'Aziz. "Khadamat al-ma'lumat." *al-Majallah al-'Arabiyah lil-Ma'lumat* 5, no. 2 (1984): 194-212.

The development of information services requires new techniques and new standards in order to achieve information retrieval.

GENERAL WORKS 49

212 "al-Nadwah al-Iqlimiyyah Hawl al-Siyasat al-Wataniyyah li-Nuzum al-Ma'lumat wa Khadamatiha fi al-Buldan al-'Arabiyah, Amman, al-Mamlakah al-Urduniyah al-Hashimiyah, June 17-20, 1989." *Risalat al-Maktabah* 24, nos. 3-4 (September-December 1989): 5-91.

A special issue on the Regional Seminar on National Policies on Information Systems and Service in the Arab Countries, held in Aman, Jordan, June 17-20, 1989. Issues discussed include the development of national information policies and networks and improving national library and information systems.

213 al-Najdawi, Amin. "Mashakil tatbiqat al-hasibat al-iliktruniyah fi al-maktabat wa-marakiz al-ma'lumat fi al-aqtar al-'Arabiyah." *al-Majallah al-'Arabiyah lil-Ma'lumat* 3, no. 1 (1982): 75-91.

The author describes the different problems facing computerization of libraries and information centers in the Arab world.

214 Rehman, Sajjadur. "National infrastructure of library and information services in Arab countries." *Library Review* 40, no. 1 (1991): 15-28.

Examines the existing situation of library and information infrastructure in Arab countries. Six factors were studied: status of the national library, state of the art of national bibliographic control, availability of indexing and abstracting services, state of inter-library cooperation, existing networking connections, and application of modern technology. The information was gathered by reviewing the relevant literature and by administering a questionnaire to selected resource persons in the relevant countries. Information collected from 15 countries revealed some inherent shortcomings in the infrastructures of these countries which impede any efforts towards networking and resource sharing. [A]

215 Salem, Shawky. "The role of information in science and technology transfer in Arab countries." *Journal of Information Science* 2, no. 5 (November 1980): 255-261.

This paper discusses the position of science and technology in Arab countries and identifies the problems and obstacles in the transfer of science and technology from the developed countries to the Arab countries. It discusses the reasons for these obstacles and proposes solutions, distinguishing the information role in science and technology transfer and the role of a national plan for information services. It considers relations with developed countries and how they should be continued. The help of international organizations should also be enlisted.

216 al-Samirra'i, Iman Fadil. "Masadir al-ma'lumat al-iliktruniyah wa-ta'thiriha 'ala al-maktabat." *al-Majallah al-'Arabiyah lil-Ma'lumat* 14, no. 1 (1993): 58-83.

Discusses the impact of information technology and online information services on libraries.

217 al-Samirra'i, Iman Fadil. "al-Ittijahat al-hadithah fi al-khadamat al-marja'iyah/khadamat al-ma'lumat fi al-maktabat wa-marakiz al-ma'lumat." *al-Majallah al-'Arabiyah lil-Ma'lumat* 16, no. 1 (1995): 65-85.

Discusses modern technologies that are reshaping libraries, especially in the reference and information services.

218 Sattar Chaudhry, Abdus, and Sajjadur Rehman. "Coverage of Islamic literature in selected indexing services." *International Library Review* 17, no. 4 (October 1985): 357-370.

To improve the dissemination of information in the Muslim world, accessibility to Islamic literature needs to be improved. This article examines reasons for the shortcomings in the bibliographic coverage by the available sources, and explores ways of developing improved apparatus. It evaluates the four major indexing and abstracting services in the West which claim to cover Islamic literature by providing a detailed and comprehensive analysis of these services.

219 Shahla Yaghmai, Nargess, Virgil P. Diodato, and Jacqueline A. Maxin. "Arab-Islamic cultures and online bibliographical systems." *International Library Review* 18, no. 1 (January 1986): 15-24.

This paper considers the inadequacy of bibliographical control of and access to information about the development of Arab-Islamic cultures. It describes the consultation of databases available through Bibliographical Retrieval Services (BRS) and DIALOG Information Services in order to determine the degree of online bibliographical support available to Arab-Islamic scholars in the non-Arab world. Databases were searched for specific information on particular Arab-Islamic cultures, as well as on the cultures as a whole. Results are discussed and recommendations are suggested.

220 al-Shorbaji, Najeeb. "Tadaffuq al-bayanat 'ibra al-hudud wa-al-qadayah dhat al-'ilaqah bi-khadamat al-maktabat wa-al-ma'lumat." *Risalat al-Maktabah* 28, no. 3 (September 1993): 4-23.

Provides definition and scope of transborder data flow with emphasis on electronic media. The technological, legal, social and economic issues

GENERAL WORKS 51

involved in transborder data flow are discussed with special reference to the national information policy and its implementation in Jordan.

221 al-Shorbaji, Najeeb. "al-Intirnit wa-al-maktabah." *Risalat al-Maktabah* 32, no. 3 (September 1997): 58-70.

The author approaches the subject of the Internet by introducing the following points: definition, services, linkage and cost of linkage. He discusses the levels of accessibility to the Internet and the tools used to find the information. Finally he discusses the services offered to libraries by the Internet.

222 Tamraz, Ahmad Ali. "al-Qiyas wa-al-taqwim lil-majmu'at al-maktabiyah: dirasah fi falsafat al-asalib bayna al-nazariyah wa-al-tatbiq." *Maktabat al-Idarah* 15, no. 3 (April-May 1988): 119-158.

223 UNESCO. *Nuzum al-Ma'lumat fi al-'Ulum al-Ijtima'iyah: al-Halqah al-Dirasiyah al-Thalithah al-Mun'aqidah bi-al-Markaz, fi al-Muddah min 10-28 Nuvimbir, 1979.* [Cairo]: Yunisku, al-Markaz al-Iqlimi al-'Arabi lil-Buhuth wa-al-Tawthiq fi al-'Ulum al-Ijtima'iyah, 1979. 275 p.

224 UNESCO. *al-Halqah al-Dirasiyah 'an Nuzum al-Ma'lumat wa-al-Tawthiq li-Mustakhdimi al-Ma'lumat fi Majal al-'Ulum al-Ijtima'iyah; 24/11-3/12/1980, Tanjah, al-Maghrib.* al-Qahirah: al-Yunisku, al-Markaz al-Iqlimi al-'Arabi lil-Buhuth wa-al-Tawthiq fi al-'Ulum al-Ijtima'iyah; Tanjah: Kafrad, al-Markaz al-Afriqi lil-Tadrib wa-al-Bahth al-Idari lil-Inma', 1980. 246 p.

INFORMATION SERVICES—SPECIAL SUBJECTS

225 al-'Askar, Fahd Ibrahim. "al-Ta'lim wa-al-ma'lumat fi majal al-arshiv fi al-Watan al-'Arabi." *Maktabat al-Idarah* 13, no. 2 (January-February 1986): 47-65.

226 Feiler, Gil. "Peace and information in the Middle East." In *Proceedings of the 19th International Online Information Meeting, London, 5-7 December, 1995*. Edited by David I. Raitt and Ben Jeapes, pp. 529-537. Oxford and New Jersey: Learned Information Ltd., 1995.

One of the main difficulties faced by potential investors in the Middle East is the lack of business information, including accurate and up-to-date information on business opportunities in the region. Even the largest global database facilities do not provide substantial information or indeed quality information on such activities in Arab countries. In order to benefit potential investors, specialized information is needed which focuses on the micro level. This requires the urgent establishment of business information database services supplying both business opportunities information and more general investment services. The creation of appropriate database services can help to overcome another problem which has stood in the way of increased investment in and grants to the occupied territories of Palestine. To date, one of the principle reasons why non-profit organizations have channeled less money than they can actually afford to Palestinian ventures has been their inability to conduct accurate feasibility studies for such projects. Ideally, every foreign loan or investment should be based on a feasibility study. Lack of such studies either delays the grant, or in many cases prevents it being given altogether. Another problem facing potential investors is the language obstacle, since most information currently available in the Middle East is either in Arabic, Hebrew or in Persian; little is translated into foreign languages and foreign investors are usually therefore dependent on local contacts for advice and information. [A]

227 Pedersen, R. C. "Networked resources on politics in the Middle East." *The Serials Librarian* 27, no. 5 (1995): 37-44.

Due to the complex nature of Middle East politics, this paper asserts that it is especially useful for students of that region to have access to information and opinion that has not yet been subjected to media filters. Describes and evaluates a highly selective list of information resources that can be accessed free of charge through the Internet.

228 Salem, Shawky. "Bibliometric aspects of medical librarianship in Arab countries." *Bulletin of the Medical Library Association* 78, no. 4 (October 1990): 339-344.

This paper discusses the current state and development of health and biomedical libraries in Arab countries. The study concentrates on the Arabic sources of medical articles, and surveys and analyzes the size of the literature and its development in the last 100 years. Two aspects of these sources are covered: the Arab medical information sources published within the Arab region, and those published outside the region. This includes the quantity of material available within and outside the region. The size of the Arab medical literature indicates that it is worthy of collection. Treatment of the Arab medical literature, a pressing and urgent issue, is needed to assist in the research and development of an Arab medical infrastructure. [A]

229 Sattar Chaudhry, Abdus. "Agricultural information in the Arab world—prospects for regional cooperation." *Quarterly Bulletin of the International Association of Agricultural Information Specialists* 32, no. 4 (1987): 185-191.

Agriculture is a major sector of the economy and social structure of many Arab countries. In spite of huge investments in this sector, agricultural development in the region is unsatisfactory. The productivity of agricultural information is very low. Whatever information is generated is not properly controlled and disseminated. Proper information sources as means of access have not been developed adequately. The information resources and services can be strengthened through cooperative efforts. It is suggested that a regional system for cooperation in agricultural information should be developed on the model of AIBA, under the sponsorship of the League of Arab States assigning coordination responsibilities to ALDOC. [A]

230   Sattar Chaudhry, Abdus. "Information exchange in agriculture." In *Building Information Systems in the Islamic World*. Edited by Ziauddin Sardar, pp. 67-76. London and New York: Mansell, 1988.

The author surveys the scope of information exchange programs in agriculture in fifteen countries of the Middle East and concludes that despite huge investments in agriculture in the region, the production of agricultural information is meager. He argues for the setting up of a regional system for sharing agricultural information on the lines of International Information System for Agricultural Sciences and Technology (AGRIS).

INFORMATION STORAGE AND RETRIEVAL

231   Abdel-Hadi, Mohammed Fathi. "Adawat al-bahth wa-al-istirja' al-bibliyughrafi fi al-'ulum al-ijtima'iyah wa ba'd qadaya al-dabt al-bibliyughrafi al-murtabit biha fi al-Watan al-'Arabi." *al-Majallah al-'Arabiyah lil-Ma'lumat* 3, no. 1 (1982): 119-142.

Different tools of bibliographic control are introduced: printed library catalogs, bibliographical lists, guides to serials and dissertations, etc. Bibliographic control problems facing the Arab countries are described too.

232   Aman, Mohammed M. *Bunuk al-Ma'lumat*. Tunis: al-Munazzamah al-'Arabiyah lil-Tarbiyah wa-al-Thaqafah wa-al-'Ulum, 1983.

233   Ellis, Larry M. "Middle East information: the Arab Information Bank." *Online* 15, no. 2 (March 1991): 41-43.

This paper gives a brief, critical review of the Arab Information Bank (DIALOG File 465), which provides access to newspaper, periodical and radio sources about the Arab world and Middle Eastern affairs. It analyzes subject areas covered and gives searching tips and search techniques (for example, all items relating to the Gulf War are indexed under 'Crisis').

234   al-Hajrasi, Sa'd Muhammad. *Qadiyat al-Ikhtizan wa-al-Istirja' al-Iliktruni lil-Ma'lumat al-Bibliyujrafiyah ma'a Namudhaj Mi'yari li-Ashkal al-Ittisal*. al-Qahirah: al-Munazzamah al-'Arabiyah lil- Tarbiyah wa-al-

Thaqafah wa-al-'Ulum, Idarat al-Tawthiq wa-al-Ma'lumat, 1977. 219 p. in various pagings, [4] leaves of plates (some folded): ill.

235   Hashim, Mud Ustfan. "Ma ba'da al-mantiq al-bulini (boolean): al-tatawwurat al-akhirah fi asalib istirja' al-ma'lumat, wa-subul istifadat al-tawthiq al-'Arabi minha." *al-Majallah al-'Arabiyah lil-Ma'lumat* 16, no. 2 (1995): 30-45.

236   al-Hasu, Ahmad 'Abdullah. "Nahwa qa'idat ma'lumat lil-watha'iq wa-al-khattiyyat al-'Arabiyah." *Risalat al-Maktabah* 27 (June 1992): 17-27.

Arab interest in documentation of manuscripts and traditional literature is reviewed. The author calls for the establishment of a database to control the vast amount of literature.

237   Ibrahim, Farid Mohammed Selim. *A Syntactically-Based Preprocessor for a Limited Experimental Arabic Document Retrieval System*. Ph.D., 1988. University of Technology, Loughborough (UK). 439 p.

Describes and discusses an experimental document retrieval system for Arabic texts using linguistic methods of analysis. Specifically, Arabic presents difficulties for the efficient retrieval of information because it is an agglutinative language, thus rendering the stop list method (as commonly used for English texts) near to useless. The system has two stages: the creation of the retrieval lexicon and the search program. The latter is done using a limited online searching which allows for partial matching. The former has four stages. Texts in the form of abstracts are processed by morphological analysis, syntactic analysis, term extraction and term manipulation modules. Each stage produces a new representation of the source text. The morphological analyzer attempts to recognize any prefixes and/or suffixes attached to the words in the corpus being processed. It also assigns grammatical labels specifying the part of speech using a contextual analysis of individual words (assuming that the inflectional features of a word are indicative of its syntactic role). An augmented transition network grammar and parser have been built for this purpose. The same parser has been developed and used in the second stage which is syntactic analysis. It takes as its input the representation of the text created by the morphological analysis, and uses a separate grammar file defined as a recursive transition network. The aim of syntactic analysis is the definition of the relations of the different constituents in the individual sentences being processed. The formation added by the morphological and syntactic analyzers is used in the term extraction module. This module uses a traversal algorithm to negotiate the structure built by syntax, utilizing a set of rules, kept on a file, specifying the type of constructs needing to be selected. The manipulative module generates new entries for each term selected by rotating its elements. The system has been implemented using the Hull V-mode Pascal compiler available on the

L.U.T. Prime System. It has been tested using 40 abstracts selected from a conference proceedings in the field of computer applications. [DAI 49/09-A: 2435.]

238 al-Kharashi, Ibrahim A. *Micro-Airs: A Microcomputer-Based Arabic Information Retrieval System Comparing Words, Stems, and Roots as Index Terms*. Ph.D., 1991. Illinois Institute of Technology. 90 p.

Experimentation with retrieval systems in Arabic language environments has been very limited. Arabization of available information retrieval systems has dealt mostly with internal representation of the Arabic data and translation of menus and system messages to Arabic. The problems of working with the Arabic language have not been confronted directly. Stemming algorithms have been widely used to enhance the retrieval behavior of information systems. In English based systems, stemming algorithms deal with the removal of suffixes to reduce the storage needed for the keyword list and to increase the recall factor by conflating word variants. In the Arabic language, both prefixes and suffixes are added to roots and stems to form related words. The number of affixes used in the Arabic language exceeds that used in English. Surface affix removal processes produce word stems while deep affix removal processes produce word root. This research studies the effect of using words, stems, and roots of Arabic words as index terms on the effectiveness of the retrieval of Arabic bibliographic records. To run the experiment for these three different retrieval methods we used 355 Arabic bibliographic records covering computer and information science, and 29 queries. The test was conducted on an IBM/AT compatible microcomputer using the Microcomputer-based Arabic Information Retrieval System, Micro-AIRS. The effectiveness of the system using word, stem, and root retrieval methods are presented using the recall and precision measures along with two non-parametric statistical tests. The system evaluation results shows the superiority of the root retrieval method over the word retrieval method, and over the stem retrieval method at high recall levels. It also shows the superiority of stem retrieval method over the word retrieval method at all recall levels. The experiments with ranking methods using dice, cosine, and Jaccard similarity coefficients shows that all three similarity coefficients produce exactly the same results when applied to a binary weighted word counts. [DAI 52/07-B: 3703.]

239 al-Kharashi, Ibrahim A., and Martha W. Evens. "Comparing words, stems, and roots as index terms in an Arabic Information Retrieval System." *Journal of the American Society for Information Science* 45, no. 8 (September 1994): 548-60.

The Micro-AIRS System, a microcomputer system for Arabic Information Retrieval, was designed as an experimental system to investigate indexing and retrieval processes for Arabic bibliographic data. A series of experiments were performed using 29 queries against a base of 355 Arabic bibliographic records, covering computer and information science from the bibliographic databank at King Abdulaziz City for Science and Technology. These experiments revealed that using roots and using stems as index terms gives better retrieval results than using words. The root performs as well as or better than the stem at low recall levels and definitely better at high recall levels. Several different binary similarity coefficients were tried: the cosine, Dice, and Jaccard coefficients. All three led to exactly the same document rankings for every query. The experiments were run on an IBM/AT-compatible microcomputer. Micro-AIRS is written in Turbo C, Version 2.0. [A]

240 al-Kindilchie, 'Amir Ibrahim. "Nizam al-ma'lumat wa-dawruha fi khidmat al-mustafidin." *Maktabat al-Idarah* 15:2 (January 1988): 27-51.

241 Madkour, M. A. K. "Information processing and retrieval in Arab countries: traditional approaches and modern potentials." *Unesco Journal of Information Science, Librarianship and Archives Administration* 2, no. 2 (April-June 1980): 97-104.

Argues that Algeria, Egypt, Iraq, Jordan, and Kuwait must not assume that they can enjoy the information revolution without active participation. Importing new technology is no substitute for indigenous technology development. As a prerequisite for participation in international information exchange, each must develop and manage its own scientific and technological information systems. Constraints include absence of bibliographies, lack of user relations, misuse and/or shortage of trained personnel, and, most seriously, the need to adapt technology to Arabic conditions. The paper outlines existing Arabic information infrastructures, efforts to improve information processing, and Arabic bibliographic databases.

242 Qasim, Nizar Muhammad 'Ali. "Hulul 'Arabiyah li-mushkilat al-istirja' al-khati' lil-ma'lumat." *Risalat al-Maktabah* 29 (March 1994): 4-16.

Problems facing Arabic language in storing and retrieving information. The author discusses the problems and offers solutions to avoid retrieval of incorrect information.

243 al-Qawasimah, Muhammad 'Abdullah. "Istikhdam al-lughah al-tabi'iyah fi-istirja' al-ma'lumat wa-mushkilat dhalika fi al-lughah al-'Arabiyah." *Risalat al-Maktabah* 27, no. 3 (September 1992): 35-39.

The article deals with the use of natural language in information retrieval and states the problems of this use in Arabic language.

244 Salem, Shawky, and Tarek El-Haddad. "Bilingual medical terminology database: design, programing and online service. In *Proceedings of the*

14th International Online Information Meeting, London, 11-13 December, 1990. Edited by David Raitt, pp. 413-422. Oxford and New Jersey: Learned Information Ltd., 1990.

The bilingual medical terminology database is one of many projects designed to develop the medical information infrastructure in the Arab World. The database collects all English and Latin terms used for the medical sciences, translates them into Arabic and standardizes the translators. Describes the database design and software considerations. Future plans are outlined briefly.

245 al-Samadi, Nasim Hasan. "Nuzum al-aqras al-basariyah al-muktanazah wa-ta'thiriha 'ala nuzum al-istirja' al-mubashar lil-ma'lumat." *Maktabat al-Idarah* 15, no. 2 (January 1988): 53-75.

246 al-Suwayna', 'Ali al-Sulayman. *Istirja' al-Ma'lumat fi al-Lughah al-'Arabiyah*. al-Riyadh: Maktabat al-Malik Fahd al-Wataniyah, [1994].

247 'Uthman, Samir. "Muhawalah li-taqrib al-mafahim bayna al-fahrasah wa-al-istirja' (al-bibliyughrafi)". *'Alam al-Kitab*, no. 55 (July-August-September 1997): 4-13.

The author stresses the importance of the relationship between the information retrieval specialist, the bibliographer and the information seeker. He describes the different problems facing automation and information centers as well as the new techniques needed to achieve information retrieval.

248 Zash, Amal Muhammad. "al-Bath al-intiqa'i lil-ma'lumat: wasilah taswiqiyah hadariyah." *Risalat al-Maktabah* 29, no. 3 (September 1994): 38-49.

The author defines the selective dissemination of information process, identifying the various tools and techniques used.

INFORMATION/LIBRARY SYSTEMS

249 al-Anzi, Khalid, and Mel Collier. "Arabisation of library and information systems." *Program* 28, no. 4 (October 1994): 395-403.

This paper analyzes the current state of Arabization of computerized library systems. It describes the problems of Arabic language and Arab scripts handling and the limitations of romanization. It brings together the areas of character encoding, standards for coding and bibliographic records, character recognition and lexical analysis. Finally, it reviews the current state of Arabization in commercial library systems and identifies areas for further research.

250 Ashoor, Mohammad Saleh. "Arabisation of automated library systems in the Arab world: need for compatibility and standardisation." *Libri* 39, no. 4 (December 1989): 294-302.

Many libraries in Arab countries have installed computerized library systems and made efforts to Arabize these systems to accommodate the unique features of the Arabic language. Problems encountered include: absence of standard coding system for data entry and display of Arabic characters; unavailability of bilingual terminals with a complete set of Arabic characters; and absence of cooperation and information exchange among institutions involved in Arabization. Describes major Arabization projects in Arab countries and problems they have encountered with the Arabization of DOBIS/LIBIS, MINISIS and STAIRS. [A]

251 Badran, Udit Marun, and Layla al-Farhan. "al-Nas al-mutarabit (al-haybirtixt): mahiyyatuhu wa-tatbiqatuhu." *al-Majallah al-'Arabiyah lil-Ma'lumat* 18, no. 1 (1997): 71-79.

252 Musa, F. A. "A system for processing bilingual Arabic/English text." *Journal of the American Society for Information Science* 37, no. 5 (September 1986): 288-293.

The production of high-quality Arabic /English text poses technical problems that are caused mainly by the high degree of syntactical flexibility which characterizes the Arabic language. This paper describes a system with adequate solutions to the problems encountered in processing bilingual Arabic /English text.

253 Razzuqi, Nu'ayma Hasan. "Qawa'id al-bayanat al-bibliyughrafiyah wa-marahil tasmimiha bi-istikhdam maykru CDS/ISIS." *Risalat al-Maktabah* 26, no. 2 (June 1991): 95-114.

The article reviews the importance of developing computer-based information systems. It also defines the related basic concepts and describes the CDS/ISIS.

254 Sakai, Yasushi, Yoichi Terashita, and Koho Takemoto. "An experimental system for creating and managing Arabic Bibliographic Database—a step toward effective international information exchange." *Libri* 36, no. 4 (December 1986): 259-275.

This paper discusses results of an experiment conducted at Knanazawa Institute of Technology, Japan, to develop a prototype system that can manage catalog records of Arabic materials in computerized form. The approach adopted is to extend the 16-bit character encoding scheme which has been developed for Japanese and other oriental languages, and is widely used in text-orientated applications, including library catalog records. The paper describes an information retrieval experiment involving a small Arabic database. It demonstrates the possibility of using the system as the technical basis for developing international bibliographic information systems capable of integrating textual materials of various languages effectively.

255 Salem, Shawky. *Nuzum al-Ma'lumat wa-al-Hasib al-Iliktruni: Mabadi' Tahlil al-Nuzum, Tasmim al-Nuzum, Tanfiz al-Nuzum, Taqyim al-Ada'*. al-Iskandariyah: Markaz al-Iskandariyah lil-Wasa'it al-Thaqafiyah wa-al-Maktabat, 1996.

The author stresses the importance and role of information and information technology. He describes the steps for an effective handling of information, the goals and objectives of information and finally, the relation of information to the decision-making process.

256 Sardar, Ziauddin (ed.). *Building Information Systems in the Islamic World*. London and New York: Mansell Publishing Limited, 1988. 170 p.

The contributions to this volume were originally presented to COMLIS 2 (Congress of Muslim Librarians and Information Scientists) held at Universiti Utara Malaysia, Kedah, Malaysia, October 20-22, 1986. Examines the reasons why Muslims have neglected to develop their own information structures; highlights areas of particular concern and instances where progress is being made and; charts a course out of the present state of information dependency. Contributors are librarians and information professionals from Muslim countries.

INTERLIBRARY LOAN

257 Aman, Mohammed M. "Document delivery and interlibrary lending in the Arab countries." *Interlending and Document Supply* 17, no. 3 (July 1989): 84-88.

The Arab countries have a long history of document delivery, although the modern process is relatively new to Arab libraries. Efforts are currently under way to establish a formalized document delivery system across the regions taking advantage of new technology and modern methods of transmission. Varying degrees of success have been achieved so far: although some networks do exist and many Arab libraries already make use of European and US document delivery services, problems have been encountered in the attempts to set up any broad-based similar local system. More data on regional and national interlibrary loan and document delivery patterns are needed, and the possibility of establishing national and regional clearing-houses, as well as verification and location tools, should be explored. In the less wealthy countries, finance could present problems. The author concludes that progress is being made, albeit somewhat slow, but there are no easy answers to some of the questions that have been raised. [A]

258 Khafagi, Muhammad Tawfiq. "Siyasat tabadul al-i'arah bayna al-maktabat 'ala al-mustawa al-qutri wa-al-qawmi." *al-Majallah al-'Arabiyah lil-Ma'lumat* 7, no. 2 (1986): 5-10.

ISLAM AND LIBRARIANSHIP

259 Badr, Ahmad Mahmud. "al-Islam wa-mafahim 'ilm al-ma'lumat." *al-Majallah al-'Arabiyah lil-Ma'lumat* 5, no. 2 (1984): 213-224.

260 Ekere, F. C. "The contributions of Islam to the spread of literacy and development of libraries in the Middle-East, North Africa and the West African Sudan." *Library Scientist* 10 (1983): 101-119.

Explains how the spread of Islam in the Middle East, North Africa and Western Sudan, led to the literacy, development of educational system and the establishment of libraries in the three areas.

ISLAMIC LIBRARIES

261 'Abdullah, Yusra 'Abd al-Ghani. "al-Fahrasah wa-al-faharis fi al-maktabat al-Islamiyah: al-dawr, wa-al-ahamiyah." *Risalat al-Maktabah* 32, no. 4 (December 1994): 71-76.

Islamic libraries have always been well organized, and almost every library had a catalog to facilitate access to books.

262 Bakhsh, Khuda. "The Islamic libraries." *Pakistan Library Bulletin* 17, no. 3-4 (September-December 1986): 1-18.

This article provides a brief account of the progress of learning among the Muslim peoples focusing on Arab countries and Spain. It regrets the destructions of the Mughals and the fact that there is no consecutive account of the establishment of libraries in the Muslim empire. It also discusses conditions of learning in India and the origins of the public library of the city of Patna.

263 Elayyan, Ribhi Mustafa. "The history of the Arabic-Islamic libraries: 7th to 14th centuries." *International Library Review* 22, no. 2 (June 1990): 119-135.

This historical study deals with the development of the Arabic-Islamic libraries in the period between the 7th and 14th century. It discusses the factors that led to the rising of the different types of libraries which are: mosques, private, public and academic libraries. The study gives, in some

GENERAL WORKS 61

detail, information about the most famous libraries in the Arabic-Islamic civilization. It also talks about management and organization of these libraries. Finally, the study discusses the factors behind the destruction of the Arabic-Islamic libraries.

264 Ibrahim, Yahya Muhammad. "Nash'at al-maktabat al-Islamiyah." *Tarikh al-'Arab wa-al-'Alam* 3, no. 35 (September 1981): 72-73.

265 Imamuddin, S. M. *Some Leading Muslim Libraries of the World*. Dhaka: Islamic Foundation Bangladesh, 1983. xvii, 217 p., xli p.

266 Imamuddin, S. M. *Arabic Writing and Arab Libraries*. London: Ta Ha Publishers, 1983. 80 p. Includes bibliographical references.

Describes the development of Arabic calligraphy and the place of calligraphy in Muslim culture. Gives an historical account of the libraries developed by the Abbassids, Fatimids and Umayyads, including a large section devoted to the building up of libraries in Muslim Spain.

267 Krek, Miroslav. "Islamic Libraries: 7th to 17th centuries." In *World Encyclopedia of Library and Information Services*. 3rd ed. (pp. 394-395). Chicago: American Library Association, 1993.

268 Merlet, Shukrieh R. "Islamic libraries of the Middle East." *Libri* 39, no. 2 (June 1989): 127-140.

269 Plumbe, Wilfred John. *Tropical Librarianship*. Metuchen, N.J.: The Scarecrow Press Inc., 1987. xv, 318 p.

Two chapters on Arab countries are included: "The libraries of mediaeval Islam" (pp. 207-216) and "Preservation of books and periodicals in Arab countries" (pp. 217-227).

270 Sibai, Mohamed Makki. *An Historical Investigation of Mosque Libraries in Islamic Life and Culture*. Ph.D., 1984. Indiana University. 447 p.

Although agreement among historians is almost unanimous that mosques were the first places where books were to be found in Muslim society and that many of these book collections gradually grew in size and quality into full-fledged libraries, very little has been written about this important segment of Muslim librarianship. There is not, either in Arabic or in any other language, a single consecutive account which explores the history of mosque libraries or their close affinity to Muslim scholarship. This is particularly significant in view of the fact that these libraries seem to have had a more diverse and dynamic life than Muslim or non-Muslim writers have thus far recognized in any meaningful detail. Purely historical in nature, this study is undertaken in an effort to remedy that situation. This thesis attempts to accomplish two primary objectives. First, there is evidence that a number of mosque libraries grew out of the Muslim custom of bequeathing copies of the Quran to favorite mosques. There is more evidence, however, that a considerable number of these libraries were born of the widespread Muslim acceptance and active utilization of the mosque as a principal learning center. An important objective of this study therefore is to investigate the institution of the mosque as it relates to Muslim scholarship. Secondly, there is evidence that many mosque libraries have reached high stages of development as well as social prominence. Being an integral part of their parent mosques, these libraries were not merely storehouses or reading rooms but working libraries in the full sense of the word. Hence, the second and main objective of this thesis is to investigate the historical growth of mosque libraries per se. This investigation therefore covers a large number of mosque libraries in an attempt to formulate a coherent picture of their functions and operations through history. [DAI 45/05-A: 1229.]

271 Taher, Mohamed. "Mosque libraries: a bibliographic essay." *Libraries & Culture* 27, no. 1 (Winter 1992): 43-48.

LIBRARIANS—DIRECTORIES

272 Bin Khamis, al-Hadi (comp.). *Dalil al-Muwaththiqin wa-al-Maktabiyin fi al-Watan al-'Arabi*. Tunis: al-Munazzamah al-'Arabiyah lil-Tarbiyah wa-al-Thaqafah wa-al-'Ulum, Idarat al-Tawthiq wa-al-ma'lumat, 1981.

LIBRARY ADMINISTRATION/MANAGEMENT

273 al-Daly, 'Abd al-Baqi. "Tanzim marakiz al-tawthiq wa-tasyiriha." *al-Majallah al-'Arabiyah lil-Ma'lumat* 4, no. 2 (December 1983): 21-31.

274 Farsuni, Fu'ad Hamad. "al-Maktabat ka-munazzamah maftuhah: nahwa tatbiq li mafhum al-nizam al-maftuh fi idarat al-maktabat." *Maktabat al-Idarah* 13, no. 3 (May-June 1986): 59-81.

275 Mustafa, Usamah. "al-Idarah al-hadithah wa ta'thiraha fi idarat al-nuzum al-maktabiyah." *al-Idarah* 18:3 (January 1986): 71-79.

276 al-Sayyid, Muhammad Kamal. "al-Idarah al-hadithah lil-a'mal al-maktabiyah ka madkhal li idarat nuzum al-ma'lumat." *al-Idarah* 18, no. 2 (October 1985): 66-75.

277 al-Takruri, Sana'. "Qanawat al-ittisal fi idarat al-maktabat." *Risalat al-Maktabah* 27, no. 2 (June 1992): 5-15.

Discusses communication between the various sections of the library and stresses the importance of training as an essential element for successful communication.

LIBRARY ASSOCIATIONS

278 Qandil, Yusuf. "Jam'iyyat al-maktabat fi Bilad al-Sham: waqi'uha wa subul taf'iliha." *al-Jadid fi 'Alam al-Kutub wa-al-Maktabat*, no. 6 (spring 1995): 84-88.

Reviews the historical development of library associations in the Arab world; their aims and objectives, the roles that they should play in the library field; and how to activate their roles.

LIBRARY BUILDINGS

279 Salem, Shawky, and Michael Dewe. "Library buildings in the 1980s: The Middle East and North Africa." *Information Development* 6, no. 3 (July 1990): 163-169.

The 6th in a series of articles on library buildings completed in the 1980s, based largely on the library and architectural literature. It describes new library buildings in the Arab states, Iran, and Israel.

LIBRARY COOPERATION

280 'Aliwi, Muhammad 'Awdah. "al-Usus al-'ammah lil-ta'awun bayna al-maktabat." *Maktabat al-Idarah* 13:2 (May-June 1986): 31-58.

281 Bu-'Ayyad, Mahmud. "al-Tabadul bayna al-maktabat al-'Arabiyah min ajl ittifaqiyah 'Arabiyah li tabadul al-watha'iq." *'Alam al-Kutub* 9, no. 4 (November 1988): 477-484.

282 *al-Tansiq bayna Marakiz al-Buhuth fi al-Duwal al-'Arabiyah—Abhath al-Nadwah al-'Ilmiyah al-Thaniyah: al-Khittah al-Amniyah al-Wiqa-'iyah al-'Arabiyah al-Ula.* al-Riyad: al-Markaz al-'Arabi lil-Dirasat al-Amniyah wa-al-Tadrib bi-al-Riyad, 1986. 61 p.

LIBRARY EDUCATION

283 Abdel-Hadi, Mohammed Fathi. "al-Wad' al-mihani li mudarrisi 'ilm al-ma'lumat wa-al-maktabat fi al-Watan al-'Arabi." *al-Majallah al-'Arabiyah lil-Ma'lumat* 3, no. 3 (1982): 125-143.

The author enumerates the professional qualifications of the teaching staff in library and information science in the Arab world.

284 Abdel-Hadi, Mohammed Fathi, and Abdelmajid Bouazza. "A survey of education for library and information science in Egypt, the Maghreb countries, and Sudan." In *Information and Libraries in the Arab World*. Compiled and edited by Michael Wise and Anthony Olden, pp. 26-40. London: Library Association Publishing, 1994. [Information and libraries in the developing world, vol. 3.]

Article included in a collection of papers presenting a comparative review of librarianship and library practices in Arab countries. Reports results of a survey of the state of library and information science professional education in Egypt, the Maghreb countries (Algeria, Morocco, Tunisia), and the Sudan, based on a questionnaire survey sent to thirteen library schools in these countries. The fact that only four library schools responded to the survey was partly compensated by the addition of supplementary information derived from recently published sources.

285 Ahmed, Munir D. "Die ausbildung von bibliothekaren, dokumentaren und archivaren im vorderen orient." [The training of librarians, documentalists and archivists in the Near East.] *Auskunft* 8, no. 4 (1988): 277-286. [In German.]

Professional librarianship was established in the Near East only after 1900. Pakistan developed a library training program after 1915, Iran after 1945. Provision for training of archivists and documentalists is varied and there is often a shortage of library textbooks in native languages. Egypt has the widest range of courses offered in the Arab world. Short courses in library science were offered by UNESCO experts in Iraq and the Sudan. Tunisia and Morocco now have library schools. In Saudi Arabia and Algeria training is provided at a university. Afghanistan, Libya, Syria, Kuwait and Lebanon have no regular library schools; most of their librarians are trained abroad. Some national and international institutions arrange seminars and short courses. [LISA]

286 el-Akhras, Mahmud. "Tadriss 'ilm al-maktabat wa-al-ma'lumat fi al-Watan al-'Arabi." *al-Majallah al-'Arabiyah lil-Ma'lumat* 3, no. 3 (1982): 11-27.

The author presents the development of knowledge over the years and then the development of library education in the Arab world. He states the problems (programs and curricula, degrees, teaching staff, cooperation and instructional material) and concludes that a policy based on cooperation and collaboration between the Arab countries, should be established.

287 Aman, Mohammed M. "al-Ta'lim al-mustamir li-ikhsa'i al-ma'lumat fi al-Watan al-'Arabi." *al-Majallah al-'Arabiyah lil-Ma'lumat* 8, no. 1 (1987): 5-30.

Reviews continuing education programs offered by a number of library schools. Describes the factors related to the professional development of librarians and the guidelines for the evaluation of the training courses offered in these schools.

288 Aman, Mohammed M. "Ta'thir al-hasub 'ala barnamij ta'lim 'ulum al-maktabat wa-al-ma'lumat." *al-Majallah al-'Arabiyah lil-Ma'lumat* 9, no. 2 (1988): 83-99.

Discusses the impact of computers on the teaching of library and information science.

289 Badrah, Ahmad Anwar. *'Ilm al-Ma'lumat wa-al-Maktabat: Dirasah fi al-Nazariyah wa-al-Irtibatat al-Mawdu'iyah*. al-Qahirah: Dar Ghrayyib, 1996.

290 al-Daly, Abd al-Baqi. "Mu'assasat wa-madaris 'ilm al-maktabat wa-al-mal'lumat fi al-Watan al-'Arabi." *al-Majallah al-'Arabiyah lil-Ma'lumat* 3, no. 3 (1982): 29-53.

A review of the programs of study of library and information science in specific countries of the Arab world.

291 Dibs, Mohammad. "Tiknulujyah al-ta'lim fi al-maktabat: imkaniyat tatbiqiha wa-al-tadarub 'alyha fi al-duwal al-namiyah." *Risalat al-Maktabah* 20, no. 3 (September 1985): 20-25.

Discusses audiovisual materials (AVM) terminology and explains the possibility of using AVM in developing countries, especially the idea of in-house production. Identifies the most-used AVM format. Considers problems of AVM such as storage, maintenance, tradition and customs. Provides a comparative table of old and new concepts of educational technology.

292 Gdoura, Wahid. "L'enseignement des nouvelles technologies de l'information dans les ecoles arabes de bibliotheconomie." [The teaching of new information technologies in Arab library schools.] *Revue de la Science de l'Information*, no. 2 (July 1995): 31-46.

Provides a background to Arab information science schools. Discusses the curricula of Arab library schools considering whether information technology has been adequately incorporated. Conducts a survey on new information technology in library automation and information science courses. Systems analysis is present in only 50% of courses, and programming in 35%. Information technology represents on average only 14% of the whole curriculum. Considers the obstacles to courses trying to keep up to date. [A]

293   Itayem, Mahmoud A. *Dalil Madaris 'Ilm al-Maktabat wa-al-Ma'lumat fi al-Watan al-'Arabi.* Reviewed by Mahmud el-Akhras. Tunis: Jami'at al-Duwal al-'Arabiyah, al-Munazzamah al-'Arabiyah lil-Tarbiyah wa-al-Thaqafah wa-al-'Ulum, Idarat al-Tawthiq wa-al-ma'lumat, 1984. 152 p.

294   Johnson, Ian M. "Education and training in the Arab States." *Journal of Education for Library and Information Science* 35, no. 1 (Winter 1994): 59-61.

This paper summarizes the proceedings of a conference on professional education and training in Arabic speaking countries, held at the Ecole des Sciences de l'Information (ESI), Rabat, May 1993. It reports on the situation in Algeria, Egypt, Jordan, Kuwait, Libya, Oman, Saudi Arabia, and Tunisia.

295   al-Kindilchie, 'Amir Ibrahim, and Iman Fadil al-Samirra'i. "Dirasat 'ilm al-maktabat wa-al-ma'lumat fi al-watan al-'arabi : al-waqi' wa-al-tumuh." *Al-Majallah al-'Arabiyah lil- Ma'lumat* 10, no. 1 (1989): 100-120.

As the role of library and information science (LIS) in society begins to increase, the curriculum of LIS in schools faculties and sections in universities needs to be studied, surveyed and compared to evaluate the curricula. There are more than 20 LIS schools in the Arab world and they grant diplomas, B.Sc. degrees, higher diplomas, Master degrees and Ph.D. degrees. The curricula differ from one country to another and the required period to obtain one of these degrees also can differ from one Arab country to another. Most of the curriculum concentrates on cataloging, classification, bibliography, library management, introduction to library science, research, introduction to information science, acquisitions, archives and scientific documentation. Suggests an ideal LIS curriculum.

296   Meherik, Mebrooka Omer. "al-'Amilun bi al-maktabat wa-marakiz al-ma'lumat wa-al-ta'lim al-mustamir." *al-Majallah al-'Arabiyah lil-Ma'-lumat* 14, no. 1 (1993): 114-121.

297   Namlah, Ali Ibrahim. "Principles in planning library education programs in the Muslim world." *American Journal of Islamic Studies* 1, no. 1 (April 1984): 101-108.

Of major importance in planning library education programs in the Muslim world are environmental needs; application of programs; cultures, backgrounds, and traditions of the nation; and predicted future changes. The Muslim world is acquiring expertise largely from non-Muslim nations, through recruiting expert planners or through sending their students to developed countries to acquire knowledge. Both approaches have problems, which are discussed. Blind application of library technology is considered the main reason for the failure of library education programs in Muslim countries. [A]

298 al-Sabbagh, 'Imad 'Abd al-Wahhab. "al-Mumarasah al-maydaniyah khilal al-baramij al-ta'limiyah li-'ilm al-maktabat." *Risalat al-Maktabah* 26, no. 2 (June 1991): 127-136.

The importance of practical and in-service training in library education is discussed.

299 al-Sharif, 'Abdullah M. "The factors which effect the development of librarianship and library education in the Arab countries." *International Library Review* 11, no. 2 (April 1979): 245-257.

Dividing the paper into two groups of factors, the author starts discussing the positive factors, including: the long history of Arab scholarship and contribution to knowledge, ALECSO's (Arab League Educational, Cultural, and Scientific Organization) activities, UNESCO's contributions, the influence of international organizations, the contribution of foreign librarians, library studies abroad, establishment of libraries at home, expansion of education, the growth of population, the discovery of petroleum and unity of cultural and social factors. The negative factors include: lack of library national planning, lack of library cooperation, absence of library standards, difficulty of purchasing foreign materials, absence of effective library legislation, lack of a national book plan, traditional system of education, lack of library associations, lack of library literature, illiteracy, and lack of recognition.

300 al-Sharif, 'Abdullah M. "The development of professional library education in the Arab countries." *International Library Review* 13 (January 1981): 87-101.

Provides a detailed review (including a historical section) of the development and current state of professional library education in the Arab countries, beginning in 1945 when a group of Egyptian librarians proposed a plan for the establishment of an Institute of Library to be attached to Fouad (now Cairo) University.

301 al-Sharif, 'Abdullah M. "al-Manahij wa-al-baramij al-dirasiyah fi 'ilm al-maktabat wa-al-ma'lumat fi al-Watan al-'Arabi." *al-Majallah al-'Arabiyah lil-Ma'lumat* 3, no. 3 (1982): 55-98.

Analyzes the teaching programs and curricula of library and information science as they are applied in different institutes in the Arab countries.

302   Swaydan, Nasser M. "Wasa'il wa-asalib tadris 'ilm al-maktabat wa-al-ma'lumat fi al-Watan al-'Arabi." *al-Majallah al-'Arabiyah lil-Ma'lumat* 3, no. 3 (1982): 99-124.

The author discusses the modern methods of instruction compared to the traditional ones used in the Arab countries.

303   Swaydan, Nasser M. "al-Munazzamat al-mutakhassissah wa dawruha fi haql al-maktabat wa-al-ma'lumat." *Maktabat al-Idarah* 14, no. 3 (April-May 1987): 63-115.

LIBRARY LEGISLATION

304   'Anani, Shukri. "al-Ida' al-qanuni wa-tashri'atuhu." *'Alam al-Kutub* 9, no. 2 (May 1988): 160-168.

305   al-Zubaydi, Majid Tuhan. "al-Ida' al-qanuni: nash'atuhu wa-ta'rifuhu, ahdafuhu wa-mazayah, ahammiyyatuhu wa-fawa'idahu." *Risalat al-Maktabah* 31, no. 3 (September 1996): 47-59.

Discusses legal deposit as a major characteristic of national libraries.

MANUSCRIPTS

306   Abu-Haybah, 'Izzat Yasin. *al-Makhtutat al-'Arabiyah: Faharisaha wa-Fahrasatiha*. al-Qahirah: al-Hay'ah al-Masiryah al-'Ammah lil-Kuttab, 1989.

307   al-Bashity, Intisar Muhammad. "al-Makhtut al-'Arabi wa-malamihihi al-madiyah." *Risalat al-Maktabah* 18, no. 2-3 (June-September 1983): 26-31.

Describes the physical elements which help to determine the dating of an Arabic manuscript.

MICROFORMS

308   Arab League. *al-Dalil al-'Amali lil-Musaghghirat al-Filmiyah*. Tunis: Jami'at al-Duwal al-'Arabiyah, al-Amanah al-'Ammah, Markaz al-Taw-thiq wa-al-ma'lumat, 1990.

309   Barnawi, Muhammad 'Ali. "al-Musaghghirat al-filmiyah fi al-maktabat wa-marakiz al-ma'lumat." *'Alam al-Kutub* 3, no. 2 (July 1982): 171-178.

The author points at the role of microfilms, their development. He describes their different formats: flat form, aperture cards, microfilm strips, jackets, microfiche, micro-opaque card, etc. and their uses.

GENERAL WORKS 69

310 al-Kindilchie, 'Amir Ibrahim. "al-Tiqaniyyat al-hadithah fi al-maktabat." *al-Majallah al-'Arabiyah lil-Ma'lumat* 2, no. 1 (1980): 57-72.

Discusses the new technologies used in libraries: microfilm, microfiche, computers, etc.

311 Shu'ayb, Bakr Muhammad Ahmad. "al-Musaghghirat al-filmiyah: mazayaha wa-istikhdamatiha al-mukhtalifah." *Makatabat al-Idarah* 14, no. 2 (January 1987): 71-87.

MOBILE LIBRARIES

312 al-Qawasimah, Muhammad 'Abdullah. "al-Maktabah al-mutanaqqilah." *Risalat al-Maktabah* 30, no. 3 (September 1995): 28-36.

The study lists the goals, features, applications, and requirements of the mobile library.

NATIONAL LIBRARIES

313 el-Akhras, Mahmud. "al-Maktabah al-'Arabiyah al-wataniyah." *Shu'un 'Arabiyah*, no. 11 (January 1982): 191-199.

314 Bu-'Ayyad, Mahmud. "al-Maktabah al-wataniyah al-'Arabiyah limadha? wa-kayfa?" *'Alam al-Kutub* 7, no. 3 (September 1986): 308-312.

A feasibility study: the establishment of an Arab national library. The author discusses the aims and objectives of such a central library and its advantages.

315 Itayem, Mahmoud A. "National libraries in the Arab World." In *Information and Libraries in the Arab World*. Compiled and edited by Michael Wise and Anthony Olden, pp. 12-25. London: Library Association Publishing, 1994. [Information and libraries in the developing world, vol. 3.]

Article included in a collection of papers presenting a comparative review of librarianship and library practices in Arab countries. Reviews the history, current status and possible future developments in national libraries in thirteen Arab countries, based on a survey of the national libraries in these countries.

316 Itayem, Mahmoud A. "National libraries in the Arab World." In *National Libraries 3: A Selection of Articles on National Libraries, 1986-1994*. Edited by M. B. Line and J. Line, pp. 187-196. London: Aslib, 1995.

NETWORKS AND NETWORKING

317   Aman, Mohammed M. "The coordination of information resources and services in developing countries with particular emphasis on the Arab world." In *The Infrastructure of an Information Society*. Proceedings of the First International Information Conference in Egypt, Cairo, 13-15 December, 1982. Edited by Bahaa El-Hadidy and Esther E. Horne, pp. 119-131. Amsterdam: North-Holland, 1984.

The establishment of specialized information centers focusing their activities on specific 'missions' of high priority and with a regional responsibility regarding collecting, processing and disseminating information have been made possible with support from international agencies. Networking is favored as a device for ensuring availability of resources of the interacting systems to any or all members when needed. The creation, development and management of a proposed Arab information network require a great deal of flexibility and support from the public and private sectors in the Arab world.

318   al-Gharbi, Ahmad. "al-Shabakah al-'Arabiyah lil-ma'lumat: nazrah nahwa mustaqbalin afdal." *al-Majallah al-'Arabiyah lil-Ma'lumat* 8, no. 1 (1987): 43-76.

According to the author, ALESCO has made important efforts in designing a regional information network for collecting, processing and disseminating information throughout the Arab region. This could be considered as a feasibility study for an information network in the areas of education, culture and sciences.

319   Haj Bakry, Saad. "A proposed computer-based methodology for planning an Arab information network." *Telematics and Informatics* 6, no. 2 (1989): 87-98.

The League of Arab States is at present involved in the initial stages of a project aimed at the construction of an Arab Information System Network (ARIS-NET). In this article, a computer-based methodology is developed for the planning and design of the communication part of ARIS-NET. The methodology is derived using the past experience of different research organizations and individuals in the field of network planning. The need for the development of mathematical and computer tools for network planning has been emphasized by the methodology.

320   Itayem, Mahmoud A. "al-Shabaka al-'Arabiyah lil-ma'lumat: bayna al-haqiqah wa-al-khayal." *Risalat al-Maktabah* 23, no. 1 (March 1988): 27-57.

Emphasizes the value of information in economic and social development and the trend towards the paperless society by the year 2000. The Arab Information Systems Network (ARIS-NET) is defined as a network of institutions concerned with information and cooperation in resource sharing, and is shown to be a decentralized, integrated, cooperative information system. Its aims and objectives are indicated and 3 subsystems described. Problem areas and obstacles are identified and current activities in the region, including national, regional and international efforts to establish information networks. Examines obstacles to implementation of networking projects in the Arab World.

321 Jirjis, Jasim Muhammad, and Nu'aymah Hasan Razzuqi. "Shabakat al-ma'lumat fi al-duwal al-namiyah." *'Alam al-Kutub* 7, no. 2 (July 1986): 146-158.

The author presents a historical development of networks, the specifications and basic concepts of library networks and classifies the different networks according to the type of network, type of source materials and type of functions performed.

322 Kamaruddin, Abdul Rahman. "Islam-Net: the development of an Islamic information network." In *Building Information Systems in the Islamic World*. Edited by Ziauddin Sardar, pp. 142-155. London and New York: Mansell, 1988.

The author presents a multi-disciplinary network linking the libraries and information centers in the entire Muslim world. The model for such a network which he presents—Islam-Net—has three prerequisites: cooperation, coordination and automation. On the basis of experience gained from the development of the Arab Information System Network (ARIS-NET) at the Arab League Documentation Centre in Tunis, the author has developed a rationale for the design and basic features of Islam-Net in some detail.

323 al-Kindilchie, 'Amir Ibrahim. "Bina' shabakat maktabat jami'iyah 'Arabiyah 'ibra al-qamar al-sina'i al-'Arabi." *al-Majallah al-'Arabiyah lil-Ma'lumat* 14, no. 1 (1993): 5-25.

Describes the benefits of library networks, the different forms of networks and their uses in a great variety of areas like cooperative cataloging, centralized acquisition, interlibrary loan, union catalogs, online bibliographic search, etc. The building of a university library network in the Arab world through ARABSAT is described too.

324 al-Makkawi, Ahmad Hasan. "Shabakat al-ma'lumat al-sina'iyah al-'Arabiyah: hadiruha wa-mustaqbaliha." *al-Majallah al-'Arabiyah lil-Ma'lumat* 4, no. 2 (December 1983): 82-94.

325 Mustafa, 'Adnan, and Hind Mustafa. "al-Shabakah al-'Arabiyah lil-ma'lumat: tasawwur jadid." *Shu'un 'Arabiyah*, no. 73 (March 1993): 69-76.

The authors stress the importance of an Arab information network. They summarize the objectives of an Arab network as: a better exchange of information and a reduction in the duplication of work.

326 Rehman, Sajjadur. "National infrastructure of library and information services in Arab countries." *International Library Review* 21, no. 4 (October 1989): 445-461.

Examines the existing situation of library and information infrastructure in Arab countries in order to generate understanding among policy makers, designers, and participants of a proposed network about the current situation which is expected to lead to more realistic plans and strategies. Analyzes data gathered during a questionnaire survey, and online literature searches on ERIC and databases on the following variables: status of the national library; national bibliographic control; availability of union catalogs, union lists, and indexing and abstracting services; arrangements for interlibrary cooperation; connections with networks; and application of information technology. The data relates to 15 Arab countries in Africa and the Middle East and analysis indicates that the development of an information infrastructure in these countries is still in the early stages.

327 Shahin, Baha'. *Shabakat al-Intirnit*. al-Qahirah: Kumpusayince al-'Arabiyah li-'Ulum al-Hasib, 1996.

The author describes the development of the Internet, its different uses. He focuses on the role of networking as a device for ensuring the availability of resources.

328 Zoltai, S. "Information transmission and the translation of medieval Islamic science." *Libri* 48, no. 1 (1998): 35-48.

Poised on the edge of a new millennium, electronic information networks are assuming a cardinal place in the dissemination of global information. Information networks were, however, of no less importance in the ancient world. This paper examines the role of translating activity as a vehicle for the transmission of one element in Islamic learning, science, via the single most important transmission conduit, the Arab conquest of Spain. Several broad channels by which information transmission occurred in medieval Europe are identified: Spain (the primary transmission route), Sicily and southern Italy, the Crusader states of Palestine-Syria, Byzantium and possibly North Africa. However somewhere between the recognition of broad streams of information flow and the specificity of a particular aspect of information transmission lies another level of analysis. Information networks, though lacking clear definition, are nonetheless identifiable. Such networks comprise discrete eddies within the overall direction of information flow involving isolable instances of information transmission and dissemination. They illustrate the means of information transfer in this pre-electronic age. [A]

329   Younis, Abdul Razeq Mustafa. "Resource-sharing networks in developing countries." In *Encyclopedia of Library and Information Science*. Vol. 41 (pp. 304-320). New York: Marcel Dekker, Inc., 198.

Reviews the literature and discusses the state of the art of library cooperation in Egypt, Jordan, and the Sudan, among other developing countries.

PRESERVATION

330   al-Mahasini, Sama' Zaki. "Siyanat al-kutub wa-al-muhafazah 'alayha." *al-Majallah al-'Arabiyah lil-Ma'lumat* 2, no. 1 (1980): 73-88.
This article deals with the historical interest of the Arabs in manuscripts and their preservation. It enumerates the methods and techniques used in the restoration and preservation processes.

PRINTING

331   Albin, Michael W. "Recent studies in Middle Eastern printing history: a review essay." *Libraries & Culture* 23, no. 3 (Summer 1988): 365-373.

332   Bulliet, Richard W. "Printing in the medieval Islamic underworld." *Columbia Library Columns* 36 (May 1987): 13-20.

333   Mahdi, Muhsin. "From the manuscript age to the age of printed books." In *The Book in the Islamic World: The Written Word and Communication in the Middle East*. Edited by George N. Atiyeh, pp. 1-16. Albany: State University of New York Press, 1995.

A paper originally presented at a conference held at the Library of Congress, Washington, D.C., November 8-9, 1990. The author confirms the need for more information on the history of books in the Islamic world. He explains the reasons why the printing of religious books by Muslims came late, as late as the nineteenth century, and wonders why the excellent scribal traditions of dictation, collation, and illustration have not been applied to the exigencies of modern book production. He systematically raises many issues resulting from the introduction of printing, such as the impact of translations on the development of the sciences, languages, and even orthography. Furthermore, he calls for the preservation and sustenance of scholarly traditions and systems while looking forward to the new technologies in the editing and preservation of the great wealth of manuscripts remaining in the Islamic world.

334 Partington, David H. "Arabic printing." In *Encyclopedia of Library and Information Science*. Vol. 24 (pp. 54-75). New York: Marcel Dekker, Inc., 1978.

Topics discussed include: Arabic printing in Europe, Arabic printing by the Melkites, Arabic printing in Istanbul, Egypt, Lebanon, Syria, Iraq, Palestine, Jordan, Arabian Penninsula, North Africa, and India. Also discussed are problems in the history of Arabic printing.

335 Roper, Geoffrey. "Faris al-Shidyaq and the transition from scribal to print culture in the Middle East." In *The Book in the Islamic World: The Written Word and Communication in the Middle East*. Edited by George N. Atiyeh, pp. 209-232. Albany: State University of New York Press, 1995.

A paper originally presented at a conference held at the Library of Congress, Washington, D.C., November 8-9, 1990. The transition from scribal to print culture, as exemplified by Ahmad Faris al-Shidyaq, is ably presented by the author, who has shown that al-Shidyaq personifies in his career, as well as in his attitudes, the dawn of a new cultural era for the Arab and Islamic worlds, an era in which the communications revolution caused by the printing press brought radical changes to intellectual, political, and social life.

PUBLIC LIBRARIES

336 'Aliwi, Muhammad 'Awdah, and Majbal Lazim Musallam al-Maliki. "al-'Anasir al-asasiyah li-najah al-khidmah al-maktabiyah fi al-maktabat al-'ammah." *Risalat al Maktabah* 27, no. 1 (March 1992): 46-66.

The goals and objectives of the public library are discussed, as well as the basic elements for the success of the library.

337 Bin 'Isa, 'Abdullah Salih. "Tatwir khadamat al-maktabah al-'ammah." *'Alam al-Kutub* 6, no. 2 (June 1985): 162-167.

An overview of the public library, its purposes and objectives, its administration, and the different services it offers to users.

PUBLIC RELATIONS

338 Alqudsi, Taghrid M. "al-'ilaqat al-'amah: qadayah hadithah fi al-maktabat." *al-Majallah al-'Arabiyah lil-Ma'lumat* 13, no. 1 (1992): 5-14.

Library public relations, a new growing field in communication techniques.

PUBLISHING

339 Botros, Salib. "Problems of book development in the Arab world with special reference to Egypt." *Library Trends* 26, no. 4 (Spring 1978): 567-573.

Starts with examining some general problems in the development of book industry in the Arab worlds, then, discusses exonomic, commercial and institutional, legal aspects abstructing the development of the production of books in Arabic in the Arab world as well as book distribution among Arab countries.

340 Mawlawi, Radwan. "Arab scientific journalism: achievements and aspirations." *Impact of Science on Society* 38, no. 4 (1988): 397-409.
This paper traces the growth of a successful publishing industry in the Arab world. It considers that the key to successful science publishing in Arabic is the development of a standardized technical vocabulary and the adoption of modern equipment for the transmission of information.

341 Rosenthal, Franz. "'Of making many books there is no end': the classical Muslim view." In *The Book in the Islamic World: The Written Word and Communication in the Middle East*. Edited by George N. Atiyeh, pp. 33-56. Albany: State University of New York Press, 1995.

A paper originally presented at a conference held at the Library of Congress, Washington, D.C., November 8-9, 1990. The author discusses Muslim attitudes toward books and the dilemma caused by the abundance of books in terms of quantity and quality. Books were often so plentiful that one could think of discarding some, but this was generally considered wrong. The destruction of books is discussed, when and why it occurs, the meaning and scope of originality, and the relationship between knowledge and books. The author points out the persistent distinction between oral and written information, a theme that appears in several papers.

RARE BOOKS

342 al-Sari', Sari' Muhammad. "al-Kutub al-nadirah: ta'rifiha, masadiriha, hifziha wa-istirja'iha." *Maktabat al-Idarah* 14, no. 1 (September-October 1986): 25-39.

RESEARCH METHODS

343 al-'Anani, Sarah Yunis. "Min adawat al bahth al-'ilmi: al-muqabalah." *Risalat al-Maktabah* 25, no. 1(March 1990): 37-50.

Information for scientific research can be collected by different tools and techniques such as observation, questionnaires, interviews, etc. This paper defines the concept of the interview and its different types and discusses the various steps and requirements for conducting them. It also discusses the use of interviews in library studies.

344 Zash, Amal Muhammad. "al-Bahth al-'ilmi al-'Arabi: al-mu'tayat wa-al-tatallu'at." *Risalat al-Maktabah* 31, no. 1 (March 1996): 15-26.

The study highlights scientific research, its functions, factors of success, role in community development and the difficulties facing scientific research in the Arab world.

SCHOOL/CHILDREN'S LIBRARIES

345 Abdel-Hadi, Mohammed Fathi. "Nahwa tatwir maktabat al-atfal." *al-Majallah al-'Arabiyah lil-Ma'lumat* 16, no. 1 (1995): 5-11.

346 Abdel-Hadi, Mohammed Fathi. "al-Istikhdam al-tarbawi wa-al-ta'limi lil-maktabah al-madrasiyah." *al-Majallah al-'Arabiyah lil-Ma'lumat* 18, no. 1 (1997): 5-17.

Provides a review of the role and responsibilities of school libraries as well as their organization. The author stresses on library services that meet the educational and instructional needs of both students and teachers.

347 Abdel-Hadi, Mohammed Fathi, et al. *Maktabat al-Atfal*. al-Qahirah: Maktabat Ghrayyib, 1989.

The book is divided into four chapters: library services for the children, the professional librarian in the children's libraries, children's books published in the Arab world, and cataloging of children's literature.

348 'Abd al-Hadi, Zaynuddin Muhammad. *al-Hasub fi al-Maktabah: Dirasah 'an Idkhal al-Hasub fi al-Maktabah al-Madrasiyah*. al-Qahirah: al-Dar al-Sharqiyah, 1993.

The author reviews the role of the school library in this age of information, the services offered by the school library and the aims and objectives of using computers in these libraries.

349 'Abd al-Hamid, Khalid Rashid. "al-Barmajiyyat al-ta'limiyah al-tarfihiyah fi maktabat al-madaris." *Risalat al-Maktabah* 30, no. 4 (December 1995): 4-17.

This paper examines a new term: edutainment, a term that falls into the field of educational software and how it relates to the school library when a school library functions as a part of the educational program.

350 Dyab, Miftah Muhammad. "al-Khidmah al-maktabiyah wa-al-atfal al-'Arab." *al-Majallah al-'Arabiyah lil-Ma'lumat* 5, no. 2 (1984): 175-183.

Library services for children in the Arab world.

351 al-Hajrasi, Sa'd Muhammad. *al-Maktabat wa-al-Ma'lumat bi al-Madaris wa-al-Kulliyyat*. al-Qahirah: al-Dar al-Misriyah al-Lubnaniyah, 1993.

A study of the role of the school library as a center for reading and for developing education.

352 Hamadneh, 'Umar M. "Fahrasat al-matbu'at fi al-maktabat al-madrasiyah." *Risalat al-Maktabah* 25, no. 1 (March 1990): 31-36.

The whole process of cataloging is discussed. School libraries being considered as the center of the process of education, cataloging the collections of the these libraries is important for offering better technical and public library services.

353 Hamshari, 'Umar Ahmad. "Athar al-maktabah al-madrasiyah fi tathqif al-nasha' wa-al-shabab." *al-Jadid fi 'Alam al-Kutub wa-al-Maktabat*, no. 1 (winter 1994): 113-118.

The author presents the concept of the school library, its educational role, the activity programs in school libraries, the creative activities.

354 Karam al-Din, Layla Ahmad. "Dawr al-maktabah fi khidmat wa-ri'ayat al-atfal dhawi al-hajat al-khassah." *'Alam al-Kitab*, no. 44 (October 1994): 15-30.

355 al-Majarha, Muhammad. "Idarat al-maktabah al-madrasiyah." *Risalat al-Maktabah* 26, no. 1 (March 1991): 31-40.

This article defines the concept of "management" and explains its function in the context of school libraries.

356 Meherik, Mebrooka Omer. "Hawla taqyim fa'iliyyat al-maktabah al-madrasiyah." *al-Majallah al-'Arabiyah lil-Ma'lumat* 4, no. 2 (December 1983): 95-106.

357 al-Shaykh, Muna Muhammad 'Ali. "al-Intirnit wa-al-maktabah al-madrasiyah." *Risalat al-Maktabah* 32, no. 1 (March 1997): 25-33.

Discusses the importance of using the Internet to obtain information in the various fields of knowledge emphasizing the role of the Internet in school libraries.

358 Shubbar, Mayy Makki. "Athar al-maktabah 'ala muyul al-tifl al-qira'iyah." *al-Majallah al-'Arabiyah lil-Ma'lumat* 16, no. 1 (1995): 12-22.

359 Shubbar, Mayy Makki. "al-Maktabah al-madrasiyah qalb al-barnamij al-tarbawi." *Risalat al-Maktabah* 32, no. 1 (March 1997): 13-24.

The author shows the importance of the school library, its role, objectives, and collections.

360 Tuqan, 'Ali Muhammad Wasif. "al-Maktabah al-madrasiyah wa-dawruha fi tashji' 'adat al-qira'ah wa-ta'ziz al-minhaj al-madrasi." *Risalat al-Maktabah* 30, no. 3 (September 1995): 4-27.

Discusses the school library and its role in supporting and promoting the reading habit and in enhancing the curriculum.

SERIALS

361 Ali, Syed Nazim. "Serials acquisition in the Middle East." *The Serials Librarian* 14, no. 3-4 (1988): 133-146.

The publishing of periodicals in the Middle East over the last decade is very noteworthy. Unfortunately, a lack exists of proper bibliographical tools normally useful for the selection and acquisitions of periodicals, and vendors who specialize in supplying periodicals are few. In consequence, librarians have to use many channels in obtaining periodicals. As many periodicals published in the Middle East are non-commercial, publications, gifts and exchange methods must be resorted to in acquiring such publications.

362 Anees, Munawar Ahmad. "Periodical literature." In *The Oxford Encyclopedia of the Modern Islamic World*. Edited by John L. Esposito, vol. 3, pp. 308-311. New York: Oxford University Press, 1995.

An excellent survey of Islamic periodical literature published over the last 100 years, from the time of al-Afghani to the present.

363 Zayid, Yusriyah. "al-Dabt al-bibliyughrafi li muhtawayat al-dawriyyat: al-nash'ah wa-al-tatawwur." *al-Majallah al-'Arabiyah lil-Ma'lumat* 4, no. 1 (1983): 77-92.

A review of the origins and development of bibliographic control of periodical literature is presented.

SPECIAL COLLECTIONS

364 el-Akhras, Mahmud. "ALECSO and special library collections in the Arab countries." *Unesco Journal of Information Science, Librarianship and Archives Administration* 3, no. 1 (January-March 1981): 55-59.

Arabic-Islamic civilization flourished in the Middle Ages. The intellectual achievements of this civilization in all fields of knowledge were recorded in manuscripts. In the twentieth century small proportion of the million surviving manuscripts has been edited and printed by interested individuals and institutions, mainly publishers in the Arab counties. It has, however, become necessary that an authority should exist to undertake responsibility for various aspects of the preservation, processing, maintenance, and restoration of unpublished manuscripts and for making them known worldwide. ALECSO (Arab League Educational, Cultural and Scientific Organization) is the authority to undertake such responsibility through its two organs, the Institute of Arab Manuscripts and the Department of Documentation and Information. The activities of these organs are described in this article.

SPECIAL LIBRARIES

365 Badr, Ahmad Mahmud. "al-Maktabat al-mutakhassisah: tarikhuha, ta'rifuha, ahdafuha wa-tahawwuliha al-mu'asir ila marakiz al-ma'lumat." *'Alam al-Kutub* 9, no. 4 (November 1988): 466-476.

A history of special libraries: their roles, organization and development to information centers.

366 Leroy, J. "L'Institut du Monde Arabe." [The Institute of the Arab World.] *Bulletin d'Informations de l'Association des Bibliothecaires Francais*, no. 132 (1986): 21-22.

Paper presented at a French Librarians Association congress on International relations and French libraries, in Lyon, May-June 1986. The Institute was jointly founded in 1980 by France and 19 of the 22 Arab states, with the objective of improving knowledge about the Arab world in France and Europe. The work of building a library collection began in 1982, with the purchase of works in France, Western Europe, and the Arab countries. Buying from Arab publishers is difficult - production is generally small, national bibliographies few and delayed, and publishers' catalogs inaccurate. In addition transmission of payment is complex and postal delivery slow. Exchange systems with institutions in France and North Africa, using lists, are proving more viable. The Institute has now succeeded in some cases in setting up formal agreements, which include (in the case of French institutions) joint database and cataloging projects.

367 Maliha, Nuhad, et al. "Dawr maktabat Ikarda wa khadamat ma'lumatiha fi da'm tatawwur al-zira'ah fi mantaqat al-Sharq al-Awsat wa-Shamal Afriqiyah." *Risalat al-Maktabah* 32, no.4 (December 1997): 4-16.

This study deals with the agricultural information and those who benefit from them, as well as the information technology that affect its libraries. The objectives of ICARDA Library are reviewed as well as the information circulation and the efforts to set up an agricultural information network in the Middle East and North Africa.

368 al-Maliki, Majbal Lazim Musallam, and Muhammad 'Awdah 'Aliwi. "Maktabat al-mustashfayat: ahammiyatiha, ahdafiha wa-khadamatiha." *Risalat al-Maktabah* 27, no. 3 (September 1992): 21-34.

Discusses the role, nature, and type of services rendered by hospital libraries and calls for the activation of hospital libraries in the Arab world.

THESAURI AND OTHER REFERENCE BOOKS

369 Habaili, Hussein. "al-Makaniz muta'addidat al-lughat wa-manhajiyyat i'dadiha." *al-Majallah al-'Arabiyah lil-Ma'lumat* 8, no. 1 (1987): 77-133.

The author analyzes the linguistic foundation of thesauri construction and the role of multilingual thesauri in the exchange of information between Arab and international networks. Problems involving Arabic language while constructing multilingual thesauri are discussed.

370 Habaili, Hussein. "al-Makaniz muta'addidat al-lughat: min al-nazariyah ila al-tatbiq: al-waqi' wa-al-tumuh." *al-Majallah al-'Arabiyah lil-Ma'lumat* 9, no. 2 (1988): 100-129.

The author deals with the practical part of multilingual thesauri. According to him, a well revised linguistic criteria on which thesauri building and developing depends are determined.

371 Itayem, Mahmoud A. "I'dad al-makaniz wa-tatwiriha." *al-Majallah al-'Arabiyah lil-Ma'lumat* 5, no. 2 (1984): 81-106.

The author reviews the establishment and development of thesauri, and the different Arabic efforts in constructing thesauri and the problems involved.

372 Itayem, Mahmoud A. *Bina' al-Makaniz wa-Tatwiriha*. Tunis: Jami'at al-Duwal al-'Arabiyah, al-Amanah al-'Ammah, Markaz al-Tawthiq wa-al-Ma'lumat, 1987.

373 Itayem, Mahmoud A. "al-Makaniz fi al-Watan al-'Arabi." *Risalat al-Maktabah* 28, no. 4 (December 1993): 4-13

The paper discusses Arab efforts to build thesauri since the 1970s. Twenty-one thesauri are covered by the study.

374 Roper, Geoffrey. "Reference books." In *The Oxford Encyclopedia of the Modern Islamic World*. Edited by John L. Esposito, vol. 3, pp. 415-420. New York: Oxford University Press, 1995.

The author provides and excellent overview of the history and development of reference books among Muslim nations. He also discusses in detail the different kinds of reference books being produced by Muslims, including biographical dictionaries, encyclopedias, historical tables, language dictionaries, reference grammars, bibliographies and guides to the literature. He also provides a significant list of sources used some of which are annotated.

375 Salem, Shawky. "Computerized bilingual thesauri: problems of thesauri construction and development in Arabic languages - case studies." *Microcomputers for Information Management* 8, no. 1 (March 1991): 27-44.

This paper introduces two vital case studies in which thesauri in bilingual "Arabic and English" construction were established. The Arabic language has special features that differ from many other languages. These features create problems that require special methods of handling to solve. The objectives, resources, and rules of each case have been mentioned in detail. The first case, which occurred in 1982, involved the establishment of a bilingual thesaurus for the documents and decrees of the Council of Ministers in Kuwait, and was implemented on an IBM mainframe. The second case, which was in 1985, involved the establishment of a bilingual petroleum thesaurus for the Arab Petroleum Training Institute (APTI), and was implemented on a Hewlett-Packard 3000 with a Mini-ISIS package. The creation of the second thesaurus was more efficient, and avoided some of the problems that arose in the creation of the first thesaurus. This paper describes, in detail, the gathering of the terms, the Arabic and English translation of these terms, the grouping of the terms, the logical hierarchy of the trees, and the preparation of the broad, narrow, and related terms in one logical sequence according to thesaurus construction rules and indicators. A new program was used to determine the Arabic permutation keywords during this work. Although the Arabic language is a difficult one to use for thesaurus construction, the Arabic auto-posing indexing, and the technique used for this work prove that it is possible to control the Arabic language and to set workable rules. [A]

376   Samahah, Imil, and Mahmoud A. Itayem. "Ikhtiyar al-mustalahat lil-maknaz." *al-Majallah al-'Arabiyah lil-Ma'lumat* 15, no. 1 (1994): 5-22.

Discusses the ways of choosing terms in building thesauri.

TRANSLITERATION

377   Farsuni, Fu'ad Hamad. "al-Intisakh." *'Alam al-Kutub* 11, no. 2 (May 1990): 169-188.

Transliteration is playing an important role, being a linguistic channel deemed to make information transfer easy among different countries. The author considers the linguistic and bibliographic aspects of transliteration as well as the practices, standards, and obstacles encountering it.

CHAPTER 2

ARABIAN GULF

GENERAL

378 Abdel-Hadi, Mohammed Fathi. "al-Isham al-khaliji fi majal al-maktabat wa-al-ma'lumat: dirasah tahliliyah wa qa'imah bibliyughrafiyah." *'Alam al-Kutub* 3, no. 4 (January-February 1981): 545-565.

A review of library and information science literature published in the Arabian Gulf Region.

379 *A'mal Nadwat Mas'uli Marakiz al-Tawthiq al-Tarbawi li-Dirasat Tanmiyat Nuzum al-Ma'lumat al-Tarbawiyah fi Duwal al-Khalij al-'Arabiyah wa-Taqniniha min ajl Ta'awun Mushtarak; al-Riyad, 15-17 Jumada al-Ula 1401 H, 21-23 Mars, Adhar 1981 M*. [al-Riyad]: Maktab al-Tarbiyah al-'Arabi li-Duwal al-Khalij, Idarat al-Baramij al-Tarbawiyah wa-al-'Ulum, 1981. iv, 89 p.

380 Aman, Mohammed M. "Libraries and information systems in the Arab Gulf States: after the war." *Journal of Information Science* 18, no. 6 (1992): 447-451.

Part of a special issue devoted to library and information services in the Arab countries after the Gulf War. It describes the situation of libraries and information centers in the Arab countries after the Gulf War. It also discusses the impact of the Gulf War on revenues and manpower, as well as the prospects for increased information access, improved use of technology, greater cooperation between libraries, the setting up of national library agencies and greater international and pan-Arab interaction. [A]

381 Shearer, Kenneth D. "The Arabian Gulf plans its library future." *International Library Review* 13, no. 3 (July 1981): 259-273.

This study highlights the necessity of forging new relationships between the Arab World and the West. The Arabian Gulf has great financial resources, has become familiar with Western achievements in library and information services in the English language, and desires to establish comparable services in the Arabic language. This requires new initiatives and the allocation of greater priority to the publication of books in Arabic.

ACADEMIC LIBRARIES

382 Abdo, Mekhag B. *The Academic Library in the Electronic Age: The Case of Six Arabian Peninsula Countries*. Ph.D., 1987. State University of New York at Buffalo. 345 p.

The study identified the impact of the electronic age on the form and services of the academic library at present and its implications in the future. In the light of it, the present status and future plans of the academic libraries of the six Arabian Peninsula countries were surveyed. The purpose of the study was to identify through a questionnaire, the automation projects of the thirteen academic libraries of the six states. In doing so the organizational set-up was studied as well as their plans for future automation and regional cooperation in doing so. The questionnaire was sent to the Deans of Library Affairs and Directors of Libraries for the thirteen universities. Analysis of the three parts of the questionnaire was made, namely, the Library Profile, Library Automation Status and the Future. Answers to each question were tabulated and findings presented. Comparison findings of the three parts of the questionnaire were made and the results were: (1) Types of Automated Libraries. The trend seemed to be that the libraries of the more technical/specialized universities were automated while the libraries of the comprehensive universities were not. (2) Arabic Bibliographic Standards and Bibliographic Tools. One of the basic problems of academic library automation seemed to be the lack of standardized bibliographic tools for the control of Arabic bibliographic information. (3) Bilingual Systems. The narrow choice of only two presently available systems that can handle the automation of a bilingual collection. (4) Trained Manpower. The lack of trained competent librarians seemed to be another problem for automation. Drawing upon the above findings, guidelines were presented for the automation of the University of Qatar Library and recommendations made on the regional level for the thirteen academic libraries under study. [DAI 48/02-A: 239.]

383 Ali, Syed Nazim. "Academic libraries and their services in the Arabian Gulf." *Library Review* 35, no. 4 (Winter 1986): 238-244.

This paper outlines the current situation and the development which has taken place in the libraries of the seventeen universities of the Arabian Gulf countries. It examines their administration, manpower, technical services, and reader services. The author states that libraries and information services at the universities have developed more actively in a short time than any other type of library in the Arabian Gulf, but, with a few exceptions, have yet to reach an international standard.

384 Zehery, Mohamed H. "University library development in the Arab Gulf region: a survey and analysis of six state university libraries." *International Information & Library Review* 29, no. 1 (March 1997): 13-44.

This study examines the development of six state university libraries in the Arab Gulf countries of Bahrain, Kuwait, Oman, Qatar, Saudi Arabia, and United Arab Emirates. Despite the relatively short history of higher education in these countries, these libraries have made some significant progress. It should be noted that in terms of library organization, size of collections, number of staff, service activities, and computer applications, these libraries are considered by default the main libraries in their respective countries. At present, only Saudi Arabia has a national library. This study employed a survey questionnaire which was sent to all Gulf university libraries to identify and gather pertinent and current information necessary to establish an accurate profile on each one of these libraries. The study provides basic information on library organization and analysis of collections, services, staffing, budgeting, expenditures, automation, and information technology The study findings suggest that further research is needed to examine and evaluate collections, service activities and instructional programs, staff development and training, co-operation among Arab Gulf universities, and library education programs in the region.

AUTOMATION

385 Khurshid, Zahiruddin "System migration: challenges for libraries in the Arabian Gulf region." *The Electronic Library* 16, no. 3 (June 1998): 171-174.

With the availability of some innovative second generation systems in the Arabian Gulf marketplace, several libraries in the region are considering system migration. However, they are faced with a number of challenges some of which have continued from the time of implementation of the first generation systems. The paper aims to highlight those challenges and emphasizes the need to address them in a planning stage (which includes vendor support, data conversion, and training) so that the process of changing systems does not turn into a futile exercise.

386 Symposium on New Technology in Libraries (1982: Dahran). *Proceedings of the Symposium on New Technology in Libraries: Prospects and*

Problems for Libraries in the Gulf States, 26, 27, 28 April 1982. Jami'at al-Bitrul wa-al-Ma'adin, 'Imadat Shu'un al-Maktabat. Dhahran, Saudi Arabia: UPM Press, 1982. iv, 284, 3 p.

BIBLIOGRAPHIC CONTROL

387   al-Samadi, Nasim Hasan. "al-Dabt al-bibliyughrafi lil-dawriyyat fi al-Khalij al-'Arabi: al-istirja' al-kulli." *'Alam al-Kutub* 3, no. 4 (January-February 1983): 566-574.

The author discusses four basic things: bibliographic control, periodicals, information retrieval and the Arabian Gulf. He reviews the most important periodicals published in the Gulf Region, the level of bibliographical control as well as the periodical directories and the serial bibliographies that are published there.

BIBLIOMETRIC STUDIES

388   Lammers, W., and A. Tahir. "Profile of medical research publications from the GCC countries, 1990-1994." *Annals of Saudi Medicine* 16, no. 6 (November 1996): 666-669.

Using the CD-ROM system of MEDLINE, which contains the origins of articles that are published in about 3500 international medical journals, a survey was performed of the medical publications from the six countries in the Gulf Cooperating Council (GCC) over a period of five years (1990-1994). The Kingdom of Saudi Arabia was the largest producer of publications, with approximately 400 papers each year. In the same period the output from Kuwait declined from about 200 to lower number, an effect probably caused by the invasion. In contrast, the United Arab Emirates, and to a lesser extent the Sultanate of Oman, have shown a growth in their publication record due to the initiation of new medical schools in these two countries. In the six GCC countries, all the colleges of medicine together were responsible for 34% of the total number of publications, hospitals and health centers published 45% of all papers, while non-medical colleges and other institutions published smaller amounts.

CATALOGING AND CLASSIFICATION

389   Khalid, Farooq A. "On your MARC, get set, go [status of machine readable bibliographic control in the Arabian Gulf countries.]" *Information Technology and Libraries* 15, no. 2 (June 1996): 99-103.

Reports the decision, taken at the 'Workshop on Arabic Online Cataloging Network', United Arab Emirates University, 5-6 October 1993, to create a committee to develop a MARC standard for the handling of Arabic computerized bibliographic records. Lists measures to be taken in establishing standards for Arabic computerized data with particular reference to: the Arabic character set; authority files; mandatory MARC fields; holdings format; and acquisitions (BISAC and SISAC).

390 Khurshid, Zahiruddin. "Preparing catalogers for the electronic environment: an analysis of cataloging and related courses in the Arabian Gulf region." *Journal of Education for Library and Information Science* 39, no. 1 (Winter 1998): 2-13.

The advent of library automation in the 1960s and subsequent developments in information technology have changed the role of catalogers. How catalogers are being prepared by American library schools to meet the challenges of the electronic environment is discussed. This is followed by an analysis of cataloging courses offered by library science departments in the Arabian Gulf region to see whether they have been designed to develop the desired competency in catalogers for present and future trends in cataloging.

COLLECTION DEVELOPMENT/ACQUISITION

391 Ali, Syed Nazim. "Acquisition of scientific literature in developing countries: Arab Gulf countries." *Information Development* 5, no. 2 (April 1989): 108-115.

Reviews the current state of the art with regard to policies, procedures and problems in the acquisition of scientific literature by libraries in the Arabian Gulf region.

INDEXING AND ABSTRACTING SERVICES

392 al-Samadi, Nasim Hasan. "Takshif al-dawriyyat fi duwal al-Khalij al-'Arabi: al-itar al-nazari." *Maktabat al-Idarah* 11, no. 1 (October 1983): 20-37.

INFORMATION RESOURCES

393 Burkhart, G. "The Internet gains acceptance in the Persian Gulf." *Communications of the ACM* 41, no. 3 (March 1998): 19-25.

The number of countries with Internet access have increased dramatically over the last 20 years. However, large areas have been slow to acquire or absorb this technology. Within the Organization of the Islamic Conference (OIC), the slowest to join the world's Internet community have been the nations of the Persian Gulf. Research information is presented of the nine petro-chemically endowed countries of the Persian Gulf, to discover why there is so little of the Internet in this part of the world for so long and what has brought about its acceptance in so many countries in a short time. The Persian Gulf countries examined include: Bahrain , Iran, Iraq , Kuwait , Oman , Qatar , Saudi Arabia , United Arab Emirates (UAE), and Yemen . The research demonstrates that all nine countries are characterized by strong forms of state control, including rule over the content and distribution of information. The exact forms of control vary from country to country, usually deriving from military, religious authority, hereditary monarchies, or other oligarchic sources. Two broad, overlapping categories of concern and cautious acceptance of the Internet in these countries are described, including: national/cultural/religious values, and national security.

394   al-Hubayl, 'Abd al-Qadir Muhammad. *Masadir al-Ma'lumat fi Duwal al-Khalij al-'Arabi*. Baghdad: Markaz al-Tawthiq al-I'lami li-Duwal al-Khalij al-'Arabi, 1983. 107 p.

INFORMATION STORAGE AND RETRIEVAL

395   Dewachi, Abdulilah. "Computer-based industrial information systems for the Arabian Gulf region." In *4th International Online Information Meeting, London, 9-11 December, 1980* (pp. 509-518). Oxford and New York: Learned Information, 1980.

In the Arabian Gulf where information systems and access to international telecommunication networks for information are hardly known, the intergovernmental Gulf Organization for Industrial Consulting--GOIC (founded in 1976 and based in Doha) has developed an indigenous Industrial Data Bank, offering socio-economic and industrial information to its member states. It also succeeded in accessing international data centers through TYMNET. The paper outlines the facilities at GOIC.

INTERLIBRARY LOAN

396   al-Ibrahim, Baha. "Interlibrary loans in the Arabian Gulf: issues and requisites." *Interlending and Document Supply* 21, no. 2 (1993): 21-5.

This article studies the regional interlibrary loan process among the Arabian Gulf universities and other institutions, and covers the following broad aspects: (1) Historical development of the regional ILL process since the early 1980s, with a critique thereof; (2) Basic requisites, specifically a specialized ILL unit, union list and document delivery mechanism; and (3) The impact of the Gulf war on the Kuwait University library system - one of the leaders of regional ILL activity in the 1980s.

397   Siddiqui, Moid A. "Regional interlibrary loan network of Arabian Gulf academic libraries." *Resource Sharing & Information Networks* 11, no. 1-2 (1996): 143-158.

All six Arabian Gulf countries are signatory to the Arab Bureau of Education for the Gulf States Interlibrary Loan Code developed in 1983, but resource sharing and library cooperation among Gulf academic libraries is still minimal and of great concern. This article discusses the background, as well as the present resource-sharing situation in the Arabian Gulf. Based on the results of a questionnaire survey of thirteen Arabian Gulf academic libraries, the article looks into the feasibility of establishing an interlibrary loan network (ILLN) among Gulf academic libraries. In addition, it discusses the networking requirements and suggests an ILLN plan for consideration and implementation by the Arabian Gulf academic libraries to encourage, strengthen and streamline resource sharing.

LIBRARY ADMINISTRATION/MANAGEMENT

398 Badri, M. A. "Critical issues in information systems management: an international perspective." *International Journal of Information Management* 12, no. 3 (September 1992): 179-191.

Evaluates critical information system (IS) issues from an international perspective. The study reveals that an information revolution is sweeping through the economies of member countries of the Gulf Cooperation Council. Strategic issues in IS management are given top priorities. The perception of critical issues depends greatly on environmental characteristics and the backgrounds of the chief executives. [A]

LIBRARY COOPERATION

399 Bouazza, Abdelmajid. "Resource sharing among libraries in developing countries: the Gulf between hope and reality." *International Library Review* 18, no. 4 (October 1986): 373-387.

Examines the obstacles to cooperation which are common to developed as well as developing countries. Considers barriers caused by political, human and professional, social and cultural factors. Stresses that cooperation is doomed to failure unless the importance of information for solving social and economic problems is realized.

400 Bukhari, A. A. "Resource sharing in Gulf academic libraries '95." *Library Hi Tech News* 130 (March 1996): 9-12.

Reports the 3rd annual conference of the Special Libraries Association (SLA) Arabian Gulf Chapter, al-Ain, United Arab Emirates, 15-17 March 1995. The topic of the conference was 'Strengthening resource sharing in libraries and information centers in the Arabian Gulf region'. Over 500 delegates attended from the USA, UK, Kuwait, Bahrain, Oman, Saudi Arabia, and several other countries. Papers covered the following topics: information policy and resources: international, regional, and national perspectives; standards for resource sharing; technology and resource sharing; databases and systems for resource sharing; and interlibrary loan and document delivery.

LIBRARY EDUCATION

401 Qari, Abdulghafoor A. "Electronic library and library and information science departments in the Arabian Gulf region." *Journal of Education for Library and Information Science* 39, no. 1 (Winter 1998): 28-37.

Advances in networking and communication technologies have been widely discussed as having the potential to radically change library systems. The term "electronic library" has been accepted by most of the university libraries providing electronic information services. The library educational system is being affected by this technology, and new methods of teaching/learning activities are needed. The aim of this paper is to provide a clear picture of how the Arabian Gulf region library appears today and how the library educational system can meet the changes to provide skilled and trained librarians to manage, operate, and plan future electronic library systems.

402 al-Sabbagh, 'Imad 'Abd al-Wahhab. "Waqi' wa-mustaqbal al-ta'lim al-akadimi fi 'ilm al-ma'lumat wa-al-maktabat fi Duwal al-Khalij al-'Arabi." *Risalat al-Maktabah* 32, no. 3 (September 1997): 23-37.

Academic programs of library and information sciences in the Arabian Gulf region need to be improved and the curricula revised in order to meet the technological innovations.

NETWORKS AND NETWORKING

403 Ashoor, Mohammad Saleh. "Bibliographic networking in the Gulf region." In *Building Information Systems in the Islamic World*. Edited by Ziauddin Sardar, pp. 116-124. London and New York: Mansell, 1988.

The author describes the evolution of Gulf-Net, a computer-to-computer network established to link computer centers of academic and research institutions in the Gulf region. He considers this development as a major breakthrough and argues that if such problems as lack of bibliographic control and adequate provision of telecommunication facilities can be overcome, the example and success of Gulf-Net can be repeated in other regions of the Muslim world.

404 Ashoor, Mohammad Saleh. "Bibliographic networking in the Arabian Gulf Region: prospects and problems." *Resource Sharing & Information Networks* 4, no. 2 (1989): 13-25.

The development of a bibliographic network to serve the needs of the academic, research and special libraries in the Arabian Gulf region has long been the dream of professionals in the field. The formulation of Gulf Cooperation Council (GCC), introduction of automation in libraries, and strong networking capabilities of the DOBIS/LIBIS Library Automated System, hold the promise of shared access to library resources. It is hoped that recent improvements in telecommunications in the region would further advance the chances of development of a bibliographic network. Introduction of Gulfnet, a computer-to-computer communication link among academic institutions in the Gulf region, should contribute to the development of such a network by facilitating interlibrary loan services. In this venture toward greater regional library cooperation, the King Fahd University of Petroleum and Minerals Library (KFUPM) can serve as a central node by providing a central database for online cataloging, cooperative acquisition, interlibrary loan, and other resource-sharing activities. There is a need, interalia, for agreement on standards for bibliographic procedures among libraries in the Gulf for achieving a reasonable level of cooperation and resource-sharing. However, the creation of an effective bibliographic network will only be possible with the provision of a legal base by delegating the authority for networking to a region-based organization like GCC and administrative support of individual governments of the Gulf states.

405 Khalid, Farooq A. "At the threshold of a library network." *Information Technology and Libraries* 15, no. 4 (December 1996): 241-6.

The Arabian Gulf Libraries stand poised at the threshold of networking, which promises the sharing of resources through cooperation and provides the individual library with greater access to resources. Several libraries in the Gulf region have acquired sophisticated systems and there is a great potential to develop library networks. Highlights both the benefits and the problems associated with networking in libraries and discusses the circumstances that are forcing several information centers in the Gulf region to begin thinking seriously about library networking. Describes briefly the development of an important networking tool, the Union List of Scientific and Technical Periodicals in the Gulf Region, which should serve as a springboard for further discussions related to library networks in the Gulf.

SPECIAL LIBRARIES

406 Tedd, Lucy A. "Report on the second annual conference of the Arabian Gulf Chapter of the Special Libraries Association, January 1994." *Program* 28, no. 3 (July 1994): 295-299.

Reports on the papers presented at the second annual conference of the Arabian Gulf Chapter of the Special Libraries Association, January 1994.

CHAPTER 3

ALGERIA

GENERAL

407 Boumarafi, Behdja B., and Peter Havard Williams. "Problems affecting the development of libraries in Algeria." *Focus on International & Comparative Librarianship* 14, no. 2 (1983): 15-17.

The development of library services has a low priority in the national development policy of Algeria. Other factors which have contributed to the poor standard of provision are: a lack of reading habit even amongst the educated elite; the lack of a strong professional body; the absence of library legislation; poor library stock; lack of cooperation between libraries; lack of qualified staff; an educational system geared to teaching through textbooks only.

408 Boumarafi, Behdja M. "Libraries and information in Algeria: past, present and future prospects." In *Transforming Libraries and Educating Librarians. Essays in Memory of Peter Havard-Williams*. Edited by John Feather, pp. 123-144. London: Taylor Graham, 1997.

Reviews the past history and current developments in libraries in Algeria focusing on: the work of the National Library of Algeria (Bibliographie de l'Algerie); academic libraries; public libraries; school libraries; special libraries and documentation centres; the Algerian book publishing industry; and new developments in the information infrastructure, including information technology. Lists the factors affecting the development of Algerian libraries and notes four paradigm shifts that will shape this development: educational growth and change; political and economic change; institutional changes in the use of information; and globalization of economics.

409 Chait, R. "Algeria." Translated by Charles S. Fineman and Mary Niles Maack. In *World Encyclopedia of Library and Information Services*. 3rd ed. (pp. 44-46). Chicago: American Library Association, 1993.

Discusses the history of libraries and library education in the country and gives a description of its national, academic, public, school, and special libraries.

ACADEMIC LIBRARIES

410 Boumarafi, Behdja B. *Tatawwur al-Maktabat al-Jami'iyah fi al-Jaza'ir*. Tunis: al-Ma'had al-A'lah lil-Tawthiq, 1986.

COPYRIGHT/INTELLECTUAL PROPERTY

411 Bu-'Ayyad, Mahmud. "Huquq al-ta'lif fi-al-Jaza'ir." *'Alam al-Kutub* 2, no. 4 (January-February 1982): 671-674.

INFORMATION SYSTEMS

412 Bahelli, Y. "Algerian Scientific Abstracts, an information system to heighten awareness of Algerian scientific research." *Documentaliste - Sciences de l'Information* 34, no. 4-5 (July-October 1997): 253-257.

Scientific and technical publications are the indispensable vehicle for increasing awareness of research results. To ensure that such information transfer really takes place presupposes that the means of access and exploitation exist; in other words, an information system designed to the highest standards that systematically and comprehensively announces these publications. Algeria's national system for disseminating scientific and technical information was not functioning optimally. The ASA program, initiated by the CERIST in 1993, set out to improve things. A bibliographic database called Algerian Scientific Abstracts was created to list and describe articles published in Algeria in all scientific and technical fields. A preliminary core of references was prepared and recorded on a prototype CD-ROM, still being tested, to be used to promote the ASA program among all concerned parties-universities, scientific societies, enterprises, governmental bodies, etc.

413 Idruj, al-Akhdar, and Kamal Bu-'Anjah. "al-Faharis al-mushtarakah lil-dawriyyat: manhajiyyat rasd al-ma'lumat: dirasat halah al-fahras al-jaza'iri lil-dawriyyat." *al-Majallah al-'Arabiyah lil-Ma'lumat* 15, no. 2 (1994): 75-97.

414 Tekfi, Chaffai. *Design of a Computer Information System for the Algerian National Archives.* Ph.D., 1990. City University (United Kingdom). 449 p.

The main purpose of this project is to investigate the state of the art of the Algerian National Archives (ANA) so as to design an automated system that responds to the needs of this institution. The effects of computerization on archives are investigated. Some automated archives systems, around the world, are examined. The various obstacles impeding the development of a technology capable of processing Arabic script are reviewed. Some solutions are also discussed. The case of Algeria in the context of the Arab World is taken as an example. A number of problems hampering the transfer of technology are identified. The study is concentrated on the state of the art of the ANA. It is carried out using a variety of data collection techniques; including questionnaires, interviews, observation and the author's own experience of the ANA. Several problem areas are identified; including: the lack of resource sharing between the various institutions and the access speed to documents, to name just a few. The objectives of the system to be designed and implemented are identified. A prototype user-friendly system, using the query language, dBASE III PLUS and Clipper, is developed to simulate some of the various tasks carried out within records management institutions. An explanation of how can the system be operated is provided. An evaluation of the prototype system is carried out. A number of recommendations to improve the system are presented. Amongst these, is the necessity to provide a much faster system. The prototype system is thus redeveloped using, this time, Turbo Pascal. Apart from speed, no alterations or additions are introduced to the one developed using dBASE. Because the project has not been taken to the last stages of the System Development Life Cycle (SDLC), a number of recommendations are made regarding the steps that the ANA should observe to ensure a smooth system implementation and maintenance. [DAI 52/12-A: 4128.]

LIBRARY EDUCATION

415 Boumarafi, Behdja B., and J. Haythornthwaite. "Library information education in Algeria." *International Library Review* 20, no. 4 (October 1988): 469-475.

Addresses the history of library and information science education in Algeria which is modeled on the French system. Describes the development of the following courses: the training of para-professionals; the training of library assistants; the training of library technicians; training of professionals; a course leading to a first degree; the post-graduate program; and the master program. Outlines problems facing library and information science education in Algeria: curriculum improvement; staff development; lack of material facilities; and the lack of computers in libraries.

416 Lajeunesse, Marcel. "Education and training of information specialists in French-speaking countries: a comparative study." *Unesco Journal of Information Science, Librarianship and Archives Administration* 1, no. 2 (April-June 1979): 124-137.

Compares the education and training of information specialists in Algeria, Belgium, France, Morocco, Canada, Senegal, Switzerland and Tunisia, and tabulates the results. Differences are apparent in the organization of the teaching institutions and their incorporation into the national structure; the nature and content of curricula; standards of study and diplomas; and the link between theory and practice in the teaching of librarianship, documentation, computerization of documentation, and information science.

417 Semra, Halima. "The education and training of librarians in Algeria." *Inspel* 21, no. 4 (1987): 219-225.

In the period between 1960 and 1970, after many African states had become independent, the need to take advantage of the knowledge recorded in literature for economic and sociological development was not forgotten. A connection was seen between illiteracy and living standards. In addition, new standards of scientific training had to be set, leading to the need to create libraries, documentation services and archives. These were to be run by staff trained for the job on special courses. The author describes the current training situation in Algeria and makes serious suggestions regarding the possibility of further development in other Third World countries.

418 Semra, Halima. "Education and training of librarians in the Maghreb (Algeria, Morocco, Tunisia)." In *Information and Libraries in the Arab World*. Compiled and edited by Michael Wise and Anthony Olden, pp. 41-54. London: Library Association Publishing, 1994. [Information and libraries in the developing world, vol. 3.]

An article included in a collection of papers presenting a comparative review of librarianship and library practices in Arab countries. It reviews the main aspects of professional library and information science education and training in Algeria, Morocco, and Tunisia.

419 Yacine, Badiaa. "L'enseignement theorique et pratique de la biblioth-conomie a l'Institut de Bibliotheconomie et Sciences Documentaires d'Oran." [Theoretical and practical teaching of librarianship at the Institute of Library and Information Science in Oran.] In *Theorie et pratique dans l'enseignement des sciences de l'information*. [Bridging the gap between theory and practice.] Universite de Montreal. Ecole de Bibliotheconomie et des Sciences de l'Information, 1988.

LIBRARY LEGISLATION

420   Lajeunesse, Marcel, and Henri Sene. "Les problemes de legislation en matiere d'information dans les pays africains." *Libri* 34, no. 4 (December 1984): 271-288.

Outlines the comparative development of library and information services in African countries with French influences, with particular emphasis on legislation of direct relevance to national institutions and services, including: national libraries; legal deposit; national bibliographic agencies; bibliographic control; national bibliographies; and the status of the library profession and its professional associations.

PUBLIC LIBRARIES

421   Gandon, Francis. "La lecture publique en Algerie: l'exemple d'Oran." [Public libraries in Algeria: the example of Oran.] *Mediatheques Publiques* 46 (April-June 1978): 39-44.

The author, a lecturer in the Faculty of Arts of Oran, being surprised by his students' limited reading, surveyed the resources of two public libraries in the town. Es-Senia, a suburb, has a one-room library with 2,300 books. Oran Municipal Library, founded in 1935, has 40,700 books (for a population of 700,000) of which 37,000 are in French and 3,000 in Arabic. All non-fiction is for reference only. The library is open 5 hours daily, has no qualified staff, and provides only an author catalog. Additions average 700 yearly. There are 4,000 adult and 6,000 adolescent members (mainly grammar school pupils). Public libraries are considered a marginal activity, hence their inadequacy. The state Arabization policy and antipathy to Western influences create other difficulties.

SCHOOL/CHILDREN'S LIBRARIES

422   Bouderbane, Azzedine. "Children's library services in Algeria." In *Information and Libraries in the Arab World*. Compiled and edited by Michael Wise and Anthony Olden, pp. 55-67. London: Library Association Publishing, 1994. [Information and libraries in the developing world, vol. 3.]

Article included in a collection of papers presenting a comparative review of libraries and library practices in Arab countries. Reviews the status of children's libraries and library services in Algeria with particular reference to their contribution to the cultural and educational development of Algerian society: a society still in the process of defining its cultural policy. Discusses the role of public libraries, cultural centers, foreign cultural centers, school libraries and children's literature.

SPECIAL LIBRARIES

423   Menant, J. "Une bibliotheque dans le camps de refugies sahraouis?" [A library in the Saharan refugee camps?] *Bulletin d'Informations de l'Association des Bibliothecaires Francais* 166 (1st Quarter, 1995): 68-70.

Western Sahara, formerly a Spanish colony, though legally independent, is now occupied by Moroccan troops and some 165,000 refugees live in south west Algeria, chiefly women, children and old people. At the request of the Saharan Democratic Arab Republic, a French delegation made a visit in October 1994 with a view to creating a library to support the Women's School, which trains 800 women annually on matters ranging from national culture to organizing camp life. The visit raised the question of the appropriateness of traditional library science models in Arab contexts, and in addition to supplying books, plans are in hand to develop a Franco-Arab library science manual.

USER EDUCATION

424   Yakoubi, Bechir. "User education at the Oran University of Science and Technology." *IATUL Quarterly* 1, no. 1 (March 1987): 63-67.

Contribution to an issue devoted to papers presented at the 3rd International Association of Technological University Libraries (IATUL) Online User Education Seminar held at the Technological University of Compiegne, France, July 1986. The Oran University of Science and Technology (OUST) was created in 1975 as a training center for engineers in Western Algeria. Describes the OUST Library, and creating awareness of its problems among the central administration, the teaching staff and students. Discusses methods used to keep users informed, and training courses for the library staff, the teaching staff and researchers, and the students. Outlines plans for automation.

CHAPTER 4

BAHRAIN

GENERAL

425 Ali, Syed Nazim. "Bahrain." In *World Encyclopedia of Library and Information Services*. 3rd ed. (pp. 98-100). Chicago: American Library Association, 1993.

Discusses the history of libraries and library education in the country and gives a description of its national, academic, public, school, and special libraries.

426 al-Rumayhi, Fu'ad 'Abd al-Latif, and Sarah Yusuf Naji. "al-Maktabat wa-marakiz al-ma'lumat bi dawlat al-Bahrayn: al-waqi' wa-al-tatallu'at al-mustaqbaliyah." *al-Majallah al-'Arabiyah lil-Ma'lumat* 10, no. 2 (1989): 5-32.

In Bahrain, libraries face common problems that are identified as follows: different perceptions of library service; lack of access to information sources; funds for library development have low priority; absence of new information technology; absence of library legislation, library cooperation, and planning on a national level; shortage of qualified librarians. Bahrain has adopted different methods in the training of library personnel, but these methods have not yet provided Bahrain with the required quality of professional staff.

427 Young, Harold C., and Syed Nazim Ali. "The Gulf War and its effect on information and library services in the Arabian Gulf with particular reference to the State of Bahrain." *Journal of Information Science* 18, no. 6 (1992): 453-462.

Part of a special issue devoted to library and information services in the Arab countries after the Gulf War. The existing development of libraries and information centers in Bahrain in terms of collections, library manpower and the national information policy are provided as a setting to discuss the impact that the Gulf War has had on the regional growth of information and library services. The regional information flow prior to and after the Gulf War is discussed to highlight the impact upon researchers, and research generation. Some suggestions and recommendations are made to focus on collection development, inter-library lending, and the benefit that would accrue from the establishment of national libraries in the large Gulf States to disseminate national publication information and standardized Arabic cataloging. [A]

CD-ROM DATABASES INFORMATION SERVICES

428 Ali, Syed Nazim. "CD-ROM databases as an alternate means to online information: the experience of a university library in developing country." *Microcomputers for Information Management* 5, no. 3 (September 1988): 197-202.

Also appears under the title "CD-ROM databases as an alternative means to online information: the experience of a university library in developing countries" in *Proceedings of the 12th International Online Information Meeting, London, 6-8 December, 1988* (pp. 569-573), Oxford: Learned Information Ltd., 1988. Optical disc technology, especially the CD-ROM, has provided a new dimension to information professionals because of its enormous storage and retrieval capabilities. As a result of that, publishers have begun to produce most of the frequently used reference and non-reference material on optical media. Libraries and information centers in most developing countries have limited resources and they cannot afford to provide access to online searching for their users. Databases on optical media appear to be a good alternative means for online searching. Describes briefly the ways in which this technology has been utilized as an alternate means to online database searching at the University of Bahrain.

429 Ali, Syed Nazim, and Harold C. Young. "Information access through CD-ROM and its impact upon faculty research output: a case of a university in Third World countries—University of Bahrain." *Microcomputers for Information Management* 9, no. 3 (1992): 177-189.

An analysis of data on the use of CD-ROM for database searching, as well as data of interlibrary loan activities in the past five years, shows that there is a strong relationship between the use of CD-ROMs with the increase in faculty publication output. Although there are many contributing factors to the increase in faculty productivity, such as the emphasis placed by the University upon research publications for tenure considerations, and the increased financial support for research endeavors, this study shows that the library's dramatic increase of access to the world's bibliographical information resources is due to the acquisition of CD-

ROM databases. It is also a significant factor for the increase in faculty research publication output. The use of CD-ROM technology in libraries has also greatly improved the quality of the library users' bibliographical citations. This has enabled the library to achieve a better fulfillment rate in terms of interlibrary loan requests. [A]

430   al-Qaisi, M., and Syed Nazim Ali. "Searching CD-ROM databases for non-English-speaking users." *New Library World* 96 (1995): 24-27.

Describes how access to English language information by non-English speaking students and faculty at a Middle Eastern university (Bahrain University) is being facilitated by making available a variety of computerized sources, particularly CD-ROMs, and also how use of the information retrieved is made possible by several means, including the provision by faculty and library staff of translations into English of information requests made in Arabic; the publication of bilingual dictionaries covering a wide range of scientific, technological and other disciplines; and the recent development, by other institutions, of a number of online, multilingual databases covering computer terms and science and technology fields, accessible via Gulfnet and the Internet. Anticipates the development of an all sources database accessible through all public search and retrieval terminals. [A]

INFORMATION SYSTEMS

431   Klunder, Frederick. "Designing micrographics systems in Bahrain." *Journal of Micrographics* 15, no. 6 (June 1982): 33-36.

The recent tempo of socioeconomic development in Bahrain has placed strong demands on the government information system. The Ministry of Justice and Islamic Affairs retained a consulting firm, Arcadia Associates, to design a microfilm production/use system to function as part of a flexible long-range information systems plan involving several technologies. It was decided to microfilm the land registration and court case files and the case indexes. Describes the procedure, promotion of user acceptance, and the importance of environmental considerations. [A]

LIBRARY EDUCATION

432   Alian, R. M. "Library science programs in the State of Bahrain." In *Information and Libraries in the Arab World*. Compiled and edited by Michael Wise and Anthony Olden, pp. 68-80. London: Library Association Publishing, 1994. [Information and libraries in the developing world, vol. 3.]

Article included in a collection of papers presenting a comparative review of librarianship and library practices in Arab countries. Focuses on the state of professional library and information science education and the training of library staff in Bahrain. Notes the library and information science education programs of various organizations in Bahrain, including Bahrain University, and the problems associated with these programs.

CHAPTER 5

DJIBOUTI

GENERAL

433 American Library Association. "Djibouti." In *World Encyclopedia of Library and Information Services*. 3rd ed. (p. 254). Chicago: American Library Association, 1993.

SPECIAL LIBRARIES

434 Dawe, M. P. St. J. "Creation d'une bibliotheque a l'Assemblee nationale de Djibouti." [Creation of a library at the National Assembly of Djibouti.] *Bulletin d'Informations de l'Association des Bibliothecaires Francais* 142 (1989): 15-20.

Paper presented at the IFLA Congress in Sydney, August 1988. Djibouti (Africa) became independent in 1977, and elected its first parliament in 1982. The project to create a library for the National Assembly was first submitted to the Inter-parliamentary Union in 1983. Member countries, most notably Italy, lent support and aid for drawing up plans, providing training, and supplying an initial minimum collection of books and periodicals. The project was put in hand in 1985, and the library finally opened in January 1988, with a staff of seven trained professionals and a collection of some 1,500 books and 25 periodicals. [A]

CHAPTER 6

EGYPT

GENERAL

435 Aman, Mohammed M. "Egypt." In *World Encyclopedia of Library and Information Services*. 3rd ed. (pp. 265-267). Chicago: American Library Association, 1993.

Discusses the history of libraries and library education in the country and gives a description of its national, academic, public, school, and special libraries.

436 al-Arini, Muhsin. "Egyptian libraries." *Pakistan Library Bulletin* 21, no. 2 (June 1990): 23-33.

This paper describes the library system in Egypt against the background of its geography, population, history, education and cultural life. An historical review, including that of national library planning, gives a survey of existing library resources, including the National Library, public libraries, school libraries, college and university libraries, government and special libraries, and foreign libraries. The paper also describes bibliographic control, the library profession and library education in Egypt. It finally recommends to increase libraries' funds, integrate the philosophy of modern library service, strengthen library training, encourage bibliographical tools, link reference library networks and develop technical manuals and set forth resource-sharing programs among similar institutions.

437 Lees, Nigel. "Library and information work in Egypt: perspective of a volunteer working in Assiut." *Journal of Information Science* 16, no. 2 (1990): 99-105.

Personal experiences of the author whilst working as a Libraries Coordinator in the libraries of the Faculty of Science, Assiut University are discussed. Difficulties and shared problems faced by volunteer librarians are described which include: staffing, library stock, library building, library usage, cooperation and status of library work. A brief history of volunteer input to the Faculty of Science is given with special reference to the years 1986-1988, when the author was involved. Problems relating to research work in Egypt, again with reference to experience in Assiut, are described. The work of the National Information System (ENSTINET) and its various information nodes, especially NIDOC, is also described. The work of other library and information centers (American University Library, Cairo University Department of Librarianship, the National Library and the British Council) is briefly described and compared to development in Assiut. [A]

438 Tedd, Lucy A. "Report on a visit to Egypt, April 1993." *Program* 28, no. 1 (January 1994): 77-82.

Reports on some of the libraries and information institutions visited in Egypt during a study tour, organized by the British Council at the instigation of the Department of librarianship, information and archival studies, Cairo University.

ACADEMIC LIBRARIES

439 Kaufmann, Ita. "Bedeutended Bibliotheken der Welt (XXXIX): Zentralbibliothek der Uni Kairo." [Important libraires of the world (XXXIX): Central Library of Cairo University.] *Borsenblatt fur den Deutschen Buchhandel* 41, no. 59 (1985): 1886-1888. [In German.]

In 1908 Cairo gained its first Egyptian university for every man. By 1912 its library had 700 volumes. Grants soon raised the stock to 70,000. The major early contributions included those from the eye specialist Dr. Max Meierhof, and the archaeologist, Professor Junker. In 1925 the university was taken over by the state. In 1929 the library acquired the 4,000 volume collection of the Orientalist, Hermann Sybold. Other books have come from Prince Ibrahim Helmy (19,000) and Prince Kamal el Din Hussein (5,000). By 1935 Cairo University Library (CUL) had 4,000 Arabic, Persian and Turkish manuscripts. The year 1972 saw the publication of a bound catalog. A card catalog immediately followed. Theses are now microfilmed. CUL publishes an annual bibliography in English and Arabic. [LISA]

440 Macmillen, Sandy. "Egyptian university libraries." In *Information and Libraries in the Arab World*. Compiled and edited by Michael Wise and Anthony Olden, pp. 81-95. London: Library Association Publishing, 1994. [Information and libraries in the developing world, vol. 3.]

Article included in a collection of papers presenting a comparative review of librarianship and library practices in Arab countries. Presents an overall study of university libraries in Egypt, covering: ancient and modern history; characteristics of Egyptian universities; role and organization of libraries and their collections, library staff, library buildings, and users. Concludes with a brief discussion of cooperation and foreign assistance.

ALEXANDRIA LIBRARY

441   el-Abbadi, Mostafa. *The Life and Fate of the Ancient Library of Alexandria*. 2nd ed., rev. Paris: Unesco/UNDP, 1992. 250 p.

442   al-'Ajlouni, Tha'ir. "Maktabat al-Iskandariya al-jadidah: markaz thaqafi hadari yahya min jadid." *Risalat al-Maktabah* 23 (June 1988): 40-46.

Discusses the renovation of the Alexandria Library which was established by the Greeks 2,000 years ago in Egypt. The historical background of the library is described and how the idea of renovation began, and the way it took place with the assistance of UNESCO and the various international libraries is outlined. Describes in detail the renovation policy and procedures.

443   Aman, Mohammed M. "Bibliotheca Alexandrina" In *The ALA Yearbook of Library and Information Services: A review of Library Events 1988*. Vol. 14 (1989), pp. 81-82. Chicago: American Library Association, 1989.

444   Aman, Mohammed M. "Alexandrian Library rises again." *Herald of Library Science* 29, no. 1-2 (January-April 1990): 3-11.

States the past history of the great Alexandrian Library established in 332 B.C. in Alexandria, Egypt. Describes the type of literature forming its rich holdings in the ancient past and discusses its significance as a center for scientific research and scholarship. Narrates the eventual destruction of the library and its collection. Evaluates the project for the establishment of a new Alexandrian Library based upon a winning design in an international competition, with support from Unesco and the United Nations development program. Discusses the subject orientation of the proposed collection, the administrative organization and structure envisaged and the creation of an International School of Information Studies. Provides cost estimates of the project and the contributions made to raise its funds.

445   Aman, Mohammed M. "Rebuilding the Library of Alexandria." *Journal of Information, Communication, and Library Science* 2, no. 3 (Spring 1996): 13-28.

Based on two earlier works: the first appears in *DOMES: Digest of Middle East Studies*, vol. 4, no. 1 (1995), pp. 14-15, under the title: "The intellectual content, collection development, and services of the Bibliotheca Alexandrina. A report on the International Symposium hld on November 1-7, 1994 at the Alexandria Conference Center, Alexandria, Egypt." The second work appears in *World Encyclopedia of Library and Information Services*, 3rd ed. (pp. 123-124), Chicago: American Library Association, 1993, under the title: "Bibliotheca Alexandrina (Modern)." The article presents a brief history of the ancient library, including its foundation; acquisitions policy; users; the tradition of the librarian/scholar; collections and theories of its demise. It describes the progress to date of the revival project for the Bibliotheca Alexandrina including: the international architectural competition for the new building and the winning design by Snohetta Arkitektur and Landskap from Oslo, Norway; the scope of the new library's collections; and its organization. An International School of Information Studies (ISIS) housed in the new library building will offer a number of graduate programs for students from around the world as well as engaging in research in information science. When completed in 1998, the library will restore to Alexandria its world prominence as the city where East meets West and where science and ideas flourish.

446 Aman, Mohammed M., Ahmed H. Helal, and Jacques Jean Marie Tocatlian. "The new Biblioteca Alexandrina." *Alexandria* 2, no. 3 (December 1990): 1-10.

A new Bibliotheca Alexandrina is planned in the city of Alexandria, Egypt, where the famous Alexandrian Library of antiquity was situated. The winning design for the building, by Snohetta Arkitektur Landskap of Norway, is in the form of a circle inclined towards the sea, partly submerged in the ground. Unesco has launched an international appeal to meet the cost of the building, the collection and computerization of the library, and the establishment and staff of an International School of Information Studies. With annual operating costs the estimated sum totals $160 million.

447 Blum, Rudolf. ***Kallimachos: The Alexandrian Library and the Origins of Bibliography***. Translated from the German by Hans H. Wellisch. Madison, Wis.: University of Wisconsin Press, 1991. ix, 282 p.

448 Burkard, Gunter. "Bibliotheken in alten Agypten." [Libraries in ancient Egypt.] ***Bibliothek: Forschung und Praxis*** 4, no. 2 (1980): 79-115. [In German.]

There are various Egyptian words for 'library' all occurring frequently in literary citations which leave no doubt as to the existence of such an institution in ancient Egypt. Yet there is a remarkable contrast to these findings regarding library buildings as far as archaeological and/or epigraphic proof is concerned. Presents an outline method which may be applied to the treatment of archaeological or epigraphic findings and offers a practical application of this method. [LISA]

449 Canfora, Luciano. *The Vanished Library*. Translated by Martin Ryle. Berkeley: University of California Press, 1989. ix, 205 p. Includes bibliographical references and index.

450 Canfora, Luciano. *La Bibliotheque d'Alexandrie et l'histoire des textes*. [Liege]: Universite de Liege, Centre de documentation de papyrologie litteraire, 1992. 69 p.

451 Chen, Ching-chih. "Bibliotheca Alexandrina comes to life again after 2,000 years: is there a place for new information technology?" *Microcomputers for Information Management* 7, no. 1 (March 1990): 75-82.

Describes the project to build a new Library of Alexandria in Egypt with notes on the design of the building and the main departments planned.

452 Chepesiuk, Ronald J. "The eighth wonder reborn: the new Alexandrian Library." *Wilson Library Bulletin* 68, no. 6 (February 1994): 42-44.

Describes the Bibliotheca Alexandrina project to build a new library in Alexandria as a successor to the first library founded in 295 BC. The project is now at the fundraising stage. Describes the planned design and services of the future library and fundraising efforts which include support from UNESCO and friends groups in the US and Europe.

453 Clavel, Jean-Pierre, Jan Meissner, and Francois Lombard. *Bibliotheca Alexandrina: programme architectural et reglement du concours*. Paris: Unesco, 1988. 2 vols.

454 Ede, Stuart. "The Alexandriana Library: a new opportunity in international cooperation." In *International Library Cooperation: 10th Anniversary Essen Symposium, 19 October-22 October 1987*. Edited by Ahmed H. Helal and Joachim W. Weiss, pp. 1-16. Essen: Universitatsbibliothek Essen, 1988.

455 Geh, Hans-Peter. "Die Wiederentstehung der Alexandrina." [The recreation of the ancient library of Alexandria.] *Zeitschrift fur Bibliothekswesen und Bibliographie* 36, no. 1 (January-February 1989): 65-67. [In German.]

The Egyptian government, Unesco and Alexandria University plan to rebuild the old libraries at a cost of 160 million dollars as a center for research and culture in the Mediterranean, Africa and the Arab states. Stocks, mainly on humanities and social sciences, should total 200,000 at the opening of the first section in 1995 and ultimately 4 million. A conference center nearby will be part of the infrastructure. Electronic data processing will link the library with others in the area. The library will contain a center for manuscript restoration and an international library school will be established locally. Since Egypt has financial problems, other countries will be asked for money and for help with librarianship training. [LISA]

456 Haarala, A-R., and E. Tornudd. "Biblioteca Alexandrina." *Signum* 28, no. 2 (1995): 37-40. [In Finnish.]

The cultural exchange program between Finland and Egypt, 1993-1995, mentions support for the Library and also participation of two library experts to help in the planning process. The General Organization of the Alexandria Library (GOAL) asked for assistance for planning information services in general, acquisitions and training of staff. Describes the work of the two Finnish consultants in these processes. Biblioteca Alexandrina will be functional in 1997. GOAL is particularly interested in Finnish library furniture and microcomputers. [LISA]

457 Ibrahim, Ferhad. "Der 'Wiederaufbau' der Bibliothek von Alexandria." [The rebuilding of the library of Alexandria.] *Bibliotheksdienst* 22, no. 11 (1988): 1079-1081. [In German.]

The library is being rebuilt on the original site. UNESCO is contributing 80 million US dollars, half the building costs; it is hard for Egypt to find the remainder, because of economic problems. Present stocks total 30,000 volumes, with space for four million. There are three reading-rooms and seats for 1,000 readers. The project should be completed in 1995; it is hoped that stocks will have expanded to 200,000 volumes by then. These targets may not be achieved since the Egyptians are already involved in modernizing the Egyptian national library and completing the new building of the Islamic al-Azhar university. [LISA]

458 Jackson, Sidney L. "Alexandrian Library (Ancient)" and "Egypt (Ancient)." In *World Encyclopedia of Library and Information Services*. 3rd ed. (pp. 42-44; 98-100). Chicago: American Library Association, 1993.

459 Lazzari, Giovanni. "La nuova biblioteca di Alessandria d'Egitto." [The new library in Alexandria, Egypt.] *Bollettino d'Informazioni* 30, no. 3-4 (July-December 1990): 221-227. [In Italian.]

Describes the international competition to design the new research library in Alexandria, Egypt. Some 1200 architects from around the world participated in the competition. Discusses the design by Manfredi Nicoletti, an Italian architect which won second prize in the competition. The first prize was won by a Norwegian firm, Snohetta Arkitektur and Landskap. [LISA.]

460 Muhadat, Mohammed M. "Hariq maktabat al-Iskandariyah." *Risalat al-Maktabah* 13, no. 2 (June 1978): 20-25.

Discusses eight different points of view concerning the burning of the Library of Alexandria, concentrating on that presented by Abdul-Latif Bughdadi in his book *Mawdi-al-Aetabar*. Some historians accuse the Arabs of destroying it when they occupied Egypt in the 1st century; it is believed that the incident was not generally known of for about 1,500 years.

461 Mutahhari, Murtaza. *The Burning of Libraries in Iran and Alexandria*. Translated by N. P. Nazareno and M. Nekoodast. Tehran, Iran: Islamic Propagation Organization, 1983. 96 p.

462 Romerio, G. F. "Antiquity's most famous library to be re-born." *Logos* 5, no. 3 (1994): 141-147.

The ancient library of Alexandria, one of the most celebrated centers for research and study in the whole Mediterranean area, was founded during the reign of Ptolemy I (323-285 BC) and destroyed by an edict of the Emperor Theodosius in 391 AD. Now a project is under way to reincarnate the Alexandria Library as a modern center of learning and research. The Bibliotheca Alexandrina will cover both human heritage and science and technology and its mission will be both national and international. It will be both a public and a research library. In association with the Alexandria Conference Centre, the library will constitute a unique complex of buildings and infrastructures which could be put at the disposal of cultural and scientific initiatives of national and regional interest. Discusses possible strategies for building up the collections. The following subjects will be given priority: the Pharaonic period; Ancient Greece and the Hellenistic civilization; Roman civilization; Renaissance and modern civilization; mathematics; physical sciences; applied sciences and technology; economics and management sciences; and ecology and environmental sciences. The library is scheduled to be fully operational after the year 2005. [A]

463 Ruby, Carmela M. "Bibliotheca Alexandrina: the world community helps to build a new library." *California State Library Foundation Bulletin*, no. 38 (January 1992): 14-19.

464 Salem, Shawky. "GOAL network design for the Bibliotheca Alexandrina." In *Proceedings of the 15th International Online Information Meeting, London, 10-12 December, 1991*. Edited by David I. Raitt, pp. 507-516. Oxford and New Jersey: Learned Information Ltd., 1991.

Describes the project aimed at the creation of a new Alexandria Library, in Egypt (Bibliotheca Alexandrina) with particular reference to the GOAL

(General Organisation of the Alexandria Library) information network and the computers and software required to build the network.

465 Salem, Shawky. "The revival of the Alexandria Library (Bibliotheca Alexandrina): a unique project of the twenty-first century." *Journal of Information Science* 17, no. 6 (1991): 385-393.

Traces the history of the Ancient Library of Alexandria, Egypt, and describes the project to establish a new library, the Bibliotheca Alexandrina. Illustrates the layout of the building and its operations.

466 Shubert, Steven Blake. "The oriental origins of the Alexandrian Library." *Libri* 43, no. 2 (April-June 1993): 142-172.

This article examines the contribution of Near Eastern libraries to library history through their relationship to and possible influence on the ancient Alexandrian Library. Although not denying the substance of the traditional Greek thesis for the origin of the Alexandrian Library, the Oriental origins of the library are presented in a new light, relying upon Egyptian and Mesopotamian evidence. [A]

467 Siewert, Peter. "Geschichte Alexandrias und seiner antiken Bibliothek." [History of Alexandria and its antique library.] *Biblos* 39, no. 4 (1990): 274-277.

468 Thiem, Jon. "Myths of the universal library: from Alexandria to the postmodern age." *The Serials Librarian* 26, no. 1 (1995): 63-74.

469 Tocatlian, Jacques Jean Marie. "Bibliotheca Alexandrina. Une bibliotheque pour le troisieme millenaire nait des cendres de l'antiquite." [The Alexandria Library: a library for the third millenium born from the ashes of antiquity.] *Bulletin des Bibliotheques de France* 36, no. 5 (1991): 384-90, 392.

Briefly recalls the historical and cultural context of the Alexandria Library of ancient Egypt and considers whether the new Alexandria Library can turn myth into reality. Discusses the political, financial, and organizational problems of the library with emphasis on the library building and its organization into two divisions and six departments.

470 Tocatlian, Jacques Jean Marie. "Bibliotheca Alexandrina—reviving a legacy of the past for a brighter common future." *International Library Review* 23, no. 3 (September 1991): 255-269.

After briefly recalling the creation, organization, role and destruction of the Ancient Library of Alexandria, this article describes the scope and objectives of the new Bibliotheca Alexandrina and its functions and organization in six departments. It explains the symbolic and aesthetic values of the winning design for the new library, the budget required for its creation, and the international support so far obtained. It summarizes the steps undertaken by Egypt, UNESCO and the United Nations Development Program (UNDP) and briefly explains the future strategy for proceeding with the implementation of the project. It concludes by highlighting the meaning of the new Bibliotheca Alexandrina for Egypt, UNESCO and the International Community. [A]

471 Zahran, Mohsen."Bibliotheca Alexandrina: revival of the Ancient Library of Alexandria Project." In *Towards a Worldwide Library: A Ten Year Forecast*. Proceedings of the 19th International Essen Symposium 23 September - 26 September 1996. Edited by Ahmed H. Helal and Joachim W. Weiss, pp. 41-52. Essen, Germany: Universitatsbibliothek Essen, 1997.

ARCHIVES

472 Albin, Michael W. "The National Archives of Egypt." *Bulletin of the International Association of Orientalist Librarians*, no. 24-25 (1984): 46-47.

Translation of the Arabic brochure on the goals, organization, facilities, and statistics on the use by scholars of the National Archives of Egypt.

BIBLIOGRAPHIC CONTROL

473 Alawady, Sana M. *Bibliographic Control and Services in Egypt: A Survey and Study with Emphasis on the Role of the Egyptian National Library*. Ph.D., 1978. Texas Woman's University. 168 p. DAI 40/01-A: 11.

BIBLIOMETRIC STUDIES

474 Sattar Chaudhry, Abdus. *Relationship Between Political Alignment and Scientific Communication: A Bibliometric Study of Egyptian Science Publications*. Ph.D., 1985. University of Illinois at Urbana-Champaign. 156 p.

This thesis reports the results of a bibliometric study of Egyptian science publications. Data for the study were collected through citation analysis. A total of 1182 Egyptian science papers were randomly selected from a variety of Egyptian and non-Egyptian sources. These papers contained 15,222 bibliographic references that formed the sample for the study. Egyptian scientists mostly cited literature from the developed world. Citations to literature from third world countries, especially to neighboring Arab and Muslim countries, were infrequent. The comparison of citation proportions showed that citations to a particular bloc did not increase or decrease quite in accordance with the increase or decrease of political influence of that bloc. The changes in the citation proportions were not consistently correspondent to the changes in political influence. Therefore, the hypothesis that there exists a positive relationship between political alignment and citation behavior was rejected. The citation behavior of Egyptian scientists was not found independent of the sources in which they published. They were more likely to cite sources from the countries and political blocs in which they published their papers than they were to cite these countries or blocs in other circumstances. Collaboration was also shown to be related to the citation behavior of Egyptian scientists. They cited more sources from the countries and political blocs of scientists with whom they collaborated than they did in other circumstances. Further research is suggested to refine the results of the study by expanding the sample size or extending the scope of the study, and by replicating the research on the model of the present study for other countries such as Cuba, Sri Lanka, Ethiopia, and the East European countries. [DAI 46/07-A: 1767.]

CHILDREN'S LITERATURE

475 Alqudsi-Gharba, Taghreed M. *The History of Published Arabic Children's Literature as Reflected in the Collections of Three Publishers in Egypt, 1912-1986*. Ph.D., 1988. University of Texas at Austin. 223 p.

In order to trace the historical development that occurred in published Arabic children's literature between 1912-1986, this dissertation examines the changing attitudes and trends as reflected in the themes published by al-Kilani, Dar al-Ma'aref and Dar al-Fata al-'Arabi publishing houses. A content analysis of selective major themes and values present in children's books published by the three named above publishers was performed. A list of eight thematic categories was developed as follows: (I) Concept Books, (II) Nursery Rhymes and Bedtime Stories, (III) Human and Social Issues, (IV) Conflict Issues, (V) Stories of Other Peoples and Cultures, (VI) Entertainment and Escape Books, (VII) General World History and Geography, and (VIII) Sciences. Material was analyzed at two levels: first, by a general analysis of each category within the collections under study; second, and more specifically, by an in-depth analysis of two of the thematic categories, namely the Human and Social Issues Category and the Conflict Issues category. Family, State and Heritage were analyzed under the former thematic category and politics, war and foreign domination under the latter. Current published Arabic children's literature is moving toward realism even though results of the content analysis reveals an emphasis on moralizing, social morals and values. Many current issues of life in the Middle East are completely omitted from books written for children. Egypt's economic dilemma, poverty, pollution, and relations with other countries of the world are topics discussed in every house in Egypt. Yet none of these topics seems to appear in children's books. The Iraqi-Iranian war, the ongoing Lebanese civil war, and the inter Arab relations and conflicts are all topics that are avoided in the literature. The Palestinian-Israeli conflict is the exception and it is treated only by Dar al-Fata al-'Arabi. Publishing of religious themes is increasing and it is causing the reprinting of old published series by Dar al-Ma'aref in addition to issuing of newer series. [DAI 50/02-A: 285.]

476 Naguib, Ahmad. "Arab children's literature in the Republic of Egypt." In *Printed for Children: World Children's Book Exhibition* (pp. 106-110). Munich: K. G. Saur, 1978.

INFORMATION POLICY

477 Kabesh, Ahmad and Ahmed Abdel Bassit. "Towards a national information policy for Egypt." In *Information, Knowledge, Evolution*. Proceedings of the forty-fourth FID Congress held in Helsinki, Finland, 28 August-1 September, 1988. Edited by Sinikka Koshiala and Ritva Launo, pp. 407-419. Amsterdam: North-Holland, 1989.

Traces the emergence of a national information policy in Egypt against the background of the activities of individual Egyptian library and information organizations (National Research Council, National Information and Documentation Centre (NIDOC), and the Egyptian National Scientific and Technical Information Network (ENSTIENT).

478 Kamel, S. "IT diffusion and socio economic change in Egypt." *Journal of Global Information Management* 3, no. 2 (Spring 1995): 4-16.

Analyzes the experience of the Egyptian government in spreading awareness of information technology and its use in managing development planning for socioeconomic change. The experience has been one of building multiple information handling and decision support systems in messy, and turbulent environments. Suggests analytical methods and guidelines for the future implementation of similar projects in developing countries which may benefit from the successes of Egypt's Cabinet Information and Decision Support Center. [A]

INFORMATION SERVICES

479 Abdel Bassit, Ahmed, Nadia el-Shishiny, and J. S. Nour. "Computerised information services of ENSTINET: an Egyptian perspective. In *Proceedings of the 18th International Online Information Meeting, London, 6-8 December, 1994*. Edited by David I. Raitt and Ben Jeapes, pp. 173-190. Oxford and New Jersey: Learned Information Ltd., 1994.

This paper analyzes the computerized information services of the Egyptian National Scientific and Technical Information Network (ENSTINET) of the Egyptian Academy of Scientific Research and Technology (EASRT). The paper is organized into three main sections. Section I is an overview of the development of information services in Egypt in general, together with background information on the purposes, functions, organizational structure and services of ENSTINET. Section II discusses the technical and user services of ENSTINET, including the local databases, database searching services of local, CD-ROM and international online databases, document delivery services of local and international resources, ENSTINET's remote user system, and ENSTINET's publications and training services. Finally, section III overviews ENSTINET's computer and telecommunication facilities in relation to technical service requirements and economic constraints.

480 Abdel-Shafi, Hasan Muhammad. *Khadamat al-Ma'lumat bi-Qita' al-Ta'lim fi Misr: Waqai'iha wa Mustaqbaliha*. Ph.D., University of Cairo, 1991.

481 el-Hadi, Mohamed M. "Library and information services in Egypt, 1979." In *The Bowker Annual of Library & Book Trade Information*. 25th ed., 1980. Edited and compiled by Filomena Simora, pp. 501-506. New York: R. R. Bowker Company, 1980.

482 el-Kholy, Aziz, and Salah Mandil. "The relevance of microcomputers to health improvement in developing countries." *Information and Management* 7, no. 4 (August 1984): 177-182.

Based on observations and conclusion drawn from a joint World Health Organization-Egypt study in support of that part of the 5-year health plan (1979-82) of the Ministry of Health of Egypt which dealt with the strengthening of health information systems for the management of health resources. The joint study included the actual pilot operation in two Egyptian provinces of microcomputer-supported health data collection, validation, processing, printing and distribution, from and to users. It discusses how current and foreseen developments in the medical approaches to many of the major health problems in the developing countries appear to coincide with tremendous breakthrough in the information technology which in turn contribute to alleviating many of the impediments to the two-way process of information collection, processing, printing and distribution. It briefly discusses the loaded techno-political issue of micro-informatics technology transfer, and how an international effort could assist in this respect. [A]

483 Mutwalli, Nariman Isma'il. "Tatawwur khadamat al-ma'lumat lil-makfufin wa-du'af al-basar, ma' dirasat halah 'an Misr." *'Alam al-Kutub* 17, no. 3 (May-June 1996): 220-240.

A study of the library services for the blind and physically handicapped individuals with Egypt as a case study.

484 Sadiq, Umniyah Mustafa. ***Dawr Khadamat al-Ma'lumat fi Tahqiq al-Tanmiyah al-Idtisadiyah wa-al-Ijtima'iyah fi Misr***. Ph.D., University of Cairo, 1989.

485 Slamecka, Vladimir, Nadia El-Shishiny, and Ahmed Abdel Bassit. "A longitudinal profile of a national database search service." ***Information Processing & Management*** 22, no. 3 (1986): 203-216.

This paper presents a performance analysis of the retrospective database search service operated by the Egyptian National Scientific and Technical Information Network (EINSTINET) between April 1982 and May 1985. During the 38-month period, the service executed 4,965 searches, accessing nearly 100 US databases. Because of the unavailability of packet-switched telecommunications, the service operated in a 'delayed online' mode; search queries, prepared in Egypt, were forwarded to the US and executed at the Georgia Institute of Technology. Tabulates extensive statistics regarding service demand trends, characteristics of searches and their results, usage of US databases, service turn-around time and costs. As all of the searches were monitored throughout the period, this case study provides empirical data profiling the evolution and performance of a specific national information service in a developing country. [A]

486 Te'eni, Dov. "Towards effective information processing in high office: an analysis of decision support systems in the national governments of Israel and Egypt." ***Government Publications Review*** 17, no. 5 (September-October 1990): 429-440.

Evaluates the analysis of support systems for high office from the perspective of an information-systems analyst. Compares two cases of information systems for government policy making institutions, one in Egypt and the other in Israel, to demonstrate the unique character of the decision-making activities in such institutions. The underlying model of decision processes that is assumed in the design of conventional decision support systems is inadequate for very high-level policy making environments. Presents a broader view of the decision-making activities which suggests that support systems for high level policy making require an unconventional approach for their development. [A]

INFORMATION STORAGE AND RETRIEVAL

487 Abdel Bassit, Ahmed, Nadia El-Shishiny, and J. S. Nour. "The scientific and technical archiving system of ENSTINET: 'STARS'. In ***Proceedings of the 19th International Online Information Meeting, London, 5-7***

December, 1995. Edited by David I. Raitt and Ben Jeapes, pp. 371-381. Oxford and New Jersey: Learned Information Ltd., 1996.

This paper reviews the Egyptian experience in building a full text database of national scientific journals. ENSTINET's Scientific and Technical Archiving System 'STARS' started as a project in mid-1994 to provide an efficient and improved method of retrieving and disseminating Egyptian scientific information. The paper is organized into three main sections. The first section is an overview of the document supply services available in Egypt in general, supported by statistical analysis of ENSTINENT's document delivery services. The second section reviews 'STARS' in detail: the subjects and range of the Egyptian research and development journals, the technology used and the overall flow of system development. The third section discusses the prospective use of digital storage of documents together with developments in data networks in developing countries.

488 el-Hadidy, Bahaa. "Delayed online search: an alternative access mode for developing countries." *Journal of Information Science* 5, no. 5 (February 1983): 173-185.

This paper discusses the design and implementation of a pilot experiment to introduce commercially available online services to Egyptian users from a geographically distant location in the U.S. With the lack of international data communication networks for online transmission in Egypt, a delayed online search technique is used as an alternative mode for accessing the service from the United States. A document delivery support system from abroad is also discussed. A critical analysis and evaluation of the project activities is presented. Factors affecting the performance of the service, and users' reactions and expectations are also analyzed.

INFORMATION SYSTEMS

489 el-Gamal, S. S. "A computer-based clinical information system." *Methods of Information in Medicine* 26, no. 4 (October 1987): 189-194.

Describes the Clinical Hospital Information System developed at the Urology-Nephrology Center, Mansoura University in Egypt. The system used specially tailored programs that permit the analysis of unrestricted, non-codified medical text and it can be operated by non-specialized hospital staff. It comprises 4 modules which are described in detail: Patients Information System; Reporting Module; Hospital Activity Analysis; and special detailed sub-files for subgroups of patients.

490 Machaly, Horeya Ibrahim. *A Prescriptive Model for Planning a National Scientific and Technical Information System for Egypt*. Ph.D., 1979. University of Pittsburgh. 274 p.

This study has attempted to survey the prevailing conditions of the present system for handling scientific and technical information in Egypt, justify whether there is a need for establishing a national scientific and technical information system, and propose a model for a plan of action to establish a national technical information system for Egypt. The methodology utilized for data collection in this research consisted of analysis of the literature, questionnaires, and interviews. A questionnaire was sent to librarians in Alexandria, Egypt, to gather information relevant to the local and regional setting. The questionnaire was devised to secure data on users and institutions handling information in regard to administration, acquisitions, processing, services, and personnel. Data gathered from the questionnaire were supplemented by interviews conducted in the field of research with top government officials, administrators, and librarians. In order to justify the need and the desirability for the establishment of a national technical information system, the data gathered were compared with the standards pertaining to library services in colleges and research libraries in the United States and with situations described in the literature concerning similar systems in other countries. To draw meaningful conclusions, a second questionnaire was devised to elicit opinions of worldwide knowledgeable experts on the objectives, functions, administrative, and operational requirements necessary for establishing a national technical information system in Egypt. The analysis of the different classes of data indicated that libraries have been functioning in Egypt for a long time, but their impact and role in the socio-economic ventures is far less than it should be for the following reasons: (a) absence of library services legislation; (b) insufficient funds; (c) lack of needed resources; (d) unnecessary duplication of materials; (e) shortage of qualified manpower; (f) lack of cooperative efforts. Based on the findings, a model has been proposed for a plan of action to establish a national technical information system. [DAI 41/02-A: 446.]

491 Romerio, G. F. *Arab Republic of Egypt: A Teledocumentation System for the National Information and Documentation Centre*. Paris: Unesco, 1977, 35 p. illus. tables. bibliog

Presents the results of a Unesco/UNISIST consultative mission to Cairo in April 1977, undertaken at the Egyptian government's request. Two problems are examined: the design of a national information system which could be developed into a regional teledocumentation system serving the Middle East; and an analysis of NIDOC (National Information and Documentation Centre) library management procedures, particularly the lending system and the exchange of publications unit.

492 Slamecka, Vladimir. "Development of a national information system in Egypt." *International Information, Communication and Education* 1, no. 2 (September 1982): 242-244.

Report of a project to design and implement a national system of scientific and technical information in Egypt being undertaken by the Egyptian Academy of Scientific Research and Technology and Georgia Institute of Technology. The overall goal of the project is the establishment and maintenance of a national infrastructure in Egypt for the husbanding and use of scientific, industrial and economic data and information so as to bring these resources to bear on the country's socio-economic development.

INTERLIBRARY LOAN

493 Osman, Fawzia Mostafa. *A Proposal for Planning an Interlending System for the Libraries of Cairo City in Egypt*. Ph.D., 1981. University of Pittsburgh. 233 p.

A study was conducted to make explicit the factors responsible for the present state of the art of interlibrary loan (ILL) in Cairo and to propose a system for formal interlibrary lending which can be modified for other developing countries. A questionnaire survey, interviews, visits, and analysis of the literature comprised the methodological tools utilized for data collection in this research. The questionnaire was designed to obtain data related to library collections, users, budgets, library techniques, and the extent of interaction among the national, special, academic libraries located in Cairo. Ten libraries which reported they participate in some form of ILL activity were selected for further analysis. The directors of these libraries were interviewed. These interviews identified some of the problems which hinder an effective ILL system: inadequate resources, budget constraints, lack of standardization, prohibitive library regulations, lack of bibliographic tools and nonexistent formal lending agreements. The choice of Pittsburgh Regional Library Center (PRLC) for investigation was based on the fact that this network is geared toward facilitating access to library resources and delivery services. The goal and objectives of the system, its organizational structure, roles and functions, operational requirements, expected services, and its international lending function are presented. The proposed system is supported by two major roles. The coordinator role of the national library will be characterized by the following responsibilities: (1) retention of the country's last document copy and its availability for loan; (2) acquisition of foreign materials; (3) coordination of the operational function for the establishment of standardized bibliographic form; (4) international lending function; and (5) coordination of the acquisition programs of the member libraries. The other role will be played by the member libraries. It will consist of: (1) cooperative acquisition programs for monograph and serial based on subject specialization of the collections already on existence; (2) assumption of the responsibility for making these collections available for loan. [DAI 42/08-A: 3334.]

ISLAMIC LIBRARIES

494 al-Arini, Muhsin. "al-Azhar University library." *Pakistan Library Bulletin* 20, no. 1 (March 1989): 33-45.

In an account of the historical background of al-Azhar University, this article examines ancient Egypt, Egypt in the Islamic era, and the modern era and outlines methods of teaching. It discusses the origins, objectives, legislation, building, finance, staff, collection development, and the nature of the collection of al-Azhar University Library.

495 al-Arini, Muhsin. "The Azhar Library: state of the art." *Pakistan Library Bulletin* 25, no. 3-4 (July-December 1994): 10-22.

Reviews the sources of data available on the history of the Azhar Mosque and its Library, founded in Egypt in the 10th century, which has never been systematically studied. The author plans to visit the site to examine the physical remains of the Mosque and Library in addition to the primary and secondary bibliographical sources. The Azhar Library ranks as the second largest in Egypt, coming after the Egyptian National Library in regard to its collection and valuable manuscripts.

LIBRARY EDUCATION

496 Halwagy, A. S. "Recent changes in library education in Egypt." *Journal of Education for Library and Information Science* 33, no. 3 (Summer 1992): 255-259.

Traces the history of library education in Egypt as a background to a discussion of recent trends in teaching methods and aids, grading and evaluation of library students, postgraduate studies, and library staff.

497 Palmer, R. P., U. E. Mahmoud, and Michael W. Albin. *Department of Librarianship and Archival Studies and University of Cairo Libraries: Fact Resource Paper and Evaluation and Recommendations*. Cairo: US Agency for International Development, Bureau for Near East, 1978. 90 p.

An evaluative report of library and archival education as offered by Cairo University and the University library.

MICROFICHE

498 al-Amlah, Ismail. "Dalil istikhdam jihaz al-maykrofish fi al-Munazmah al-'Arabiyah lil-'Ulum al-Idariyah." *Risalat al-Maktabah* 20, no. 1-2 (March-June 1985): 26-35.

Examines the characteristics and importance of microfiche in library use. Discusses its advantages, characteristics, disadvantages, the instruction of photocopying by microfiche, cataloging and documentation of microfiche, examples of microfiche available at the Arab Organisation of Administrative Sciences (AOAS), and describes examples of microfiche hardware, fiche, microfiche readers, reader printers, microfiche envelopes, flexible disk storage, and rotary stands.

MUSEUMS

499 Saleh, Fathi, Mohammed Saleh, Nahed Refaat, and Nora Ebeid. "The Egyptian museum registration project: the challenge and the implementation." *Program* 27, no. 4 (October 1993): 399-409.

The article describes an important project in the history of preservation of Egypt's culture heritage. Initiated by the Egyptian Ministry of Culture and executed by the Cabinet Information and Decision Support Center (IDSC), the project involves the Cairo Egyptian museum that contains the world largest collection of ancient Egyptian antiquities (160,000 objects). A major problem in the museum is the lack of a standardized approach for registration, resulting in a variety of unrelated registration schemes and the non-existence of efficient tools for information dissemination. This project aims to resolve these problems. A team of Egyptologists, museum curators and system analysts, designers and developers defined the basis for work and specified project challenges which included the indexing of all museum objects ensuring cross-referencing between already used registration schemes. The result has involved the use of multimedia computer technology to establish a complete database of museum objects (text, image and sound) and various cultural products, in addition to the establishment of required procedures and standards to organize the internal museum work flow and the provision of training programs for staff. The outcome of the project is expected to be profound in enabling researchers and curators to have instant access to any object in the museum and providing the museum's visitors and public with a wealth of information about ancient Egypt. [A]

NATIONAL LIBRARIES

500 Abdul-Reheim, Olfat. "The National Library of Egypt." In *Encyclopedia of Library and Information Science*. Vol. 45 (pp. 125-127). New York: Marcel Dekker, Inc., 1990.

501 Kaufmann, Ita. "Bedeutende Bibliotheken der Welt (XXIX): die NB in Kairo; ein Koran 1000 Kilogramm." *Borsenblatt fur den Deutschen Buchhandel* 41, no. 22 (1985): 753-756. [In German.]

Founded in 1870 by the Minister of Education, Ali Mubarak Egypt's National Library (ENL), Dar-el-Kutub, acquired books and manuscripts from mosques, schools and government ministries. In 1873 ENL received the Egyptological Association bequest. By 1899 the first floor of the Khedive's palace had been filled. In 1904 ENL moved to a new building by the Islamic Museum. It now has two large catalogs: One for Arabic and the other for foreign languages, arranged by author, title and subject terms. ENL has its own classification system. Reference works include a bibliography from 1862, listing 851 Arabic first editions. ENL's music department has 5,000 records and 22,000 cassettes. ENL has around 3,000 papyri, mainly originating in Egypt -the largest collection of Arabic papyri by far. In 1984 ENL had 27,000 readers-a high number, especially as Egypt has an 80% illiteracy rate. [LISA]

502   Salih, 'Izzat Yasin. "Dar al-kutub al-Misriyah wa-al-maktabat al-mulhakah biha." *'Alam al-Kutub* 6, no. 3 (September 1985): 317-334.

503   Wien, Charlotte. "Det egyptiske nationalbibliotek: eller noget om arabisk informationsstruktur." [The Egyptian national library: or something about Arab information structure.] *DF Revy* 17 (Feb. 1994): 7-9. [In Danish.]

The General Egyptian Book Organization is responsible for the National Library, public and research libraries, and the national archives. The National Bibliography has received legal deposits since 1954. The National Library, founded in 1870, is with its 5 million volumes the largest in the Arab world. The manuscript collection has copies of the Koran, 2000 other manuscripts, 300 papyri and 500 parchments. While there are 430 Danish libraries for 3.4 million adults, Egypt has only 1051 for its 15 million people with some form of education. The situation is not helped by the lack of a union catalog or interlending, and the national bibliography is unsuitable for verification, while the greatest problem is the lack of experience of computer-based catalogs and networking. [LISA]

PUBLIC LIBRARIES

504   Bouri, Elizabeth Nicolas. *The Development and Decline of Public Libraries in Egypt: A Shift in National Development Priorities (UNESCO)*. Ph.D., 1993. University of Texas at Austin. 467 p.

This study analyzes the circumstances leading to the development and current decline of public libraries in Egypt and advances a new interpretation of this phenomenon, based on a "problem context" approach. In addition to the internal dynamics that have provided the rationale for the establishment of the public libraries, Egypt, like many other developing countries, was also exposed to external influences. The convergence between the national and international forces is at the core of the proposed interpretation of development and current decline of public libraries in

Egypt. After 1945 UNESCO's international discourse encouraged fundamental education and the development of public libraries as operational tools of education. The linkage between education and national development ushered in an era of "education for development" during which public libraries witnessed remarkable growth in Egypt. Public library development has come to a standstill and even declined since the early 1970s, however. Traditionally, public library decline is attributed to local factors and issues of scarcity. In the case of Egypt, however, factors of scarcity are better interpreted as symptoms rather than as underlying causes of the decline of public libraries. This study maintains that the current state of decline of public libraries in Egypt is primarily a consequence of public policy choices precipitated by a shift in national and international development priorities, not of factors inherent in the country's political, social and cultural fabric. [DAI 54/04-A: 1133.]

505 Bouri, Elizabeth Nicolas. "Public libraries development reconsidered: the case of Egypt." *International Information & Library Review* 26, no. 3 (September 1994): 151-68.

This paper advances a new interpretation of the development and current decline of public libraries in Egypt based on the study of international influences which helped to shape national discourses about development and provided the context for policy mandate for resource allocation in Egypt. The current state of decline of public libraries in Egypt is primarily a consequence of public policy choices precipitated by a shift in international as well as national development priorities, not of factors inherent in the country's political, social and cultural fabric. [A]

PUBLISHING

506 Rizk, Nadia A. "The book-publishing industry in Egypt." *Library Trends* 26, no. 4 (Spring 1978): 553-565.

507 Rodenbeck, John. "A scholarly publisher in Egypt." *Scholarly Publishing* 16 (July 1985): 316-340.

SERIALS

508 Zayid, Yusriyah. "al-Ma'ayir al-muwahhadah lil-dawriyyat al-Misriyah." *'Alam al-Kitab*, no. 18 (April-June 1988): 6-11.

SPECIAL COLLECTIONS

509 Tovell, Joyce Pressey. "The Creswell Library in Islamic Art and Architecture at the American University in Cairo. Part one: in the presence of the original owner, 1956-73." *Art Libraries Journal* 17, no. 4 (1992): 13-22.

This paper describes the history of the Cresswell Library which remained uncataloged and accessible to a very limited number of students and faculty until the Suez War when permission was secured to move the books to the American University in Cairo (AUC) by telling the Egyptian Government that the Collection was a gift. It discusses other libraries at AUC, Cresswell's teaching career and the teaching program. [A]

510   Yamauchi, Edwin M. "The Nag Hammadi Library: a collection of Coptic works discovered in Upper (southern) Egypt in 1945." *The Journal of Library History, Philosophy & Comparative Librarianship* 22 (Fall 1987): 425-441.

SPECIAL LIBRARIES

511   Dimitroff, Alexandra. "Information access in a developing country: special libraries in Egypt." *Special Libraries* 84, no. 1 (Winter 1993): 25-29.

Describes two special libraries in Egypt with special note of each library's attempts at overcoming some of the barriers to information access.

512   Freudenthal, Juan R. "The art library scene in Egypt." *Art Libraries Journal* 6, no. 1 (Spring 1981): 7-18.

Art libraries in Egypt, as part of a broader art information context, do not play a vital role in the preservation, survey, and dissemination of art information in the country. These information centers lack the recognition and financial support necessary to allow them to become active, up-to-date art information clearinghouses. Two major art documentation centers in Cairo are discussed: the Egyptian Museum Library and the Cresswell Collection and Library at the American University. Common problems among art libraries are identified and a few steps which could lead to improved conditions are suggested.

TRAINING, STAFF

513   al-Arini, Muhsin. *Tanmiyat Maharat al-'Amilin fi al-Maktabat wa Marakiz al-Ma'lumat bi-Misr: Dirasah Nazariyah Tatbiqiyah*. Ph.D, 1992. Jami'at al-Qahirah.

The author discusses the importance of training and continuing education for library personnel in Egypt and the different programs that are offered.

514 el-Hadidy, Bahaa. *Training of Egyptian Information Specialists: A Multifaceted System Approach*. Washington, D.C., Catholic University of America, 1982, 226 p.

This paper discusses the design and development of a two-year, non-degree training system to train Egyptian information specialists in the USA. The major objectives of the training system were to train a core group of information specialists in the technical skills required for the development of the national information services in Egypt. Based on the analysis of the training requirements, an integrated, multifaceted training system was developed utilizing several training strategies.

515 Khaled, Maged. "Information manpower development program in Egypt." *Journal of Information Science* 18, no. 6 (1992): 463-469.

Part of a special issue devoted to library and information services in the Arab countries after the Gulf War. The Information Manpower Development Programme is a major component of the Egyptian National Scientific and Technological Information Project, the goal of which is to implement a national network of scientific and technical information Systems in Egypt. The principal USAID contractor, the Georgia Institute of Technology, is assisting the Egyptian Academy of Scientific Research and Technology in all phases of this three-year program. The program objective is to train 1,000 trainees to manage, operate, and make effective use of the national information network. The training plan includes eight different courses for: top management, professionals, and paraprofessionals. Courses have different durations and different frequencies. The total training days of the program exceeded 800. [A]

CHAPTER 7

IRAQ

GENERAL

516 Francis, Simon. *Development of Documentation and Academic Library Services, Iraq*. Paris: Unesco, 1977, 55 p.

Contains a consultant's observations on the state of documentation centres and academic libraries in Iraq at the time of his visit in late 1976, as well as his recommendations for their development.

517 al-Kindilchie, Amer Ibrahim. "Libraries in Iraq and Egypt: a comparative study." *International Library Review* 9, no. 1 (January 1977): 113-123.

A brief examination of the ancient history of Egypt and Iraq shows that temples organized library collections thousands of years B.C. Comparisons made between the various types of library reveal that at present there are many similarities between the two countries, particularly in the areas of finance and administration. Differences are notable in the public and academic sectors, where Iraq appears to be in a better position, but Egypt has the most comprehensive library education and training system in the Arab world.

518 al-Kindilchie, Amer Ibrahim. "al-Maktabat wa-marakiz al-tawthiq fi al-'Iraq." *al-Majallah al-'Arabiyah lil-Ma'lumat* 5, no. 1 (1984): 42-53.

519 al-Kindilchie, Amer Ibrahim. "Iraq." In *World Encyclopedia of Library and Information Services*. 3rd ed. (pp. 390-392). Chicago: American Library Association, 1993.

Discusses the history of libraries and library education in the country and gives a description of its national, academic, public, school, and special libraries.

520   al-Kindilchie, Amer Ibrahim. "Libraries in Iraq: a short report." In *Information and Libraries in the Arab World*. Compiled and edited by Michael Wise and Anthony Olden, pp. 96-103. London: Library Association Publishing, 1994. [Information and libraries in the developing world, vol. 3.]

Article included in a collection of papers presenting a comparative review of librarianship and library practices in Arab countries. A very brief outline of the history of libraries in Iraq is followed by statistics covering: book publishing; growth of national library collections; academic libraries; school libraries; public libraries; special libraries; and National Network for Libraries and Information Centers.

521   Salih, Muhannad Muhammad, et al. "al-'Anasir al-asasiyah lil-siyasah al-wataniyah li-nuzum al-ma'lumat wa-khadamatiha fi al-jumhuriyah al-'iraqiyah." *Risalat al-Maktabah* 26, no. 2 (June 1991): 5-23.

The study reviews the development of libraries in Iraq and discusses in details the elements of a national information policy in Iraq.

ACADEMIC LIBRARIES

522   Ismail, Saad Ahmad. "Marakiz al-ta'lim bayna al-nazariyah wa-al-tatbiq fi jami'at al-Khalij al-'Arabi, ma' isharah khassah li-markaz al-ta'allum fi jami'at al-Musil." *Al-Majallah al-'Arabiyah lil-Ma'lumat* 10, no. 1 (1989): 69-99.

The Education Centre is an agency for stimulation of the human creation using available resources. The Education Centre has its own design, furniture, and maintenance. One of its main divisions is the library which can disseminate technical services combined with audio-visual tools. The situation of audio-visuals in Arab countries especially the Arab Gulf States needs to be studied. A model can be noticed concerning the Education Centre in Mousel University with its enormous collection of audio-visuals: films; videos; slides; equipment; and manuals to guide the Education Centre activities.

523   Manzoor, Suhail. "Trends of users: a study in Iraqi scene." *Indian Librarian* 35, no. 1 (June 1980): 9-17.

A study based on personal experience illustrating user trends in Iraq's academic libraries. Discusses awareness of services, reader expectations, non-use, factors responsible for non-use and their possible solutions. Stresses the need for a more effective Iraqi library movement.

524   Manzoor, Suhail. "Academic libraries in Iraq." *International Library Review* 17, no. 3 (July 1985): 283-291.

Tremendous growth has taken place in the field of education during the past 20 years and the demand for library services is being recognized in Iraq. This paper describes the developments which have taken place in academic libraries and examines their potential for fulfilling the needs of the academic community of the country. It reviews the library movement, suggests ways and means to improve library services, and highlights the importance of libraries in learning and teaching programs.

525 Mohamed, Mahmoud Girgis, Mahmoud Saleh Ismail, and Saad Ahmad Ismail. "al-Maktabah al-akadimiyah fi al-'Iraq bayna al-waqi' wa-'am 2000." *al-Majallah al-'Arabiyah lil-Ma'lumat* 10, no. 1 (1989) : 121-150.

The design of infrastructure of academic libraries in Iraq is an essential matter for future development. The borrowing services, references services are main features of the academic libraries in Iraq. The obstacles which face academic libraries must be confronted for librarians to solve them and to avoid creating other obstacles. A detailed comparison between academic libraries in developed countries and 3rd World countries is discussed in detail, to show the differences and requirements, to follow the developmental topics in developed academic libraries such as: recent communication media; online systems; online searching; SDI and current awareness.

526 al-Wardi, Zaki Husayn, and Muhammad 'Awdah 'Aliwi. "al-Su'ubat allati tuwajih talabat al-dirasat al-'ulyah fi majal al-khidmah al-maktabiyah: dirasat halah li-maktabat jami'at al-Basrah." *Risalat al-Maktabah* 28, no. 4 (December 1993): 36-58.

The study describes the services offered by Basrah University libraries to higher studies and the obstacles facing them.

ARCHIVES

527 Jirjis, Jasim Muhammad. "al-Dirasat al-arshiviyah fi al-'Iraq." *Makatabat al-Idarah* 14, no. 2 (January 1987): 37-57.

CATALOGING AND CLASSIFICATION

528 'Aliwi, Muhammad 'Awdah. "al-Tatbiq al-'amali li tasnif diwi al-'ishri fi maktabat jami'at al-Basrah: dirasah midaniyah." *Risalat al-Maktabah* 28, nos. 1-2 (March-June 1993): 37-52.

Problems which appeared by using Dewey Decimal Classification at Basrah University.

529 Qarahghawli, 'Afaf Sami. "Tasnif al-'ulum al-sihhiyah fi al-maktabat al-tibbiyah: dirasat halah li-maktabat kulliyyat tub Baghdad." *Risalat al-Maktabah* 32, no. 1 (June 1997): 4-20.

The paper describes the different catagories of medical libraries and the specialized classification schemes that are established. The library of medicine at Baghdad University is used as a case study.

COPYRIGHT

530 al-Sudani, 'Abdullah 'Abd al-Rahim. "Haq al-mu'allif fi al-'Iraq." *'Alam al-Kutub* 2, no. 4 (January-February 1982): 653-665.

DATABASE MANAGEMENT SYSTEMS

531 Alak, Safa M., and Sabah A. Ali. "Use of database management systems at the University of Basrah Library." *Program* 22, no. 3 (July 1988): 275-283.

Basrah University, Iraq, has nine colleges in five campuses, each with its own library. A computerized acquisitions, cataloging and circulation control system, for books and periodicals, was installed (NEC-800s) with two database management systems (DBMS): ADBS (Advanced Database Management System) and INQ (Information Query). The article presents details of the DBMS and the system structure.

532 Muhsin, Sabah Rahmah, and Muhammad Hasan Qasim al-Khafaji. "Nizam ma'lumat idari lil-markaz al-watani lil-watha'iq fi al-'Iraq: muqtarah khittat tasmim." *al-Majallah al-'Arabiyah lil-Ma'lumat* 15, no. 1 (1994): 124-140.

INDEXING AND ABSTRACTING

533 Salih, G. Khamas. "Tatbiq al-qawa'id al-duwaliyah fi faharis al-maktabat al-jami'iyah fi al-'Iraq: dirasah taqwimiyah." *Risalat al-Maktabah* 31, no. 4 (December 1996): 20-32.

The author studies the extent to which Iraqi university libraries apply international rules of bibliographic description in their indexes.

INFORMATION SERVICES

534 Jacso, Peter, and Faik Abdul S. Razzaq. "Computerizing information services in Iraq." *Information Development* 2, no. 2 (April 1986): 85-92.

A large scale computerization project was initiated in Iraq to automate library and information work in support of the accelerating research and development work in the country. It was jointly implemented by the Iraqi

Scientific Documentation Center and the Hungarian Computer Applications and Service Company under the auspices of Unesco. Four databases were implemented initially: the local versions of the BIOSIS and INSPEC databases, a union catalog of monographs from LC/MARC records and a union catalog of serials from the ISDS tapes. The background and justification of the project are reviewed and an overview given of the design concepts, implementation and the major characteristics of the databases, services and products. The results of the project are evaluated and future developments discussed. [A]

535 al-Kindilchie, Amer Ibrahim. "Istikhdam al-hawasib fi khadamat al-ma'lumat: malamih 'an al-tajribah al-'iraqiyah." *al-Majallah al-'Arabiyah lil-Ma'lumat* 15, no. 1 (1994): 55-81.

536 Razzuqi, Nu'ayma Hasan, and Rubak Muhammad 'Ali. "Khadamat al-bath al-intiqa'i: dirasat ijra'atiha wa mutatallibatiha wa taqyim mukhrajatiha." *al-Majallah al-'Arabiyah lil-Ma'lumat* 9, no. 2 (1988): 24-59.

The author explores the methods and processes used by the Iraqi Centre for Scientific Documentation when offering selective dissemination services. These methods are also used by other documentation centers.

537 Zado, Victoria Yousif. *The General Information Programme (PGI) and Developing Countries: A Case Study of Iraq*. Ph.D., 1990. University of Technology, Loughborough (United Kingdom). 231 p.

The existing information services in Iraq are inefficient and inadequate. They are contributing very little to the development process in the country. Therefore, they need to be improved and developed. The majority of the developing countries, of which Iraq is one and with which we are especially concerned, are undergoing a development process which, in itself, forms a force that develops demand for information services (libraries, documentation and archives centers). This study (a) investigates the present situation of information services in Iraq, examines their deficiencies, and considers the possibility of establishing effective guidelines for their development within the conceptual framework of the General Information Programme (PGI) of Unesco, so that they can contribute to the national development plans of the country; (b) explains the vital role of information services in development and the functions of collecting, organizing, retrieving and disseminating information at the national, regional and international level; (c) identifies the factors that are hindering the development of information services; (d) identifies the measures and steps that must be taken to bring about a fundamental change in the development of these services in Iraq and that might be useful for other developing countries, especially Arab countries. [DAI 53/09-A: 3025.]

INFORMATION STORAGE AND RETRIEVAL

538 al-Kindilchie, Amer Ibrahim. "Tiqaniyyat al-bahth bi al-ittisal al-mubashar wa-al-aqras al-muktanazah wa-istikhdamatiha fi jami'atay Baghdad wa-al-Musul." *Risalat al-Maktabah* 26, no. 2 (June 1991): 25-42.

Discusses the importance of both online information retrieval and CD-ROM technology in developing countries. The article includes a case study from Baghdad University which uses online services and Mosul University which uses CD-ROM technology.

INFORMATION SYSTEMS

539 'Abd al-Razzaq, Amirah Haqqi, and Ghassan Hamid 'Abd al-Majid. "Nizam maktabah mumaknan bi-istikhdam al-hasibah al-maykruwiyah "al-Warka'." *Risalat al-Maktabah* 26, no. 2 (June 1991): 115-126.

The article discusses al-Warka', a computer-based library system, developed in Iraq in order to meet the demands of small libraries.

540 Rahan, G. I. "Outlook on the new information system of petroleum products distribution in Iraq." *Economic Computation and Economic Cybernetics Studies and Research*, no. 3 (1982): 71-86.

This paper describes an information system to aid distribution of petroleum products. The structure of the system is described and the indices system is discussed in detail. The system is classified by product type, sort of sale station, deposit etc., and thus coding is delineated. The structure of the database is given.

541 al-Samirra'i, Iman Fadil. "al-Baramijiyyat al-jahizah wa-al-musammamah mahalliyyan fi al-maktabat wa-marakiz al-ma'lumat fi al-'Iraq." *Risalat al-Maktabah* 32, no. 4 (December 1997): 17-52.

A survey study of computer programs used in libraries and information centers in Iraq. The study stresses the problems and weaknesses of the locally designed softwares, specifically in their application to documentation.

LIBRARY ADMINISTRATION/MANAGEMENT

542 'Aliwi, Muhammad 'Awdah. "al-Idarah al-'ilmiyah al-hadithah fi al-maktabat al-jami'iyah ma' dirasah lil-waqi' al-idari li maktabat jami'at al-Basrah." *Risalat al-Maktabah* 26, no. 2 (June 1991): 65-94.

The author discusses the advantages of applying scientific management in university libraries. Basra University is used as a case study.

LIBRARY EDUCATION

543 al-Farhan, Layla, Udit Marun Badran, and Salim Husayn al-'Azzawi. "al-Ittijahat al-mawdu'iyah li rasa'il al-majistir fi 'ulum al-maktabat wa-al-ma'lumat fi al-jami'ah al-Mustansariyah: 'ard wa tahlil." *Risalat al-Maktabah* 29, no. 4 (December 1994): 11-25.

A review of dissertations in library and information science presented to al-Mustansiriyah University.

544 al-Sabbagh, 'Imad 'Abd al-Wahhab, and Margarit B. Husib. "al-Ta'lim al-jami'i fi haql al-maktabat wa-al-ma'lumat: muqaranah bayna al-'Iraq wa-al-Sa'udiyah wa-Misr." *Risalat al-Maktabah* 27, no. 1 (March 1992): 18-33.

According to the authors, interest in library and information science education, at the university level, was manifested only recently. The study introduces the educational programs in library and information science in Iraq, Saudi Arabia and Egypt.

LIBRARY INSTRUCTION

545 Manzoor, Suhail. "Instruction in the use of academic library." *IASLIC Bulletin* 24, no. 1 (March 1980): 23-26.

The importance in the use of the academic library is discussed with particular reference to Iraq. Emphasizes the need for instruction to be an integral part of the curriculum. Methods of library instruction are considered, such as personal assistance or the use of television. The need for library/faculty cooperation is emphasized.

LIBRARY LEGISLATION

546 al-Zubaydi, Muhammad 'Abbud. "al-Tashri'at al-maktabiyah fi al-'Iraq." *Risalat al-Maktabah* 30, no. 2 (June 1995): 24-48.

Different aspects of library legislation in Iraq are discussed.

NATIONAL LIBRARIES

547 Hashmi, Syed Ali. "Iraq and its National Library." *Libri* 33, no. 3 (Summer 1983): 236-243.

Also appears in *National Libraries 2: 1977-1985*, edited by Maurice B. Line and Joyce Line, pp. 220-226 (London: Aslib, 1987). Gives the history of the modern national library established in Baghdad in 1961, its growth, organization, and activities.

NETWORKS AND NETWORKING

548   Qasim, Nizar Muhammad 'Ali. "(Nahwa) al-shabakah al-wataniyah lil-Ma'lumat fi al-'Iraq." *Risalat al-Maktabah* 31, no. 3 (September 1996): 60-76.

Discusses efforts being made for the establishment of a national information network in Iraq.

PRINTING

549   Albin, Michael W. "Iraq's first printed book." *Libri* 31, no. 2 (August 1981): 167-174.

Examines critically three frequently cited opinions regarding Iraq's first printed book in order to propose a firm date for the introduction of printing to that country. The 3 dates concerned are: 1816, when the Mamluk governor of Iraq, Da'ud Pasha is said to have brought a lithographic press to Baghdad to print a newspaper called *Jurnal al-Iraq*; 1830-1831 when a history of this same Da'ud Pasha's governorship was printed in Baghdad; and 1856, when presses were set up almost simultaneously in Mosul, Kerbala, and Baghdad. Argues that bibliographical and historical evidence leads to the conclusion that the 1830-31 publication of Dawhat-al-Wuzara, the history written in praise of Da'ud Pasha was the first printed book in Iraq and that claims for other dates are based on historical errors, or ignore strong bibliographical evidence.

SCHOOL/CHILDREN'S LIBRARIES

550   'Aliwi, Muhammad 'Awdah, and Majbal Lazim Musallam. "al-Khadamat al-maktabiyah lil-atfal ma' dirasah li maktabat al-atfal fi al-'Iraq." *'Alam al-Kutub* 10, no. 4 (November 1989): 506-519.

TRAINING, STAFF

551   Amin, Abdul-Karim. "Tadrib al-maktabiyyin fi al-Jumhuriyah al-'Iraqiyah." *Rissalata al-Maktaba* 12, no. 3 (September 1997): 7-15.

CHAPTER 8

JORDAN

GENERAL

552 Mansour, Farouq. "Jordan." In *World Encyclopedia of Library and Information Services*. 3rd ed. (pp. 418-419). Chicago: American Library Association, 1993.

Discusses the history of libraries and library education in the country and gives a description of its national, academic, public, school, and special libraries.

553 Qandil, Yusuf. "al-Maktabat wa-al-harakah al-maktabiyah fi al-Urdun." *al-Jadid fi 'Alam al-Kutub wa-al-Maktabat*, no. 2 (spring 1994): 116-121.

According to the author, the first library established in Jordan was at the Sult Secondary School, in 1926; and by 1970, Jordan had 38 specialized libraries, 44 school libraries, 8 college libraries and 3 public libraries.

554 al-Qawasimah, Muhammad 'Abdullah. "al-Maktabat fi al-Urdun." *Risalat al-Maktabah* 28, no. 4 (December 1993): 14-35.

The author discusses the status and development of all kinds of libraries in Jordan.

555 al-Shorbaji, Najeeb. "Library and information services in Jordan." In *Information and Libraries in the Arab World*. Compiled and edited by Michael Wise and Anthony Olden, pp. 104-130. London: Library Association Publishing, 1994. [Information and libraries in the developing world, vol. 3.]

Article included in a collection of papers presenting a comparative review of librarianship and library practices in Arab countries. Addresses the issues of library and information services in Jordan within the general framework of the country as a developing country and as a country with special features and characteristics. Includes discussion of: geography, history and development; school libraries; college libraries and university libraries; public libraries; national libraries; the National Documentation Centre; and other libraries and information centers. Concludes with notes on the aims and objectives of the Jordan Library Association.

556 Younis, Abdul Razeq Mustafa. "Jordan Libraries." In *Encyclopedia of Library and Information Science*. Vol. 26 (pp. 339-362). New York: Marcel Dekker, Inc., 1979.

Topics discussed include: (1) Historical Background; (2) Development of Library and Information Services in Jordan—school, public, academic, and special libraries; (3) The Jordan Library Association; (4) The Department of Libraries at the Ministry of Education; (5) The Department of Libraries and National Archives; (6) Library Education; (7) Information Needs and Networking in Jordan; and (8) Assessment: Libraries in Jordan.

557 Zash, Amal Muhammad. *al-Maktabat fi al-Urdun: Waqi' wa-Tumuhat*. 'Amman: A.M. Zash, 1989. 313 p.

ACADEMIC LIBRARIES

558 Elayyan, Ribhi Mustafa. "al-Khadamat al-maktabiyah: dirasah li-khadamat al-qurra' fi maktabat al-Jami'ah al-Urduniyah." *Risalat al-Maktabah* 16, no. 2 (June 1981): 28-41.

The effectiveness of any library is measured mainly by its collections and the services it offers to its clientele. Describes the services offered by the University of Jordan Library, including borrowing, reference, periodicals and photocopying services; reading facilities; user education programs; publicity and bibliographical services; and extra services such as exhibitions, lectures and meetings.

559 Hamshari, 'Umar Ahmad. *Job Satisfaction of Professional Librarians: A Comparative Study of Technical and Public Service Departments in Academic Libraries in Jordan*. Ph.D., 1985. University of Michigan. 161 p.

The main objectives of the study were to investigate job satisfaction of Jordanian professional academic librarians employed in technical and public service departments and to determine the applicability of Herzberg's two-factor theory of job satisfaction to academic library environments in Jordan. The following two main hypotheses were tested: (1) professional librarians in technical service departments in academic libraries in Jordan attain a higher level of satisfaction than do those of public service departments and (2) the motivator factors (satisfiers) are more likely to increase job satisfaction than they are to decrease it, and the hygiene factors (dissatisfiers) are more likely to contribute to job dissatisfaction than to job satisfaction. The population for the study consisted of all professional librarians employed in the two major library departments in Jordanian academic libraries. A questionnaire was distributed to participants in eight university and twelve community college libraries in the East and West Bank of Jordan. 109 persons returned completed usable questionnaires; of those, 74 were technical service librarians and 35 were public service librarians. Results supported the first main hypothesis and revealed that technical service librarians were more satisfied with their work than were public service librarians. Statistically significant differences between the two occupational departments were found on: ability utilization, achievement, activity, authority, co-workers, creativity, independence, moral values, recognition, responsibility, social status, supervision-human, supervision-technical, variety, comfort, challenge, communications and career satisfaction. Technical service librarians scored significantly higher on those dimensions than did public service librarians. A multiple regression analysis was performed to test the second major hypothesis. The results of the study partially supported Herzberg's theory of job satisfaction and showed that both motivators and hygienes contributed to overall satisfaction of the two occupational groups of Jordanian librarians. [DAI 46/11-A: 3179.]

560 Mohammed, Amal. "Maktabat Jami'at Mu'tah: rafid thaqafi mumayyaz fi janub Urdunina al-'aziz: istitla' musawwar." *Risalat al-Maktabah* 23, no. 1 (March 1988): 111-118.

Describes the University of Mu'ta Library based upon an interview with the director, Mr. al-Najdawi. Discusses general organization, collections available, classification, cataloging and circulation systems, and describes library services offered to both the university and the local community. Examines the professional activities of the library in the various areas of library and information science.

561 al-Qawasimah, Muhammad 'Abdullah. "Waqi' maktabat kulliyyat al-mujtama' fi al-Urdun." *Risalat al-Maktabah* 26 (December 1991): 5-54.

The author surveys 53 libraries at community colleges in Jordan. He emphasizes the importance of these libraries and their roles.

562 Shniour, Farouk, and Abdalla Damdom. "Istittla' hawla khidmat al-taswir fi maktabat al-Jami'ah al-Urduniyah." *Risalat al-Maktabah* 20, no. 1-2 (March-June 1985): 36-38.

Describes services offered by the photocopying section of the University of Jordan Library. Lists hardware equipment available in the library which facilitates photocopying services. Provides a summary of student opinion of these services.

AUDIOVISUAL MATERIALS

563 Abu al-Ruz, Mohammad. "al-Mawad al-sama'iyah wa-al-basariyah: ahamiyyataha wa-mutatalibatiha." *Risalat al-Maktabah* 20, no. 1-2 (March-June 1985): 3-6.

Focuses on the development of the following types of audiovisual materials (AVM): audio materials, visual materials and audiovisual materials. Outlines the advantages of AVM in library collections and discusses the problems associated with introducing AVM. Emphasizes the need for the 3 universities in Jordan to familiarize users with AVM in libraries.

564 Hamadneh, 'Umar M. "Masadir al-ma'lumat: al-suwar." *Risalat al-Maktabah* 18, no. 4 (December 1984): 26-28.

Discusses pictures as an information source in libraries and gives help in their selection, acquisition and storage. Discusses classification and cataloging of pictures. Recommends that Jordanian librarians establish picture collections and have good and comprehensive bibliographical control over these collections.

AUTOMATION

565 Younis, Abdul Razeq Mustafa. "Library automation in Jordan." *International Library Review* 22, no. 1 (March 1990): 19-29.

This study reviews the historical development and factors affecting the library movement in Jordan and explores the extent of computer applications in 333 libraries in Jordan. Of the 255 libraries that responded, only 3.9% of them use computers for cataloging, circulation, serials check-in, acquisitions records and correspondence. Problems, solutions, and future plans are pointed out. The problems that obstruct the use of computers are the lack of trained staff, funds, physical facilities, software, users' indifference, and administrative factors. The study recommends solutions to improve libraries' chances to adapt new computer technologies to improve their functions and services to users. [A]

BIBLIOGRAPHIES

566 el-Akhras, Mahmud. "al-Biblioghrafia al-Filastiniyah al-Urduniyah, 1978." *Risalat al-Maktabah* 14, no. 1 (March 1979): 39-72.

JORDAN

The Palestinian-Jordanian Bibliography of 1978 includes 175 entries. Consists of works written by Palestinian and Jordanian authors regardless of place of publication and language used. Entries are arranged according to the 18th edition of Dewey Decimal Classification with slight modifications to the subjects of interest (especially Islam, Arabic language and literature, and Islamic and Arabic history). The International Standard Bibliographic Description (ISBD) is given for all entries with special attention to the qualities significant to Arab publications. There are three alphabetical indexes-author, title, and subject. Includes government publications and school textbooks.

567   'Awf, Zahidah Izzat. "The Jordanian National Bibliography." *Risalat al-Maktabah* 20, no. 3 (September 1985): 6-9. [In English.]

Paper presented at the 7th International Middle East Libraries Committee Conference held at the Chester Beatty Library, Dublin, on 16-19 April 1985. Describes the historical background of the Jordanian National Bibliography outlining aspects of the new arrangement in 1979 such as a list of participants in the compilation process, numbers of Arabic and English titles included, and a description of its contents. Examines factors affecting the book production industry in Jordan; the high number of academic institutions, research organizations, government bodies and private institutions that are involved with their own publishing programs; the increase in the number of commercial publishing houses; and the fact that authors often pay their own expenses for printing, marketing and distribution of their books. Considers difficulties confronting the book production industry, and summarizes activities relating to manuscripts in Jordan.

568   Itayem, Mahmoud A. "al-Tarkibah al-urduniyah al-muwahhadah." *Risalat al-Maktabah* 27, no. 4 (December 1992): 30-44.

The author calls Jordanian libraries to adopt one flexible format to be used for constructing their bibliographic databases.

BOOK DISTRIBUTORS

569   Akel, Adeeb. "Taqrir hawla awda' markaz tawzi' al-kitab al-Urduni." *Risalat al-Maktabah* 20, no. 1-2 (March-June 1985): 39-40.

The Jordan Library Association (JLA) established the Jordanian Distribution Centre in 1983. Its aims and objectives are explained.

CATALOGING AND CLASSIFICATION

570   Abu al-Ruz, Mohammad. "Taqrir 'an al-dawrah al-thaniyah lil-mu'alajah al-faniyah lil-ma'lumat: al-fahrasah wa-al-tasnifat wa-al-arshif." *Risalat al-Maktabah* 20, no. 3 (September 1985): 44-47.

Describes an advanced course in technical processing organized by the Jordan Library Association and held at the University of Jordan. Details of venue, lectures, curriculum and participants are provided.

571   Hamshari, 'Umar Ahmad. "al-Fahrasah athna' al-nashr wa-al-bibliughrafia al-wataniyah al-Urduniyah." *Risalat al-Maktabah* 15, no. 4 (December 1980): 10-13.

Overview of the CIP concept, listing its benefits, and suggesting that the appropriate bibliographic data be sent to the Jordanian National Bibliographic Centre between 6-9 weeks prior to publication for inclusion in the National Jordanian Bibliography.

572   Hamshari, 'Umar Ahmad. "Fahrasat al-kitab al-'Arabi: mashakil wa-hulul muqtaraha." *Risalat al-Maktabah* 17, no. 1 (March 1982): 11-16.

Cataloging problems in Jordan as well as the other Arab countries are very varied. Discusses these problems such as the lack of Arabic cataloging code, the problems of Arabic/Muslim names, filing, style of entry, marginal works, government publications and subject headings. Suggests some solutions such as the introduction of centralized cataloging, the cataloging in publication, the compilation and publication of a standard subject heading list in Arabic and the establishment of a standard authority list for the names of Arabic authors.

CHILDREN'S LITERATURE

573   el-Akhras, Mahmud. "Children's books in the Hashemite Kingdom of Jordan." In *Printed for Children: World Children's Book Exhibition* (pp. 245-246). Munich: K. G. Saur, 1978.

CLIPPINGS

574   al-Kindilchie, 'Amir Ibrahim. "Istikhdam nizam CDS/ISIS fi bina' qawa'id bayanat al-qasasat al-suhufiyah wa-al-shakhsiyyat: tajribat markaz al-riyadah lil-Ma'lumat wa-al-dirasat/'Amman." *al-Majallah al-'Arabiyah lil-Ma'lumat* 16, no. 1 (1995): 39-64.

Describes the use of CDS/ISIS in building clippings and biographical databases in a center in Jordan.

COMPUTERS IN LIBRARIES

575   al-Natour, Nahla. "Istikhdam al-kumpiutar fi maktabat wizarat al-takhtit—al-majlis al-qawmi lil-takhtit sabiqan." *Risalat al-Maktabah* 19, no. 4 (December 1984): 68-69.

As a result of the information explosion and the huge increase in the number of documents in the Ministry of Planning (Previously known as the National Planning Council) Library, a computer was installed. A database has been created including a full bibliographical description of documents held in the library. A card catalog is produced by the computer and retrieval will be via terminals in the future. The computer will be used for circulation, current awareness services, a union list of periodicals and archive control.

576 Younis, Abdul Razeq Mustafa. "The use of computers in libraries and information centres in Jordan: a survey." *Program* 22, no. 3 (July 1988): 268-274.

Provides a brief historical review of the library movement in Jordan, followed by a survey of library computerization in 333 libraries of all types. Out of 255 (76.6%) that responded, 10 (3.9%) indicated that they use computers for specific functions. The paper presents results of the survey and lists the main functions for which the computers are used. It notes the problems faced when using automation in Jordanian libraries and discusses future plans currently in hand.

INFORMATION POLICY

577 Younis, Abdul Razeq Mustafa. "Nahwa istratijiyah wataniya li-nuzum al-ma'lumat wa-khadamatiha fi al-Urdun." *Risalat al-Maktabah* 29, no. 1 (March 1994): 17-34.

The paper reviews the Jordanian government's attempts to formulate a national information policy for science and technology. Different approaches are discussed.

INFORMATION SERVICES

578 Abdul-Rahman, As'ad. "Private institutions and computer utilization in community service and education: the case of the Abdul-Hamid Shoman Foundation." *Advances in Library Administration and Organization* 7 (1988): 263-274.

579 Soufan, Hani'a Jarallah. "al-Khidmah al-marja'iyah wa-qism al-maraji' ... wa-maktabatina." *Risalat al-Maktabah* 17, no. 1 (March 1982): 26-35.

Discusses the reference section in a library; its collection and staff, the services it must give to readers and the qualifications the reference librarian must have. Also explains briefly the situation in Jordan University library and offers some suggestions to improve the reference service in the country.

INFORMATION STORAGE AND RETRIEVAL

580 Qandil, Yusuf. "Bunuk al-ma'lumat fi al-Urdun: mulahazat wa-istintajat." *Risalat al-Maktabah* 32, no. 2 (June 1997): 57-66.

A review of the use of computers in Jordan, and the widespread of MINISIS and CDS/ISIS; and a review of the Jordanian experience in establishing databanks.

581 al-Qutub, S. "Dawr al-hasub fi al-anzima al-mutakamilah lil-maktabat wa-marakiz alma'alumat (al-janib al-fanni wa-altatbiq al-'amali)." *Risalat al-Maktabah* 22, no. 4 (December 1987): 105-129.

Reports a seminar held at Princess Summaya College, a Department of Computer Systems at the Royal Scientific Society in cooperation with Jordan Library Association from June 15 to July 13 1987. The following practical aspects of the seminar are discussed: the system objective; the system approach; the system components; the system performance; and the system follow-up.

582 al-Shorbaji, Najeeb. "Hazmat barmajiyyat CDS/ISIS ma hiya?" *Risalat al-Maktabah* 25, nos. 2-3 (June-September 1990): 5-46.

Origin and development of the ISIS is discussed as well as the reasons for the selection of the CDS/ISIS for the libraries in Jordan. Detailed description of the package and its applications is given.

583 al-Shorbaji, Najeeb, and Bakhit al-Bakhit. "al-Tarkibat al-bibliyughrafi-yah al-mustakhdamah fi al-maktabat wa-marakiz al-ma'lumat al-urduni-yah." *Risalat al-Maktabah* 27, no. 4 (December 1992): 4-29.

The study aims at identifying the bibliographic formats used to build databases in Jordanian libraries and to compare them with other standard international formats. The study shows CDS/ISIS in the most used package, while Common Communication Format is the most used format.

INFORMATION SYSTEMS

584 al-Sutari, 'Ali, and 'Awad 'Athaminah. "Nizam al-ma'lumat al-ali fi maktabat jami'at al-Yarmuk." *Risalat al-Maktabah* 29, no. 1 (March 1994): 35-59.

The authors discuss the different stages that the University of Yarmouk went through in order to establish and develop an automated library information system.

INTERLIBRARY LOAN

585 al-Odeh, Abdul-Rahman Mahmoud. *Feasibility and Support for an Interlibrary Loan Network among the West Bank and Gaza Academic Libraries (Jordan)*. Ph.D., 1987. University of Missouri–Columbia. 131 p.

The purposes of this study were to investigate the present status of the West Bank and Gaza (WB/G) academic libraries and to explore the degree of support for the establishment of an Interlibrary Loan Network (ILLN) in relation to the size of the library administered and the academic degree of the directors of the WB/G academic libraries combined with their experience. Two methods have been used for collecting information for this study. A written questionnaire survey was administered to the WB/G academic library directors and an analysis of the literature related to ILL developments, particularly in the developing countries, was undertaken. The WB/G academic libraries vary greatly in resources available to the students and faculty who are potential users. Most of the books and serials are in the major university libraries and the same is true for the library staff. Library directors also report inadequacy in number of professional staff. Although some of the libraries are involved in informal borrowing and lending among themselves, a formal interlibrary loan system does not exist in the WB/G academic libraries. It was reported by the respondents that all directors but one support the establishment of an ILLN among the WB/G academic libraries. Lack of advanced planning has been reported as the number one obstacle that needs to be overcome before most of the libraries can participate in an ILLN. The need for adequate resources, strong leadership, support of organizations, adequate finances, spirit of cooperation and effective communications were reported in that order as factors which libraries need to address in order to enrich library services in the WB/G academic libraries. It is hoped that this study will contribute to the development of the academic libraries of the WB/G by presenting information about problems and difficulties which need to be overcome in order for an ILLN to be established in the WB/G. [DAI 48/10-A: 2480.]

LIBRARIES AND LIBRARIANS—DIRECTORIES

586 Abu 'Ajamiyah, Yusra, Muhammad Mahmud Midhat, and 'Umar M. Hamadnah. *Dalil al-Maktabat wa-al-Maktabiyin fi al-Urdun, 1984*. 'Amman: Yusra Abu 'Ajamiyah, 1985. 255 p.

LIBRARY ASSOCIATIONS

587 al-'Azab, 'Issa. "Jam'iyyat al-maktabat al-urduniyah: dirasat halah." *Risalat al-Maktabah* 30, no. 2 (June 1995): 64-75.

The paper presents a historical background of the Jordanian Library Association, its aims, achievements and objectives.

588   Elayyan, Ribhi Mustafa, and Anwar Akrush. "Jordan Library Association (JLA) in twenty years 1963-1983." *Risalat al-Maktabah* 18, no. 4 (December 1983): 3-7. [In English and Arabic.]

Briefly describes library development in Jordan during the 20th century. Describes the aims and activities of the Jordan Library Association which was established in December 1963.

589   al-Shorbaji, Najeeb. "The Jordan Library Association." *Information Development* 10, no. 1 (March 1994): 38-40.

Describes the activities of the Jordan Library Association and its impact on the library and information movement in Jordan.

LIBRARY COOPERATION

590   Younis, Abdul Razeq Mustafa. *Components of a Proposed Resource Sharing and Information Network for Academic and Special Libraries in Jordan*. Ph.D., 1983. University of Pittsburgh. 355 p.

Based on the assumption that resource sharing would allow libraries in Jordan to achieve levels of services and efficiency by working in a cooperative mode, and that a favorable climate exists to establish a network, this study attempts to achieve two objectives: determine the feasibility of an information network, and to formulate the networks' components. Analysis of the literature, questionnaires, interviews and site visits comprised the methodology for obtaining data. The questionnaires were designed to collect: current data on academic and special libraries, resources, and the nature and extent of cooperatives among them; librarians' opinions and attitudes of resource sharing and networking, functions, obstacles, solutions, and factors contributing to establishing the network; and steps for linkage with other networks abroad. Experts' opinions were probed on planning practical ideas and steps for implementation to assess the desirability, need, and extent of support, government officials were interviewed. Site visits to OCLC, MEDLINE, and Pittsburgh Regional Library Center (PRLC) furnished firsthand information and ideas to help in planning various aspects of the network. Major findings of the study indicate that a wealth of current and historical information exists. The two university libraries are the largest and richest in resources, staff, and budget. However, most libraries suffer economic constraints, thus maintaining poor collections, facilities, and providing less than optimal services. Cooperatives among libraries are informal and limited to interlending, gift and exchange, and photocopying. Nevertheless, resource sharing, cooperation, and networking concepts are well understood, and analysis of data indicate a favorable atmosphere to establish a network. Librarians and officials perceived the network as most needed for the flow of the world's knowledge and to further education, research, and development. Librarians voiced their concern for the need of a deposit law, national bibliographies, and leadership. Supported by the findings, a "plan for action" was proposed. Network modules would comprise of cooperative acquisitions, processing, interlending, storage, and delivery of services. Network rationale, goals, objectives, functions, governance, linkage, and operational requirements were discussed. [DAI 45/02-A: 333.]

LIBRARY EDUCATION

591   Akroush, Anwar. "Hawla tadris 'Ilm al-maktabat." *Risalat al-Maktabah* 16, no. 2 (June 1981): 3.

The Jordan Library Association (JLA) has supplied Jordanian libraries with trained staff since its librarianship courses began in 1964, and the Library and Information Centre was later established to take the responsibility in this field. Suggests that library education is hampered by excessive interest in financial concerns and lack of proper planning. Contends that: academic qualifications and field experience of instructors should be standardized; institutions qualified to teach librarianship must be defined; the real library needs of the country should be considered; quality must not be sacrificed to output of graduates; and coordination between individual institutions and the JLA would be advantageous.

592   Jordanian Library Association. "Tadris 'ilm al-maktabat wa-al-ma'lumat fi kuliyat al-mujtama'." *Risalat al-Maktabah* 18, no. 4 (December 1984): 29-32.

Gives results of a study of librarianship and information science education in community colleges in Jordan. There are 9 colleges offering such courses in Jordan. Their curriculum is approved by the Ministry of Education. Comments on the curriculum, teaching methods, training, teaching staff, resources and libraries in these colleges, teaching aids and tools, the examinations and the evaluation methods.

593   al-Kharuf, Yunis Isma'il. "Takhassus al-masadir al-ta'limiyah wa-al-maktabat bi-kulliyyat al-mujtama' al-urduniyah: dirasah naqdiyah." *Risalat al-Maktabah* 25, no. 1 (March 1990): 17-30.

Analyzes and criticizes the new curricula of the specialty "Libraries and Educational Resources" applied at the community colleges in Jordan.

594   Mansour, Farouq. "Takhassus al-masadir al-ta'limiyah wa-al-maktabat fi kulliyyat al-mujtama'." *Risalat al-Maktabah* 25, no. 1 (March 1990): 5-16.

A comprehensive and detailed study about the new program entitled "Educational resources and libraries" applied at the community colleges in Amman. The plan of the program as well as its requirements, courses, etc. are discussed.

595 Qandil, Yusuf. "al-Tadris al-jami'i li-'ilm al-maktabat wa-al-hajah al-urduniyah." *Risalat al-Maktabah* 30, no. 1 (March 1995): 16-25.

The paper shows available information on teaching library and information science in the Arab world, with emphasis on Jordan.

596 al-Shorbaji, Najeeb. "Dirasah hawla asbab ikhtiyar al-talabah al-Urduni-yyin li-takhassus al-maktabat wa-al-tawthiw wa-al-ma'lumat." *Risalat al-Maktabah* 19, no. 4 (December 1984): 46-51.

The relationship between motivation, employment and job satisfaction is discussed. 6 previous studies-from the UK, USA, Canada, Australia, and Jordan -were surveyed and analyzed. Describes results of a questionnaire survey of 160 community college students in Jordan in order to establish their reasons for choosing librarianship, documentation and information science courses. Outlines the main reasons which were found to be similar to those of students in other parts of the world: an opportunity to improve general knowledge; a suitable profession for women; belief in the value of books and information for social development; and a desire to help other people.

597 Younis, Abdul Razeq Mustafa. "Professional library development, manpower education and training in Jordan." *International Information & Library Review* 24, no. 1 (March 1992): 15-43.

Library education in Jordan falls into three categories: professional, at the post-graduate level, sub-professional, at the community colleges level, and in-service training. The primary institution concerned with in-service training is JLA. Detailed accounts of programs, syllabus, curriculum and course contents offered at all levels are given. The historical account of the library movement in Jordan indicates that Jordan's libraries are in transition from traditional to advanced library and information functions and practice. Continuous course evaluations and assessments resulted in the development of curricula endeavoring to advance trends in library and information science. Thus, more libraries are implementing computer systems. The post graduate curriculum introduces courses on advanced topics in information science and technology' besides library automation. JLA is shifting its emphasis towards specialized courses on computerization and library software packages such as CDS/ISIS. Community colleges' library education has also changed to include advanced topics. Statistical analysis of students and trainees at all levels is given. The impact of information technology on several library aspects and information services is highlighted to disclose what should be incorporated into the new library education curricula to equip the future generation of library and information professionals to practice the profession in Jordan. [A]

MAPS

598   Hamadneh, 'Umar M. "al-Khara'it wa-al-wad' fi maktabatina." *Risalat al-Maktabah* 17, no. 1 (March 1982): 42-49.

Discusses one of the most important non-book materials, namely, maps. The map is defined as a guide to information such as geographical features and natural resources. It is also used as a guide for users in library service. Discusses how to select maps and the problem librarians face in map selection, how to classify maps, the means of maps preservation and map resources. Introduces recommendations concerning maps in Jordan libraries.

599   al-Shorbaji, Najeeb. "al-Dabt al-biblioghrafi lil-khara'it al-jiulujiyah wa-al-wad' fi al-Urdun." *Risalat al-Maktabah* 18, no. 2-3 (June-September 1983): 36-52.

Describes the general problems associated with maps and the steps needed to ensure bibliographical control of maps. Lists the government departments, academic institutes, and private mining companies in Jordan which have map collections. Recommends that the librarians at these institutes should be trained in modern systems which deal with the organization and care of maps, and should prepare catalog cards for maps which will lead to the establishment of a union catalog.

NATIONAL LIBRARIES

600   Grolier, Eric de. *Development of the National Documentation Centre, Hashemite Kingdom of Jordan*. Paris: Unesco, 1977. 72 p.

The development of a National Documentation Centre in the Hashemite kingdom of Jordan's East Bank is described in five major sections including basic data (geographical background, historical background, population, natural resources, services, finance, research and development, and planning); the information situation (user studies, media, data banks, and libraries); recommendations; unsettled problems; and conclusions. A list of institutions and/or persons visited is included.

601   Hamshari, 'Umar Ahmad. "al-Maktabah al-wataniyah: waqi' wa-ru'ya mustaqbaliyah." *Risalat al-Maktabah* 30, no. 4 (December 1995): 43-53.

The National Library of Jordan was established in 1990. The author describes its role in organizing, preserving the national heritage through an organizational and administrative structure within the Ministry of Culture.

PERSONNEL

602   Mustafa, Suleiman Hussein. "Current library manpower situation in Jordan and projection of demand: a case study for a developing country." *Risalat al-Maktabah* 18, no. 1 (March 1983): 5-11.

An overview of the library system in Jordan concentrating on levels of stock and manpower. There is no national library as yet but the Department of Libraries and National Archives' collection of 30,000 books is intended to form the basis for one. Public libraries have only 180,000 volumes (0.18 volumes per literate inhabitant), of which 2/3 are in Amman. The 40 special libraries and documentation centers have been recently established; many are no more than collections of books maintained by untrained staff. School libraries, which were the very early components of the modern Jordanian library system, have a high ratio of books to pupils but no non-book media. Few full-time librarians are professionals, although many have had training. There are only 15 professional staff in the 27 college libraries and 11 professionals in the two university libraries. However Jordan University library has a structure comparable with those of developed countries.

603   Mustafa, Suleiman Hussein. "Current library manpower situation in Jordan: factors affecting demand for manpower." *Risalat al-Maktabah* 18, no. 2-3 (June-September 1983): 8-19.

Analyzes some of the factors which are closely related to the demand for library workers, both professional and supportive, in Jordanian libraries during the next 10 years. These include: population growth and shifts in population patterns; student enrolment trends in schools and further education; financial support and public demand for services; introduction of the new technology; and natural and voluntary wastage of staff. Provides estimates for library staff demands 1981-90 in the following areas: public libraries; special libraries; school libraries; and academic libraries.

604   Soufan, Hani'a Jarallah. "al-Istiqrar al-wazifi 'ind al-maktabiyyin." *Risalat al-Maktabah* 18, no. 2-3 (June-September 1983): 18-21.

The instability of librarians in their jobs is a dangerous phenomenon in Jordan, as well as in other developing countries. Reasons outlined in the paper include: librarians are not appreciated, working hours are long and conditions bad, lack of material or moral motives, continuing higher education, incompatible teaching and library salaries, and marriage of female librarians. Describes the effect of this instability on libraries and suggests solutions.

605   Younis, Abdul Razeq Mustafa. "Manpower shortage and education for librarianship in Jordan." *International Library Review* 14, no. 4 (October 1982): 417-425.

Intends to pinpoint the basics for future projections of manpower needs in Jordanian libraries where there is a shortage of trained staff. Reviews training courses offered in Jordan including annual Jordan Library Association (JLA) courses. Describes a manpower study of a small sample of libraries using an American classification of library jobs. Reports the findings, assessing the need for, and functions of, professionals in special, academic, public and school libraries in Jordan. Recommends a full-scale study to project future manpower needs and determine the curriculum and criteria for admission to courses.

PUBLIC LIBRARIES

606   Abu Dayeh, K. "Maktabat baladiyat Tulkarm—'al-maktaba al-'amma'." *Risalat al-Maktabah* 19, no. 4 (December 1984): 70-72.

Tulkarm is a town in the occupied West Bank (Jordan). The library, which is part of the municipality services, serves the local community and neighboring villages. Describes its location, design, organization and staffing and discusses services provided: reference, circulation, community information services, and cooperative programs with other libraries. Examines the shortcomings of the library: lack of a special room for audiovisual materials and media; lack of a special room for children; and unsuitable positioning of the catalogs.

607   Akroush, Anwar. "Maktabatuna al-'Amma wa-al-haja al-massa lil-tatwir." *Risalat al-Maktabah* 15, no. 4 (December 1980): 3.

Findings of a 1979 survey by the Jordan Library Association and Amman Municipal Public Library showed that Jordan cities lack library services and in some cases have none. 89 municipalities and 238 village councils have only 9 public libraries, which do not meet expected standards. Negative attitudes hinder library development. The Jordan Library Association has set aside an annual monetary award for the best library of the year and has communicated with the media, municipal mayors, ministerial personnel and others to encourage cooperative library development. If libraries are to improve both qualitatively and quantitatively, the matter requires serious attention at the national level.

608   Akroush, Anwar. "Qaddim kitaban tunshi' maktaba." *Risalat al-Maktabah* 17, no. 3 (September 1982): 4-7.

'Donate a book...and establish a library', is the project undertaken by the Jordan Library Association to promote public libraries. Its objectives are to expand library services via municipal libraries, to make people aware of libraries and their importance, and to develop a cooperative spirit among citizens. Various needs to implement such a project are mentioned. Under this project, the 1st library was inaugurated on September 20, 1982. The library consists of 3,000 books donated by the minister, citizens, and other institutes.

609 al-'Amad, Hani. "Waqi' al-maktabat al-'ammah fi al-Urdun." *Risalat al-Maktabah* 25, no. 4 (December 1990): 5-90.

A special issue devoted to study the present status of public libraries in Jordan. Public libraries are divided into five categories: libraries of municipal councils, libraries of official institutions, libraries of rehabilitation centers, prisons, libraries of diplomatic missions and libraries funded by the private sector. The author concludes that public libraries in Jordan are of a low standard and calls for the application of international standards.

610 al-Natour, Nahla. "Abdul-Hameed Shoman Public Library." *Advances in Library Administration and Organization* 7 (1988): 275-278.

PUBLISHING AND TRANSLATION

611 el-Akhras, Mahmud, and Sidqi Dahbur. "Harakat al-ta'lif wa-al-tarjamah wa-al-nashr fi al-Urdun 1967-1976." *Risalat al-Maktabah* 12, no. 2 (1977): 3-9.

SCHOOL/CHILDREN'S LIBRRAIES

612 Abu-'Ajmiyah, Yusra, and Ribhi Mustafa Elayyan. "Waqi' maktabat al atfal fi al-Urdun." *al-Jadid fi 'Alam al-Kutub* wa-al-*Maktabat*, no. 5 (winter 1995): 70-77.

The author discusses the present status of children's libraries in Jordan, focusing on their aims and objectives, building, equipment, collections, services; their problems and the obstacles that hinder their development.

613 Ali, Muhammad Sa'id al-Shaykh. "Waqi' Maktabat al-Madaris al-Thanawiyyah fi al-Urdun." [Special issue.] *Risalat al-Maktabah* 24, no. 2 (1989): 1-118.

Originally a Master's thesis, this study examines and compares Jordanian secondary school libraries with their British counterparts in terms of furniture, size and locations, holdings, staff, budget, and services.

614 Ayyub, Aminah. "al-Maktabah al-'ammah li baladiyyat al-Zarqa': fir' al-atfal: dirasat halah." *Risalat al-Maktabah* 31, no. 4 (December 1996): 40-58.

The article focuses on the children department in al-Zarqa' Municipal Library: its location, building, furniture, equipment, staff and services.

615 Debbas, Isma'il. "al-Maktabat al-madrasiyah fi al-Salt." *Risalat al-Maktabah* 15, no. 4 (December 1980): 47-63.

Attempts to define the problems which hinder library services in Salt schools in Jordan suggests possible solutions. A questionnaire was sent to 24 schools-21 responded. Schools were divided into 3 educational levels: elementary, preparatory and secondary. Their library services are compared to international standards for school libraries. Only three trained librarians work in these schools—1 to 2750 students. No special library facilities exist, collections are poor, and finances minimal. There is no cooperation or interlibrary loan, and teacher/librarians have to pay for missing books. No non-book materials are available. Suggestions are made for the improvement of the situation.

616 Fasheh, Mary Jamil. "Jordan." In *School Libraries: International Developments*. 2nd ed. Edited by Jean E. Lowrie and Mieko Nagakura, pp. 236-252. Metuchen, N.J.: Scarecrow Press, 1991.

First discusses education in general and then examines the history of school library development, school library administration and management, school library programs, and school librarians/teacher-librarians. It also discusses school library standards, professional support, and lists journals and publications related to libraries and librarianship in Jordan.

617 Frayhat, Maryam. "Maktabat al-madaris al-thanawiyah fi liwa' 'Ajlun." *Risalat al-Maktabah* 20, no. 3 (September 1985): 56-61.

Surveys the current status of the secondary school libraries in Ajlun by using a questionnaire designed to collect data about: present status, staffing holdings, buildings, furniture and budget. Compares results with international standards.

618 Mustafa, Mohammad Hassan. "Waqi' al-khidma al-maktabiyah fi madaris Wikalat al-Gawth." *Risalat al-Maktabah* 15, no. 4 (December 1980): 21-26.

UNRWA has about 195 preparatory and elementary schools serving 140 thousand pupils. Twelve cents per head is assigned for book purchasing—an inadequate amount. Library service is not centrally supervised and has no technical organization. Rooms are unsuitable for libraries, and no librarians, with no encouragement to pupils to benefit from the library service. A proper budget, better book selection, book binding, sufficient space, suitable furniture, posts for librarians, good supervision are just some of the needs of the service.

619   al-Sufi, 'Abdullah. "al-Maktabat al-madrasiyah fi al-Urdun." *Risalat al-Maktabah* 30, no. 4 (December 1995): 54-63.

A study of the school libraries in Jordan, the role of the Ministry of Education, and the school library department.

SERIALS

620   Abu 'Ajamiyah, Yusra. "al-Qa'ima al-muwahada lil-dawriyat al-ajnabiyah fi al-Urdun." *Risalat al-Maktabah* 23, no. 1 (March 1988): 129-135.

The importance and number of periodical titles necessitates bibliographic control. This may be achieved with a union list which is defined and its objectives and services listed. By the end of 1987, Shoman Public Library issued the first part of a union list of foreign periodicals in Jordan which comprises 6194 titles in all subjects, and represents 30 libraries. Explains steps taken in the compilation of the list.

621   Farsuni, Fu'ad Hamad. "Hasr al-matbu'at al-dawriyah al-Urduniyah: waqfah 'ind hadhihi al-qadiyah wa-mu'alajat al-tashri'at al-Urduniyah laha." *Risalat al-Maktabah* 15, no. 4 (December 1980): 34-41.

Considers the question of bibliographic organization, and specifically concentrates on periodical control in Jordan and the role of Jordanian legislations in that process. Since Jordan formed a part of the Ottoman Empire before World War 1, Ottoman press laws have been examined with regard to periodical control. Also dare Jordanian press laws from 1927-1973, and suggestions are made to achieve better control over periodical and non-periodical publications.

622   al-Shorbaji, Najeeb. "The Message of the Library." *Information Development* 11, no. 1 (March 1995): 46-49.

Reviews the history and development of the library and information science periodical: *Risalat al-Maktabah,* the periodical published by the Jordan Library Association since 1965. Discusses the reasons for the survival and success of the periodical in terms of economic and financial aspects and intellectual and content aspects. Concludes that the story of *Risalat al-Maktabah* shows that library periodicals in developing countries can survive with effective management and support from the profession. [A]

623   Shraim, Omaima. "Dirasah tarikhiyah lil-dawriyat al-Urduniyah, 1920-1980." *Risalat al-Maktabah* 17, no. 1 (March 1982): 36-41.

Handles the development of periodicals in Jordan 1920-80. Introduces the different factors that influenced the nature and subject of the periodicals

SPECIAL LIBRARIES

624 Abu Laban, Nawzat. "al-Mujamma' al-malaki li-buhuth al-hadarah al-Islamiyah (Mu'assasat al-Bayt) wa maktabatihi." *Risalat al-Maktabah* 25, nos. 2-3 (June-September 1990): 83-92.

625 Abu al-Ruz, Mohammad. "Maktabat al-munazamat al-'Arabiyah wa-al-duwaliyah wa-al-marakiz al-thaqafiyah fi al-Urdun." *Risalat al-Maktabah* 19, no. 4 (December 1984): 32-35.

The Jordan Library Association (JLA) has recognized the importance of the regional and international organizations in playing a major part in the social and economic development of the country. Library and information services are major parts of these organizations. The libraries and information centers play a major role in serving and promoting the activities practiced by these organizations. A survey was conducted by JLA to collect data on library and information services in these organizations. Seven libraries responded with full details about their establishment, organization, staffing and services. Libraries, according to their parent institutions, were divided into 2 categories: special libraries in pan-Arab and international organizations whose aim is to serve staff members; and libraries of the foreign cultural centers whose aim is to promote cultural ideas of their countries and serve as information centers for their countries.

626 Ahmad, Alaa-Aldin A., and Steven D. Zink. "Information technology adoption in Jordanian public sector organizations." *Journal of Government Information* 25, no. 2 (March 1998): 117-134.

Based on the relatively scarce data and literature on information technology (IT) utilization, as well as a sample survey of 44 Jordanian public agencies, this study examines the adoption and uses of IT in the Jordanian public sector. The findings show that the majority of Jordanian public organizations have access to computers, and most of the agencies have in-house systems. Microcomputers were found to be the most common computer platform, and agency use of IT was consistently intense in the area of financial management. Most public organizations with in-house computers employ on-staff programmers, whose numbers range from one to four or fewer. Software being used in the agencies was primarily commercially produced, but there was evidence of considerable internal development of software as well. The study concludes that current, specific agency use of computing is associated positively with plans to acquire additional microcomputer technology. In addition, an overview of emerging Internet activity in Jordan and the government's role in this still-emerging phenomenon is presented. [A]

627 Elayyan, Ribhi Mustafa, and Yusra Abu 'Ajmiyah. "Waqi' al-maktabat al-tibbiyah fi al-Urdun." *'Alam al-Kutub* 11, no. 1 (January 1990): 11-19.

A survey of medical libraries in Jordan, their collections, services and performance.

628 Mustafa, Suleiman Hussein. "Maktabat ma'had al-bulitiknik." *Risalat al-Maktabah* 12, no. 2 (June 1977): 14-22.

Describes Amman Polytechnic Library.

629 Salah, T. M. "Istittla' 'an ba'd marakiz al-mu'aqin fi 'Amman." *Risalat al-Maktabah* 19, no. 4 (December 1984): 27-31.

The Jordanian Society through its official organization has recognized the importance of providing various services for handicapped individuals. The University of Jordan, the Ministry of Social Development and Queen Alia Fund for Social Welfare are taking a leading role in these services. Describes five centers concerned with these services their establishment, fellowship, development and elaborates on library and information services provided by each.

USE STUDIES

630 Elayyan, Ribhi Mustafa. *An Investigation into the Use of Sources of Medical Information by the Practicing Jordanian Physicians of Selected Hospitals in Jordan*. Ph.D., 1986. University of Pittsburgh. 160 p.

This study investigated the use of information sources by the full-time practicing physicians in four selected hospitals representing the government, military, private and teaching hospitals in Jordan. The main objectives of the study were: (a) to investigate the needs for medical sources and libraries, (b) to identify the medical sources and libraries used by physicians, (c) to determine what methods and sources physicians used to locate needed information, and (d) to determine potential variables that may affect the frequency of use of library and non-library related sources. A questionnaire was used as the main instrument for collecting data. It was pre-tested using a sample population of twelve Arab health professionals. Four hundred and ten questionnaires were then distributed to the physicians working in the four selected hospitals. A total of 289 completed questionnaires were returned, resulting in a 70.5% response rate. Various packages of the SPSS were used for the statistical analysis of data. The one-way analysis of variance (ANOVA) and the t-test were used to test five hypotheses. The level of significance was set at .05. Of the five hypotheses, four of them were supported by the results of the analysis of data and one was rejected. The major findings of the study are: (1) Physicians who have longer years of experience use non-library related sources of information more frequently than their colleagues who have shorter periods of experience. (2) Internists, surgeons, pediatricians, obstetricians and gynecologists, and radiologists do not differ statistically from one another in their frequency of use of information sources. (3) Specialists use information sources more frequently than do general practitioners. (4) Physicians involved in research use all library related-sources (excluding newspapers) more frequently than their colleagues engaged in clinical practice. (5) Practicing physicians educated in English-speaking countries use libraries and library-related sources more frequently than those educated locally, or in the Arab States or in non-English speaking countries. [DAI 47/10-A: 3600.]

CHAPTER 9

KUWAIT

GENERAL

631 al-Freih, Ferial. "Shabakat al-ma'lumat al-wataniyah al-mutakhassisah fi al-Kuwayt: nash'atiha, tattawuriha, ma'uqat tanmiyatiha." *Risalat al-Maktabah* 23, no. 1 (March 1988): 58-84.

Emphasizes the role of information in national development and defines the role of the Kuwait Institute for Scientific Research. Discusses the aims and objectives of the national information network and investigates the information situation in special libraries in Kuwait by means of a questionnaire to gather data on library collections, organization, staffing, facilities, equipment, budget and finance. Sixteen libraries were surveyed, a plan of action submitted to implement the project, and a national seminar was held to discuss survey results.

632 el-Hadi, Mohamed M. "Kuwait." In *World Encyclopedia of Library and Information Services*. 3rd ed. (pp. 431-432). Chicago: American Library Association, 1993.

Discusses the history of libraries in the country and gives a description of its national, academic, public, school, and special libraries.

ACADEMIC LIBRARIES

633 Kelly Brewin, C. "An American librarian in Kuwait." *College & Research Libraries News* 52, no. 4 (April 1991): 226-228.

First published in *Louisiana Library Association (LLA) Bulletin* 53, no. 3 (Winter 1991), this paper briefly describes experiences and achievements at Kuwait University Libraries as part of a task force of five U.S. librarians recruited to assist in upgrading library services and automating library functions.

AUTOMATION

634 Khalid, Farooq A. "Automation in a special library in Kuwait." *Information Technology and Libraries* 2, no. 4 (December 1983): 351-363.

This paper traces the introduction of automation in the National Scientific and Technical Information Center (NSTIC) of the Kuwait Institute for Scientific Research. The growth from a modest remote batch-mode environment to online applications in both English and Arabic are highlighted. Provided is a brief discussion of the systems designed and developed by NSTIC, which include the bibliographic control programs, the circulation control system, KWOC indexes and online databases of NSTIC's English and Arabic collections. The use of STAIRS for an integrated database approach for library automation is envisaged.

BIBLIOMETRIC STUDIES

635 al-Kharafi, Faiza, Nizar El Rayyes, and George Janini. "Science research in Kuwait—a bibliometric analysis." *Journal of Information Science* 13, no. 1 (1987): 37-44.

Presents a review of the scientific output of the State of Kuwait on the occasion of the 25th anniversary of its independence. Prior to 1970, only about 100 publications were credited to Kuwaiti institutions. The majority of these papers were medical reports published in local journals. In contrast, the 1970s and 1980s witnessed a steady growth with an average doubling time of three years. In 1983, 185 publications were credited to Kuwaiti institutions, and 80% of these appeared in international journals. This represents 1.1 articles per 10000 populations, a respectable figure in comparison to Third World standards. While Third World countries put more emphasis on research in the life sciences, the distribution of research publications of Kuwait closely match that of the World's scientific publications as a whole as seen from the Science Citation Index. 59% of all Kuwaiti authored articles are in the life sciences as against 55% of the international literature. 62.6% of Kuwaiti publications appeared in journals with impact factors ranging from 0- <1 as against 46.6% of the international literature, and 3.3% of Kuwaiti publications appeared in journals with impact factor > 4 as against 6.5% of the international literature. Furthermore, 43% of Kuwaiti publications were not cited at all as against 25% of the international literature, and Kuwaiti publications averaged 1.8 citations per publication over a 5 year period as against a world average of 4.8 and a Latin American average of 2.9. Overall, the average citedness of papers published from Kuwait comes close to matching that of India, but is inferior in comparison with the standards set by the scientifically advanced co tries. On the positive side Kuwaiti science appears to be steadily improving. [A]

CENSORSHIP

636 Alqudsi-Ghabra, Taghreed M. "Information control in Kuwait: dialectic to democracy." *Journal of South Asian and Middle Eastern Studies* 18 (Summer 1995): 58-74.

Explores the nature, characteristics, and mechanisms of press censorship in Kuwait before and after the 1990-1991 Arabian Gulf crisis.

GULF WAR AND INFORMATION SERVICES

637 Abdel-Motey, Yaser Y., and Nahla A. Hmood. "Librarianship in Kuwait after the Gulf War." *DOMES: Digest of Middle East Studies* 2, no. 1 (1993): 40-49.

Based on an earlier article which appeared in *Journal of Information Science*, vol. 18, no. 6 (1992), pp. 441-446, under the title: "An overview of the impact of the Iraqi aggression on libraries, information and education for librarianship in Kuwait." A general view of the field of librarianship in Kuwait is presented with special emphasis on the impact of Iraqi aggression on libraries and information centers in the country. First, a review of the Central Library of Kuwait, school, public, academic and central libraries and their future plans, is presented, followed by a summary of the effect of the Iraqi occupation on education in library and information science.

638 Aman, Mohammed M. "Damage to Kuwait's information and library services: report of October 1991 visit." *Bulletin of the American Society for Information Science* 18, no. 4 (April-May 1992): 24-25.

639 Muhammed, Abdulbasit Abduljaleel. *The Uses of Mass Communication Under a Crisis Situation: A Comparative Study of Kuwaiti's Utilization of Information Sources Before and During the Iraqi Occupation of Kuwait*. Ph.D., University of Oregon, 1994. 192 p.

This study investigates the impact of the Iraqi invasion of Kuwait upon the communication habits of Kuwaiti civilians under occupation. The way Kuwaiti families utilized official media channels during the normal times prior to the occupation is compared to their use of available information sources following the sudden Iraqi invasion of Kuwait. The study examines a crisis situation in which word of mouth/rumor plays an important role as an information source. The uses and gratifications approach to the study of mass communication (asking what people do with media rather than what media do to people) is utilized as part of the theoretical framework. The ideological function of news is considered in addition. Personal interviews were conducted with sixteen Kuwaiti families who were in Kuwait from the first day of the invasion until liberation day. In addition to collection of demographic information, the interviews solicited families' pre-invasion and occupation patterns of media usage. Findings indicate that crisis situations seem to level out former usage differences associated with gender, age and education. Also people appear to reject media whose ideological bias differs greatly from their own or whose interpretation of events differs from the people's direct experiences. In times of crisis rumor becomes an increasingly important source of information, however inaccurate that information turns out to be, because people are living in a state of fear and desperately hoping for positive change. Further studies are needed to verify these preliminary findings because of the small selected sample studied. [DAI 55/11-A: 3342.]

640 Salem, Shawky. "Inside the Gulf crisis: destruction and looting in Kuwait." *Information Development* 7, no. 2 (April 1991): 70-71.

Provides a brief personal account of the destruction and looting of library and information facilities in Kuwait during the Iraqi invasion.

641 Salem, Shawky. "Tables and photos on the Iraqi aggression to the library and information infrastructure in Kuwait." *Journal of Information Science* 18, no. 6 (1992): 425-440.

Part of a special issue devoted to library and information services in the Arab countries after the Gulf War. In this paper the tables and photos clearly show the effects of the Iraqi aggression on the Library and Information Infrastructure in Kuwait in different sectors such as university libraries, special libraries, school libraries, the destroyed and missing collections, equipment, furniture and manpower as well (Kuwaiti nationals as well as foreigners). The tables give detailed figures about the catastrophe and the photos reflect the actual situation. [A]

INFORMATION SERVICES—SPECIAL SUBJECTS

642 Salem, Shawky. "The impact of the Gulf crisis on business information." In *Proceedings of the 14th International Online Information Meeting, London, 11-13 December, 1990.* Edited by David Raitt, pp. 507-514. Oxford and New Jersey: Learned Information Ltd., 1990.

The lack of statistics, descriptive data and accurate and extensive surveys is a major problem facing the Arab planner in the field of information. Kuwait is considered a pioneer in the region and is leading the information revolution there. Although the country is small the movement of library information and computer activities is more developed than in any other part in the Arab region. The main educational organizations in Kuwait are: Kuwait University (KU); Kuwait Institute for Scientific Research (KSIR); General Organisation for Applied Education and

Training (GOAET); Kuwait Foundation for the Advancement of Science (KUFAS); National computer and Microform Centre (NCMC). [A]

INFORMATION STORAGE AND RETRIEVAL

643 Choudhury, M. H., M. A. Shah, and M. T. Bojanczyk. "PC-based research-oriented clinical information system: a case study of Kuwait." *Medical Informatics* 16, no. 4 (October-December 1991): 323-329.

Describes the design and application of a clinical information system (CIS) in a tertiary care facility (Kuwait Center for Cancer Control) using low-cost microcomputers (personal computers). The facility focuses on the collection and use of clinical information for prospective application in clinical trials, individual therapy and research. In order to meet this requirement the patient treatment and follow-up system (PTFS) was developed, based on recent database management technology. The exercise demonstrates that low-cost microcomputer systems can be used effectively in meeting the clinical management information and research needs of care facilities. It is anticipated that the application of the system will be replicated on other health care facilities. [A]

644 Salem, Shawky. "The design of a microfilm information system for a petroleum well file." *Microdoc* 18, no. 2 (1979): 35-36, 38-40, 42, 44.

The Ministry of Oil, Kuwait, holds a number of documents providing information on oil well operations. Although the statistical data of these documents is stored and analyzed on computer, it was decided that microfilming the original documents would provide a means of storing and preserving documents, unify the system of handling the well file in oil companies and enable the distribution of well files to oil companies in Kuwait. Describes the organization of documents into subject categories, the use made of flash cards on the microfilm and the frame reference used to correspond to code numbers used for detailed indexing. Provides a brief description of microfilm equipment and operations. [A]

645 al-Turkait, Adla A., Sabika A. Bin Naser, and M. I. Ismail. "The handicapped in Kuwait and the role of the Internet." In *Proceedings of the 18th International Online Information Meeting, London, 6-8 December, 1994*. Edited by David I. Raitt and Ben Jeapes, pp. 121-129. Oxford and New Jersey: Learned Information Ltd., 1994.

The benefits to the handicapped from information stems available in Kuwaiti libraries are highlighted with reference to advanced information systems such as the Internet and the online services. There are several non-governmental (NGO) institutes in Kuwait which care for various classes of handicapped persons. The number of handicapped increased as a result of the August 1990 invasion of Kuwait. Moreover, all the infrastructure was destroyed. Most of the library and information systems have now been rehabilitated. Handicapped people suffered more than others, particularly in the loss of information resources. Handicapped people have the attention of several ministries such as the Ministry Social Affairs, the Ministry of Education, the Ministry of Health and others. Several NGO's are interested in providing information services to handicapped persons in Kuwait. Electronic information retrieval from the Internet and online are used to help the handicapped in Kuwait. Online and Internet are reliable sources for quality information for the handicapped, as well as for decision-makers in governmental and NGO agencies. Certain CD-ROMs are also of potential interest to the handicapped in Kuwait. E-mail, currently used widely in various sectors, will dominate and serve a large number of users in Kuwait in the near future, with the support of the Kuwaiti government. There is a society in Kuwait which cares for handicapped people and supports them in governmental and private institutions. Most libraries and information centers concerned with the handicapped in Kuwait are aiming at quality information services from online and the Internet. [A]

646 al-Turkait, Adla A., M. I. Ismail, and Sabika A. Bin Naser. "Online and Kuwait." In *Proceedings of the 15th National Online Meeting, New York, 10-12 May, 1994*. Edited by Martha E. Williams, pp. 29-31. Medford, N.J.: Learned Information, Inc., 1994.

The objective of this article is to focus on the online database use in Kuwait before and post the Gulf War. In the 1980's the online services were introduced to the users in Kuwait University as well as to the other users in public organizations such as The Public Authority for Applied Education and Training and some oil companies in Kuwait. The paper says that online services in Kuwait are now better than before the invasion but better use of online or CD-ROM searching is necessary for development. [A]

LIBRARY EDUCATION

647 Abdel-Motey, Yaser Y. "A glimpse of library education in Kuwait." *Journal of Education for Library and Information Science* 36, no. 4 (Winter 1995): 353-355.

Briefly reviews the state of professional education in library and information science in Kuwait with a list of courses and their distribution. Concludes with the hope that, in the near future, a comprehensive library education program will be available in Kuwait, beginning with the associate's degree program at the Public Authority for Applied Education and Training and continuing to the master's level at Kuwait University.

648 Hague, Howard. "Medical librarianship course, Kuwait, March-April 1984." *Health Libraries Review* 1, no. 2 (1984): 114-116.

Describes the health care system in Kuwait and the recent planning for the development of hospital library services and training of staff some of whom were already working in health care libraries. Discusses the provision of a wide range of postgraduate and continuing education courses and the heavy use of facilities. Suggests that practical work is an essential part of this course and gives examples of topics covered during the sessions. Discusses the project and visits to other libraries. Stresses the need for the continuing education of library staff and the provision of a firm base for the future development of good hospital library services in Kuwait. [A]

649 al-Khabbaz, Ali Fakher. *Assessment of the Undergraduate Library and Information Science Program in the College of Basic Education in the State of Kuwait Through the Development and Application of Global Standards: A Case Study*. Ph.D., 1996. Florida State University. 360 p.

The purpose of the first stage of this study was to formulate global standards for undergraduate library and information science programs in the developing countries. This was accomplished by surveying an international panel of 64 individuals in 39 countries who were expert in education for library and information specialists. Fifty (78%) usable questionnaires from 34 countries were returned. The questionnaires contained 147 proposed statements grouped in 14 standards covering locus, goals, general and specific objectives, administration, financial support, physical facilities, library, faculty, staff, curriculum, continuing education, admission of students, and completion requirements. Of the 147 statements, 123 (83.7%) obtained a mean score of 4.0 or higher, allowing them to be accepted as standards. These standards were then used in the second stage of the study to determine the current status of the Library and Information Science program at the College of Basic Education in Kuwait, the adequacy of the library and information science curriculum in that program, and how the program deals with new developments in the field. A case study methodology was selected for the second stage. Research data were collected on site through document examination, interviews, and observation. According to the study findings, the Library and Information Science program met only two of the 14 standards: Locus and Completion Requirements. The number and content of the courses in the curriculum were not sufficient to graduate qualified librarians. The curriculum lacks topics that deal with specialization and information technology. The curriculum content is old and out of date and does not conform to the modern approach to library and information sciences. [DAI 57/08-A: 3308.]

650 Stockham, Kenneth A. *The Establishment of a Two-Years Course in Library and Information Studies: A Report to the Ministry of Education in Kuwait*. Kuwait: Ministry of Education, 1977, 19 p. table. bibliog.

The purpose of the report is to identify the educational needs of middle manpower in Kuwait libraries, with particular reference to school and public libraries. Middle manpower is defined as staff with library duties falling between the professional librarian's and the clerk's (i.e., the assistant librarian or library technician). With many of the basic decisions already taken the report is concerned with the staffing of the course and the development of a basic curriculum.

PERSONNEL

651 al-Ansari, Husain A. *A Study of Supply and Demand of Library and Information Workers in Kuwait: Five-Year Projections and Recommendations for Human Resources Planning*. Ph.D., 1992. Florida State University. 208 p.

The purpose of this study was to investigate the current status of library and information workers in Kuwait after the Iraqi invasion, to project future manpower requirements for the next five years (1997), and to propose recommendations for the future. Data were collected with (a) a questionnaire sent to respondents in five types of library and information centers and (b) interviews with key officials, head librarians, and directors of libraries and information centers. A manpower forecasting model was used to generate the projections. The findings of the study indicate that the current supply of library and information workers in Kuwait is deficient in number and necessary skills. The majority of library and information center staff are paraprofessionals. The study projects the manpower requirements for five types of library and information centers at three levels: high, middle, and low projections. According to the study findings, the shortage of library and information workers in Kuwait is very real and will increase sharply by 1997. To address this shortage a number of changes should occur: (a) The level of library and information science education should improve; (b) Current staff should be given intensive training; (c) Salaries and incentives should be improved; (d) Work conditions and environment should be improved; (e) Professionals and subject specialists from other fields should be recruited; (f) A national committee should be established for information manpower planning. [DAI 53/10-A: 3399.]

652 al-Ansari, Husain A., and Charles William Conaway. "Projections of library and information workers in Kuwait in its post-war development." *Technical Services Quarterly* 13, no. 2 (1996): 25-39.

During the invasion of Kuwait by Iraqi troops in August 1990, the libraries of the University of Kuwait and the public and school libraries were looted or destroyed. Manpower is the key element in the rebuilding and sustained development of the information infrastructure of Kuwait. This article describes a study conducted to survey and assess Kuwait's current and future needs in an effort to rebuild the infrastructure of Kuwait's libraries. The purpose, methodology and findings of the study are described and recommendations for meeting future personnel needs are given. [A]

653 al-Hassan, S., and A. Jack Meadows. "Improving library personnel management." *Library Management* 15, no. 1 (1994): 19-25.

An investigation of personnel management in Kuwait libraries prior to the Gulf War showed that serious problems existed in most libraries. A further study was carried out to try to define actions which might help to alleviate these problems. A soft systems methodology was used for the first time in this context and subsequent discussion of the study with senior library management was delayed by the advent of the Gulf War. However, the changed conditions in Kuwait brought about by the war are found to have imparted particular significant to the conclusions and to their implementation. [A]

SCHOOL/CHILDREN'S LIBRARIES

654 Ali, Abdulrazzaq Hussain. *A Comparative Study of the Perceptions of the School Library Media Specialist's Role as Perceived by Principals, Teachers, and School Library Media Specialists in Public Schools in the State of Kuwait*. Ph.D., 1997. Florida State University. 160 p.

The purpose of this study was to investigate the divergence and congruence in the role perceptions of the school library media specialists (SLMS) held by principals, teachers, and SLMS at elementary, intermediate, and secondary school levels in the State of Kuwait. Another attempt of the study was to determine whether differences in role perceptions of the SLMS occurred among SLMS at different education levels and different school levels. An attitude questionnaire developed for studying media specialists' perceptions of role was used in this study. On a five point Likert-type scale, respondents were asked to indicate their strength of agreement or disagreement with the way things really are in their school library media centers. The questionnaire was handed to a sample of 600 respondents and a total of 83% response rate was obtained. The Statistical Package for the Social Sciences (SPSS) computer program was used in this study. Factor analysis was performed and four factors emerged: Teaching/Instructional Consultant Role, Management Role, Traditional Role, and Media Role. T-tests and Levene's tests were performed to test for differences between groups and within the SLMS group. Findings indicated that there were no significant differences between teachers and principals as to their perceptions of role of the SLMS. Significant differences in perceptions were found between teachers and SLMS for the Teac/Instructional Role, and Management Role, and no significant differences were found between them for the Traditional Role and the Media Role. At the 0.05 level, role perceptions held by principals were statistically significant from the perceptions of SLMS for all roles except for the Traditional Role. No significant differences in perceptions were found among the SLMS themselves at different school levels. Also, no significant differences were found among SLMS of different education levels. Thorough analysis of Information Power (1988), revealed that the guidelines identified and supported the Teaching/Instructional Role, the Management Role, and the Media Role that emerged in this study. [DAI 58/02-A: 329.]

655 al-Musalam, Muna Abdullah. *A Study of the Libraries in Girls' Credit Hour Secondary Schools in Kuwait*. Ph.D., 1988. University of Denver. 188 p.

The fostering of self-education is a major goal of Kuwait's Ministry of Education. In support of the philosophy, the new credit-hour high schools, established in 1979, were encouraged to use their libraries as active facilitators of independent study. Required courses in library and research methodology were established, and library research was built into regular credit-hour courses. Haidar's previous 1974 study was of these libraries, however, revealed inherent difficulties in their potential as modern educational centers. These included inadequate facilities and services and poor integration with existing curricula. No recent study has analyzed the current ability of school libraries to support the new curriculum. Four research questions were specified: (1) What is the current typical physical layout of Kuwait's credit-hour school libraries? (2) To what extent does the credit-hour high school curriculum interact with the school library program? (3) How do the librarians perceive their roles in the schools? (4) How do the librarians describe their preferred roles? The subjects of this study were the population of head teachers (116) and librarians (21) working in Kuwait's eight credit-hour secondary schools for girls. Three instruments were used to collect data: (1) an observation guide used by the researcher to record the physical layout and contents of each library; (2) an interview protocol for the head teachers; and (3) a librarians' questionnaire to determine their actual activities and the differences, if any, from those they would prefer. This questionnaire, developed by Veronica Cooper, was pre-tested in a pilot study conducted in Kuwait in April 1988. The study revealed that although the typical physical layout of the libraries has changed, it remains far from ideal. Most libraries still need more space, and better organization, as well as additional equipment, books, and materials. Existing conditions hinder complete utilization of the libraries by students and teachers. The majority of the head teachers interviewed expressed serious complaints about library deficiencies in their subject areas. They made many recommendations for improvements in library materials and services. Librarians want improvements in each of their eight official areas of duty as well as recognition or reward for their skills and services. [DAI 49/12-A: 3596.]

656 Zehery, Mohamed. H. "School libraries in Kuwait: before and after the Gulf War." In *Information and Libraries in the Arab World*. Compiled and edited by Michael Wise and Anthony Olden, pp. 131-139. London: Library Association Publishing, 1994. [Information and libraries in the developing world, vol. 3.]

Article included in a collection of papers presenting a comparative review of librarianship and library practices in Arab countries. Traces the development of school libraries in Kuwait, before and after the Gulf War, with statistics for different types of school library. Concludes that the Kuwait school library system has made remarkable progress in support of the country's educational system and has exceeded the achievements of the public libraries.

SPECIAL LIBRARIES

657 Dessouky, Ibtesam A. "Libraries in Kuwaiti financial institutions: their functions and potentials." *Special Libraries* 76, no. 3 (Summer 1985): 198-203.

The purpose of this study is to examine the expanding role of libraries and information centers in Kuwait's financial institutions, to explain their potential and prospects in a changing financial and technological world. This study illustrates how a particular class of special libraries is striving to grow in a developing country with immense financial resources. The role of information in financial institutions in Kuwait are studied.

658 Salem, Shawky. "Arab Center for Medical Literature." *Journal of Information Science* 14, no. 1 (1988): 57-58.

Provides a description of the Arab Center for Medical Literature and its structure, objectives, and activities.

659 Sullivan, Marilyn Gorman, and Patrick W. Brennen. "Medical library services in Kuwait: history and future prospects." *Bulletin of the Medical Library Association* 72, no. 1 (January 1984): 12-17.

Despite immense resources and a growing interest in education and libraries, library development in Kuwait has been restricted by the problems common to all developing countries. These include an overdose of bureaucracy, lack of trained librarians, and little perception of the library's importance in the educational system. Medical librarianship is virtually a new field. The only medical library of any significance in the country is the Faculty of Medicine Library established in 1974 to serve the newly organized Faculty of Medicine of Kuwait University. In recent years, the Faculty of Medicine Library has gone through several reassessments and many changes. It has expanded its collection, begun computerized searching, and recruited several professional librarians. Now semiautonomous from the university's Libraries Department and housed in a new, modern building, the library has the potential to become the main medical library in the Persian Gulf area. [A]

USER TRAINING

660 Ismail, M. I., Adla A. al-Turkait, and S. B. Naser. "Internet training and utilization by young researchers and creative students in Kuwait." In *Proceedings of the 17th National Online Meeting, New York, 14-16 May, 1996*. Edited by Martha E. Williams, pp. 167-173. Medford, N.J.: Information Today, Inc., 1996.

The objective of this work is to present the state of the art of training of young researchers and creative children and Internet utilization for retrieval of useful data. In Kuwait training on the use of Internet, e.g. International Gulf Net "SPRINT" and Kuwait Gulf Net. Other non-governmental organizations offer the training on the Internet at nominal cost or even for free. The awareness of the importance of the Internet is at its highest level in Kuwait compared to other Developing Countries. Young researchers are motivated by the quality achievement of research programs when they share their plans and research data with experts in the field. The project of common interest is proposed by the volunteer professor(s) for joining and sharing its objectives with the young researchers. Simple and accelerated research tools are proposed for achievement of the results needed to satisfy the pre-set objective(s) of the selected research project. Several examples from both social and applied fields are discussed and detailed data are presented. Refereed publications on the topic are presented with focus on volunteer programs from Kuwait and with author's contribution.

CHAPTER 10

LEBANON

GENERAL

661 Hashim, Mud Ustfan. "al-Maktabat al-Lubnaniyah: waqi' marir wa afaq mahdudah." *al-Jadid fi 'Alam al-Kutub wa-al-Maktabat*, no. 4 (Fall 1994): 49-55.

The research is based on a survey undertaken by the Lebanese Library Association, which covered 490 libraries in Lebanon. The author discusses the different types of libraries, their geographical distribution and the problems faced by the Lebanese libraries. She concludes that the government should take the initiative to promote library services.

662 Naaman, Aida Salman. "Lebanon." In *World Encyclopedia of Library and Information Services*. 3rd ed. (pp. 352-353). Chicago: American Library Association, 1993.

Discusses the history of libraries and library education in the country and gives a description of its national, academic, public, school, and special libraries.

663 Vernon, Elizabeth. "Librarianship in Lebanon in the post-civil war period." *Third World Libraries* 4, no. 2 (Spring 1994): 36-41.

Describes how Lebanese librarians coped with the impact of the civil war (1975-1991) and their post war efforts to rebuild the library infrastructure. Despite damage from bombing, triple digit inflation, and staff shortages, many libraries functioned throughout the conflict. Describes new library initiatives at the American University of Beirut, Lebanese American University (formerly Beirut University College), the Lebanese University, the national archives, and the Lebanese Library Association.

ACADEMIC LIBRARIES

664 Fustukjian, Samuel. "American University of Beirut." *College & Research Libraries News* 45 (April 1984): 172-174.

Describes the scope and functions of the American University of Beirut Library, acclaimed for the unique character and quality of its collections, and how it functions in war-ravaged Lebanon. Maintains that the conflict has had a profound effect on staff, students, and the library. Discusses observations concerning difficulties experienced by staff: collection losses, censorship, library hours, privileges for non-university users, and annual leave. Expresses doubt about re-opening of the university which was closed during the recent Beirut crisis.

665 Khalaf, Nadim, and John Rubeiz. "Economics of American University of Beirut library." *Libri* 28 (March 1978): 58-82.

Attempts to analyze the main determinants of library costs in order to estimate future financial needs and develop guidelines for allocating resources at the American University of Beirut Library. According to the authors, the methodology used and some of the statistical findings and conclusions may contribute to a better understanding of library economics, and provide insight into the operations of comparable institutions.

COPYRIGHT/INTELLECTUAL PROPERTY

666 Maktab Juzif Mughayzil. "al-Milkiyah al-adabiyah wa-al-faniyah fi Lubnan." *'Alam al-Kutub* 2, no. 4 (January-February 1982): 666-670.

GOVERNMENT PUBLICATIONS

667 'Abd al-Samad, Nasib. *al-Watha'iq al-Lubnaniyah bi al-Mikrufilm*. Bayrut: Muassassat al-Mahfuzat al-Wataniyah, 1982.

INDEXING AND ABSTRACTING SERVICES

668 Ali, Syed Nazim. "Arabic periodical indexing." *Outlook on Research Libraries* 9 (April 1987): 9-11.

Prior to 1981 there was virtually no indexing services, available in the Arabic language, exclusively for Arabic periodicals. The Lebanese service, *Al-Fihrist*, was launched in 1981 and currently indexes 216 periodicals from 21 countries (5 non-Arabic speaking). Saudi Arabia and Iraqi periodicals are indexed heavily with the next group being Egypt and Lebanon.

669 Hashim, Mud Ustfan. "Dabt muhtawa al-suhuf al-lubnaniyah: tajribat markaz al-tawthiq wa-al-buhuth al-Lubnani." *al-Majallah al-'Arabiyah lil-Ma'lumat* 5, no. 2 (1984): 235-240.

An assessment of the trilingual index, covering newspapers, published by the Lebanese Documentation and Research Center.

LIBRARIES—DIRECTORIES

670 Jam'iyyat al-Maktabat al-Lubnaniyah. *Dalil al-Maktabat wa-Marakiz al-Ma'lumat fi Lubnan*. Bayrut: Jam'iyyat al-Maktabat al-Lubnaniyah, 1995.

LIBRARY EDUCATION

671 Muhyiddin, Hassanah. "Haykaliyyat al-takhassus fi 'ilm al-ma'lumat fi Lubnan: waqi' wa-afaq." *al-Majallah al-'Arabiyah lil-Ma'lumat* 15, no. 2 (1994): 5-29.

PUBLISHING

672 Atiyeh, George N. "The book in the modern Arab world: the cases of Lebanon and Egypt." In *The Book in the Islamic World: The Written Word and Communication in the Middle East*. Edited by George N. Atiyeh, pp. 233-254. Albany: State University of New York Press, 1995.

A paper originally presented at a conference held at the Library of Congress, Washington, D.C., November 8-9, 1990. The author surveys the history of book publishing in the modern Arab world, describing the general attributes of book production and dissemination, and the prevalent trends that characterized the different periods of the last two centuries.

673 Thoumy, Aimee Salim. *University Publishing in Lebanon: A Historical and Comparative Study of the Publishing Programs of the Five Universities in Lebanon*. Ph.D., 1981. Indiana University. 175 p.

The purpose of this study was to survey university publishing in Lebanon. Five universities of different backgrounds are established in the country, the American University of Beirut, the University of Saint Joseph, the University of the Holy Spirit at Kaslik, the Lebanese University, and the Beirut Arab University. The study was intended to investigate the publishing program of each university and to examine the publications to determine the lines along which the publishing programs developed. Seven hypotheses were proposed to guide the study. They addressed particularly the relationship of the university publishing program to the governing body of the university, the policies concerning the number of titles published, the language and subject areas covered by the publications, and the policies and procedures for selecting manuscripts for publication. They also addressed the relationship of university publications to the scholarly activities of the faculty members, and to the total book production of the country. It was found that the publishing programs of the five universities developed in distinct ways rather than in any uniform pattern. Each program reflected the interests of the university from which it emanated. Several factors affected the growth and development of the publishing programs. Some of these were external, such as the political and economic environment of the country. Others were internal, related to the attitude of the universities toward their programs. The number of titles published by the universities fluctuated considerably. Their publications are small compared to the number of titles issued by Lebanese general publishers. University publications provided only a partial outlet for the scholarly publication activities of faculty members. In regard to subject fields of publications, it was found that the universities published in a wide variety of fields. Some fields were of special interest because of their regional character. [DAI 42/12-A: 4964.]

674 Thoumy, Aimee Salim. "University publishing in Lebanon." *Scholarly Publishing* 13 (July 1982): 355-362.

Discusses the publishing programs of the five universities in Lebanon. Each program was developed in a different way and reflected the interests of the university from which it emanated.

CHAPTER 11

LIBYA

GENERAL

675 Colvin, Peter. "Organizing a library in Libya." *Focus on International & Comparative Librarianship* 9, no. 2 (1978): 17-19.

The author, in 1977, helped to establish a library of books on Islam and the Islamic world at the Department of Antiquities of the Libyan Ministry of Culture, at the Castello, Tripoli. Catalogs were planned in both Arabic and Roman scripts, but shortage of time, equipment and personnel allowed only one author entry card for each item to be produced, with added title and author entries. The classification scheme was drawn up by the author in parallel Arabic and English texts, based on the books in the collection. Explains certain difficulties encountered, e.g. in the integration of classical and modern subjects in one sequence. Suggests that such 'coarse librarianship' could become a useful branch of the art for use in the developing world, although few countries are like Libya in having a paucity of people and skills but no shortage of money.

676 Fannoush, Mohammed Omar, and Ahmed Mohammed Gallal. "Libraries in Republic of Libya." In *Encyclopedia of Library and Information Science*. Vol. 25 (pp. 241-247). New York: Marcel Dekker, Inc., 1978.

Topics discussed include: origins of libraries—national, university, public, special, school, and other libraries— national bibliography, and library education.

677 Gallal, Ahmed Mohammed. "Libya." In *World Encyclopedia of Library and Information Services*. 3rd ed. (pp. 516-517). Chicago: ALA, 1993.

Discusses the history of libraries in the country and gives a description of its national, academic, public, school, and special libraries.

678 el-Hush, Abu Bakr Mahmood, and Mebrooka Omer Meherik. *Hawla al-Maktabah wa-al-Kitab: Maqalat wa-Dirasat*. Tarabulus, Libya: al-Munsha'ah al-'Ammah lil-Nashr wa-al-Tawzi' wa-al-I'lan, 1986. 130 p.

679 Meherik, Mebrooka Omer, Abu Bakr Mahmood el-Hush, and Yunis Aziz Mohamed. "Libraries and library services in the Socialist People's Libyan Arab Jamahiriya." *International Library Review* 13, no. 1 (January 1981): 73-85.

The authors describe the current development of all types of libraries in Libya, and the ways in which the traditions of the country are being applied to their development.

680 al-Sharif, 'Abdullah M. "al-Tatawwur al-tarikhi lil-maktabat fi Libya min aqdam al-'usur." *al-Majallah al-'Arabiyah lil-Ma'lumat* 2, no. 2 (1980): 93-114.

A historical account of all types of libraries in Libya, covering ancient, medieval, and modern ages until the year 1950.

ACADEMIC LIBRARIES

681 Dukaly, Ali Mohammed, and Syed Iftekar Ali. "University libraries in Socialist People's Libyan Arab Jamahiriya: an introduction to Sebha university library." *Libri* 35, no. 2 (June 1985): 119.

A brief history of libraries in Libya is followed by a description of the library at Sebha University. The account includes details of book selection, classification and cataloging, staff and services, and publications. Problems hindering the development of Libyan university libraries are noted.

ARCHIVES

682 al-Sharif, 'Abdullah M. "al-Watha'iq al-tarikhiyah al-Libiyah wa-amakin tawajudiha dakhil al-Jamahiriyah al-'Arabiyah al-Libiyah al-Sha'biyah al-Ishtirakiyah." *al-Majallah al-'Arabiyah lil-Ma'lumat* 5, no. 2 (1984): 225-234.

Discusses the role of the different types of historical documents in Libya and their locations.

DATABASES

683 al-Janafawi, Ahmad Mustafa. "Bunuk al-ma'lumat wa-khadamatiha: tajribat al-Jamahiriyah." *Risalat al-Maktabah* 30, no. 2 (June 1995): 49-63.

The paper discusses the experience of Libya in using databank techniques and services. Emphasis is on marketing information and cooperation among different institutions.

INFORMATION SEEKING BEHAVIOR

684 Dawi, 'Ali 'Abd al-Rahman. *Manhajiyat al-Bahth al-Qanuni: Turuq I'dad al-Rasa'il al-Jami'iyah fi al-Qanun wa-al-Ta'liq 'ala al-Ahkam wa-Kitabat al-Istisharat wa-Istikhdam al-Maktabah al-Qanuniyah*. [Tripoli, Libya]: Majma' al-Fatih lil-Jami'at, 1989. 298 p.

LIBRARY EDUCATION

685 Dyab, Miftah Muhammad. "Library education in Libya." *Information Development* 13, no. 3 (September 1997): 142-4.

Briefly reviews the development of formal library and information science education at the Department of Library and Information Science, El-Fateh University, Libya (the country's first library school. Provides information on the educational programs, faculty members, curriculum development, information technology and material facilities of the library school. [A]

NETWORKS AND NETWORKING

686 Lind, P. "An information network project in Libyan industry: a critical review." *Information Technology for Development* 5, no. 4 (December 1990): 413-420.

The Secretariat for Strategic Industry in Libya, responsible for the development of the fast-growing non-oil industry sector, has launched an ambitious program to introduce personal computer-based information networks throughout the industry. The goals are twofold. First, to improve the possibilities of monitoring industry performance from the Secretariat's level; and secondly, to improve productivity in office work so that office personnel can be released and transferred to production in industry. The purpose of the paper is to discuss some of the opportunities and difficulties encountered in the first implementation phase of this project. The author has been involved in the project as an advisor to the Secretariat. [A]

PUBLIC LIBRARIES

687 'Azu, Majidah Hamid. "Dawr al-marakiz al-thaqafiyah wa-al-maktabat al-'ammah bi baladiyyat Tarablus fi taqdim al-thaqafah lil-tifl: dirasah midaniyah." *al-Majallah al-'Arabiyah lil-Ma'lumat* 15, no. 2 (1994): 110-132.

SCHOOL/CHILDREN'S LIBRARIES

688 el-Hush, Abu Bakr Mahmood. "al-Tifl wa-al-qira'ah wa-al-khidmah al-maktabiyah al-'ammah." *al-Majallah al-'Arabiyah lil-Ma'lumat* 11, no. 1 (1990): 7-15.

SERIALS

689 Ghani, Abdul. "Newspaper journalism in Libyan Jamahiriya: a review." *The Serials Librarian* 15, no. 1-2 (1988): 207-220.

The history of Arabic newspapers is outlined, and the beginning and development of Libyan newspaper journalism described. The article also discusses the publication policy under Colonel Muammar Al Gadhafi and sets out the theories put forward in his Green book. Includes a bibliography of current Libyan newspapers.

690 Ghani, Abdul. "Serials in the Libyan Jamahuriya, past and present." *The Serials Librarian* 20, no. 2-3 (1991): 151-176.

The article deals with serials publication and their acquisition and management of serials in libraries in the Great Socialist Peoples' Libyan Arab Jamahiriya. The introduction of printing and the earliest serials published in Arabic are detailed. Recent changes in government policies affecting general conditions in the country and expected changes in publication policies are discussed. Two lists containing serials published prior to 1975 and a third, consisting of current serials published under Green Book theories, are annexed.

CHAPTER 12

MAURITANIA

GENERAL

691 Diouwara, Oumar. "Mauritania." In *World Encyclopedia of Library and Information Services*. 3rd ed. (p. 545). Chicago: American Library Association, 1993.

Discusses the history of libraries and library education in the country and gives a description of its national, academic, public, school, and special libraries.

INFORMATION SYSTEMS

692 Thiam, Amadou Khoudiedji. *Geographic Information Systems and Remote Sensing Methods for Assessing and Monitoring Land Degradation in the Sahel Region: The Case of Southern Mauritania*. Ph.D., Clark University, 1988. 490 p.

MANUSCRIPTS

693 Heymowski, Adam. "En samkatalog over Mauretaniens arabiska handskrifter-ett forsta forsok." [A union catalogue of Arabic manuscripts of Mauritania.] *Tidskrift for Dokumentation* 37, no. 5-6 (1981): 115-118. [In Swedish.]

The first catalog of Arabic manuscripts by Mauritanian scholars may be considered a by-product of the author's first Unesco mission to Mauritania in 1964/65. During this mission the legal basis of a National Library in Nouakchott had to be created. During the two subsequent missions, in

1971 and 1975/76, a nationwide manuscript survey was officially included into the project concerning the development and organization of Mauritania's National Library. Thanks to this catalog, it is possible to divide the authors involved into roughly three categories: (1) scholars whose works are found in practically every part of the country (and most probably even outside Mauritania); (2) scholars of local importance whose fame seems to be limited to one of the provinces; and (3) scholars whose works have never reached beyond the tribe or family circle. In Mauritania, the catalog has already started playing the role of a bridge between the traditional culture and the new era represented by the National Library. [LISA]

CHAPTER 13

MOROCCO

GENERAL

694 Benjelloun-Laroui, Latifa. *Les Bibliotheques au Maroc* [The libraries of Morocco.] Paris: G.-P. Maisonneuve et Larose, 1990. xiv, 413 p.

This French publication constitutes the only major comprehensive volume on Moroccan libraries and the materials which they hold. It includes details of materials held in the libraries in Rabat, Tetouan, and the Al-Quairouan Mosque in Fez as well as in private libraries. Manuscripts, films, photographs, and archival materials are included.

695 Binebine, Ahmed-Chouqui. *Histoire des Bibliotheques au Maroc* [History of libraries in Morocco.] Rabat: Faculte des lettres et des sciences humaines, 1992. 255 p.

696 Hajji, M. "Jawlah fi maktabat al-Sahra' al-Maghribiyah." *al-Manahil*, no. 28 (December 1983): 8-20.

697 Ibn al-Khayat, Nazha. "Nazrah 'ala al-awda' al-rahinah lil-maktabat fi al-Mamlakah al-Maghribiyah." *al-Majallah al-'Arabiyah lil-Ma'lumat* 5, no. 1 (1984): 26-41.

698 Souad, Lola. "Morocco." In *World Encyclopedia of Library and Information Services*. 3rd ed. (pp. 585-586). Chicago: ALA, 1993.

Discusses the history of libraries and library education in the country and gives a description of its national, academic, public, school, and special libraries.

ARCHIVES

699 al-Mannuni, M. "'An al-khizanah al-malakiyah bi al-Maghrib." *Majallat al-I'lami*, no. 2 (April 1982): 121-143.

700 Schroeter, Daniel. "The Royal Palace archives of Rabat and the Makhzen in the 19th century." *Maghreb Review* 7, no. 1-2 (1982): 41-45.

After many years in storage the copious archives of the 19th-century Makhzen are now being placed on the shelves of the Royal Palace Library, and access to researchers made possible. Works on pre-colonial Morocco are often lacking in quantitative sources, or lack Moroccan sources altogether. These works provide much useful material, as shown in this article.

BIBLIOMETRIC STUDIES

701 Ouazani, H. E. "Questions sur la production culturelle au Maroc: lecture preliminaire du 'repertoire des ecrivains marocains membres de l'union des Ecrivains du Maroc'." [Issues concerning cultural production in Morocco: a preliminary reading of the 'directory of Moroccan writers who are members of the Moroccan Union of Writers'.] *Revue de la Science de l'Information* 1 (February 1995): 9-24.

DOCUMENTATION

702 Fihri, Ahmad Fasi. "al-Mustaqbal yaqtarin bi al-hadir." *al-Majallah al-'Arabiyah lil-Ma'lumat* 2, no. 1 (1980): 29-36.

The future of documentation in the Arab countries is elaborated, considering the Moroccan experience since 1968 when the National Documentation Center was established. The author concentrates on the modern techniques used in documentation.

INFORMATION SEEKING BEHAVIOR

703 Koenig, Luciana Marulli, and Michael E. D. Koenig. "Use of international documents in developing countries." *Unesco Journal of Information Science, Librarianship and Archives Administration* 5, no. 4 (October-December 1983): 211-220.

This paper is a summary of a survey carried out in three countries, Colombia, Malaysia, and Morocco, to determine the availability and utilization of the documentation produced by the organizations of the United Nations system.

INFORMATION SERVICES

704   Balkhayyat, Nazhah, and Safar Rijan. "Taswiq khadamat nuzum ma'lumat al-tanmiyah fi-Ifriqiyah wa-al-Maghrib al-'Arabi: dirasah muqaranah." *al-Majallah al-'Arabiyah lil-Ma'lumat* 13, no. 1 (1992): 46-63.

705   Clark, J. G., and V. S. Lai. "Internet comes to Morocco." *Communications of the ACM* 41, no. 2 (February 1998): 21-23.

The appearance of the Internet in the Kingdom of Morocco is described. Morocco is the most recent African country to enter cyberspace. Obstacles to achieving Internet service are considered, including major infrastructure complications and the fact that full Internet connectivity was nonexistent in Morocco. The role of Al-Akhawayn University in bringing the Internet to the country is discussed, and the university's four-stage plan for Internet connection is presented. The development of the service is addressed.

706   Johnson, Peggy. "Information for development: a model for the delivery of information in developing countries." *Quarterly Bulletin of the International Association of Agricultural Information Specialists* 39, no. 1-2 (1994): 76-80.

Paper presented at the IAALD International symposium on new information technologies in agriculture, Bonn, Germany, 10-12 November 1993. This paper analyzes the implementation of a CD-ROM database project at the Institut Agriculture et Veterinaire Hassan II (Rabat, Morocco) as a model for similar projects. Rather than a simple "how-to-do-it" report, this paper explores the broader concerns of training, sustainability, continuing linkages, and support through document delivery that must accompany all access to bibliographic databases in developing countries. The paper concludes with a list of recommendations to provide guidance for successful implementation of new information technologies for agricultural information in developing countries. [A]

INFORMATION STORAGE AND RETRIEVAL

707   al-Daly, 'Abd al-Baqi. "al-Nizam al-Maghribi lil-ma'lumat "Maghribnet": mahattah mumayyazah lil-ta'awun al-'Arabi al-Urubbi." *al-Majallah al-'Arabiyah lil-Ma'lumat* 13, no. 1 (1992): 15-45.

708   Fihri, Ahmad Fasi. "al-Tajribah al-Maghribiyah li-maknanat al-mu'tayat al-bibliyughrafiyah." *al-Majallah al-'Arabiyah lil-Ma'lumat* 3, no. 1 (1983): 48-74.

The paper enumerates the activities and achievements of the Moroccan National Documentation Centre which was established in 1966.

709 Squalli, Hassan. "Presentation du projet de creation d'une banque maghrebine d'information industrielle." [Introduction to the plan for creating a Moroccan industrial information bank.] *Documentaliste* 15, no. 3 (July 1978): 27-31.

The data bank envisaged is initially limited to industrial information. The information available will be both bibliographic and informative, to cater for varying needs, and will cover business, procedures, economics and technical information. It will be supplied from literature searches and from specialist organizations. Following indexing and recording, information will be available through publication and by special request. A feasibility study envisages at least a year of preparatory work followed by a period of limited operation. After three years the bank will be linked to computer networks, including TYMSHARE, CYLADES and EURONET. The ultimate development of the bank will depend on an evaluation of its early effectiveness and cost. An appendix comprises an index to the full report on the conception of the project and the feasibility study.

INTERLIBRARY LOAN

710 Fihri, Ahmad Fasi. "Interlibrary loans in Morocco." In *Interlending and Document Supply for Developing Countries*. IFLA pre-session seminar, Paris, August 1989. Edited by Graham P. Cornish and Sara Gould, pp. 127-140. Boston Spa, West Yorkshire, England: IFLA, Program for Universal Availability of Publications, 1994.

Paper presented at Interlending and document supply for developing countries. IFLA Pre session Seminar, Paris, August 1989. Interlibrary lending has long been the most usual way of cooperating and sharing resources. Interlibrary loans require bibliographical tools and services, communication channels and an organizational framework. In Morocco there is no national code regulating interlibrary lending, and the practice is not widespread. There is some cooperation between university libraries. The General Library and Archives (Bibliotheque Generale et Archives) acts as a national library but does not make loans. The Center National De Documentation is working to implement a national information network, and set up an interloans system.

LIBRARY EDUCATION

711 Loughridge, Brendan. "Library and information science education in Morocco: observations on a recent visit to the 'Ecole des Sciences de l'information' and the 'Center National de Documentation' in Rabat." *Education for Information* 5, no. 1 (March 1987): 27-39.

The contribution of the Centre National de Documentation (CND) and the Ecole des Sciences de l'Information (ESI) in Rabat to the development of library and information services and the education of a professional workforce in Morocco is reviewed. The work of both institutions has to be seen in the context of national economic and social development planning in Morocco, with particular reference to the development of education and encouragement of science and technology research. Since the first national development plan of 1973-1977 much emphasis has been placed on the expansion of education at all levels and on vocational and professional education in particular. The CND's role in document collection and indexing, its publication of numerous indexes and bibliographies and its role in the development of a national information network are highlighted. ESI's three-year undergraduate program for information science and its two-year postgraduate program for information specialists are described. While the undergraduate program has expanded beyond projected numbers, the postgraduate program has not yet achieved the numbers estimated as necessary by CND. As funding from outside bodies decreases, efforts are being made to expand stafff development and research, including an agreement with the Department of Information Studies, University of Sheffield, United Kingdom. [A]

712   Loughridge, Brendan. "Library and information science education in Morocco: notes on a recent visit." *Journal of Education for Library and Information Science* 28, no. 1 (Summer 1987): 62-64.

Discusses formal education for professional library and information work in Morocco since the foundation in 1974 of the Ecole des Sciences et de l'Information (ESI), Rabat. Gives a brief history of the ESI and outlines its contact with the Center National de Documentation, responsible for the development of a central document collection and the production of appropriate bibliographical records and finding aids. Outlines details of courses run by the ESI leading to professional qualifications. [A]

713   Miski, Abdelhamid. *Prognosis of Academic Achievement in Library and Information Science in Morocco: Comparison of Examinatorial and Nonexaminatorial Prediction Models.* Ph.D., University of Pittsburgh, 1986. 144 p.

In regard to academic achievement in library and information science in Morocco, the objective of this study was to determine the predictability of two prediction models. The examinatorial model was based on a set of scores on ESI Entrance Examination, a costly, verbal ability, written and oral set of entrance tests of the national school of library and information science. The biographical model utilized a set of readily available, potential, cognitive and noncognitive predictors. The research was designed to compare the two models on three alternative criterion variables, overall grade point average (GPA) in all components of the curriculum, freshman year GPA in all components of the curriculum and overall GPA in the core curriculum, courses in library and information science. Data was analyzed for a three-year-plus-practicum undergraduate program and a two-year-plus-thesis graduate program. The sample consisted of all graduates of both programs on whom data was available; more than 70 per cent of the total population. Stepwise multiple regression was used to derive the predictive models which were cross-validated on the last class of each program. No conclusive findings were reached for the graduate program due, mainly, to small screening and calibration samples. For the undergraduate program, the biographical model consistently accounted for more variance, in each criterion variable, than did the examinatorial model. For the three criterion variables listed above, R('2)s of .22, .15 and .25 were arrived at through the utilization of the biographical model. The examinatorial model yielded R('2)s of .08, .06 and .09. The prediction in the biographical cross-validated model were found to be: standing on the high school diploma, major, marital status, age and work experience in information related fields. The testing of a supplementary cognate research question supported the conclusion that ESI Entrance Examination was not a predictor of academic achievement. The crude predictions which may be obtained by application of the biographical model should be complemented by other selection criteria. Further research is highly needed in this area to consolidate its theoretical base. DAI 47/10-A: 3600.

714 Mokhtari, M. "Library and information science education in Morocco: curriculum development and adaptation to change." *Journal of Education for Library and Information Science* 35 (Spring 1994): 159-66.

This paper describes the curriculum development and changes made by the Ecole des Sciences de l'Information, the main library school in Morocco, caused by the changing nature of library and information science and the environment as a whole.

MANUSCRIPTS

715 al-Mannuni, M. "Marakiz al-makhtutat wa adillatuha di al-Maghrib al-Aqsa." *Da'wat al-Haqq* 5 (1980): 21-26.

716 al-Mannuni, M. "al-Makhtutat al-Maghribiyah." *Az-Zaman al-Maghribi* 6-7 (1981): 125-140.

NETWORKS AND NETWORKING

717 Bennani, A. "Pour l'implantation d'un reseau d'information sur l'urbanisme et l'amenagement du territoire." [Towards the implementation of an information network on urban studies and regional management.] *Revue de la Science de l'Information*, no. 1 (February 1995): 47-62.

Presents a study on the establishment in Morocco of an information network on urban and national development through pre-existing information units. Provides a cost analysis of the operation. Results show that even if the material is relevant, there is not enough of it. Users prefer services to be nearby and to hold maps, plans, technical reports and periodicals with factual information. Explains how time may be cut by 56% and expenses by 45%. Such a project aims to ensure adequate knowledge transfer, initiate communication and promote public information. A coordination council is vital for keeping close contact between members of the network.

SERIALS

718 Bekkari, O. "Le periodique agricole au Maroc: production, diffusion et accessibilite." [The agricultural periodical in Morocco: production, distribution and access.] *Revue de la Science de l'Information*, no. 1 (February 1995): 11-29.

Discusses the problems of producing and distributing scientific and technical information. Publications in general, and periodicals in particular, closely reflect the scientific development of their country of origin. Evaluates the scientific development of the agricultural community in Morocco by analyzing characteristics of agricultural periodicals including production, distribution and access.

TRAINING, STAFF

719 Abid, Abdelaziz, and Mohamed Benjelloun. "La formation des specialistes de l'information au Maghreb et au Senegal." [The training of information specialists in Maghreb and Senegal.] *Bulletin des Bibliotheques de France* 30, no. 1 (1985): 62-67.

In developing countries with no official policy on information, and inadequate library infrastructures, provision for training information workers is inevitably rudimentary and ill-adapted to the real needs of the country. Outlines courses available at universities and librarianship schools in Algeria, Morocco, Senegal and Tunisia for technicians and professionals, giving details of course content and duration. The chief problem is lack of properly trained teaching personnel. The situation will not be improved, however, until the governments concerned become aware of the importance of information for economic and social development.

CHAPTER 14

OMAN

GENERAL

720   Karim, Bakri Musa A. "The emergence of libraries in the Sultanate of Oman." *International Library Review* 23 (September 1991): 229-236.

The purpose of this article is to report library developments that took place in the Sultanate of Oman during the seventies and eighties. Rapid social and economic development in Oman has not been matched by adequate improvements in library and information infrastructure. Still in their infancy, libraries in this country suffer from deficiencies in human and physical resources. There is no designated national library. Public libraries are few and appear to function within a rather limited scope. Academic libraries got off to a good start. The Sultan Qaboos University Library is in the front line and is likely to have considerable potential as a research library. Several special libraries exist mainly in government ministries and other government-supported institutions. These are also not yet fully developed and provide only limited services. School libraries are also deficient in resources. The dearth of qualified school librarians seems to be a major problem. The effort to collect ancient manuscripts is making steady progress with two libraries already set up. Education for librarianship has started in earnest. Thus, the first batch of locally-trained Omani professional librarians is due to graduate this year. [A]

721   Simons, Ian. "Oman." In *World Encyclopedia of Library and Information Services*. 3rd ed. (pp. 636-637). Chicago: ALA, 1993.

Discusses the history of libraries and library education in the country and gives a description of its national, academic, public, and school libraries.

ACADEMIC LIBRARIES

722   Varnet, Harvey. "Sultan Qaboos University in Oman." *College & Research Libraries News* 45, no. 4 (April 1984): 175-177.

Describes the geographical disposition of the Sultanate of Oman. Discusses plans to construct a modern, technologically-oriented university to be opened in autumn 1986. Outlines the process of hiring a library consultant to prepare a brief for a comprehensive and fully automated library, and the additional responsibility of overseeing the development of the Computer Centre, Centre for Educational Technology, the Medical Library and some aspects of the College of Education. Discusses further challenges to be met such as liaisoning with the architect and contractor, how to equip the university, staffing, education, and communication delays.

ARCHIVES

723   el-Mallah, Issam. "Archiving at the Oman Centre for Traditional Music, Muscat." *Phonographic Bulletin*, no. 55 (November 1989): 32-48.

Paper presented at the International Association of Sound Archives (IASA) Conference, Radio Sound Archives Committee Open Session, Oxford, 1989. Outlines the reasons for the lack of archives for traditional music in the Arabic countries. Describes the foundations of the Oman Centre for Traditional Music (OCTM) in 1985 the main goals of which are to preserve the heritage of musical culture of Oman and to extend the collection. Describes the design of the archiving system.

CD-ROM DATABASES INFORMATION SERVICES

724   Johnston, Colin S. "The development of CD-ROM provision at the Sultan Qaboos University in the Sultanate of Oman." *Program* 26, no. 2 (April 1992): 177-182.

High telecommunications costs caused the Sultan Qaboos University Library to consider CD-ROM as an alternative to online searching. Initially three titles were installed: AGRICOLA, ERIC, and MEDLINE: all from SilverPlatter Information Inc. Guidelines were drawn up for use by students on the principle that the service should be open to all, although students are encouraged to perform manual searches first as part of the educational process. Although a full online service has been given full approval, the feeling is that CD-ROM will continue to be used for the bulk of searches with online being used to top up a CD-ROM search. Future developments planned, including further CD-ROM titles and CD-ROM. [A]

725 Johnston, Colin S. "CD-ROM database quality: some observations based on experience at Sultan Qaboos University library." *Program* 28, no. 4 (October 1994): 379-394.

Over the past four years Sultan Qaboos University Library in Oman has increased its CD-ROM collection to 10 databases. It quickly became apparent to both the staff and end users that discs varied in quality. This paper reports results of a study to evaluate the quality of the indexes and abstracts in these CD-ROM databases. These revealed: variations in the availability of abstracts and descriptors, spelling mistakes, mis-typing or inconsistent policy on hyphenation; inconsistent indexing policy; and thesaurus quality. The paper presents specific examples of these errors and inconsistencies. It also reports differences between some CD-ROM databases and their printed and online counterparts in terms of: coverage and the selective indexing of periodical titles. Also the limitations of the search software on some CD-ROM products are highlighted. Few product reviews include comments on all these shortcomings although their effects can have significant impact on search results. [A]

CENSORSHIP

726 Gardner, Stanley A. "Censorship and librarianship in Oman." *Library Journal* 114, no. 19 (November 15, 1989): 54-56.

Describes the program of modernization embarked upon in 1975 by Sultan Qaboos in Oman which culminated in the opening of Sultan Qaboos University in September 1986. Discusses the setting up of an Audiovisual Media Library at the university and the very stringent checks to which choices of books and audiovisual materials were subjected by the Ministries of Information and National Heritage and Culture. The censorship procedure and the problems concerning lack of professional status and sexism which confront librarians are described. Stresses the conviction, based upon experience gained in Oman, that there should be no erosion of the basic right of every adult to choose his or her information sources.

LIBRARY EDUCATION

727 al-Mufaraji, Moosa N. "Libraries and library education in Oman." *Journal of Information Science* 18, no. 6 (1992): 471-479.

This article surveys the current status of librarianship in the Sultanate of Oman. Similar to any other developing country, Oman faces problems in librarianship, such as shortage of professional librarians, lack of well-equipped libraries, and the absence of a professional library organization. The article deals with the various types of existing libraries in the Sultanate, with emphasis on the Sultan Qaboos University Libraries, the largest in the country. The article also reviews the foundation of the librarianship and Documentation Department at Sultan Qaboos University and discusses other informal training programs for librarians. [A]

PUBLIC LIBRARIES

728   Shehadeh, Lilly. "I Oman er der kun en bibliotekar." [In Oman there is only one librarian.] *Bibliotek* 70, no. 6 (1982): 179-180. [In Dannish.]

Describes the library service in Oman. The National Islamic Library, Muscat, is the only public library at present. The 30,000 Arabic, 1,000 English and 3,000 children's books are being cataloged and classified according to the Dewey system. The books are for reference only at the moment. The country's only librarian is in charge of the manuscript collection and the development of the library in general. There are plans to develop a public library system on the basis of this library beginning with three branches in Nizwa, Salalah and Sohar. Describes the development of Oman since 1970. Many of the elite were born and educated abroad, including the office trained cataloger and the librarian. [LISA]

SPECIAL LIBRARIES

729   Bhatti, A. M., and S. M. Tariq. "The health system and medical information services in the Sultanate of Oman." *Health Libraries Review* 10, no. 1 (March 1993): 31-37.

Outlines the geographic, social and economic background of the Sultanate of Oman and describes its health care system and the role of the ministry of health and of Sultan Qaboos university in the development of health information services. Recommends the establishment of a consortium of biomedical libraries with the co-operation of the ministry, the university and the regional office of the World Health Organization to improve resource sharing and to provide a cost-effective document delivery system throughout the Gulf region. [A]

730   Woodward, A. M. *Development of Agricultural Library and Documentation Services in the Sultanate of Oman*. Report of a mission (25 April–11 May 1986). Rome: FAO, 1986. 22 p. (FAO Accession No. XF8878327.]

A report of a special Food and Agriculture Organization mission to Oman to advise on the setting up of libraries for the Ministry of Agriculture and with proposals for development of information services to the sector.

CHAPTER 15

PALESTINE

GENERAL

731 Abu-Ghush, 'Asma', and Mufid al-Sharif. "Waqi' al-khadamat al-maktabiyah fi maktabat al-mukhayyamat al-filastiniyah fi al-Diffah al-Gharbiyah." *Risalat al-Maktabah* 28, no. 3 (September 1993): 32-60.

The study describes the situation and services of the libraries in the camps of the West Bank. It discusses the problems and obstacles faced by the libraries under occupation.

732 al-'Asali, Kamil Jamil. *Ajdaduna fi Thara Bayt al-Maqdis*. 'Amman: Mu'assassat Al al-Bayt, 1981.

An account of Islamic tombs, funerary monuments, and cemeteries in Jerusalem, including material on several buildings which are now libraries, and on persons who founded them.

733 Chepesiuk, Ronald J. "Field trip to Palestinian libraries yields audience with Arafat." *American Libraries* 29 (January 1998): 40-42.

734 Majmu'ah min al-Maktabiyyin al-Mutakhassisin. *al-Maktabat fi Filastin: Dirasah Mashiyah Hawla Waqi' al-Maktabat wa-al-Maktabiyyin fi Filastin*. al-Quds: al-Majlis al-Thaqafi al-Baritani, 1996.

BIBLIOGRAPHIC CONTROL

735 al-Kharuf, Yunis Isma'il. "Adawat dabt al-intaj al-fikri al-filastini 1876-1986: dirasah wa-tahlil." *Risalat al-Maktabah* 30 (March 1995): 49-58.

Tools of bibliographic control of Palestinian intellectual heritage from the late 19th century to the present time are reviewed. The need to compile a national bibliography is stressed.

BIBLIOGRAPHIES

736   Albrecht, Lisa. "Bibliography: Jewish/ Palestinian Middle East peace perspectives." *Collection Building* 12, no. 1-2 (1993): 75-8.

CENSORSHIP

737   Berman, Sanford. "Israeli censorship, Palestinian rights, and antisemitism." In *Alternative Library Literature, 1990/1991: A Biennial Anthology*. Edited by Sanford Berman and James P. Danky, pp. 82-83. Jefferson, N.C.: McFarland & Company, Inc., Publishers, 1992.

738   Ismail, Noha. "Israeli censorship in the Occupied Territories." In *Alternative Library Literature, 1990/1991: A Biennial Anthology*. Edited by Sanford Berman and James P. Danky, pp. 79-81. Jefferson, N.C.: McFarland & Company, Inc., Publishers, 1992.

CHURCH LIBRARIES

739   Kusa, Vira, and Valiri Ruk. "Maktabat al-adyirah fi mantaqatay al-Quds wa Bayt Lahm: dirasat halah." *Risalat al-Maktabah* 29, no. 3 (September 1994): 65-94.

The paper describes monastery and church libraries in the Jerusalem and Bethlehem regions and shows the specificity and rarity of their collections. Fourteen libraries are covered.

DOCUMENTATION

740   Shbib, Samih. "al-Tawthiq wa-al-tawthiq al-Filastini." *Shu'un Filastiniyah*, nos. 146-147 (May-June 1985): 122-129.

741   Shbib, Samih. "al-Tawthiq wa-sultat al-isdar." *Shu'un Filastiniyah*, no. 160-161 (July-August 1986): 115-122.

INFORMATION SERVICES

742   Tamari, Salim. "Problems of social science research in Palestine: an overview." *Current Sociology* 42, no. 2 (Summer 1994): 68-86.

Identifies some current problems related to social science research in Palestine, focusing on the lack of a tradition and milieu of critical inquiry in the Palestinian academic context. Research efforts in Palestine are hampered by: an absence of a form wherein social scientists can exchange findings and discuss relevant issues, lack of a professional association, and the absence of a critical audience that can facilitate the development and accuracy of polemics. Also discussed are methodological obstacles, noting the lack of research facilities, i.e., major libraries, and the inaccessibility of official records. Several problems related to conducting survey research in Palestine are examined, and comments offered on the expansive industry that has grown up around commissioned reports and "packaged" research on Palestine. A listing of important Palestinian journals and bibliographies is offered, and it is suggested that more attention needs to be given to class formation, popular culture, Diaspora studies, and sociology of media. [A]

INFORMATION SYSTEMS

743   Harb, 'Afaf Ghassan. "Istikhdam al-hasub fi al-maktabat al-jami'iyah al-Filastiniyah li-iqamat shabakat ma'lumat bibliyughrafiyah wataniyah bi-istikhdam CDS/ISIS." *Risalat al-Maktabah* 28 (March-June 1993): 4-17.

The need for the development of a computer-based library system in Palestine's university libraries is stressed. The computerization of those libraries will solve problems such as library cooperation and networking. The author proposes the use of CDS/ISIS in all Palestinian libraries.

ISLAMIC LIBRARIES

744   Abu-Layl, Amin Sa'id. "al-Maktabat al-Islamiyah fi Bayt al-Maqdis." *Risalat al-Maktabah* 31, no. 2 (June 1996): 25-35.

A description of the Islamic and Arab libraries in Jerusalem, their status and a call to save these libraries in order to safeguard Arab culture.

745   al-'Asali, Kamil Jamil. "Dur al-kutub fi al-Quds." *al-Majallah al-'Arabiyah lil-Ma'lumat* 2, no. 1 (1980): 13-28.

The article deals with the old Islamic libraries in Jerusalem, their history and present status.

MANUSCRIPTS

746   al-'Asali, Kamil Jamil. "Athar al-Quds wa-makhtutatiha." *Shu'un 'Arabiyah*, no. 15 (May 1982): 304-309.

747   al-Munajjid, Salah al-Din. *al-Makhtutat al-'Arabiyah fi Filastin*. Bayrut: Dar al-Kitab al-Jadid, 1982.

Discusses manuscript collections in Jerusalem and Nablus.

PERSONNEL

748 Tuqan, 'Ali Muhammad Wasif. "al-Namat al-qiyadi li-mudiri wa-mudirat al-maktabat al-'ammah wa-al-jami'iyah fi al-Diffah al-Gharbiyah kama yatasawwaruhu al-'amilun fi hadhihi al-maktabat." *Risalat al-Maktabah* 29, no. 4 (December 1994): 26-49.

Discusses leadership pattern practiced in library work as viewed by public and university library employees in the West Bank.

749 Tuqan, 'Ali Muhammad Wasif. "Ittijahat al-'Amilin fi al-maktabat al-'ammah fi Filastin nahwa hawafiz al-'amal wa-ta'thiriha fi kafa'at al-ada'." *Risalat al-Maktabah* 32, no. 4 (December 1997): 53-70.

The author analyzes the effect of work incentives on the attitudes of public libraries' staff and their performance. He also suggests a number of recommendations.

PUBLIC LIBRARIES

750 Abul-Haj, Ghaleb. "Library services and political uprising in Eastern Jerusalem." *Yad La-Kore* 25, no. 1 (October 1990): 42-43.

Since the uprising, the East Jerusalem Public Library, branch of the Jerusalem Municipal Public Library Network has been fulfilling a triple mission: as a public library to all the Jerusalem Arab readers, as a school library to all the schools in East Jerusalem, and as a college library to hundreds of college students. This has necessitated an open book budget to enable the continuous addition of new books in all fields and of all standards, and increasing the number of staff to enable the opening of the branch libraries from the morning hours until late afternoons, to allow all concerned to use the library regardless of curfews or political disturbances. [LISA]

751 al-'Asali, Kamil Jamil. *Ma'ahid al-'Ilm fi Bayt al-Maqdis*. 'Amman: Jami'at al-Urdun, 1981.

A detailed account of private and public libraries in Jerusalem.

752 Schidorsky, Dov B. "The emergence of Jewish public libraries in nineteenth century Palestine." *Libri* 32, no. 1 (March 1982): 1-40.

Examines the development, in 19th century Palestine, of various types of public library: those which strove to gather and assemble the spiritual heritage of the Jewish people; libraries created for use by immigrants of the 1st *aliyah*; and those established to meet the educational needs of pupils and teachers. Discusses the growth of these libraries in their socio-historical context, traces their historical roots in Europe, and analyzes the factors which stimulated their establishment, as well as those which had a retarding effect on their development.

753 Schidorsky, Dov B. "Modernization and continuity in library development in Palestine under the British Mandate (1920-1948)." *Libri* 45, no. 1 (March 1995): 19-30.

This article examines Jewish public libraries during the British Mandate period (1920-1948), focusing on processes of modernization and change which were evident in (a) the development and the shaping of a Jewish national and university library, (b) the emergence of centralized library services for workers in rural and urban regions, (c) the voluntary provision of services to the urban population by municipalities, (d) the beginning of special library services in support of applied work and research activity, in the areas of agriculture, technology, and medicine, and (e) the beginnings of librarianship a profession. [A]

754 Schidorsky, Dov B., and Heinrich Loewe. "Heinrich Loewe's conception of the role of public libraries in Palestine." *Yad La-Kore* 18, no. 1-2 (January 1979): 90-101.

Loewe directed the Tel-Aviv municipal library network (1933-47), but his interest in Palestinian libraries dates to the turn of the century. Focuses on his conception of the role of public libraries in the spiritual and cultural development of the people. He advocated a centralized national system in which the national library would aid and supervise the development of local collections, suited to meet local needs. He emphasized the service aspects of public libraries-long opening hours, circulation and interlibrary loans, all geared towards making collections readily available to the public. Loewe was influenced in his thinking by developments in the Prussian library system, especially the trend toward centralization on the one hand, and the development of the multi-purpose Einheitsbibliothek on the other. [LISA]

755 Sever, Shmuel. "The Arab library in Israel." [pre-1967 boundaries.] *Library Quarterly* 49, no. 2 (April 1979): 163-181.

The Arab population of Israel has distinctive features. It belongs to the Arab world and culture but for more than a generation it was separated from the mainstream of Arab culture and from its own intellectual leadership who left Israel when Israel was established. Owing to the high birthrate of the Israeli Arabs, and the socio-cultural conditions prevailing in Israel the level of literacy of the Israeli Arabs is higher than that of other Arab populations. A rapid change in education has influenced reading and may influence library development in the Arab sector of Israel. Until the end of the seventies whatever library development had occurred in the

Arab sector had been initiated from outside by government or private Jewish organizations. Among Christian Arabs there may be signs of local initiative for library development, but this is still lacking in the Moslem communities. [A]

SCHOOL/CHILDREN'S LIBRARIES

756 Harb, 'Afaf Ghassan. *Dirasah Hawla Awda' al-Maktabat al-'Ammah wa-Maktabat al-Atfal fi al-Diffah al-Gharbiyah wa Qita' Ghazzah.* al-Quds: Maktab al-Yunicif, [1994].

757 MacMillan, S. "Books for children in Palestine." *Focus on International & Comparative Librarianship* 26, no. 3 (December 31, 1995): 132-135.

Describes a visit to Israel/Palestine to assess the libraries making bids for Welfare Association funding and to suggest ways in which they could be developed further. Discusses two exciting and innovative projects under way in the region; the Nablus Public Library program; and the Arab Children Friends Association project.

CHAPTER 16

QATAR

GENERAL

758 Farhan, Hamad Hasan. *Hawla al-Maktabat fi Qatar*. [Qatar]: H. H. al-Farhan, 1989. 204 p.

759 Khalifa, Sha'ban 'Abd al-'Aziz. "Libraries and librarianship in Qatar." *Journal of Information Science* 18, no. 6 (1992): 481-489.

Part of a special issue devoted to library and information services in the Arab countries after the Gulf War. The infrastructure of libraries and information centers in Qatar consists of a national library, 24 public libraries, 20 school libraries, 6 university libraries, 150 special libraries and 150 private collections. Statistics on the collections, man-power and services in these libraries are presented. Private libraries and library education in Qatar are discussed in detail, while curricula, courses and credits in library education are dealt with especially thoroughly. [A]

760 al-Nassr, Mohammad Hamad. "Qatar." In *World Encyclopedia of Library and Information Services*. 3rd ed. (p. 696). Chicago: ALA, 1993.

Discusses the history of libraries in the country and gives a description of its national, academic, public, school, and special libraries.

761 Rashid, Haseeb F. "Qatar library services: present problems and future prospects." *Libri* 38, no. 3 (September 1988): 210-220.

Provides a brief introduction to Qatar and its educational system. Describes the two main libraries in the Qatar Library System: the Qatar

National Library, and the Qatar University Library. Also discusses school libraries, the budget for the library system, and problem areas. Recommendations for future improvements and applications are listed.

762 Shehadeh, Lilly. "Biblioteker i Qatar." [Libraries in Qatar.] *Bibliotek* 70, no. 10 (1980): 311-314. [In Danish.]

Describes the educational system in Qatar. A school library was set up in Doha in 1954; the Doha Public Library, established in 1956 under the Ministry of Education, was intended mainly to serve educational purposes. The Qatar Public Library opened in 1963, and the Doha library became the main library, serving in 1978 35,000 students in 138 institutions including the university, which was opened in 1974. There is a staff of 8 librarians, and the library receives 5 legal deposit copies of Qatar imprints. It cooperates with other libraries throughout the Gulf area, compiles bibliographies, and arranges exhibitions. There are plans for more branches, for women staffed by women. [LISA]

INFORMATION SERVICES

763 Brum, I. M. (comp.). *Irshadat li-Tatwir Khadamat al-Maktabat wa-al-Ma'lumat fi Dawlat Qatar: Taqrir min al-Majlis al-Thaqafi al-Baritani ila Wizarat al-Tarbiyah wa-al-Ta'lim, Qatar*. al-Nuskhah al-munaqqahah. [Doha]: al-Wizarah, 1980. 114 leaves.

INFORMATION SYSTEMS

764 Lang, L. "Qatar's progressive GIS program." *URISA Journal* 5, no. 2 (Fall 1993): 88-92.

The tiny state of Qatar, no bigger than Connecticut, increased its stature in the geographic information systems world, receiving URISA's Exemplary Systems in Government (ESIG) Award and hosting the first GIS conference ever in the Middle East. Sheikh Ahmed, together with Zul Tiwani, the Canadian national who now heads Qatar's Center for GIS, created a centralized mapping agency responsible for developing digital mapping standards. In just four years, this organization has smoothed the mapping chaos and defined a national digital map database tying together many government ministries. This database is also serving as a foundation for many public-access map products from the agency. The author considers the background to the project, and the development of the high-resolution digital map database. [A]

LIBRARY EDUCATION

765 Khalifa, Sha'ban 'Abd al-'Aziz "Library education in Qatar." *Journal of Education for Library and Information Science* 34, no. 2 (Spring 1993): 162-164.

Reviews the history of education and libraries in Qatar and the institution of professional library education and qualifications in 1973, with the founding of Qatar University. Details the courses involved in the bachelor degree in history and library science and the postgraduate diploma.

NATIONAL LIBRARIES

766 al-Nassr, Mohammad Hamad. "Qatar national library." In *Encyclopedia of Library and Information Science*. Vol. 44 (pp. 274-276). New York: Marcel Dekker, Inc., 1989.

CHAPTER 17

SAUDI ARABIA

GENERAL

767   Ashfaq, Ahmad, and Simon Samoeil. "First conference of Saudi librarians." *MELA Notes*, no. 23 (May 1981): 14-17.

Reports briefly the proceedings at the first conference of Saudi Librarians, held at the University of Riyadh. Summarizes the main points of the conference's discussions concerned with: manpower problems; interlibrary cooperation in the sphere of technical services; public libraries in the Kingdom; cooperation with international library and documentation institutions and organizations; and library automation. Also noted the decisions taken by the Conference to form a library association in the Kingdom, and to publish a national bibliography.

768   Kahtani, Abdullah Salem Mossa. *Plans for Establishing and Developing the Social Research Studies and Information Center Libraries in Saudi Arabia*. Ph.D., 1990. North Texas State University. 183 p.

The problem was to define the present status of the Social Research Studies and Information Center libraries in Saudi Arabia and to suggest ways in which they could be improved. The purposes of the study were two-fold: (1) to analyze and evaluate the current status of these libraries and to develop and improve the role and functions of these libraries; and (2) to consider the possibility of cooperation between these libraries. The triangulation method consisting of questionnaires, interviews, and observations was used in the study. The study consisted of two questionnaires sent to twenty-five Social Research Studies and Information Center libraries in Saudi Arabia. The first questionnaire consisted of forty-four questions and was limited to fill-in responses. It was directed to the librarians. The second questionnaire consisted of thirty questions and was directed to employees of government agencies and information centers who use the libraries. Secondly, interviews with the librarians were held in which the library's administration, organization, and its strengths and weaknesses were discussed. Thirdly, observations of the twenty-five libraries were made. The intent of the questionnaires was to ascertain the present status of Social Research Studies and Information Center libraries in Saudi Arabia. The triangulation method is one of comparison so as to determine whether there is corroboration and to assess the sufficiency of the data with respect to the convergence of multiple data sources or multiple data collection procedures. The methodology used for this study was a descriptive community survey which is applicable to all types of libraries and information centers. The major limitations of the twenty-five Social Research Studies and Information Center libraries are: (1) inadequate funding, (2) non-uniformity in cataloging; (3) improperly designed buildings; (4) lack of suitable reading areas; (5) inadequate space for books and periodicals; and (6) inadequate space for staff. On the basis of the questionnaires' findings, a plan for establishing, developing, and improving the role and functions of these libraries is explained. [DAI 51/09-A: 2906.]

769   Khurshid, Zahiruddin. *Libraries & Librarianship in Saudi Arabia*. Karachi: Mahmood Khan, 1980. xii, 30 p.

770   Khurshid, Zahiruddin. "Libraries and information centers in Saudi Arabia." *International Library Review* 11, no. 4 (October 1979): 409-419.

Describes Saudi Arabian progress towards the provision of school, public, university and special libraries, information centers, and a national library. The national library is substandard. Recommends that it be developed as a key factor in developing resource sharing: the country's libraries cannot reach peak efficiency without the backing of a strong and resourceful national library.

771   Khurshid, Zahiruddin. "Application of modern technologies in Arab libraries." *Libri* 33, no. 2 (June 1983): 107-112.

Further comments on the proceedings of a symposium on new technology in libraries: prospects and problems for libraries in the Gulf States, held by the University of Petroleum and Minerals (UPM) at Dahran, Saudi Arabia, 26-28 April 1982. Gives an account of the steps in the program of automation at UPM and other Arab libraries: online searching; computer produced periodical lists; installation of DOBIS/LIBIS automated system; machine readable cataloging database; information systems. Computer technology has caused some problems: shortage of skilled manpower;

lack of bibliographic standards for Arabic material; difficulty of Arabic script; and lack of inter-library cooperation.

772 Namlah, Ali Ibrahim. *Infrastructure of Information Needs and Resources in the Country of Saudi Arabia: An Assessment.* Ph.D., 1984. Case Western Reserve University. 293 p.

The objective of this research is to determine the information situation of the country of Saudi Arabia as it is related to other development sectors of the country. It is intended to provide a framework for the formulation of a national information policy for Saudi Arabia based on the insight gained into the factors influencing the infrastructure of information in the country. The methodology employed for data analysis involves the application of a recently developed technique, known, as the Index of Information Utilization Potential, or I.U.P. This technique is based on 21 Structural and 17 Functional Groupings. Out of 230 variables that are used in the technique, 201 variables were found relevant for the case Saudi Arabia. However, only 171 variables were selected to match the corresponding variables used in the technique. More pertinently, in order to present realistic profiles of the information situation in Saudi Arabia, eleven previously studied cases, pertaining to other countries, were included in this study, which required destandardization of the data of these cases, and restandardization of the raw data after the inclusion of Saudi Arabia. Linear regression and factor analysis techniques were used to analyze the data, pertaining to Structural Groupings and the Information Factors, for determining the most representative Groupings of the infrastructure. The use of eleven cases was found useful to determine the ranking of Saudi Arabia. Also, various indexes were derived from these Groupings which provide insight into the information situation of the country. The interpretation of the various indexes and the profiles obtained in the study, reveal that the country is relatively well equipped in the background conditions, and lacking in the information needs and uses, as well as in the information activities and services. It also highlights the strength of the potential users, which suggests that the infrastructure of information needs and resources is heading in the right direction provided that other components of the infrastructure are met, such as the information professionals and information policies. For an emerging country like Saudi Arabia, this study attempts to emphasize the need to further redefine, reorganize and restructure the components of information infrastructure, such as the information institutions, the information technologies and the information users and uses. [DAI 45/08-A: 2287.]

773 Namlah, Ali Ibrahim. "Infrastructure of information needs and resources in the country of Saudi Arabia: an assessment." In *Challenges to an Information Society*. Proceedings of the 47th ASIS Annual Meeting, Philadelphia, Pennsylvania, October 21-25, 1984. Compiled by Barbara Flood, Joanne Witiak, and Thomas H. Hogan; indexed by Linda Cooper, Pat

Heller, and Andre Salz. White Plains, NY: Published for The American Society for Information Science by Knowledge Industry Publications, 1984.

Aimed at determining the information situation of Saudi Arabia and its relationship to other development sectors. It is intended that the research should be used to produce a national information policy.

774 Sardar, Ziauddin. "Saudi Arabia: indigenous sources of information." *Aslib Proceedings* 31, no. 5 (May 1979): 237-244.

Development planning in Saudi Arabia is carried out by five agencies: the Ministry of Planning, Ministry of the Interior, Saudi Arabia Monetary Agency, Ministry of Petroleum and Mineral Resources, Industrial Studies and Development Centre and the Saudi National Centre for Science and Technology. Four Saudi universities are active in research and all but one have their own journals. Most government ministries and agencies have special departments to collect, analyze and publish statistics. English language commercial information is available in newspapers, monthlies and quarterlies. At present Saudi Arabia lacks a national bibliography or union listings. The appendix lists indigenous published information sources.

775 Swaydan, Nasser M. "Saudi Arabia." In *World Encyclopedia of Library and Information Services*. 3rd ed. (pp. 734-735). Chicago: American Library Association, 1993.

Discusses the history of libraries and library education and gives a description of the national, academic, public, school, and special libraries.

776 Tashkandi, Abbas Saleh. "Libraries in Saudi Arabia." In *Encyclopedia of Library and Information Science*. Vol. 26 (pp. 307-322). New York: Marcel Dekker, Inc., 1979.

Topics discussed include: (1) Public Libraries; (2) University Libraries; (3) School Libraries; (4) Special Libraries; and (5) Library Training.

ACADEMIC LIBRARIES

777 Ajlan, Ajlan Mohammad. *The Effectiveness of Two Academic Libraries in Saudi Arabia: An Enquiry into the Main Factors Affecting their Services*. Ph.D., 1985. Case Western Reserve University. 120 p.

This study was conducted to assess the effectiveness of two academic libraries in Saudi Arabia: the University of Petroleum and Minerals, and King Saud University. The main objectives of the study were to determine the rate of book availability as a measure of effectiveness of library services, and to identify, in quantitative terms, the operational factors that affect the availability of materials. The study also suggests some steps for the improvement of book availability in the two libraries. For the collection of data in this study, a survey was carried out in the form of a brief questionnaire at each library. In this survey, (a) a sample of specific title searches was used, (b) the number of fulfilled requests and the number of unfulfilled requests were recorded, and (c) the status and/or location of the unfulfilled request was determined. The data were analyzed using the branching technique developed by Paul Kantor to measure the various factors affecting availability of books in the library. The study included six distinct factors that affect availability, namely, user bibliographic skills, collection development policy, user catalog skills, circulation policy, circulation management functions, and user search skills. The results of the data analysis showed that the overall rates of book availability in the University of Petroleum and Minerals and the King Saud University libraries were almost the same. That is, each library was able to fulfill approximately over 50% of user requests for books. However, the causes of unavailability differed significantly in the two libraries: (a) of the factors that were studied at the University of Petroleum and Minerals library, circulation policy performance followed by circulation management functions performance were found to be the lowest and were the most common causes of unavailability, and (b) of all the factors that were examined in the King Saud University survey, collection development policy and user search skills performance were found to be the lowest and were mainly responsible for the unavailability of library materials. [DAI 46/03-A: 543.]

778 Alghamidi, Falih Abdullah. *Planning for an Automated Cooperative Library Network of University Libraries in Saudi Arabia: An Exploratory Study*. Ph.D., 1988. Florida State University. 272 p.

The purpose of this study was to investigate the existing status of Saudi university libraries and examine the attitudes and opinions of university librarians and some university officials toward an automated cooperative university library network in the Kingdom. Data were collected with a five-part questionnaire, interviews, and analysis of relevant literature. The questionnaire was distributed to all library staff working in the seven Saudi university libraries. The questionnaire collected information on the existing status of libraries, and on the attitudes and opinions of library staff concerning a number of network functions, barriers, and requirements as well as the need, value, and feasibility of a library network. Interviews were conducted with selected university officials to learn the universities' experience with networking and network planning, support, and possible obstacles. The findings indicate that each university library performs a variety of activities and provides many types of services and programs to its users. Cooperation among libraries was found primarily in the areas of inter-library lending, gift and exchange, photocopying, and union lists and catalogs. Only minimal efforts were given to interlibrary cooperation and coordination. From a technological point of view, libraries were found to be capable of being involved in an automated cooperative network. The majority of respondents saw an automated cooperative library network as feasible and expressed willingness to participate in it. The major impediments for establishing a network were found to be human factors, lack of cooperative planning, institutional leadership, bibliographic control, standards, and communication. Based on the findings, the investigator believes that with a higher level of cooperation, coordination, and commitment, these impediments can be overcome. Also, an automated cooperative library network should be organized to contribute to solving these problems and improving existing services and activities. [DAI 49/07-A: 1608.]

779   Ashoor, Mohammad Saleh. "The University of Petroleum and Minerals: a model for an academic library." *College & Research Libraries* 42, no. 5 (September 1981): 456-460.

The University of Petroleum and Minerals Library, located in Dhahran, Saudi Arabia, is a science-engineering library that strives to maintain high standards of library service. The library passed through four phases of development (1965-1981) under the administration of four American-trained librarians. The collection is organized according to the Library of Congress classification scheme and AACR. The current collection numbers 160,000 volumes with 75% in science and engineering and 25% in humanities and social sciences. In addition, there are more than 300,000 non-print items and 3,800 periodical titles. The library offers access to external resources, photocopying, library orientation programs, and literature searching. DOBIS/LIBIS, an online, integrated interactive system, is being implemented for the automation of all library functions.

780   Ashoor, Mohammad Saleh. "University library planning: the experience of the University of Petroleum and Minerals." *International Library Review* 15, no. 3 (July 1983): 273-289.

The planning of a university library is illustrated with reference to the University of Petroleum and Minerals Library, Saudi Arabia. The objectives of the library and its relationship to the University is defined in its 5-year plan and 10-year forecast of 1973. Data is presented for space and facilities, and professional manpower needs for developing the library system. Using this plan the University administration, in consultation with the American Consortium of Universities, was able to set up a program for developing the collection, personnel, library space and facilities.

781   al-Baridi, Saleh A. *Strategic Planning in University Libraries in Saudi Arabia: An Exploratory Study*. Ph.D., 1994. Florida State University. 192 p.

Recent research in the library and information fields highlights the concept of "strategic planning" as a possible framework for planning a library's future. This concept now is slowly emerging in many developing countries, as it emerged in industrialized countries several years ago. This study attempted to reveal insights into library planning initiatives. The major goal of this study was to provide a comprehensive exploration of library planning in university libraries in Saudi Arabia. The study was to determine the degree to which university presidents, library deans, and librarians understand strategic planning and the degree to which they report that their universities or libraries are practicing strategic planning. It also examined the relationships of some variables and the understanding and reporting of the practicing of strategic planning. A research survey design utilizing questionnaires was chosen as the most appropriate and effective method for gathering the data needed to answer the study's six research questions. Three different but related populations were queried. These groups were university presidents, library deans, and librarians employed in the seven Saudi university libraries. Descriptive statistics, Pearson Correlation Coefficient, Analysis of Variance, and t-test procedures were used for data analysis. It was found that a majority of the respondents understand traditional planning more than strategic planning. Also, it was found that the majority of the respondents believe that they apply traditional planning more than strategic planning in their universities or libraries. Regarding the variables, some of them had a strong impact and some had a slight but not significant impact on the understanding and the practicing of strategic planning by the respondents. The findings of this investigation provided the means for the development of the suggested models of strategic planning for university libraries and universities presented in this study, and speak to the issue of diffusion of strategic planning innovation in these institutions. [DAI 55/12-A: 3672.]

782 Isma'il, Fu'ad Ahmad. "Maktabat jami'at al-Malik Sa'ud fi al-mizan." *'Alam al-Kutub* 6, no. 1 (April 1985): 59-67.

783 Isa, Abdulla Saleh. *Proposed Standards for University Libraries in Saudi Arabia*. Ph.D., 1982. University of Pittsburgh. 210 p.

The primary objective of this research is to give a clear picture of the existing resources in the university libraries of Saudi Arabia, and to provide a basis for the formulation of proposed realistic minimum standards for university libraries in Saudi Arabia. These proposed standards if applied will play a very significant role in the future development of university libraries in Saudi Arabia. In the field of university libraries not many studies have been done relating to developing countries. Since most of the developing countries have similar problems, it is hoped that this study will provide guidelines for the librarians of other developing countries to examine their own university libraries with the necessary modifications. In this sense it has the potential to be a significant contribution to the area of world librarianship. The study is divided into seven chapters. The first chapter provides an introduction of the methodology and the need for the study. Chapter II reviews the related research and literature of standards for academic libraries. Chapter III provides a general overview of Saudi Arabian history, and socio-economic, educational and cultural background. Chapter IV discusses the higher educational system and its influence on the present state of the university libraries. Chapter V includes presentation and interpretation of data about the present state of university libraries in the country. The sixth chapter analyzed and interpreted the data concerning standards for university libraries in Saudi Arabia. A summary, conclusion, and the recommendations of the study are in Chapter VII. The investigator invited selected librarians, library educators, and administrators from the Saudi Arabian universities to suggest tentative elements of proposed standards for university libraries in Saudi Arabia. The investigator has developed the proposed standards for university libraries in Saudi Arabia covering the following areas: objectives of the library, collections, staff, organization of materials, services, physical facilities, administration, and budget. In developing those proposed standards, the immediate needs of university libraries in Saudi Arabia, the standards suggested by experts in the field as revealed in the literature, and the financial resources available to university libraries in Saudi Arabia, are taken into consideration. [DAI 43/04-A: 962.]

784 King, Elizabeth J. "Libraries of two women's colleges in Saudi Arabia." *International Library Review* 19, no. 3 (July 1987): 243-248.

Report of a visit to two women's colleges in Saudi Arabia to assess their information needs. Some of the social and religious factors, which relate to libraries and their female users, are noted.

785 Line, Maurice B. "Libraries in Saudi Arabia: some reflections." *International Library Review* 15, no. 4 (October 1983): 365-373.

Outlines the current state of library development in Saudi Arabia with the emphasis on academic libraries. Suggests that there is an urgent need for Saudi librarians to clearly define their objectives and the basic functions which their library services should serve.

786 Obiagwu, Marcel C. "Library abuse in academic institutions: a comparative study." *International Information & Library Review* 24, no. 4 (December 1992): 291-305.

The abuse of library materials, defined in terms of theft, mutilation, unauthorized borrowing and vandalism was investigated in University of Port Harcourt, (Uniport) in Nigeria and King Fahd University of Petroleum and Minerals (KFUPM) in Saudi Arabia. The study sought to find out the ways the collections of the two institutions were abused by various classes of readers and for various reasons. By interviewing librarians, and analysis of collection use records, it was revealed that students, as well as faculty, staff and external readers all abused library materials, motivated by situational, conceptual, attitudinal factors. It was observed, however, that Uniport had greater problems than KFUPM. Recommendations relating to library building design, tightening of security, generous and flexible loan policies, etc., were made for improved collection protection. Besides, public relations campaign and multilateral cooperation on book theft detection would help to discourage in particular the uninitiated or new converts from any acts of library abuse. [A]

787   Siddiqui, Moid A. "Academic libraries in Saudi Arabia: a survey report." *The Reference Librarian*, no. 60 (1998): 159-177.

This paper argues that the lack of information in the literature about academic libraries in Saudi Arabia makes it impossible to review their systems, operations and services. It reports the results of a questionnaire survey conducted in the summer of 1994 of the seven Deans of Library Services in academic libraries in Saudi Arabia to determine the present state of affairs of their libraries. It also discusses the various constraints faced by these academic libraries and suggests how to overcome them.

788   Tameem, Jamal Abbas. "Academic libraries in the Kingdom of Saudi Arabia." *International Library Review* 20 (October 1988): 477-488.

Describes steps in the development of academic libraries and library education in the Kingdom of Saudi Arabia (KSA). These include: the founding of the first modern library as part of the establishment of King Saud University; the need for library and information services to support the educational development efforts of KSA—courses in library education and training; a study of library automation; and the offering of scholarships for study abroad and the establishment of educational links between the KSA and the USA. Evaluates the development of libraries and librarianship.

AUTOMATION

789   Ashoor, Mohammad Saleh. "Online automation at the University of Petroleum and Minerals Library, 1980." In *Proceedings of the 6th National Computer Conference* (Riyadh, November 4-6, 1980), pp. 39-64. Riyadh, Saudi Arabia: University of Riyadh, 1980.

790   Ashoor, Mohammad Saleh. "Planning for library automation at the University of Petroleum and Minerals." *Journal of Information Science* 5, no. 5 (February 1983): 193-198.

The University of Petroleum and Minerals was formed to support these industries in Saudi Arabia. Pressure to introduce computerized library systems stemmed from a critical shortage of skilled clerical and sub-professional staff; the growing number of graduate programs; and the growth of the Research Institute. Describes the planning, selection and installation of the DOBIS/LIBIS system at the University.

791   Ashoor, Mohammad Saleh. "A short account of the development of DOBIS/LIBIS Regional Centre at KFUPM." *Focus on International & Comparative Librarianship* 20, no. 2 (1989): 30-32.

Lists DOBIS/LIBIS installations in Saudi Arabia and Oman focusing on the three phases of installation at King Fahd University of Petroleum and Minerals (KFUPM) in the Eastern Province of Saudi Arabia which is a Regional Centre and a model for library automation in the Gulf States. Describes objectives of the IBM/KFUPM agreement to improve the marketing of DOBIS/LIBIS and outlines activities that have taken place within the framework of an Arabized version of DOBIS/LIBIS.

792   al-Dosary, Fahad M., and Abdurrahman H. Ekrish. "The state of automation in selected libraries and information centres in Saudi Arabia." *Libri* 41, no. 2 (June 1991): 109-120.

Use of computer technology is expanding in libraries and information centers in developing countries. In Saudi Arabia for example, little is known of this development. Based on questionnaire survey and follow up field visits, this paper describes the state of automation in selected Saudi libraries and information centers. Data on automation systems used, the user of each system, automated activities performed and major pertinent technical problems were identified and reported. An identification and assessment of technical problems received special treatment in the study. Coordination and cooperation, followed by standardization of bibliographic description of Arabic records, were found not only lacking but also have emerged to be the predominant issue among the problems explored. In the area of Arabization of hardware software systems, although it continues to be of major concern, visible progress has been made. An acceptable level of communication among local librarians and information specialists as well as an active involvement of private sector in information technology are concluded to be important steps to overcome existing problems and evolving ones. This, maybe, is the crux of the matter in this respect. [A]

793   Horton, Weldon H. "Microcomputer workstations as complements to a fully automated library system." *Computers in Libraries* 10, no. 1 (January 1990): 20-21.

SAUDI ARABIA

The King Fahd University of Petroleum and Minerals Library, Dhahran, Saudi Arabia, has a heavy investment in total library automation using a mainframe IBM computer and the DOBIS/LIBIS system. One microcomputer workstation, for searching online databases, was added to the system and two additional microcomputers were bought for staff training purposes. Use of all the workstations was logged for a month in order to determine whether they were of continuing usefulness and whether additional workstations were needed.

794 Khurshid, Zahiruddin. "Managing a library automation project." *Aslib Proceedings* 48, no. 1 (January 1996): 23-24, 26-28.

The paper begins with a brief history of library automation and the implementation of DOBIS/LIBIS at the King Fahd University of Petroleum and Minerals Library, Saudi Arabia. It also discusses the management aspects of the automation project including the composition of the project management teams, the roles of the Project Manager and the Library Systems Analyst and the relationship between the Library and the Data Processing Centre as two major partners of the project. The paper concludes that the management of library automation projects through partnerships between computer processing departments and libraries is not uncommon, but can cause problems since the library becomes dependent on a team whose composition it cannot manage. Ideally libraries should have a full-time systems person, with library automation being treated as a process, not a project.

795 Sattar Chaudhry, Abdus, and Mohammad Saleh Ashoor. "Potential of DOBIS/LIBIS and MINISIS for automating library functions: a comparative study of their potential for handling Arabic materials." *Program* 24 (April 1990): 109-128.

This paper reports the results of a comparative study of the suitability of DOBIS/LIBIS and MINISIS for library applications carried out at the King Fahd University of Petroleum and Minerals Library, Saudi Arabia. Evaluation of the systems against locally developed criteria have indicated great potential for handling all major library functions including Arabization. The study has shown that DOBIS/LIBIS scored higher in circulation and periodical control, while MINISIS scored higher in cataloging and OPAC functions. Further, DOBIS/LIBIS' support services and MINISIS' documentation require considerable enhancements. Concludes that DOBIS/LIBIS seems to be more suitable for large academic libraries, with access to the mainframe computer and adequate data processing staff. MINISIS in the meantime, may be a better choice for special libraries and information centers interested in SDI and indexing services which want to use mini or microcomputers.

796 Siddiqui, Moid A. "Installing a CD-ROM local area network in a science and engineering library." *Science & Technology Libraries* 16, no. 1 (1996): 19-33.

CD-ROM databases on stand-alone workstations have proved neither practical nor cost effective. As the number of CD-ROM databases in libraries increased, libraries were installing Local Area Networks (LANs) to provide a more reliable and convenient simultaneous multiple access to CD-ROM databases. The article reviews the literature on LAN installation and then describes the installation of a CD-ROM LAN using Novell Netware and SCSI Express at the King Fahd University of Petroleum and Minerals in Saudi Arabia. It discusses server evaluation and installation, access menu, training of users, LAN licensing, campus-wide networking, the impact of networking and future planned projects. [A]

797 Yavas, U., and M. Yasin. "Computing environment in an Arabian Gulf country: an organizational perspective." *Information Management and Computer Security* 1, no. 1 (1993): 11-18.

Examines the computing environment in Saudi Arabia and studies the trichotomy of Saudi organizations. Investigates the reasons behind the computerization of these organizations and determines their future computerization plans. Offers pointers for action to facilitate the computerization process among organizations in this Arabian Gulf country. [A]

BIBLIOGRAPHIC CONTROL

798 al-Huzaymi, Sa'ud 'Abdullah. "al-Dabt al-bibliyughrafi fi al-Mamlakah al-'Arabiyah al-Sa'udiyah." *Maktabat al-Idarah* 11, no. 2 (February 1984): 5-24.

799 Tashkandy, Abdul-Jalil. *Bibliographical Control in Saudi Arabia: An Inquiry into the Printing and Distribution of Government Publications, with Recommendations for Improvement*. Ph.D., University of Pittsburgh, 1977. DAI: 38/07-A: 3784.

BIBLIOGRAPHIES

800 Samarkandi, Abdullatif Abdulhakeem. *National Bibliography in Saudi Arabia, Egypt and Tunisia: Analytical and Comparative Study with a View to Planning a Saudi Arabian National Bibliography*. Ph.D., 1990. University of Technology, Loughborough (United Kingdom). 327 p.

The Kingdom of Saudi Arabia (KSA) has, in recent years, experienced a remarkable development in publishing, due to the expansion of education, and the encouragement of writers and publications by the government. In this context, a National Bibliography is a vital ingredient in promoting publications and encouraging their wider use. The objective of this study is three-fold: to find a model for National Bibliography in the KSA; to consider this proposal in the context of Arab national bibliographies and in the light of broader international aspects. The method of study involved reading a wide range of works on the subject. Interviews were conducted with individuals and organizations connected with the subject. Description and analysis of works in Saudi Arabia, Egypt and Tunisia were made according to the following plan: publisher; need and aim; scope of coverage; organization; bibliographical description; and depository law. Most of the bibliographic works produced in the KSA have been for specific purposes, appearing at different periods and often overlapping. They cannot themselves be regarded as a retrospective national bibliography but could be useful in producing one. Egypt and Tunisia are chosen for the study as both have experienced similar problems to the KSA and both have a tradition of regular national bibliography. In both countries, the National Library produces the National Bibliography. Their experiences are considered useful for positive adoption of successful features and avoidance of shortcomings in setting up a Saudi National Bibliography. In addition, a wider examination of Arab Bibliography and international definitions and practices has been made. Deposition law, as a vital feature of successful bibliography production, has also been considered for the main countries studied and for others. The National Library of Saudi Arabia should be the body to publish the prospective National Bibliography, benefiting from the examples given above. Recommendations are made for the administration and working of the New Bibliography. [DAI 52/10-A: 3467.]

801 Tameem, Jamal Abbas. "Saudi Arabian librarianship: an annotated bibliography (1950-1986)." *International Library Review* 20, no. 4 (October 1988): 495-507.

Lists the literature which appeared between 1950 and 1986 in English in the Kingdom of Saudi Arabia's (KSA) libraries and librarianship. Covers books, articles and reports written in English which appeared in the international literature and were published outside the KSA, and includes dissertations by students at US universities about the libraries and librarianship in the KSA.

CATALOGING AND CLASSIFICATION

802 Ashoor, Mohammad Saleh, and Abdus Sattar Chaudhry. "Bi-lingual bibliographic software for processing library materials in the Arabic language." *Program* 28, no. 2 (April 1994): 167-175.

Bibliographic processing software has been written to incorporate special capabilities but not many have proven suitable for bilingual applications. King Abdulaziz City for Science and Technology (KACST) and Imam

Mohammad Ibn Saud University are two institutions in Saudi Arabia that have written their own Arabic software for creating Arabic language databases. In contrast, several other institutions have Arabized two well known systems: DOBIS/LIBIS and MINISIS. Reports the results of a questionnaire survey of bilingual database software in use in Saudi Arabia. Concludes that in-house systems do not have much potential to provide effective support for bilingual bibliographic applications and the potential in this regard appears to lie in various Arabized versions of DOBIS/LIBIS and MINISIS. Summarizes the strengths of these systems in this field. [A]

803   Hanif, M. "Cataloging with a computer: Dobis/Libis adapted by the University of Petroleum and Minerals, Dhahran, Saudi Arabia." *Pakistan Library Bulletin* 16, no. 3-4 (September-December 1985): 63-78.

Describes the library of the University of Petroleum and Minerals (UPM) Dhahran, Saudi Arabia, and the services it provides. Discusses the decision to automate library functions and the choice of the Dortmund Library System (DOBIS) and the Leuven Integrated Library System (LIBIS). DOBIS/LIBIS is the result of cooperation between the University of Dortmund in West Germany and the Catholic University of Leuven in Belgium with IBM. Describes phase I of the implementation of the automation project: operation of the cataloging and searching modules and conversion of catalog records.

804   Khalid, H. M., and K. Mahmood. "Cataloguing practice in university libraries. A comparison of three developing countries (Pakistan, Malaysia, Saudi Arabia)." *Library Review* 46, no. 5-6 (1997): 328-338.

Surveys the status of cataloging practice in university libraries in three Asian developing countries, Pakistan, Malaysia, and Saudi Arabia. Examines the extent of the usage of international cataloging tools such as cataloging codes (AACR, ISBD), classification schemes (Dewey Decimal Classification, Library of Congress Classification) and subject heading lists (Sears, Library of Congress Subject Headings). Finds that there is an overall uniformity in the use of technical tools. There is a trend towards automation of cataloging services. With the help of new technology, more access points for catalog searching have been made available. Online catalogs are also replacing all traditional catalog forms (card, printed, and microform). Survey findings show that, in using new information technology in technical services, Malaysian university libraries are more advanced than those of Pakistan and Saudi Arabia. [A]

805   Khurshid, Zahiruddin. "Cataloguing practices in university libraries of Saudi Arabia." *International Cataloguing and Bibliographic Control* 17, no. 4 (October-December 1988): 59-61.

While the development of university libraries in Saudi Arabia has been very rapid and the application of modem technologies has added another dimension to this development, the desired results have not been achieved due to lack of planning, lack of cooperation, and shortage of professionally trained librarians. The Council of Deans of Library Affairs was formed to tackle these problems and it was recommended that the King Fahd University of Petroleum and Minerals (KEUPM) undertake a study of problems in cataloging, classifications and subject analysis of non-Arabic materials in coordination with other Saudi Arabian university libraries. The study revealed serious inconsistencies in the cataloging practices which are reviewed in detail. Heads of cataloging Departments in the seven unidentified the problems and recommended the immediate implementation of certain tasks which are listed. [A]

806 Khurshid, Zahiruddin. "Improvisations in cataloging of theses and dissertations." *Cataloging & Classification Quarterly* 20, no. 2 (1995): 51-59.

The existing subject headings lists and classification schemes are inadequate to deal with the very specific and rapidly developing subjects of theses and dissertations. As a result, libraries find it both costly and time consuming to perform original and full cataloging of these materials. Many libraries have been forced to improvise on descriptive and subject cataloging to reduce the processing cost. This article describes the improvisations of the Library of King Fahd University of Petroleum and Minerals in Dhahran, Saudi Arabia, in cataloging local and foreign theses and dissertations. [A]

807 Khurshid, Zahiruddin. "Cataloguing of audiovisual materials." *Audiovisual Librarian* 21, no. 3 (August 1995): 183-188.

Describes the practices adopted by King Fahd University of Petroleum and Minerals Library in Dhahran, Saudi Arabia, in cataloging and creating machine readable cataloging records of audiovisual materials for the benefit of other libraries interested in providing local level cataloging. Discusses some background, cataloging practices, descriptive cataloging, subject cataloging, and cataloging on DOBIS/LIBIS. [A]

808 McMurdo, George. "An analysis of UK MARC exchange tape variable data field subfield lengths, 1950-1980." *Program* 16, no. 1 (January 1982): 1-10.

The Library of the International Airport Projects of the Ministry of Defence and Aviation, Kingdom of Saudi Arabia has installed an interactive online system using MARC tapes from which records are selected and transposed into a local format using compression techniques. The investigation reported here was to determine sub-field record lengths. It was considered necessary to undertake this despite data provided by

BLAISE based on a sample of 22,569 records, since Tags often covered a number of data elements. By analyzing tapes covering the years 1950-80, it was possible to determine the maximum length of any field and frequency of occurrence. The total number of records was 633,930. The results are described and sample sets of data included. [A]

809 Moran, M. L. "Further considerations on romanization: Saudi Arabia." *International Library Review* 13, no. 3 (July 1981): 275-285.

This article deplores the romanization of Arabic characters in order that catalog entries for Arabic literature can be filed in the same sequence as those for Western literature. Maintains that Arabic entries should be in a separate sequence, and that romanization is unnecessary. Linguistic equality should be a basis for the forging of new relationships between the Arab and the Western worlds.

CHILDREN'S LITERATURE

810 Isaac, Jacob M. "The problems of Children's literature in the Kingdom of Saudi Arabia." In *Printed for Children: World Children's Book Exhibition* (p. 349). Munich: K. G. Saur, 1978.

CIRCULATION

811 Iskanderani, A. I., and Mumtaz A. Anwar. "Automated bilingual circulation system using PC local area networks." *Microcomputers for Information Management* 9, no. 3 (1992): 161-176.

Article appeared also in *Information Services & Use* 12, no. 2 (1992): 141-156. The DOBIS/LIBIS automated library system includes a highly sophisticated module to control automated circulation capable of using bar-code scanners. In order to use the LIBIS module which deals with circulation, a library must have the materials with a potential for circulation in its local database and, if possible, be linked with the student and personnel databases of the university. The libraries in the Middle East using DOBIS/LIBIS need to Arabize LIBIS. These facilities were not yet available at King Abdulaziz University, and it was very difficult to predict when they would be. Due to this reason, a local automated bilingual circulation system (ABCS) using a personal computer local area network was developed. The system is designed with fully bilingual--Arabic and English--capabilities. Important features of the system are the development of the database as it circulates documents, its ease of use, reliability, its ability to produce a variety of statistics and its capability of linking with the DOBIS/LIBIS system. [A]

812 Khurshid, Zahiruddin. "The DOBIS/LIBIS circulation control system." *Asian Libraries* 3, no. 2 (2 June 1993): 59-67.

Describes the system design, file structure, policy matrices, and various functions of the DOBIS/LIBIS circulation control system; summarizing the modifications and enhancements of the system to meet the requirements of the library at King Fahd University of Petroleum and Minerals, Saudi Arabia.

COLLECTION DEVELOPMENT/ACQUISITION

813 'Abd al-Latif, Salih 'Abd al-'Aziz. "al-Ta'awun fi majal al-tazwid bayna al-maktabat al-jami'yah fi al-Mamlakah al-'Arabiyah al-Sa'udiyah." *'Alam al-Kutub* 2, no. 1 (May 1981): 55-59.

814 Alghamidi, Falih Abdullah. "Tatwir majmu'at al-maktabat al-jami'iyah fi al-Sa'udiyah wa-taqyimiha." *'Alam al-Kutub* 17, no. 4 (July-August 1996): 291-304.

The aim of the research is to study the status of collection development in seven university libraries in Saudi Arabia. The writer states that libraries suffer from inadequate collection management and development, shortage of staff, etc. He proposes different recommendations.

815 Ashoor, Mohammad Saleh. "Evaluation of the collections of Saudi university libraries based on the ACRL Standards." *International Information & Library Review* 24, no. 1 (March 1992): 3-14.

This paper evaluates the collections of the Saudi university libraries against the Association of College and Research Libraries (ACRL) Standards of 1986. The information gathered through questionnaires to Deans of Library Affairs to provide information on library holdings and collection development programs reveals that library holdings of six Saudi university libraries are below the ACRL Standards. However, King Saud University Library collection has exceeded the Standards. The reasons for the inadequate library collections of the Saudi universities are the lack of planning, absence of collection development policies, low participation by faculty members in collection development policies, low participation by faculty members in collection building, insufficient financial support, and the absence of interlibrary loans and online information retrieval facilities in some libraries. [A]

816 Khurshid, Zahiruddin. "DOBIS/LIBIS acquisitions subsystem in operation at King Fahd University of Petroleum and Minerals." *Library Acquisitions: Practice & Theory* 11, no. 4 (1987): 325-334.

DOBIS/LIBIS is an integrated online library automation system developed jointly by the University of Dortmund in West Germany and the Catholic University of Leuven in Belgium. Its acquisitions subsystem has been in operation at King Fahd University of Petroleum and Minerals,

Dharan, Saudi Arabia, since May 1986. Provides an overview of the system design and functions available for acquisitions control, including strengths and weaknesses. [A]

DATABASE MANAGEMENT SYSTEMS

817 Siddiqui, Moid A. "A microcomputer based database management system in a university library." **Microcomputers for Information Management** 12, no. 4 (1995): 287-299.

Describes a database management system developed in the Reference and Information Services of the King Fahd University of Petroleum and Minerals Library, Dhahran, Saudi Arabia, using an IBM PC AT. The objective of creating the system was to gather, manage, sort and manipulate, efficiently and quickly, online search statistics. In addition, it reduces time spent on record keeping and maintaining statistical and financial data of online searches. [A]

DOCUMENTATION

818 *Nadwat Tawthiq al-Ma'lumat al-Idariyah (1989: Ma'had al-Idarah al-'ammah, Riyadh, Saudi Arabia)*. [Riyadh]: al-Mamlakah al-'Arabiyah al-Sa'udiyah, Ma'had al-Idarah al-'Ammah, Idarat al-Baramij al-'Ulya, 1988. 199 p.

819 *Nadwat al-Tiqniyah al-Hadithah fi Tanzim wa-Idarat al-Ma'lumat al-Mun'aqidah bi-Ma'had al-Idarah al-'Ammah fi al-Fatrah min 5-6 Rabi' al-Akhir 1407 H*. [Riyadh]: al-Mamlakah al-'Arabiyah al-Sa'udiyah, al-Ma'had, Idarat al-Baramij al-'Ulya, 1986. 102 p.

GOVERNMENT PUBLICATIONS

820 'Abdullah, Muhammad al-Ghazali. "Dawr al-ajhizah al-hukumiyah fi mu'alajat mahfuzatiha ghayr al-nashitah." **Maktabat al-Idarah** 14, no. 2 (January 1987): 59-70.

821 Swaydan, Nasser M. "al-Matbu'at al-hukumiyah al-sa'udiyah: nash'atiha wa-numuwwiha." **'Alam al-Kutub** 3, no. 4 (January-February 1983): 659-665.

822 Swaydan, Nasser M. *al-Dabt al-Bibliyughraphi lil-Matbu'at al-Hukumiyah fi al-Sa'udiyah*. Ph.D., 1984. Jami 'at al-Qahirah.

The study covers the period between 1882 and 1983 and investigates specific aspects of bibliographical control of government publications in Saudi Arabia.

823 Swaydan, Nasser M. "al-Matbu'at al-hukumiyah fi al-Mamlakah al-'Arabiyah al-Sa'udiyah: dirasah bibliyughrafiyah." *Maktabat al-Idarah* 13:1 (October 1985): 87-113.

INFORMATION POLICY

824 al-Arfaj, Khaled Abdullatif. *The Information Industry in Saudi Arabia: An Analytical Study Defining Information Industry Policy Issues and Options Through Cooperative Interaction*. Ph.D., 1993. Indiana University. 54/06-A: 1983. 288 p.

This study attempted to contribute creative insights to information policy initiatives adopted recently in Saudi Arabia. The goal of the study was to provide a systematic analysis of information industry policy issues and options through cooperative interaction among library and information professionals, information industry representatives, and planners and decision makers in Saudi Arabia. Such interactive cooperation was the underlying hypothesis of the study. Two sets of variables comprised the study's conceptual framework. The first set, identified as policy inputs, consisted of five variables: environmental indicators, economic policies, educational and Research and Development (R&D) policies, science and technology policies, and government and private sector relations policies. The second set, identified as policy outputs, included six categories of issues relating to information availability, information accessibility, information utilization, information technology, information economics, and information regulations. Study participants considered the Saudi information industry to be economically viable, although some referred to a number of obstacles that might make investment in the information industry risky. Several policy options that could stimulate information industry growth were presented from market development, regulatory, organizational, and social perspectives. Participants' appraisals of policy options highlighted the following points: (1) There is a need for a governmental policy to ease private sector investment in information services and activities. (2) Government support with respect to legal protection of the information industry need to be enhanced, and certain policy measures to direct the private sector in conducting R&D projects need to be taken. (3) A number of policy options were judged highly desirable but not likely to emerge, including a cooperative policy among Arab countries to Arabize information technology products, and establishing translation centers in Saudi universities and research institutions and a national database of works translated into Arabic. (4) In order to stimulate growth of the information industry some corrective measures to enhance the level of information use are needed. Reasons behind low information use involved professional and political factors, but socially-related problems represent the major causes for low information use in Saudi Arabia.

825 Sattar Chaudhry, Abdus. "Information policies in Saudi Arabia and Malaysia." *Information Development* 9, no. 4 (December 1993): 228-234.

Policy documents of Saudi Arabia and Malaysia were reviewed to examine provisions for library and information services and the role of libraries in formulating and implementing national policies. Concludes that, in Saudi Arabia, scattered legislative provisions need to be integrated into a unified policy and the involvement of libraries needs to be institutionalized for the effective development of an information infrastructure. The Malaysian experience of establishing an integrated national policy by involving professionals from universities and other important sectors and implementing information programs through the National Library of Malaysia has been very successful in developing an appropriate system. Suggests that this approach may provide a model for other developing countries for an appropriate policy framework and the development of services for effective utilization of national information resources. [A]

INFORMATION SEEKING BEHAVIOR

826 al-Jabri, Ibrahim M., and Muhammad A. al-Khaldi. "Effects of user characteristics on computer attitudes among undergraduate business students." *Journal of End User Computing* 9, no. 2 (Spring 1997): 16-22.

A study survey is used to investigate the computer attitudes of 238 business students attending a major university in Saudi Arabia. The findings show that computer experience, degree access, and computer ownership have a significant effect on computer anxiety, computer confidence, computer liking, computer usefulness, and overall computer attitude. Age and class standing do not appear to be related to any of the computer attitude scales. The number of computer-using courses strongly affects computer confidence, usefulness, and overall attitude, but weakly affects computer anxiety and liking. The student Grade Point Average is associated with computer confidence, and overall attitude, but not with computer anxiety, liking or usefulness. [A]

827 al-Shanbari, H., and A. Jack Meadows. "Problems of communication and information-handling among scientists and engineers in Saudi universities." *Journal of Information Science* 21, no. 6 (1995): 473-478.

A questionnaire survey has been carried out of nearly 500 scientists and engineers working at four universities in Saudi Arabia. It was aimed at establishing their communication and information-handling practices, so that these could be compared with the corresponding activities of scientists and engineers in British universities. Particular attention was paid to the role of information technology. The results of the survey show that communication and information-handling via traditional channels is subject to considerably greater limitations in Saudi Arabia than in the UK.

However, networking is developing rapidly in Saudi Arabia, and is beginning to make a significant impact on academic information activities. A detailed examination of current developments suggests that increasing employment of information technology may alleviate some of the informational problems presently experienced in the Saudi Arabian academic world. [A]

828 Tamraz, Ahmad Ali. *A Study of Availability and Actual Usage of Arabic and English Monographs in Science and Technology in Three Academic Libraries in Saudi Arabia*. Ph.D., 1984. Rutgers University: The State University of New Jersey (New Brunswick). 203 p.

No previous attempt has been made to study the availability rate of monographs in the academic libraries of Saudi Arabia. This problem statement gave rise to three questions which the study addressed: (1) Out of the whole range of monographs published in Arabic and in English—between 1978 and 1982--what has been purchased in the areas of Science and Technology? (2) Of the items purchased and prepared for use which are available on the shelves? (3) What is the actual usage of available materials? The study applied a portion of the methodology developed by DeProspo et al.—which measures the performance of public libraries in the United States—to the academic library environment of Saudi Arabia. To determine the probability of purchase, in the monographs published between 1978 and 1982, a sample of 583 English titles was drawn from the BPR. A sample of 451 Arabic titles were drawn, on-site in Saudi Arabia, from appropriate Arabic bibliographic sources. To determine the shelf availability of titles published between 1978-82, both the English and the Arabic samples drawn were checked against the central card catalog of each of the three Saudi academic libraries participating in the study: King Saud University (KSU), King Abdul-Aziz University (KAAU), and the University of Petroleum and Minerals (UPM). Documentation of the actual usage of available monographs was accomplished by perusal of the circulation files. The study demonstrated that DeProspo methodology can be generalized to academic libraries. Relative to ownership (purchase) King Saud University had the largest Science and Technology holdings in Arabic and in English. When the shelf availability of monographs was investigated King Saud University again ranked first in Arabic and in English. As to the probability of availability, three correlations pertinent to ownership and availability showed diverse results: Arabic titles ownership vs. shelf availability, $r = -0.84$; English titles ownership vs. shelf availability, $r = +0.132$; availability of Arabic vs. English titles, $r = +0.98$. Investigation of actual usage demonstrated English title circulation to be greater than Arabic. Also, in ranking the circulation, Technology place first. Physical Science, Bio-Medical Science, and Agriculture ranked second, third, and fourth, respectively. [DAI 45/02-A: 332.]

INFORMATION SERVICES

829 Basager, M. A. "Electronic information services in the libraries of the Kingdom of Saudi Arabia." *Pakistan Library Bulletin* 26, no. 2 (June 1995): 18-28.

A brief account of the introduction of electronic information services in some of the major libraries of Saudi Arabia. As early as 1977 the Kingdom set up an organization now known as the King Abdulaziz City for Science and Technology (KACST) which has played a leading role in the development of electronic information services in academic institutions and research centers throughout the country. KASCT established GULFNET in 1985, which now links 14 member institutions, including 3 in Kuwait and 1 in Bahrain. A satellite link to BITNET provides access to international databases in the US and Europe, as well as document delivery services. KACSNET is a dial up communications network linking over 60 Saudi research institutions with the central computer at KASCT, and a CD-ROM network has also been installed, currently with 73 databases. IT facilities at the King Fahd University, Dhahran and the King Abdulaziz University are described, as well as the use of IT for information services by the libraries of the Chamber of Commerce at Jeddah and Dammam.

830 Manzoor, Suhail. "Saudi Arabian National Center for Science and Technology (SANCST) Database." *International Library Review* 17, no. 1 (January 1985): 77-90.

Describes the establishment of the Saudi Arabian National Centre for Science and Technology (SANCST), its functions and objectives, and its information system. Provides statistics relating to in-house research in various disciplines carried out in universities, institutions and ministries between 1960 and 1983. Suggests that the highest research activity was in medicine, agriculture, geology, water and desalination, petroleum energy and construction engineering.

831 Munshi, Zaki, and Milton R. McRoberts. "Basic concepts, objectives and scope of online search services in Saudi Arabia." In *Proceedings of the National Online Meeting, New York, March 31-April 1, 1982*. Compiled by Martha E. Williams and Thomas H. Hogan, 411-416. Medford, N.J.: Learned Information, Inc., 1982.

A new online search and document delivery service to scientists and researchers was initiated in 1980 as an integral part of the Saudi Arabian National Centre for Science and Technology (SANCST). Basic concepts and objectives of this service were set out and an enthusiastic and progressive use of this service has been experienced. The historical background to the development of this service and the statistics describing the number of online searches conducted 1980-81 are presented. The searches are categorized into the major scientific areas to relate the emphasis of the subject requests. A summary of the universities, colleges, government ministries and other institutions utilizing these services are described. [A]

832 Marghalani, Mohammad Amin, and Abdulrasheed Abdulaziz Hafez. "Online search service at the King Abdulaziz University Library, Jeddah, Saudi Arabia." *International Information & Library Review* 25, no. 1 (March 1993): 27-41.

This study aims to investigate the perception of faculty members at King Abdulaziz university (KAAU) towards online search service in the Jeddah main campus. Survey methods were used to determine the demands of the faculty members from different faculties and to find out the subject areas for which more search requests are made. The data for this study were collected by administering a specially designed questionnaire to all the chairmen of departments within each faculty. Personal interviews were conducted with the library staff responsible for the online search service at the KAAU Central Library. Analysis of relevant data indicates that out of 73 questionnaires delivered to chairmen, 51 completed questionnaires were received, a 70% response rate. Further analysis revealed that 139 requests were made by II faculties and institutions during 1989 and 1990. Forty-five percent of respondents used online search service to conduct personal research. [A]

833 al-Tasan, Mohammed Ali. "The role of the King Abdulaziz City for Science and Technology in information services in the Kingdom of Saudi Arabia." *Journal of Information Science* 18, no. 6 (1992): 491-495.

Part of a special issue devoted to library and information services in the Arab countries after the Gulf War. The paper concentrates on one main organization which is responsible as a national center for scientific and technological information in Saudi Arabia. It describes the services prepared by this national organization, such as databases, information services, computer activities and national networks. There are many databases, covering science and technology, bibliographies, terminology and manpower, besides other services such as online services, document delivery, union lists and current awareness. [A]

INFORMATION SERVICES—SPECIAL SUBJECTS

834 Alogla, Sulaiman Ibn Saleh. *Scientific and Technical Information Transfer: Promoting Information Acquisition in the Saudi Arabian Industrial Sector (Scientific Information)*. Ph.D., 1993. Indiana University. 240 p.

The availability of scientific and technical information (STI) resulting from adequate information acquisition on as broad a scale as possible is indispensable to maintaining the vitality and international competitiveness of industry. This study therefore investigates the current status of STI transfer to the industrial sector in Saudi Arabia. The study examined the general characteristics of STI flow to Saudi industrial companies, acquisition patterns among various industries, and factors affecting information flow to the industrial sector. The study's variables were examined using a self-administered mail questionnaire supplemented by field visits to Saudi industries. A purposive sample of Saudi industries was taken by selecting those industries possessing libraries or information centers. Descriptive statistics were used for the study's data analysis. Based on the study's findings, it was found that Saudi industries acquired a large amount of information in one year, 1991. In acquiring information, Saudi industries used original producer nodes for domestic information and distributor nodes for foreign resources. Information most often was transferred directly from originating sources to industrial information centers, and the second most common means of transfer was through the use of one intermediary. Also based on the study's findings, there appeared to be many barriers affecting information transfer in the Saudi industrial sector, for instance, shortage of skilled Saudi information specialists, absence of acquisition tools, absence of professional industrial information centers, lack of cooperation between the public and industrial sectors, and lack of scientific impact on the highest levels of industrial management. These barriers can be minimized by the study's proposed information transfer system. The system presents ways in which Saudi industrial companies acquire information quickly and efficiently from foreign and domestic sources, and thus links information producers to ultimate users in Saudi industries. The system can be used by Saudi industries to improve and facilitate information service to their community users. [DAI 54/04-A: 1129.]

835 Arif, Mohammad, and A. Jack Meadows. "The provision of information to industry: a comparative study of Saudi Arabia and the UK." *Journal of Librarianship and Information Science* 26, no. 1 (March 1994): 29-33.

Reports the results of a questionnaire study to compare the methods of access to industrial information, by companies in Saudi Arabia, with similar information access in the UK. The objectives of the study were: to determine what major information sources are available to Saudi Arabian and UK industrial concerns; to examine the level of service and relevance of the information provided; to investigate how aware industries are of information sources and to what extent they use them; and to look for differences in the use of information as a function of the type of company concerned. The survey examined the size of firms, Saudi and UK government information sources, Saudi and UK non government information sources, numbers of different information sources used by firms and the industrial sector use of information, and the types of business information sources. Respondents were asked how useful they found the information that they obtained and whether they experienced any problems in acquiring it. The survey was supplemented by interviews with key information providers and users. Results suggest that current information provision in Saudi Arabia may be sufficient in terms of number and range of providers for the existing demands of industry. However, UK experience suggests that this provision will need to evolve as industrial activity develops. [A]

INFORMATION STORAGE AND RETRIEVAL

836 al-'Askar, Fahd Ibrahim. "Nizam bank ma'lumat al-watha'iq: tajribat ma'had al-idarah al-'ammah bi al-Riyad." *al-Majallah al-'Arabiyah lil-Ma'lumat* 5, no. 1 (1984): 162-173.

837 Sattar Chaudhry, Abdus, and Mohammad Saleh Ashoor. "Comprehensive materials availability studies in academic libraries." *Journal of Academic Librarianship* 20, no. 5-6 (November 1994): 300-305.

A study at the King Fahd University of Petroleum and Minerals Library, Dharhran, Saudi Arabia, (KFUPM) revealed an overall materials availability performance of 63.8 per cent. This rose to 76 per cent when library staff provided assistance. The major reasons for non availability of items were related to circulation policy, ownership and user skills. [A]

838 Siddiqui, Moid A. "Online searching in a university library of a developing country." *Microcomputers for Information Management* 8, no. 3 (September 1991): 187-195.

All university libraries are now using microcomputer technology in different forms and in varying degrees to satisfy the demands of their users. The King Fahd University of Petroleum and Minerals (KFUPM) Library is using personal computers for conducting online and CD-ROM searching, processing and controlling interlibrary loans, word processing, and so forth. This paper describes the online searching service provided by the KFUPM Library in Dhahran, Saudi Arabia and the ways in which personal computers have been used for conducting online searching. [A]

839 Siddiqui, Moid A. "Online in Saudi Arabia." *Online* 16, no. 2 (March 1992): 105-108.

Describes the online information retrieval activities of King Abdulaziz City of Science and Technology (KACST), in particular the 14 in-house databases, nine of which are directly accessible by outside users through the GULFNET network for Middle East countries. A table records DIALOG, ORBIT and KACST database usage, over the period 1983-1991, in terms of total numbers of searches and total and average costs in

Saudi Riyals and US dollars. Concludes with a list of contacts for Saudi Arabian online information. [A]

840 Siddiqui, Moid A. "CD-ROM searching in an academic library in a developing country." *CD-ROM Librarian* 7, no. 5 (May 1992): 23-28.

Describes the implementation of CD-ROM database searching in the library of the King Fahd University of Petroleum and Minerals, Saudi Arabia, as a logical procession from online searching, introduced in 1979.

841 Siddiqui, Moid A. "A study of the effect of online searching of CD index in a science and engineering library." *Library Review* 44, no. 7 (1995): 45-54.

Also published in *OCLC Systems & Services*, vol. 11, no. 4 (1995), pp. 14-21. It studies the effect of eight CD-ROM indexes on online searching at the King Fahd University of Petroleum and Minerals Library, Dhahran, Saudi Arabia, through statistical data of online searching conducted for the faculty, graduate students and researchers, before and after the acquisition of the CD-ROMs. The findings indicate a considerable decline in online searching use owing to the introduction of the CD-ROM indexes, saving a large amount of money. Discusses the impact of CD-ROM databases on staffing in the reference department. [A]

842 Siddiqui, Moid A. "A statistical study of online searches in an academic library." *International Forum on Information and Documentation* 21, no. 2 (1996): 3-20.

This article reports results of a survey to review and measure the effectiveness of the online search service, provided by the King Fahd University of Petroleum and Minerals (KFUPM), for faculty, graduate students, and researchers, between July 1988 and June 1994. Extensive statistics are tabulated by online searches conducted, costs, departments, user status, subjects, databases searched, and search type (broad and narrow). Of particular note is the detailed statistics of the distribution of online searches by subject and by DIALOG File Number (showing the most popular databases searched). Notes the database management system used for compiling online search statistics. Concludes with a brief note of acquisition of CD-ROM databases, from July 1991, and the possible implications for the online service. [A]

INFORMATION TECHNOLOGY

843 Agrawal, J. C., and S. al-Mathami. "Linguistic obstructions to scientific information in high technology areas." *Inspel* 29, no. 4 (1995): 232-239.

Paper presented at the 60th IFLA General Conference, Havana, Cuba, 21-28 August 1994. Many non-English language speaking developing countries importing information technology and computer technology face problems in information transfer caused by the foreign language barrier. Briefly describes the efforts of the College of Computer and Information Science, King Saud University, Saudi Arabia, to develop multilingual tools and techniques locally for Saudi Arabia. Developing countries need to devote greater efforts to the production of these multilingual information tools, and should work collectively to produce them. [A]

844 Jifri, Sharaf, and A. Jack Meadows. "The role of information in the information technology trade between the UK and Saudi Arabia." *Journal of Librarianship and Information Science* 28, no. 3 (September 1996): 141-148.

Many developing countries see an expansion of the use of information technology (IT) as the key to future prosperity, and hope to establish an indigenous industry which will supply at least some of their needs. Some may even develop into IT exporters. Since initially this will involve importing IT from developed countries a study was conducted which took the example of Saudi Arabia as a developing country and that of the UK as a developed country in order to study the type of importing and exporting information system that must operate to satisfy both sets of information needs. On the basis of an earlier pilot study of 28 UK IT exporters series of null hypotheses were set up to guide the investigation, namely that there were no differences in: the utilization of information sources between Saudi Arabian IT importers and UK IT exporters; the utilization of information sources between those UK IT exporters involved with Saudi Arabia and those who were not; the effect of size of the firm on the utilization of information sources; and the obstacles to accessing information sources facing both Saudi IT importers and UK IT exporters. Data collection was by means of questionnaire surveys sent to 220 likely UK exporters and 128 Saudi Arabian importers. Reports results and concludes that information transfer between the Saudi and UK IT importing and exporting systems occurs on an extensive and continuing basis but its efficiency is hampered, in part, by differing attitudes to the interface, and in part by a differing use of information channels. [A]

845 Kanamugire, Athanase B. "Implementing information technology projects in developing countries." *Information Development* 9, no. 1-2 (March-June 1993): 58-65.

Reviews the problems of implementing information technology projects in developing countries, with examples from Ethiopia, Sudan and Tanzania. Considers the advantages and disadvantages of CD-ROMs as a means of solving some of the problems of access to information experienced by developing countries, and describes the experience of the King Fahd University of Petroleum and Minerals, Saudi Arabia, in introducing CD-ROM search services to complement existing online search facilities. Reactions of users and staff to CD-ROMs are described. Concludes that, through its ability to provide appropriate information conveniently and quickly, CD-ROM may come to play a major role in the process of development of developing countries. [A]

846 Kanamugire, Athanase B. "Developing a CD-ROM service in Saudi Arabia: some lessons for developing countries." *Journal of Information Science* 20, no. 2 (1994): 99-107.

Discusses the first-hand experience of the King Fahd University of Petroleum and Minerals (KFUPM) Library in Saudi Arabia in setting up and developing a public access CD-ROM service. The article firstly gives brief background information on the University and the Library. This is followed by a discussion of the rationale for embracing CD-ROM. Then, the KFUPM Library CD-ROM system components are considered under hardware, software, databases and local area network. The other aspects of the CD-ROM service discussed include: organization and staffing, including CD-ROM search policy; publicity and end-user education; impact on services and resources, and the future direction. Finally, drawing on the KFUPM Library experience, the article advances suggestions on developing a CD-ROM service in developing countries. [A]

847 Qureshy, A. A. "Saudi Arabian national data bases and use of GULFNET/BITNET at KFUPM Library, Dhahran." *International Information & Library Review* 27, no. 3 (September 1995): 249-263.

This article traces the establishment and functions of the King Abdulaziz City for Science and Technology (KACST), Riyadh, Saudi Arabia and the development of national databases. The databases, accessible by the public, are introduced with their subject coverage and number of records. The first computer network in the Arab world, GULFNET, which provides communication among the academic communities of the Kingdom of Saudi Arabia and the other Gulf countries, including services available through GULFNET and KFUPM Library, are discussed in detail. The evaluation of the three most frequently used of KACST's databases is made by using the statistics of the last 8 years. The founding of BITNET in the USA is explained, together with its GULFNET connection in the Arab world and use at KFUPM Library with different commands. Finally, while suggesting a few points regarding the effective use of GULFNET, KACST's databases and the possibilities of INTERNET use, the future dominance of organizational networks for the purposes of educational and scientific etc., communications in the future is emphasized. [A]

848 al-Tayyeb, Muhammad Ali. *Information Technology Transfer to Saudi Arabia*. Ph.D., 1982. University of Pittsburgh. 302 p.

Information technology is studied in the context of its transfer to Saudi Arabia. The importance of a theory-based understanding of information technology and of the transfer process is stressed. As background to the problem, Saudi Arabia's past and current economic development plans are examined, along with underlying socio-cultural aspects. The nature of technology and technology transfer are examined and defined. Information technology is explored in light of Daniel Bell's concepts of post-industrial society and intellectual technology. The central role of theory in innovation and policy formulation is stressed. The Debonian EATPUT model of information systems is presented, as are C. West Churchman's determining characteristics of systems. The current status of information technology in Saudi Arabia is examined using field research methodology. Questionnaire surveys administered to information technology personnel (administrators, technicians, and users) in universities, government agencies and private companies in Saudi Arabia. Further, in-depth interviews were conducted with several key people. The data generated form the components of a comprehensive model of information technology transfer to Saudi Arabia. The model developed is juxtaposed against the theories of C. West Churchman and Anthony Debons. The model helps to identify concepts and issues. The model's role in the formulation of a national information policy is discussed. Additional areas where research is needed are suggested. [DAI 43/05-A: 1330.]

849 Thabit, Hassan J. *Information Transfer: The Diffusion of Microcomputers in Saudi Arabian Universities*. Ph.D., 1987. University of Pittsburgh. 187 p.

The study's purpose was to examine the diffusion of micros in Saudi Arabia in relation to hardware, software, users, and potential users. The study investigated the micro use by university students and faculty and identified available micro hardware and software. The study determined the source and channels of communications used and needed for the diffusions of micros and examined the vendor's role as information provider. Factors affecting the diffusion were investigated and the overall diffusion was evaluated as to: relative advantages, compatibility, complexity, trialability, and observability. Questionnaires and interviews were used, and the subjects were students and faculty members, and micro vendors. The findings showed that micros were perceived to have relative advantages, compatibility, simplicity, trialability, and observability by the study's social systems. Of the students and faculty surveyed, 28.6% used micros and the social network for micros was found to be generally established. However, vendor communication with clients was perceived as not very effective even though clients perceived vendors to have empathy and homophily. Four factors were perceived to hinder micro diffusion: limited availability of Arabic micro literature; limited availability of university courses about micros; limited services including maintenance, training, and consultation; and lack of public awareness. Conversely, the following problems were found: abnormal, vague appearance of Arabic characters on the screen; lack of Arabic software; confusing Arabic computer terminology; and difficulty programming in Arabic. The absence of copyright policy for software was also determined to affect the development of software. [DAI 49/04-A: 646.]

INFORMATION TECHNOLOGY—USE

850 Bukhari, A. A., and A. Jack Meadows. "The use of information technology by scientists in British and Saudi Arabian universities: a comparative study." *Journal of Information Science* 18, no. 5 (1992): 409-415.

Part of a special issue devoted to library and information services in the Arab countries after the Gulf War. A parallel study has been carried out of the use of information technology by scientists at universities in the UK and Saudi Arabia. A questionnaire survey on this topic was originally carried out in the UK during 1985-1986. New surveys, based on the same set of questions, have been carried out in the UK and Saudi Arabia during 1991. This provides a five-year baseline of data for the UK, which can be used to discern trends in usage and it permits a comparison of current Saudi usage with the position in the UK. The results indicate a rapid growth and diversification of information technology activities in the UK. Usage in Saudi Arabia is already approaching the level found in British universities in the mid 1980s. [A]

851 Deemer, Selden S. "Online in Saudi Arabia." *Information Technology and Libraries* 1, no. 1 (March 1982): 37-41. [Communication.]

Factors inhibiting the use of computers in Saudi libraries are outlined. The recent trend towards a growth in the use of computers, in spite of difficulties, is noted in the light of labor shortages and staffing problems. Use of computers is seen as one way to improve library services without expanding staff.

852 Mirza, Mohammad I., Moid A. Siddiqui. "CD-ROM bibliographic database searching at the KFUPM library: a use analysis." *Aslib Proceedings* 45, no. 5 (May 1993): 137-143.

The article analyzes 2,378 CD-ROM bibliographic database searches (by databases used, user status, departments, and user needs) conducted at the King Fahd University of Petroleum and Minerals (KFUPM) Library in Saudi Arabia during the period from July 1991 (when service started) to 31 December 1992. Various purposes for compiling CD-ROM statistics have also being discussed.

853 al-Musnad, Ibrahim Abdullah. *A Study of the Factors Influencing the Adoption of CD-ROM Technology in Libraries in Saudi Arabia.* Ph.D., 1994. 224 p.

The purpose of this study was to establish baseline data on the use of CD-ROM technology in libraries and information centers in Saudi Arabia. This study examined the knowledge, experience, and attitudes of library directors in the country as well as selected demographic and financial data about the libraries. A descriptive survey research method utilizing a questionnaire was chosen as the most appropriate and effective method for collecting the data needed to answer the study's research questions. Of the 68 libraries and information centers identified by the researcher, 66 (97%) provided usable responses. Descriptive statistics and the chi-square test were the statistical procedures used for the data analysis. It was found that 35% of the responding libraries were using CD-ROM technology and 32% were planning to acquire this technology in the future. The rest (33%) of the responding libraries were not using CD-ROM nor did they plan to acquire it in the future. Several reasons were given for not acquiring this technology: the library was too small, CD-ROM was never considered, CD-ROM costs too much in relation to the library budget, there was no user demand, and useful products were not available in Arabic. Institution control (public/private), student enrollment, library budget, number of professional librarians, respondents' level of education, and respondents' experience with online and CD-ROM searches were factors that significantly impacted the decision to acquire CD-ROM in a library. The study findings indicate that the majority (74%) of the libraries with CD-ROM employ additional security measures to protect their CD-ROM systems from damage and loss. Despite the large percentage employing security measures, fewer than 20% of the respondents believe that their libraries have serious security problems. The overwhelming majority (94%) of the respondents believe that CD-ROM use and evaluation should be included in the library school curricula. More than 85% of the respondents, whether their libraries have CD-ROM or not, believe that the availability of CD-ROM in libraries has a positive effect on librarians' image. [DAI 56/01-A: 15.]

854 al-Musned, Saleh Mohammed. *Microcomputer Training Guidelines for the College of Education of King Saud University: A Pilot Study Based on the Concerns-Based Adoption Model.* Ph.D., 1989. University of Pittsburgh. 145 p.

The primary purpose of this study was to assess the stages of concerns, levels of use of computers, and the variations of computer usage and applications by the faculty of the College of Education, King Saud University (KSU) in Saudi Arabia. The study utilized the Concerns-Based Adoption Model (CBAM). The CBAM is a generic diagnostic tool that provides a means by which to describe the attitudes, feelings, motivations, performances of the group as well as the individual toward an innovation, and what the innovation means to both the actual user and potential user. To answer the study research questions, a descriptive research method was employed. The population of this study was comprised of 183 faculty members of the College of Education of KSU. Of the 183, a random sample consisting of 56 subjects was drawn and administered the study questionnaire. The questionnaire consisted of four sections: (a) a demographics section, (b) a computer usage components checklist, and (c) an adaptation of the CBAM's Stages of Concern Questionnaire (SOCQ). Also, seven faculty members of the study sample were randomly selected and interviewed utilizing an adaptation of the CBAM's focused interview in order to determine their levels of use of computers. The findings of this study indicated that: (a) the respondents were a homogeneous group in terms of their demographic characteristics; (b) the respondents had low intense concerns (awareness, informational, and personal) about computers; (c) the respondents had some doubts about computers; (d) those respondents who did not use computers indicated more negative attitudes toward computers than their counterparts; and (e) those respondents who indicated low level of use had low intense stages of concerns. Based on the findings, microcomputer training program guidelines were proposed. [DAI 50/11-A: 3398.]

855 al-Salim, Salim Muhammad. "al-Tiqaniyah al-ma'lumatiyah al-mustakhdamah fi al-maktabat wa marakiz al-ma'lumat al-Sa'udiyah: dirasah lilmushkilat wa-al-hulul." *'Alam al-Kutub* 14, no. 5 (September-October 1993): 502-518.

Examines information technology used in the libraries and information centers in Saudi Arabia.

856 Siddiqui, Moid A., and Mohammad I. Mirza. "Impact of CD-ROM searching on reference and information services in a university library." *Program* 28, no. 4 (October 1994): 405-413.

Reports results of a study to determine the effects of CD-ROM searching on reference services and information services in King Fahd University of Petroleum and Minerals Library (KFUPM). The data collected before and after the introduction of CD-ROM databases was compared to analyze the CD-ROM impact on various reference services, such as interloans, online searching, reference questions, assistance with online public access catalogs (OPACs), staff requirements and development. Concludes that CD-ROM has made the nature of the reference work considerably more complex. CD-ROM searching has a direct impact on different reference activities, in terms of time and new skills required by reference librarians, and this needs to be recognized by the library management. The implementation of this new technology increased the dependence upon human resources and the need for additional reference staff should be anticipated to cope with the increased workload and stress on library staff with the implementation of CD-ROM search services. The need for more staff could be alleviated by the introduction of end user training courses. [A]

INTERLIBRARY LOAN

857 al-'Anani, Shukri. "al-I'arah al-mutabadalah bayna al-maktabat al-jami'iyah ma' dirasah li waqi' hadha al-nashat bayna al-maktabat al-jami'iyah fi al-Mamlakah al-'Arabiyah al-Sa'udiyah." *Maktabat al-Idarah* 14, no. 3 (April-May 1987): 117-162.

858 Brown, Patricia L., and Daniel Blucker. "Interlibrary cooperation in the Kingdom of Saudi Arabia: the holder-of-record system." *Bulletin of the Medical Library Association* 75, no. 4 (October 1987): 323-325.

The Saudi Arabian Ministry of Defense and Aviation, which contracts for management of military hospitals, responded to the libraries' needs for more complete and extensive journal holdings. Better journal coverage was achieved through improved communication and cooperation among neighbor libraries, and through systematic implementation of a holder-of-record system. Interlibrary loan activity was more evenly distributed, and 70% of requisitions which previously had to be handled by foreign libraries can now be filled in Saudi Arabia. [A]

859 Kanamugire, Athanase B. "Impact of CD-ROM database searching on interlibrary loans: the experience of a scientific and technological library in a developing country." *Journal of Interlibrary Loan, Document Delivery and Information Supply* 4, no. 1 (1993): 25-34.

Reports on a study conducted to determine whether there was an increase in interlibrary loan requests since the introduction of CD-ROM searching at the King Fahd University of Petroleum and Minerals Library, Saudi Arabia, and if so, the magnitude and implications of such an increase. Data collected from interlibrary loan requests received between August 1991 and September 1992 were analyzed. Results indicate that there was an increase of approximately 13%. Over 21% of all interlibrary loan (ILL) requests were prompted by CD-ROM searching. To address some of the problems encountered due to the growing number of ILL requests, recommends that the library acquire the journals indexed in most frequently used CD-ROM databases in whatever form-hardcopy, microform of CD-ROM full text databases. [A]

860 Siddiqui, Moid A. "Interlending in a university library: the KFUPM Library experience." *International Library Review* 22, no. 4 (December 1990): 329-338.

This paper describes the statistics of 1340 interlibrary loan/photocopy (ILL) requests processed by the Reference and Information Services Division of the King Fahd Unversity of Petroleum and Minerals Library, Dhahran, Saudi Arabia from April 1, 1985 to March 31, 1986. The objective of compiling the statistics is to assess the weak and strong areas of the library's collection so that necessary steps may be taken to balance it. Also, it is hoped that these statistics would provide valuable results which will help in managing ILL in future as the number of ILL requests are increasing every year. [A]

861 Siddiqui, Moid A. "Interlibrary loan policy and procedures of the King Fahd University of Petroleum and Minerals Library." *Interlending and Document Supply* 19, no. 1 (January 1991): 11-14.

The King Fahd University of Petroleum and Minerals Library, Saudi Arabia, has been finding it increasingly difficult to satisfy the growing but legitimate demand for interlibrary loan (ILL) services. This paper describes the policy and procedures established by the Library to meet the ILL needs of its clients as efficiently and rapidly as possible. An extensive ILL network has been developed and the transactions themselves are managed using an IBM PC. Statistical information is used to monitor the service and improve the local collections. [A]

862 Siddiqui, Moid A. "INTERLOAN: a microcomputer-based interlibrary loan system." *Microcomputers for Information Management* 9, no. 1 (1992): 47-59.

This article describes the functioning of INTERLOAN, the library online interloans system implemented at King Fahd University of Petroleum and Minerals Library, Saudi Arabia. The objective of creating INTERLOAN system was to manage and improve the turn around time of interlibrary loans and also to reduce the work related to manual processing and record keeping. [A]

863 Siddiqui, Moid A. "Interlibrary loan services of the King Fahd University of Petroleum & Minerals Library." *Journal of Interlibrary Loan & Information Supply* 2, no. 3 (1992): 15-31.

Interlibrary loan (ILL) is a service through which the library borrows books or obtains photocopies of articles from other libraries. The King Fahd University of Petroleum and Minerals, Saudi Arabia (KFUPM) recognizes the need users have for information and it has established ILL procedures to meet this need as efficiently and rapidly as possible. This article describes the ILL services (lending and borrowing) of the KFUPM Library supported by statistical information. [A]

864 Siddiqui, Moid A. *A Comparative Study of Interlibrary Loan Functions and the Development of a Model Interlibrary Loan Network among Academic Libraries in Saudi Arabia (Resource Sharing, Document Delivery)*. Ph.D., 1995. University of Natal (South Africa). 302 p.

The purpose of this study was to survey and analyze the condition of the present system of academic libraries, defined in this study as the seven university libraries in Saudi Arabia; determine the perceptions of academic librarians in toward cooperation; and design a model interlibrary loan network (ILLN) for the academic libraries there. An extensive analysis of international literature related to interlibrary loan developments and resource sharing networks in developed, as well as developing countries was conducted. A document review, questionnaire survey, and structured interview were used for data collection. A questionnaire was administered to the seven Deans of academic libraries to obtain data related to library personnel, collections, budgets, library equipment, the extent of cooperative interaction among the libraries, and the network opinion, etc. Interviews of the librarians of the subject academic libraries were also conducted. Major findings of the questionnaire survey are: 6 of the 7 academic libraries of Saudi Arabia do not meet the ACRL standards in respect of collections. No library indicated that 'All of the Needs' in respect of textbooks, research, and recreation are being provided by their respective libraries. All seven libraries indicated that they have cooperation with all other academic libraries, but they borrow/lend materials either occasionally or do not borrow/lend at all. Inadequate finances and inadequate resources were ranked number one as factors hindering cooperation among academic libraries. The interlibrary loan by photocopy service was ranked number one as area of cooperative activities by all academic libraries. There was also agreement that current cooperative activities were inadequate. They strongly favor participation in an ILLN and rated an ILLN as highly desirable. It was determined that the collections of the academic libraries are small and not up to any reasonable standard. Therefore, they are unable to adequately fulfill the needs of their users. The need for the immediate initiation of a cooperative and coordinated collection development policy of monographs and serials among the academic libraries is evident. This study proposed an ILLN that will both be a distributed and centralized network in which academic libraries will coordinate and communicate directly with each other. [DAI 58/09-A: 3347.]

865 Siddiqui, Moid A. "Compact disk indexes effect on interlibrary loan at a university library." *Libri* 45 (September-December 1995): 178-185.

This article is an attempt to study of the effects of CD-ROM database searching on interlibrary loans at a university library. The study is based on the statistical information compiled at the King Fahd University of Petroleum and Minerals (KFUPM) Library, Dhahran, Saudi Arabia. The data was collected over a three-year period, from July 1991 (when CD-ROM search service started) to June 1994, by analyzing the interlibrary loan requests submitted by the faculty, graduate students and researchers to the reference and information services for borrowing. The study indicates an upward trend in interlibrary loan requests due to the introduction of CD-ROM database searching; extra burdening the KFUPM Library as the borrowing cost of articles. The impact of CD-ROM database searching on staffing due to increased work load and stress is also discussed. [A]

866 Siddiqui, Moid A. "An interlibrary loan network among academic libraries of Saudi Arabia." *Journal of Interlibrary Loan, Document Delivery and Information Supply* 7, no. 1 (1996): 15-30.

This article presents a model plan of an interlibrary loan network (ILLN) among academic libraries of Saudi Arabia and discusses its organizational structure, governance, operational requirements, and finances, etc. The proposed ILLN will be formal, regular, and systematic to provide greater cooperation, coordination, efficiency, cost effectiveness, and will ensure comprehensive sharing of available resources.

ISLAMIC LIBRARIES

867 Arif, Mohammad. "Tarikh maktabat al-Haram al-Makki." *'Alam al-Kutub* 4, no. 4 (January 1984): 546-550.

868 Ibn Dohaish, Abdul Latif Abdullah. "Public and private libraries in the Hijaz up to 1925." *Pakistan Library Bulletin* 10, no. 1-2 (January-April 1979): 17-25.

Based on the author's 1974 Ph.D. dissertation for Leeds University, *History of Education in the Hijaz Up to 1925: Comparative and Critical Study*. The only Hijaz cities having libraries in 1800-1925 appear to have been Mecca and Medina. Mecca had three private and two public libraries, all containing rare manuscripts and valuable books. When the Saudi Arabia State took over after 1925, it purchased and amalgamated the libraries. Medina seems to have had many richly-endowed libraries having both public and educational functions. To preserve the rare and valuable contents of the smaller and private libraries, the Governor of Medina decreed in 1919 that all such collections should be acquired and housed together.

869 Ibn Dohaish, Abdul Latif Abdullah. "Libraries of Madina-al-Munawwarah (during the Ottoman period)." *Pakistan Library Bulletin* 11, no. 1-2 (March-June 1980): 1-12.

Provides a historical review of the development of the private and public libraries in the holy city of Madina-al-Munawwarah, Saudi Arabia, during the Ottoman period. Discusses the Library of Sultan Mahmood, established between 1223 and 1255 A.H., the Library of Arif Hikmat, established during the 13th century of Hijra, the Uthmania Library, and the Library of the Madrasah of al-Shifa.

870   Ibn Dohaish, Abdul Latif Abdullah. "Makkah al-Mukarramak Library." *Pakistan Library Bulletin* 18, no. 2-3 (June-September 1987): 7-11.

Describes the history of the Library of Haram at Makkah al-Mukaramah, Saudi Arabia, which was formally inaugurated in 1959 and eventually taken over by the Ministry of Haj and Endowment. Discusses library staffing, personal collections donated to the library, and the division of the library into administration, acquisition and technical services, readers services, photocopying and book-binding.

871   Ibn Dohaish, Abdul Latif Abdullah. "Libraries at Makkah al-Mukarramah." *Pakistan Library Bulletin* 19, no. 1 (March 1988): 21-25.

LIBRARY ADMINISTRATION/MANAGEMENT

872   Siddiqui, Moid A. "Management of libraries in Saudi Arabia: practices and constraints." *Library Management* 16, no. 6 (1995): 24-32.

Discusses the management of different types of libraries in Saudi Arabia with reference to the existing practices in the country. Indicates various problems faced by these libraries, such as absence of library legislation, absence of a library association, lack of funding, and scarcity of native librarians. Suggests how to overcome these constraints. [A]

LIBRARY COOPERATION

873   Brown, Patricia L., and Daniel Blucker. "Library co-operation in the military hospitals of Saudi Arabia." *Library Association Record* 90, no. 7 (July 15, 1988): 402-403.

Describes library cooperation in the six medical libraries of the Saudi Arabian Ministry of Defence and Aviation (MODA) which have been opened since the 1970s in Dhahran, Jeddah, Khamis Mushayt, Riyadh, Tabuk and Taif. Interlibrary loans now take about three days using the holder-of-record responsibility system agreed by the MODA libraries. Cooperation also produced the MODA Standards for hospital library services and a microform journal collection for 1970-80 which meets about 70% of requests previously sent overseas.

874   Sa'ati, Yahya Mahmud. "Subul al-ta'awun bayna al-maktabat al-jami'iyah al-sa'udiyah fi bina' al-majmu'at." *Maktabat al-Idarah* 15, no. 1 (August 1987): 7-26.

875 Sliney, Marjory. "Medical information in the Kingdom of Saudi Arabia: the case for library co-operation." *Health Information and Libraries* 2, no. 3 (1991): 140-153.

Indicates the shortage of medical journals and the underutilization of the available medical information in Saudi Arabia based upon experience gained while working in the Eastern Province. Describes the infrastructure of medical libraries and current levels of information provision both of which would point to a degree of cooperation with countries in the region such as Bahrain and Kuwait. Proposes certain cooperative ventures which would increase accessibility of information in the area of purchases, document delivery, interloans, joint periodical indexes, and microform services, and which would be economically advantageous. Examines potential problems such as copyright restrictions and those associated with document delivery, and lists the advantages of cooperation. [A]

876 Swaydan, Nasser M. "al-Ta'awun bayna al-maktabat al-Sa'udiyah fi majal al-ijra'at al-fanniyah." *Maktabat al-Idarah* 8:2 (March 1983): 5-17.

LIBRARY EDUCATION

877 Alsereihy, Hassan Awad. *Continuing Library Education: Practices and Preferences of the University and Major Research Library Personnel in Saudi Arabia with Special Emphasis on Technical Services Staff (University Library Personnel, Library Education)*. Ph.D., 1993. Indiana University. 225 p.

This exploratory study identified the continuing library education practices and preferences of university librarians and librarians at the major research centers of Saudi Arabia. It also had a comparative aspect in that it examined the available continuing education opportunities for Saudi and non-Saudi librarians. In addition, it compared technical services librarians' perceptions of continuing education needs and those of librarians from other departments in libraries under investigation. A survey research design utilizing questionnaires was chosen as the most appropriate and effective method for gathering the data needed to answer the study's twelve research questions. Three different but related populations were queried. These groups were librarians employed in the seven Saudi university libraries, or librarians employed in a purposeful sample of major research libraries plus the deans and directors of these libraries and the heads or representatives of the four existing library and information science departments in the Saudi universities. Descriptive statistics, Pearson correlation coefficient tests, and t-test statistical procedures were used for data analysis. It was found that continuing education activities and opportunities available to the librarians in the Saudi university and major research libraries were inadequate despite their strong support for the concept of continuing education. This strong support was not affected by nationality, type of library, or departmental affiliation of the respondents. The findings of this investigation provided the means for the development of the suggested successful continuing education model presented in this study. [DAI 54/04-A: 1132.]

878 Hamade, Samir N. "Computer services in libraries and information centres of Saudi Arabia." *Libri* 45, no. 1 (March 1995): 31-35.

Computer technology is flourishing rapidly in Saudi Arabia. Saudi libraries and information centers have benefited from this by implementing integrated information systems such as DOBIS/LIBIS, MINISIS and STAIRS to automate their activities. Online access and CD-ROM services are available free of charge to researchers by a large number of libraries and information centers. However, since its establishment in 1977, King Abdulaziz City for Science and Technology (KACST) has become the center for all computerized activities in the country. KACST established a local area network (KACST-NET) connecting more than 55 Saudi research institutes, libraries and information centers. A wide area network (GULF-NET) was also established by KACST connecting 11 public institutes in Saudi Arabia and Kuwait with the aim of connecting all Arab Gulf countries in the near future. Access to international networks such as BITNET and EARN is also available to GULFNET members. These computer services have some shortcomings that can be summarized by manpower shortage, language barriers and lack of cooperation. These problems should be addressed in depth in order to find suitable solutions and fulfill the information needs of end-users. [A]

879 Kanamugire, Athanase B. "Electronic information services and bibliographic retrieval education programs at King Fahd University of Petroleum and Minerals Library in Saudi Arabia." *International Information & Library Review* 28, no. 3 (September 1996): 233-248.

This article reviews various definitions of information literacy and discusses a study conducted at the King Fahd University of Petroleum and Minerals (KFUPM) Library, Saudi Arabia, to reassess the need for information literacy, to identify factors which influenced non-attendance, to evaluate the impact of the program, and comments suggestions used. The major findings include: there is a dire need for information literacy; participants found the programs useful; and one-on-one method coupled with seminars were more effective and more preferred by the participants. The article also advances a set of recommendations for improving bibliographic retrieval education programs at the KFUPM Library and other libraries in Saudi Arabia and other countries. [A]

880 Myers-Hayer, P. "Insights into automation training at a Saudi Women's College Library." *Feminist Collections* 17, no. 2 (Winter 1996): 43-44.

Reports on experiences of training women library staff at the King Abdul Aziz Women's College, Kingdom of Saudi Arabia, as part of the American Library Association's Library Fellows' Program. Describes the women's library and the staff. Currently women do not catalog online or add holdings information. Training focused on searching the online catalog, which accommodates both Arabic and English scripts. [A]

881 al-Sari', Sari' Muhammad. "Ta'lim al-maktabat fi al-Mamlakah al-'Arabiyah al-Sa'udiyah." *Maktabat al-Idarah* 13 (October 1985): 59-86.

882 Sattar Chaudhry, Abdus, Mohammad Saleh Ashoor, and Sajjadur Rehman. "Development and implementation of an in-house continuing education program in an academic library." *Education for Information* 11, no. 1 (March 1993): 47-56.

This paper reviews the preparation, planning and implementation of the Continuing Education (CE) program aimed at upgrading the skills and the competencies of the library staff at the King Fahd University of Petroleum and Minerals (KFUPM) Library, Saudi Arabia. The process of assessing the needs and strategies used for program development and implementation as well as problems faced in coordinating the various components of CE program is discussed. The CE program consisting of (1) short courses, (2) workshops, (3) symposia, (4) pre- and post-conference tutorials, and (5) local seminars - proved to be an effective means of staff development. Perhaps the key to the success of the CE program was the involvement of the library staff in assessing the needs and the structure of the program. A total of six short courses, nine workshops and 16 local seminars were conducted over a three year period as part of the CE program. An interim evaluation, follow-up to assure the utilization of training imparted, and an appropriate mechanism for continued motivation of staff have been considered necessary for future success of the program. [A]

883 al-Sharif, Abdullah M. *Education for Librarianship in the Arab Countries: Present Practices, Problems, and Possible Solutions*. Ph.D., Case Western Reserve University, 1977. 349 p. DAI 38/08-A 4425.

884 al-Shimi, Husni 'Abd al-Rahman. *Muqawwimat al-Dawr al-Tarbawi lil-Maktabat al-Madrasiyah: Dirasah Tatbiqiyah*. al-Riyad: Dar al-Mirrikh, 1987. 275 p.

885 Siddiqui, Moid A. "Library and information science education in Saudi Arabia." *Education for Information* 14, no. 3 (October 1996): 195-214.

This paper describes, in brief, the different levels of education and various types of libraries in Saudi Arabia. It reviews the state of professional library and information science education with particular reference to six library schools: King Abdulaziz University; Imam Muhammed ibn Saud

Islamic University; King Saud University; Umm al-Qura University; Girls College of Arts; and Institute of Public Administration. It concludes that in spite of the fact that there are these library schools in Saudi Arabia, the library workforce is still comprised of predominantly expatriates. Finally, it suggests steps to solve the constraints faced by LIS education in the country. [A]

NATIONAL LIBRARIES

886 al-Nahari, Abdulaziz Mohamed. *The National Library: An Analysis of the Critical Factors in Promoting Library and Information Services in Developing Countries: The Case of Saudi Arabia.* Ph.D., 1982. University of California, Los Angeles. 365 p.

This study has investigated the nature of national libraries through a study of their generally accepted functions and of those functions appropriate to the establishment of such a library in a developing country like Saudi Arabia. The author undertook the following procedures: (1) Compiled a list of the national library functions which are mentioned in the literature, and included it in a questionnaire which was sent to fifty national libraries throughout the world asking them to indicate on a scale of 1-5, the priority level of those functions they perform. (2) Reviewed and analyzed official documents in Saudi Arabia on the current state of library and information services. (3) Obtained opinions from Saudi professionals and potential users, and from the national librarians previously surveyed as to proper functions for a proposed national library in Saudi Arabia. 82% of the national libraries' questionnaires and 87.5% of the Saudi professionals' questionnaires were returned. The analysis generated a clear idea as to the functions of a national library, based on the concepts of collecting, organizing, preserving, and controlling a country's national literature. This is done through the exercise of twenty-two functions which, although implemented differently among the world's countries in response to local, social, political, and economic circumstances, are acknowledged to be valid functions of a national library. It is clear that a national library is necessary for any country which (like Saudi Arabia) has no national library nor any other institution which collects and controls the national literature. A method for planning a national library is proposed in the form of planning guidelines for Saudi Arabia which takes into consideration the current state of the nation's library and information services, as well as the opinions of Saudi professionals and of national librarians. The guidelines suggest the establishment of a national library in Saudi Arabia through a ten-year planning period, in three phases of two, three, and five years. Although the planning guidelines are devised in Saudi terms, a general framework is proposed in the form of a checklist for planning national libraries in other developing countries. [DAI 43/01-A: 6.]

887 al-Nahari, Abdulaziz Mohamed. *The Role of National Libraries in Developing Countries, with Special Reference to Saudi Arabia*. London; New York: Mansell, 1984. vi, 166 p.

An assessment of the objectives of a national library in the developing world based on Unesco planning seminars and other national library literature. Saudi Arabia, which is without a national library, is used as a case-study. The state of contemporary library and information services in Saudi Arabia is examined, and a planning process for a national library is proposed.

888 al-Nahari, Abdulaziz Mohamed. "al-Maktabah al-wataniyah fi al-Mamlakah al-'Arabiyah al-Sa'udiyah." *Maktabat al-Idarah* 13, no. 1 (October 1985): 283-296.

NETWORKS AND NETWORKING

889 Dhohayan, Abdulrahman Ibrahim. *Islamic Resource Sharing Network: A Feasibility Study for its Establishment among University Libraries of Saudi Arabia and the Republic of Turkey as Representative Islamic Nations*. D.L.S., 1981. University of Southern California.

We now live in a new library and information generation. Information is considered universally a national resource. Information has schools, centers and agencies dedicated to its study. This is true all over the world. This is a feasibility study for the establishment of an Islamic Resource Sharing Network (IRSN) among university libraries of the Kingdom of Saudi Arabia and the Republic of Turkey, two representative Islamic nations. Related literature has been reviewed for this study to help define the network concept, and the characteristics of Islamic libraries and librarianship. Technological advances provide a comprehensive response to the issues and problems facing library services and activities in both countries on two levels: (1) electronic data processing, for example, will help them gain control of their respective resources through establishing extensive and easily referenced bibliographies; (2) these advances will help to make possible the development of Islamic resource sharing networks among university libraries. This study consists of three major parts: describing the university libraries of each country, including their collections, communications technology, audio-visual materials, methods of bibliographic control and budget. These data will help to describe the existing librarianship at each university under study and the ability of these university libraries to cooperate with one another. The second section describes the relationships among the seven Saudi university libraries, which indicates that there is cooperation. However, among Turkish university libraries, there is less cooperation than there should be. This study also demonstrated that cooperation between university libraries of the two countries is limited to certain subjects and certain universities.

The Saudis and the Turks have separate cooperative programs with other foreign countries, including the United States, England, and other European countries. This cooperation, however, is limited to a very few types of service. In third section, the IRSN concept was presented. It is the main theme of this dissertation, including IRSN governance, where it should be located, the forms of the bibliographic control, technologies, and the means of communication. Furthermore, major IRSN requirements, its responsibilities, its advantages and disadvantages, obstacles facing the project and some good comments and recommendations from the respondents are discussed in order to present clearly the opinions and views of the respondents. [DAI 42/10-A: 4189.]

890 Hafez, Abdulrasheed Abdulaziz. *A Prescriptive Model for Planning and Implementing a Resource Sharing and Information Networking System among Saudi University Libraries (University Libraries)*. Ph.D., 1989. Indiana University. 300 p.

The purposes of this study were to investigate and analyze the condition of the present systems of university libraries in Saudi Arabia, to determine the perceptions of the librarians in the seven universities toward collaboration, and to design a prescriptive model for resource sharing and information network system among Saudi university libraries. The design of the study utilized the descriptive research method which comprised review of the related literature and questionnaire survey. Two sets of questionnaires were used. One was directed to the deans of the seven university libraries to collect factual data on the present systems of their libraries, and the other was directed to university librarians to elicit their opinions and perceptions toward the proposed networking system. The findings of the study revealed that the problems of Saudi university libraries stem from a lack of coordination among these libraries, an absence of national planning, an insufficient number of professionals, and the present state of shrinking budgets. University librarians perceived the proposed network activities as important factors for improving the current situation. Respondents expressed their concern for the need of a strong institutional leadership, adequate financial support and establishment of a national library and identified a number of obstacles to the establishment of cooperative systems. The majority of respondents expressed the desirability of a cooperative system and felt that it is currently possible to establish such a system. Based on the findings, the study designed a prescriptive model for establishing a network system among Saudi university libraries. The model is described as a multi-functional distributed network in which all seven university libraries will have a sense of equal being and will communicate directly with one another. The model specified the proposed system's goals and objectives, organizational structure, and network functions and programs including the need to address both current and future demands as well as a wide range of concerns revealed from the study. The model is conceived as a guideline to fill a void and to assist further planning and organization of the proposed system. [DAI 50/07-A: 1834.]

891 al-Khulaifi, M. "Gulfnet in Saudi Arabia: an overview." *Information Services & Use* 15, no. 1 (1995): 53-56.

This article contains a short overview of Gulfnet Academic Network, set in the context of development in Saudi Arabia and the establishment of King Abdulaziz City for Science and Technology (KACST). Sets out KACST's goals and objectives, it lists Gulfnet members in the Gulf states, and discusses Gulfnet management, services and facilities. [A]

892 Khurshid, Zahiruddin. "DOBIS/LIBIS network of university libraries in Saudi Arabia." *Resource Sharing & Information Networks* 9, no. 2 (1994): 101-110.

University libraries in Saudi Arabia have wasted much time and money in carrying out automation activities on their own. Four of the 7 universities in the country have acquired the same library application software, DOBIS/LIBIS, which has excellent multiple language and network capabilities waiting to be exploited. The paper presents a conceptual model based on the network structure and requirements of DOBIS/LIBIS and proposes a network of university libraries based on the existing infrastructure. The King Fahd University of Petroleum and Minerals Library has the necessary resources and capabilities to become a central node in the network and to host a union catalog of participating libraries.

893 al-Tunisi, Hammadi Ali. *Feasibility of Establishing a National Information Network System for Saudi Arabia: An Analysis*. Ph.D., 1988. University of Pittsburgh. 228 p.

This study attempts to investigate the current situation of cooperative programs and activities which exist among Saudi University and special libraries. In addition it identifies the problems and barriers encountered in developing a National Information Network System (NINS) for Saudi Arabia. The study focuses on the attitudinal factors including resistance to technology, personal ego, lack of motivation and willingness to act, and negative feelings toward sharing library resources which may exist among librarians and library administrators. Opinions of these groups in addition to library users concerning the desirability and feasibility of establishing such a network were obtained. The findings of this study present the need for a formal and scientific plan for a cooperative interlibrary system in Saudi Arabia. Additionally, the findings support the existence of several problems including fear of losing materials, competition in purchasing materials, fear of changing familiar processes and procedures as a result of using new technologies in libraries. Data, on the other hand, do not support the existence of some attitudinal problems including: fear of losing job, fear of losing information privacy, fear of using computers, dehumanizing relationships, and potential harmfulness to society. Establishing a national network was strongly requested by all the respondent groups. They perceive that it is time for Saudi Arabia to have its national information network system to improve library and information services provided by university and special libraries in Saudi Arabia. [DAI 50/04-A: 817.]

ONLINE CATALOGS

894 Deemer, Selden S. "Public access searching through DOBIS." *Software Review* 2, no. 3 (September 1983): 148-157.
DOBIS is a commercially available software package that supports a public access search function. The paper evaluates this function of DOBIS, basing conclusions on the DOBIS online catalog which has been running at the University of Petroleum and Minerals Library, Dhahran, Saudi Arabia, since April 1982. DOBIS is easy to use because of its menu-driven design and consistent display of information. Experienced users can bypass the menu system and get quicker results. Disadvantages include the rather rigid search algorithms which compare spelling, spacing and punctuation and the requirement of using IBM 3270-compatible terminals for an application usually requiring only a display screen and minimal keyboard. Explains the modifications which can be made to DOBIS. [A]

895 Khurshid, Zahiruddin. "Public access online catalogue at the University of Petroleum and Minerals Library." *Herald of Library Science* 23, no. 3-4 (July-August 1984): 192-195.

States that the University of Petroleum and Minerals Library (UPM), Dhahran, Saudi Arabia is in the middle of creating an online public access catalog. Discusses important features of the UPM online catalog, developed on DOBIS software marketed by IBM. Refers to the conventional card catalogs being maintained until retrospective conversion is completed. States the availability of a back-up COM catalog. Describes the efforts being made to develop systems capability for handling Arabic catalog data.

896 Khurshid, Zahiruddin "Arabic Online Catalog." [Communications.] *Information Technology and Libraries* 11 (September 1992): 244-251.

The article provides background information on the processing of Arabic materials using a combination of local and modified cataloging rules and the creation of the Arabic card catalog at the King Fahd University of Petroleum and Minerals Library (KFUPM). It also gives a brief history of KFPUM library automation and then presents various options considered for developing the Arabized version of DOBIS/LIBIS. Finally, the functions and features of the Arabic online catalog are described.

PERSONNEL

897 Namlah, Ali Ibrahim. "Manpower deficiency in Saudi Arabia: its effect on the library and information profession." *International Library Review* 14, no. 1 (January 1982): 3-20.

Saudi Arabia is a wealthy country with a chronic shortage of trained manpower that equally affects Saudi libraries of which there are 40 in the public sector and 11 attached to universities. At the beginning of the 1970s the shortage reached epidemic proportions, forcing the government to recruit intensively from abroad. Imported labor has not been without its drawbacks. For example, high staff turnover makes policy making in library administration difficult. Saudi Arabia already has two library schools which help to offset these difficulties. More are required, however, and there is a need for a Saudi professional association comparable to the Library Association in the UK. The establishment of a union catalog and the development of computer systems will be important in the continuing improvement of Saudi libraries.

898 Namlah, Ali Ibrahim. "al-'Ajz fi al-qiwah al-'amilah wa-ta'thirahu 'ala khidmat al-kitab." *'Alam al-Kutub* 5, no. 3 (September-October 1983): 483-492.

Public library staff deserve better incentives in the way of deserved promotion, and the chance to work in a more professional environment. They should be preoccupied with matters that affect their performance. They should feel like valued professionals.

899 Tashkandi, Abbas Saleh. "al-Qiwa al-bashariyah al-'amilah fi al-maktabat wa-marakiz al-ma'lumat fi al-Mamlakah." *'Alam al-Kutub* 6, no. 4 (December 1985): 466-480.

PUBLIC LIBRARIES

900 Abbas, Hisham Abdullah. *A Plan for Public Library System Development in Saudi Arabia*. Ph.D., 1982. University of Pittsburgh. 147 p.

This study has attempted to (1) review the background and development of public libraries in Saudi Arabia; (2) survey the current status, and to assess the present and future needs of public libraries; (3) to develop a plan of action to establish a national public library system for Saudi Arabia. The methodology utilized for data collection consisted of an analysis of the literature, questionnaires, and interviews. Questionnaires were sent to all fifty-six public library directors in Saudi Arabia to secure data in regard to administration, personnel, resources, physical facilities, and services in public libraries. These data were supplemented by interviews conducted with librarians, administrators, and top government officials.

Additional interviews were devised to elicit expert opinion on library training, the existing situation of public library system and the requirements for establishing a national public library system. Data gathered were also compared with similar systems in other countries as described in the literature. The data analysis indicated that public libraries have been functioning in Saudi Arabia for a long time, but their impact and role in the socioeconomic and educational ventures are far less than it should be for the following reasons: (1) absence of public library legislation; (2) insufficient funds; (3) lack of needed resources; (4) shortage of qualified personnel; (5) inadequate facilities; (6) lack of appreciation of the role of public libraries in the national development; (7) absence of planning; (8) lack of cooperation and coordination; and (9) inadequacy of programs and services. Based on the findings, a plan has been proposed for a plan of action to establish a national system for public libraries in Saudi Arabia. The proposed plan defines what the system should be able to do and comprises the requirements necessary for implementing the system. While several alternatives for organizational structure were presented, the centralized approach was recommended. [DAI 43/04-A: 960.]

901 Abbas, Hisham Abdullah. "Problems facing public libraries in developing countries, with special reference to Saudi Arabia: a state-of-the-art." *Libri* 36, 4 (December 1986): 297-312.

Discusses the reasons for slow growth in library development in the developing countries focusing on the situation in Saudi Arabia. These include: fostering reader interest; the production of reading materials; socio-economic conditions; recognition of the importance of library services; financial resources; physical facilities; manpower; organization of library materials; librarians' attitude towards information sources; and national library planning.

902 Abbas, Hisham Abdullah. "Public libraries in Saudi Arabia." In *Information and Libraries in the Arab World*. Compiled and edited by Michael Wise and Anthony Olden, pp. 140-154. London: Library Association Publishing, 1994. [Information and libraries in the developing world, vol. 3.]

Article included in a collection of papers presenting a comparative review of librarianship and library practices in Arab countries. Reviews the development of public libraries in Saudi Arabia in the context of the basic features of the country. Presents statistics covering public libraries, library collections, and types and languages of library materials. The study also discusses administrative organizations, goals and objectives, library staff, library materials, classification and cataloging, furniture and equipment, opening hours, and users' services.

903 Abbas, Hisham Abdullah. "al-Maktabat al-'ammah fi khitat al-tanmiyah bi al-Mamlakah al-'Arabiyah al-Sa'udiyah." *'Alam al-Kutub* 17, no. 2 (May-June 1996): 211-219.

Argues that a national policy for planning and developing library and information services should be developed in Saudi Arabia.

904 al-Misfer, Abdulaziz Mohammad. *A Combined Public/School Library System for the Educational District of Riyadh, Saudi Arabia: A Model for Planning*. Ph.D., 1988. University of Pittsburgh. 176 p.

This study investigated the current state of public and secondary school libraries under the supervision of the Educational District of Riyadh, Saudi Arabia to determine factors that hinder their development and the attitudes of the librarians, teachers, and public library patrons toward the present system. Data were gathered via the survey and interview techniques. A different questionnaire was developed and administered to each of three groups: librarians, school teachers, and patrons of the public libraries. Interviews were conducted with librarians, school principals and the heads of the Public and School Library Departments at the Ministry of Education. The findings revealed that the existing public and school libraries are not meeting the needs of their users. Specific reasons cited included the lack of awareness on the part of both the public and educational leaders of the importance of public and school libraries, a shortage of qualified professional and trained staff, and a lack of funds. Given these results, as well as recommendations from the literature, the researcher proposed a merging of public and school libraries, initially within the Riyadh Educational District and ultimately within Educational Districts throughout the Kingdom, as a solution to these problems. A planning model to facilitate this merger was also proposed. This model outlined the strategies necessary for the implementation of the recommended combined public/school library system. [DAI 49/12-A: 3539.]

905 al-Salim, Salim Muhammad. *al-Khadamat al-Marja'iyah wa-al-Irshadiyah fi Maktabat al-Malik 'Abd al-'Aziz al-'Ammah bi al-Riyad: Dirasah Taqwimiyah*. al-Riyad: Maktabat al-Malik 'Abd al-'Aziz al-'Ammah, 1995.

A review of the services offered by the Abdel Aziz Public Library in Saudi Arabia.

PUBLISHING AND PUBLICATIONS PATTERN

906 Ashoor, Mohammad Saleh, and Abdus Sattar Chaudhry. "Publication patterns of scientists working in Saudi Arabia." *International Information & Library Review* 25, no. 1 (1993): 61-71.

A literature review of the publishing behaviors of scientists in developing countries indicated that they preferred to publish in English in foreign journals. In Saudi Arabia, also, English is used as the main language of scientific communication. Not much scientific research is reported in the Arabic language. A study based on a computerized database of journal articles derived from the Science Citation Index (1980-1984) was conducted to investigate the publishing patterns of scientists working in Saudi Arabia. Publication productivity of the Saudi scientists was found quite strong with teaching institutions contributing most of the publications. While biological and medical sciences dominate the research activities, chemists seem to be the single most productive group. Publication outlets in the USA and the UK are preferred by scientists working in Saudi Arabia. The ranking of journals by declining frequency of contribution show wide scattering of journals where Saudi scientists publish their research. It was found that most of these journals, which may be considered core titles, are available in academic and specialist libraries. Ranking by productivity was also in line with the impact factor and in-house use data confirming the selection and deselection criteria for journal subscriptions. [A]

907 al-Dobaian, Saad A. "Trade book publishing in Saudi Arabia past and present." *Libri* 40, no. 3 (September 1990): 203-216.

This article concentrates on private book publishing in Saudi Arabia. At the beginning, it gives a historical background about the emergence of printing presses in the Hijaz. The first printing press to be established in Mecca was al-Wilayah in 1883. Later on some private printing presses were founded. These presses played an essential part in the intellectual life of the country particularly in Hijaz. The study divides the development of book industry into two periods: the early Saudi Era (1924-60) and the late Saudi Era (1960 to the present). A number of modern commercial publishers emerged especially in the 1970s and 1980s.

908 Islam, Manzurul. "Research and scientific publishing in Saudi Arabia." *International Library Review* 21, no. 3 (July 1989): 355-361.

Research and scientific studies are being encouraged in Saudi Arabia for its planning strategies and for rapid progress. Statistics for 1985-86 show that the largest number of online searches carried out were on medical sciences and medicine as a single discipline had the largest number of publications, mainly as journal articles and conference papers. Most of the professional and scholarly journals are published in English only, some with Arabic abstracts. Some journals are published bilingually in Arabic and English, and a few are in Arabic only. The economic restrictions of the 1980s have contributed to an increase in quality of publications.

SCHOOL/CHILDREN'S LIBRARIES

909   Hashim, Hashim 'Abdu. "al-Maktabat al-madrasiyah fi al-Mamlakah al-'Arabiyah al-Sa'udiyah." *Maktabat al-Idarah* 13, no. 1 (October 1985): 297-349.

910   Marghalani, Mohammed Amin. *A Systematic Design of a Proposed Model for School Library Media Center Programs in Saudi Arabia.* Ph.D., 1986. University of Pittsburgh. 234 p.

The purpose of this study was to investigate, assess, and analyze the present condition of secondary and comprehensive school libraries; to investigate and determine the attitudes of secondary and comprehensive school principals toward school library media center programs; and to design a model that could be regarded as a general guide for developing school library media center programs in Saudi Arabia. Two research instruments were used: questionnaires and supplemental interviews. The conclusions of this study were: (1) the concept of the school library media center program as an essential element in the secondary and comprehensive school program does not presently exist in the education system in Saudi Arabia; (2) school libraries do not play an important role in the teaching, learning, and the curriculum of the secondary and comprehensive schools; and (3) most secondary and comprehensive school principals have positive attitudes towards school library media center programs. The major findings of this study were: (1) Most library media personnel had work experience in libraries between 1-5 years. Eleven per cent of the library media personnel had library qualifications. (2) Sixty-six per cent of the library media personnel were teacher-librarians, whereas, twenty-three per cent of the school library media personnel have been acting as librarians. (3) Most school libraries lacked non-print materials and equipment. (4) The majority of secondary and comprehensive school libraries lacked adequate and appropriate print and non-print materials for teachers, staff, and students. (5) The majority of principals expressed positive comments about the need for a library media center in every school. (6) There was no significant difference in attitudes toward school library media center programs between principals who had bachelor degrees as compared with principals who had advanced degrees. (7) The analysis, design, implementation, and evaluation (ADIE) proposed model was designed to be a guide for school library media program development for Saudi Arabia. [DAI 47/10-A: 3600.]

SERIALS

911   Atram, Mohammed A. *Availability of Periodicals in Major Saudi Arabian Libraries: A Descriptive Study of Factors Contributing to Availability within the Framework of National Librarianship.* Ph.D., 1984. University of California, Los Angeles. 258 p.

Periodicals are a primary source of important and fresh information. For many reasons, a library cannot match rapid increases in the quantity of periodicals and, therefore, national governments should get involved. Saudi Arabia, however, has yet to formulate a national information policy and there is evidence that existing collections are too small to meet national needs. This study is designed to evaluate these collections in order to demonstrate the need for such a policy. A 4450-title sample was compiled. 1165 of them relate to the Saudi culture. The other 3285 at-large titles were taken from citation, interlibrary loan data, and two selection tools. Availability of the titles in 15 major Saudi Arabian libraries was determined. Data analysis showed that, except for scientific titles, Saudi libraries are not very strong in periodicals. This is especially so for culturally related titles. Generally, a correlation exists between availability of periodicals and the institution's level of development. Most periodicals are acquired by modern libraries which acquire mostly English titles dealing with modern sciences, and issued in the industrialized world. However, titles in Arabic, from developing nations, and in the humanities and social sciences are not as well attended. Newly issued titles are also an area of thin coverage. Academic libraries are the richest, while public libraries are extremely poor in periodicals. As for regions, the Central region has a modest edge over the other two regions. In conclusion, there is a real need to improve existing periodicals collections and integrate them in an organized national system whose goals and objectives should be defined within the framework of a comprehensive national library policy. [DAI 45/06-A: 1561.]

912 Khurshid, Zahiruddin. "Automated serials control at the University of Petroleum and Minerals using DOBIS/LIBIS periodicals module." *Serials Review* 12, no. 1 (Spring 1986): 49-52.

The installation and operation of the DOBIS/LIBIS online periodicals control system, at the University of Petroleum and Minerals, Saudi Arabia, is described. The system employs four files: copies file; vendor file; periodicals file; and borrower file. Elements of the model described consist of: prediction patterns; check in issues; periodicals holdings; issue receipt history; claim policy; claim overdue issues; routing lists; finding volumes ready for binding; preparing, receiving and claiming binding orders and volumes. The greatest benefits are expected to be increased availability of current information on periodicals holdings and the binding control functions.

913 Mansfield, Jerry W. "Arab medical journals: a review." *The Serials Librarian* 16, no. 3-4 (1989): 155-176.

Presents a comprehensive listing of 56 Saudi Arabian medical periodicals.

SPECIAL LIBRARIES

914 Alogla, Sulaiman. "A study of hospital and medical libraries in Riyadh, Kingdom of Saudi Arabia." *Bulletin of the Medical Library Association* 86, no. 1 (January 1998): 57-62.

This study reports results of a questionnaire survey of the status of hospital libraries in Saudi Arabia, together with their sponsoring organizations, their staff, the academic qualifications of the heads of the libraries, collections size, available space, library buildings, and services. The study was limited to the hospitals with libraries for staff in Riyadh, the capital of Saudi Arabia. The data were collected through questionnaires sent to a sample of fifteen hospitals with medical libraries and twelve libraries responded. This is the first of its kind in Saudi Arabia and it is hoped that similar surveys will be done covering the whole kingdom. [A]

915 Celli, John P. "Special libraries of the Kingdom of Saudi Arabia." *Special Libraries* 71, no. 8 (August 1980): 358-364.

Briefly describes the libraries of the Institute of Public Administration, Saudi Arabian Consulting House, Saudi Arabian Industries Corporation, Ministry of Planning, Saudi Arabia Monetary Agency, Ministry of Finance and National Economy, Saudi Airlines, Islamic Development Bank, King Abdul-Aziz University, King Faisal University, King Faisal Specialist Hospital, University of Petroleum and Minerals, Aramco, British Consul, and International Communications Agency (US).

916 McMurdo, George. "The IAP Library at King Abdulaziz International Airport." *Aslib Proceedings* 33, no. 9 (September 1981): 363-367.

The scope and activities of the International Airports Projects (IAP) office of the Ministry of Defence and Aviation, Saudi Arabia, are described. The IAP Library has favored the application of technology-intensive techniques, including the development of a computerized library administration system which makes use of UK and LC MARC tapes. Future developments may include interfacing with a computer-indexed automated microfiche retrieval system. Suggests that library and information provision in Saudi Arabia may be entering a period of rapid expansion.

917 Manzoor, Suhail. "Library and information services at the King Faisal Centre for Research and Islamic Studies at Riyadh." *International Library Review* 21, no. 2 (April 1989): 193-200.

Describes the constituent libraries and in-house computerized databases, on Islamic subjects, of the King Faisal Centre for Research and Islamic Studies, Saudi Arabia.

918 Sardar, Ziauddin. "The Information Unit of the Hajj Research Centre." *Aslib Proceedings* 30, no. 5 (May 1978): 158-164.

The Centre was set up in 1975 at the King Abdul Aziz University, Jeddah, Saudi Arabia, to study the environment of Hajj, the annual pilgrimage to Mecca performed by all Moslem adults once in their lifetime. Gives examples of specific questions which have been studied. The Information Unit is one of four units at the Research Centre, and is the key unit, taking an active part in research. It not only collects information in printed form, but also carries out its own surveys, interviews, etc. A decentralized information retrieval system is in operation, separating the technical material from the non-technical. The latter is classified using a special faceted classification developed for the collection. A thesaurus has been developed for indexing the technical material. The Modelling Unit simulates a model of the Hajj, and the Holy Cities of Mecca and Medina. Information gathered at the Centre is repackaged and produced as reports, monographs, journals, books, and pamphlets.

919 al-Suwayna', 'Ali al-Sulayman. "Istikhdam al-muwazzafin lil-maktabat al-hukumiyah." *Maktabat al-Idarah* 13:1 (October 1985): 115-140.

920 Tameem, Jamal Abbas. "The Institute of Diplomatic Studies (IDS) library at the Ministry of Foreign Affairs in Saudi Arabia." *Aslib Proceedings* 40, no. 4 (April 1988): 123-129.

Also appears in *International Library Review*, vol. 20, no. 4 (October 1988), pp. 489-493. The study covers the development of the Institute of Diplomatic Studies (IDS) Library from 1979 to 1986. The IDS functions under the auspices of the Ministry of Foreign Affairs of the Kingdom of Saudi Arabia. The IDS Library has a two-fold mission: to prepare a basic training program for providing new diplomats with the knowledge and skills needed for diplomatic assignments; and to prepare training programs for senior diplomats to bring them up-to-date. The following aspects are discussed in the study: the IDS library building, the acquisitions program, classification, cataloging, holdings, staffing, users, and plans for the future.

921 Tameem, Jamal Abbas. *User Satisfaction in a Government Library: A Case Study of the Ministry of Foreign Affairs in Saudi Arabia (Library Services)*. Ph.D., 1991. North Texas State University. 217 p.

The problem of this study was the lack of knowledge about user satisfaction with the library services which are provided at the library of the Ministry of Foreign Affairs (MFA) in Saudi Arabia. The purposes of the study were twofold: (1) to measure, evaluate, and analyze user satisfaction with the library services provided at the MFA Library for the employees; and (2) to develop a model for evaluation of user satisfaction of library services in government libraries in Saudi Arabia. The data gathering instrument of this study was distributed to 425 employees from the MFA in Saudi Arabia. Usable questionnaires were returned by 280 or 65.88% of the participants and were analyzed using Statistical Package for the Social Sciences which included the chi-square test, one-way analysis of variance (ANOVA), Scheffe test, crosstabulation of each variable, frequency distribution. Significance was at the .05 level. The results of the survey showed that the more education an employee had and the longer the employee had worked at the Ministry of Foreign Affairs, the more dissatisfied the employee was with the library's services. Significant differences were also found depending on the rank of the employee, the employee's age, the nationality of the employee, and the country granting the respondent's last educational degree. Recommendations are proposed for the Ministry of Foreign Affairs Library, and a model is presented for the use of other government libraries in Saudi Arabia. Topics for further studies on librarianship for government libraries in Saudi Arabia are also suggested. [DAI 52/08-A: 2740.]

USER SERVICES

922 Chaudhry, M. R. "User services at the KFUPM Library, Dhahran, Saudi Arabia." *Library Review* 43, no. 2 (1994): 7-23.

Describes the developments of collections and services at the King Fahd University of Petroleum and Minerals Library. Indicates services to the institution's own users and to other neighboring libraries and institutions. Describes the use of information technology in the Library and considers collection development and control and other services to users. [A]

USER STUDIES

923 Ashoor, Mohammad Saleh. *A Survey of User's Attitudes Toward the Resources and Services of Three University Libraries in Saudi Arabia.* Ph.D., 1978. University of Pittsburgh. 246 p. DAI 39/08-A: 4567.

924 Ashoor, Mohammad Saleh, and Athanase B. Kanamugire. "Responding to researchers' and faculty use patterns and perceptions of CD-ROM services." *Online & CD-ROM Review* 20, no. 4 (August 1996): 171-180.

This paper provides a brief report of a study of faculty and researchers' use patterns and perceptions of CD-ROM services at King Fahd University of Petroleum and Minerals (KFUPM) Library, Saudi Arabia as background information to measures taken as a result of the study. The main objectives were to ascertain use patterns and perceptions of CD-ROM services and to elicit comments which would be used in developing a planning strategy to expand and enhance CD-ROM services. Two main methods were used in the study: CD-ROM search forms and a questionnaire survey. The results of the study revealed that the majority of the faculty had used CD-ROM services; they felt satisfied with the service but also felt that there was a strong need for user training. Several problematic areas were identified including need for more modern CD-ROM hardware and software systems, publicity, user training, and document delivery. The report then considers the measures that have been taken to address the problematic areas and discusses how effective those remedial actions have been. The paper concludes that the KFUPM Library planned and developed user orientated services in response to the findings of the study, but still faces further challenges in developing a CD-ROM service that is fully integrated with other electronic resources and services.

925 Ashoor, Mohammed Saleh, and Zahiruddin Khurshid. "User reactions to the online catalog the University of Petroleum and Minerals Library." *Journal of Academic Librarianship* 13 (September 1987): 221-225.

This article presents results of an OPAC user survey at the University of Petroleum and Minerals (UPM) Library in Dhahran, Saudi Arabia. Compared to their counterparts studied by the Council on Library Resources, UPM users showed a preference for known-item searches over subject searches. Levels of satisfaction with searches were high even without an instructional program or an updated manual. [A]

926 Nofal, Adil Mohammed. *The Use of Information Sources by Faculty in the Physical Sciences and Social Sciences at King Abdulaziz University (Saudi Arabia)*. Ph.D., 1989. University of Pittsburgh. 185 p.

The purpose of this study was to investigate the use of formal and informal sources of information by the Saudi faculty at King Abdulaziz University and to assess whether there was a difference in information sources use by the physical science and social science faculty members at three stages of research and two stages of teaching activities. The three stages of research activities were preliminary or proposal stage, data collection stage, and data analysis stage while the two stages of teaching were developing a new course and lecture preparation. Data were collected by means of self-administered questionnaires to 254 faculty members, and face-to-face interviews with six other faculty members. Data analysis was based on 159 valid questionnaires, 97 from the physical sciences and 62 from the social sciences and all six interviews. Data from the returned questionnaires were analyzed using descriptive statistics (means, standard deviation and proportions), inferential statistics (t-test) which was used to test the hypothesis at the .05 level of significance. The findings of this study showed that faculty members in the physical sciences and social sciences use both formal and informal sources of information, but they rely more on formal sources. Among the formal sources, they rely heavily on personal files, journals, and books, while personal contact with colleagues is considered as the most important informal source of information. Also it was found that the two groups of faculty members use similar sources of information at different stages of a research project. Another important finding of this study was that faculty members in the physical sciences and social sciences differ significantly from each other in their use of formal sources of information at the preliminary or proposal stage, the data collection stage of a research project, and when developing a new course. [DAI 51/06-A: 1814.]

927 Tameem, Jamal Abbas. "The employees' attitudes regarding library services and facilities at the Ministry of Foreign Affairs Library in Saudi Arabia." *Aslib Proceedings* 43, no. 10 (October 1991): 305-330.

A research study was formed in the Spring of 1991 to survey the perceptions of Ministry of Foreign Affairs (MFA) employees in Saudi Arabia concerning their needs and their attitudes regarding library services. The problem of this study was the lack of knowledge about user satisfaction with the library services which are provided at the library of the MFA in Saudi Arabia. The purposes of the study were two fold: (1) to measure, evaluate, and analyze user satisfaction with the library services provided at the MFA Library for the employees; and (2) to develop a model for evaluation of all governmental libraries in Saudi Arabia. The data gathering instrument of this study was distributed to 425 employees from the MFA in Saudi Arabia. Usable questionnaires were returned by 280 or 65.88% of the participants and were analyzed using the Statistical Package for the Social Sciences. The results of the survey showed that the more education an employee had, the more dissatisfied the employee was with the library's services. Significant differences were also found depending on the rank of the employee, the employee's age, the nationality of the employee, and the number of years the employee had worked at the Ministry of Foreign Affairs. The most serious problem was the lack of space and adequate funding.

CHAPTER 18

SOMALIA

GENERAL

928 Abdulla, Ali D. "Somalia's reconstruction: an opportunity to create a responsive information infrastructure." *International Information & Library Review* 28, no. 1 (March 1996): 39-57.

This article envisions the development of an effective information infrastructure in future Somalia that would contribute to the economic and social renewal of that country. The article highlights the role of information in Somalia 's reconstruction. It then reviews the state of the information infrastructure before the collapse of the government in 1990, examining both existing and proposed components of the infrastructure and identifying associated problems. In its final section, the article delineates an "appropriate" information infrastructure which would be consistent with the conditions and needs of information users in that environment. This contains an outline of the attributes of such an infrastructure and offers specific recommendations to future Somali development planners and international donors supporting information development activities. [A]

929 Abdulla, Ali D. "The role of libraries in Somalia's reformation." *Libri* 48, no. 1 (1998): 58-66.

This article is based on a presentation for the Annual Meeting of the African Studies Association (ASA), San Francisco, California in November 996. The subject of libraries and information services in Somalia has received no attention in Somali studies, and little or no attention in either the literature on Africa or that of international librarianship. Through discussions of Somalia's renewal, the author aims to make a contribution to information development in Somalia by addressing the topic of information and library development in Somalia as it relates to the country's reconstruction after the collapse of the government and the communal warfare which followed. This paper highlights the role that libraries and information services can play in Somalia's revival: in creating functioning and stable institutions and in setting a permanent path toward a dynamic social and economic development. Discussions of Somalia's information and library development are placed in an African context. Somalia's experience in library development is reviewed from an historical perspective. By reexamining formerly existing library and information services systems in the country, it demonstrates their weaknesses. Finally, the paper makes a case for a different approach to establishing library and information services in Somalia and shows what the new model may mean for the rebuilding and development of the Somali society.

930 Gowda, G. Thimme. "Somalia." In *World Encyclopedia of Library and Information Services*. 3rd ed. (pp. 779-780). Chicago: American Library Association, 1993.

Discusses the history of libraries and library education in the country and gives a description of its national, academic, public, school, and special libraries.

ARCHIVES

931 Geshekter, Charles Lee. "Archival sources concerning modern Somali history: an introduction." In *Proceedings of the Fifth International Conference on Ethiopian Studies, 1978* (pp. 629-640). Chicago: University of Illinois Press, 1980.

This is a select compendium of documentary sources concerning modern Somali history.

932 Xirsi, Cali Cabdiraxmaan, and Charles Lee Geshekter. *Documentary Materials in Northern Somali Repositories: A Preliminary Listing*. Somalia: Ministry of Culture and Higher Education, 1979. 15 p.

A listing of the locations, conditions, and contents of documentary sources from the British colonial period currently available in northern Somali towns of Hargeisa, Berbera, and Burao.

CATALOGING AND CLASSIFICATION

933 Andrzejewski, B. W. "Recommendations for Somali entries in library cataloguing systems." *African Research and Documentation* 11, no. 22 (1980): 21-22.

Appears also in *International Cataloguing*, vol. 11, no. 2 (1982), pp. 23-24. The article briefly notes on the Somali naming system, divergences in the spelling of names, and honorific titles, produced to aid both catalogers in their choice of name entries and library users.

TRAINING, STAFF

934 Abidi, S. A. H. "Library training programs in East Africa: an evaluation." *Unesco Journal of Information Science, Librarianship and Archives Administration* 2, no. 3 (July-September 1980): 159-169.

Describes library training facilities in East Africa (the Sudan, Ethiopia, Somalia, Kenya, Uganda, Zambia, Botswana, Lesotho, Swaziland, Mauritius, and Tanzania). Professional library training programs reflect the past colonial educational structure, with an emphasis on subjects with little or no relevance to African librarianship. The existing syllabi should be evaluated and harmonized in accordance with the requirements of these countries.

CHAPTER 19

SUDAN

GENERAL

935   Aman, Mohammed M., and Sha'ban 'Abd al-'Aziz Khalifa. "Sudan." In *World Encyclopedia of Library and Information Services*. 3rd ed. (pp. 799-800). Chicago: American Library Association, 1993.

Discusses the history of libraries and library education in the country and gives a description of its national, academic, public, school, and special libraries.

936   Istasi, Cecile Wesley. "Libraries in Sudan." In *Encyclopedia of Library and Information Science*. Vol. 29 (pp. 228-241). New York: Marcel Dekker, Inc., 1980.

Topics discussed include: (1) Background; (2) Current Status of Library Services in the Sudan—the National Documentation Center, special libraries and documentation centers, public libraries, school libraries, bibliographic control, the Sudan Library Association, library legislation, and library education; (3) Regional and International Assistance; and (4) Library and Information Systems Development.

937   Istasi, Cecile Wesley. "Library and information services in the Sudan." In *Information and Libraries in the Arab World*. Compiled and edited by Michael Wise and Anthony Olden, pp. 181-189. London: Library Association Publishing, 1994.

Article included in a collection of papers presenting a comparative review of librarianship and library practices in Arab countries. Discusses the state of library and information services in the Sudan against the backdrop of recent economic and ecological disasters. Lists the obstacles to the development of libraries and the national information system, briefly describes the work of the Documentation and Information Centre, and notes the activities in professional library and information science education.

ACADEMIC LIBRARIES

938 Karim, Bakri Musa A. "Higher education libraries in Sudan: an overview." *African Journal of Academic Librarianship* 3, no. 2 (December 1985): 73-77.

Outlines the history of higher education in the Sudan up to 1982 and discusses the shortcomings of the library situation. Examines the characteristics of the collections of various Sudanese higher education libraries; describes acquisition problems and considers 4 aspects of user services: borrowing; reference and bibliographic services; user instruction; and audiovisual media. Also considers the staffing of libraries.

939 Shatir, Ibrahim. "Maktabat jami'at al-Nilayn: taqrir wa-khuttat 'amal." *al-Majallah al-'Arabiyah lil-Ma'lumat* 17, no. 1 (1996): 93-106.

A description of one of the largest university libraries in the Sudan: the departments, staff, collection, etc.

ARCHIVES

940 'Abdullah, Muhammad al-Ghazali. "Kayfa 'alajat ba'd duwal al-'alam al-mahfuzat al-muntahiyah?" *Maktabat al-Idarah* 8, no. 3 (April-May 1980): 25-37.

941 Cory, E. S. B., and Lesley E. Forbes. "Resources for Sudanese studies: the Sudan archive of the University of Durham." *African Research and Documentation*, no. 31 (1983): 1-11.

Describes the circumstances of the formation of the Sudan archive since 1957. The contents of the archive are explained in detail, its research use is analyzed and its potential for research assessed. The archive includes not only papers of the Sudan Political Service but also of most government departments. There are also substantial groups of non-government papers and a comprehensive collection of photographs. The collection covers pre-Mahdist times, the Mahdist period and the reconquest. Finally some historic artifacts and printed items are described. An appendix gives details of opening hours and finding aids.

942 Forbes, Lesley E. "The Sudan Archive of the University of Durham." In *Middle East Studies and Libraries: A Felicitation Volume for Professor*

J. D. Pearson. Edited by B. C. Bloomfield, pp. 49-57. London: Mansell, 1980.

Provides a brief survey of the history and holdings of the archive.

943 Grabler, Susan. "Government archives in northern Sudan." *History in Africa* 12 (1985): 363-368.

The National Records Office (NRO) of the Republic of the Sudan was organized by the eminent Sudanese scholar P. M. Holt and opened in its Khartoum location, the former residence of al-Saiyid Abd Rahman el Mahdi, in 1956. The NRO includes a MAHDIA section on the Mahdist era 1881-98, sections organized according to central administration departments during the Anglo-Egyptian Condominium era, and 11 series of records from the provinces. The archive of the Gezira Board is located at Board headquarters in Barakat and contains records pertaining to the Gezira Scheme.

944 Hodnebo, Kjell. "A report on some archives in Equatoria Province, Sudan." *History in Africa* 8 (1981): 327-332.

Political situations and governmental structures have caused problems in organizing the archives of Equatoria Province, Sudan. Individual archives are listed with some detailed information.

CONSULTANCY AND CONSULTANTS

945 Mustafa, Alhaj Salim. "LIS consultancy in the Arab world: the Sudanese experience." In *Information and Libraries in the Arab World*. Compiled and edited by Michael Wise and Anthony Olden, pp. 155-180. London: Library Association Publishing, 1994. [Information and libraries in the developing world, vol. 3.]

Traces the recent history of library consultancy and consultants in Arab countries, focusing on the missions of P. H. Sewell (1960), J. S. Parker (1971 and 1978), T. S. Rajagopalan (1972), J. A. Dagher (1976), R. Munn (1978), and D. K. Lindley (1986).

DOCUMENTATION

946 Shatir, Ibrahim. "al-Tawthiq al-tarbawi bi al-Sudan." *al-Majallah al-'Arabiyah lil-Ma'lumat* 11, no. 1 (1990): 25-32.

The author reviews Sudan's experience in the field of documentation, its cooperation with a number of international organizations specialized in this field, and finally the problems and obstacles.

INFORMATION SERVICES

947 Istasi, Cecile Wesley. "Information on current research in the Sudan." *Information Development* 1, no. 4 (October 1985): 217-222.

Information on current research and development (R&D) is vital to science policy makers, R&D managers and the scientific community as a whole. In 1982, a Unesco pilot project for the creation of an information service on research in progress was initiated in the Sudan. A major element of this project is the compilation of a National Register of Current Research. The methods of data collection and analysis used in compiling the register, and its main characteristics, are described and illustrated.

948 Sewell, Philip Hooper, and Cecile Wesley Istasi. "The development of library and information services in the Republic of Sudan in relaion to international developments." In *Information Consultants in Action*. Edited by J. Stephan Parker. London: Mansell Pub., 1986.

INFORMATION TECHNOLOGY

949 Calhoun, Craig, William Drummond, and Dale Whittington. "Lessons from the design and implementation of a computer system for the Sudanese Planning Ministry." *Third World Planning Review* 9, no. 4 (November 1987): 361-379.

A discussion of information management issues related to development planning in Third World ministries. Effective information management is crucial if domestic policymakers are to be able either to plan for or to monitor the performance of externally funded development projects. Microcomputer-based management information systems are now being implemented in a wide variety of settings to deal with these problems. Here, the development of such a system in the Sudan is described, with focus on implications for future implementations in system-poor technical environments & organizational contexts highly dependent on external funding sources

950 Weyers, Yousif. "Friend or foe? The microcomputer in developing countries." *Microcomputers for Information Management* 7, no. 3 (September 1990): 217-226.

Addresses the vexed question of the appropriateness of information technology (IT) in developing countries, considers the technical and human problems involved in the use of microcomputers in these countries taking the case of the Sudan as an example, looks at the justification and desirability of using IT for certain information applications using low-cost communications technology linked to the microcomputer, and argues that use of such technology may help to overcome the social constraints impeding the flow of information. [A]

NATIONAL LIBRARIES

951 Weyers, Richard W. "Sudan's National Documentation Centre." *African Research and Documentation*, no. 49 (1989): 10-15.

The National Documentation Centre (NDC) in Khartoum was set up by the Sudanese Government in 1974 to provide information in order to facilitate government research. In the absence of an information infrastructure and a national library, the NDC has taken on the task of collecting and making available the national imprint and documents relating to the Sudan published outside the country. Describes the implementation of a three-year project to set up a National Information System which has been funded by three organizations. Discusses achievements to date, which include: improvements in the dissemination of information such as the publication of Sudan Science Abstracts and the National Register of Current Research; the development of the Sudan Collection Library; representation of the Sudan in international information systems; setting up of a network of special libraries; and more efficient acquisition of material.

SCHOOL LIBRARIES

952 Abdelgadir, Hamad Abdalla. *An Evaluation of Secondary School Library Media Collections in Khartoum Province, Sudan*. Ed.D. Temple University, 1983. 181 p.

The purpose of this study was to evaluate the school library media collections (SLMCs) in selected Sudanese academic secondary schools. A secondary purpose was to determine the significance of relationships between certain characteristics of schools, libraries, and teachers. Perspective: The problem was viewed through a systems analysis perspective interrelating characteristics of the three populations of schools, libraries, and educators. An overlapping perspective was implicit in three dimensions of librarianship; intellectual, social, and psychological. A third perspective was provided by a three-stage (descriptive, relational, and implemental) analysis. Data were collected from random samples of twenty schools, their library situations, and 338 respondent educators from schools in the Khartoum province of the Sudan. The teachers responded to a questionnaire which asked about their perceptions and utilization of their SLMCs. Data about the schools and their library situations were collected through on-site visits observation and through two questionnaires. The two major conclusions were that: (1) There was wide gap between the ideal school library situation as perceived by teachers and the library collections that were actually available. The book collections in the sample schools, were worn, scant, and limited in variety and value. There was a lack of audio-visual materials and a lack of a sufficient budget allocation. Teachers were dissatisfied with this situation and suggested major improvements. (2) Significant relationships existed between: (a) the type of school financial support and the perceived effectiveness of the SLMC; (b) the sex of a school's students and the availability of an SLMC; and (c) perceived effectiveness of the SLMC and educator utilization of the SLMC. Sudanese educational planners were urged to give top priority to the development of school libraries for the improvement of the educational system. Specific recommendations suggested the allocation of ten percent of each school's budget for libraries. In addition, a vigorous local, national, and international campaign should be launched to solicit funds for the provision of library services and resources. [DAI 44/07-A: 2108.]

TRAINING

953   Istasi, Cecile Wesley. "Human resources for Information Development in Sudan." *Information Development* 18, no. 3 (July 1992): 159-163.

Outlines the scope, function and process of human resources development (HRD). Describes the HRD situation in the information sector in Sudan and identifies lack of effective training and misuse of trained personnel as causes of the poor state of information resources and services in the country. Discusses problems in connection with training. Factors contributing to realizing the full potential of HRD are identified and the need to establish national institutional machinery for HRD is emphasized.

954   O'Connor, Brigid. "The role of training in development: some reflections from Sudan." *Focus on International & Comparative Librarianship* 17, no. 1 (1986): 4-5.

A nation's economic progress partly depends on improved education for its people. This in turn depends partly on the availability of books, which depends almost entirely in poorer countries on effective library organization. This article describes, from a personal point of view, the experiences of a library training officer under the sponsorship of the Voluntary Service Overseas at the University of Juba, Sudan, from February 1983 to July 1985. The main goal was to build library services from the ground up, integrate it into existing institutions, schools, government ministries, training institutes and other support organizations. This would hopefully be achieved by the organization and teaching of a 16-month course in librarianship for library assistants at para-professional level.

SUDAN

955 O'Connor, Brigid, and Diana Rosenberg. "Training at the grassroots: an integrated approach to training library assistants in Southern Sudan." *Information Development* 4, no. 1 (January 1988): 14-20.

Since training of library staff in Southern Sudan began in 1978, a training structure has evolved to meet the country's specific needs. Training axioms must be based on an awareness of the social and economic limitations of the country. Three levels of courses were developed for library staff by the University of Juba library, which also plays a vital role in advising on library development in Southern Sudan. Examines the problems that arose in regard to training: selection of suitable candidates; lack of organizational support; practical application of training; poor level of English expression; lack of local examples of good library practice.

956 White, Linda. "Training library assistants at the University of Juba." *Focus on International & Comparative Librarianship* 14, no. 2 (1983): 18-19.

Outlines the training programs which have been organized at the University of Juba in the Sudan for library assistants working in libraries in the Southern Region of Sudan. Courses of one month and one year duration have been run, the latter being taught partially by lecturers from the UK.

CHAPTER 20

SYRIA

GENERAL

957 Estanbouli, M. Nidal. "Libraries in Syria." In *Encyclopedia of Library and Information Science*. Vol. 29 (pp. 394-453). New York: Marcel Dekker, Inc., 1980.

Topics discussed include: (1) History of the Syrian Arab Republic and its Library Services; (2) The Influence of UNESCO, the Arab League, IFLA, WHO, and FID on Library Development in the Arab World; (3) Present Situation and Recent History of Libraries in Syria—national, university, school, public, and special libraries, and documentation centers, training of librarians, Syrian Library Association, bibliography, cataloging and classification, and library legislation; and (4) Conclusions—library development in relation to book development, a review of the present state of development of libraries in Syria, positive factors in Syrian library development, and library planning.

958 Jabr, Kamal. "Waqi' al-maktabat wa-al-harakah al-maktabiyah fi Suriyah." *al-Jadid fi 'Alam al-Kutub wa-al-Maktabat*, no. 10 (spring 1996): 61-67.

959 al-Lahham, Ghassan. "Libraries and information infrastructure in Syria." *Journal of Information Science* 18, no. 6 (1992): 497-504.

Part of a special issue devoted to library and information services in the Arab countries after the Gulf War. Reviews the development of libraries in Syria. Describes public, school, academic, and specialist libraries. Examines library personnel and the work of the Syrian Libraries and Documents Society. Describes the role of the al-Asad National Library. With increased automation of library and information services the Syrian Scientific Society of Informatics was established to encourage communication between computer and information specialists. [A]

960 al-Lahham, Ghassan. "Syria." In *World Encyclopedia of Library and Information Services*. 3rd ed. (pp. 808-809). Chicago: American Library Association, 1993.

Discusses the history of libraries and library education in the country and gives a description of its national, academic, public, school, and special libraries.

961 al-Mahasini, Sama' Zaki. "al-Maktabat fi-Suriyah: hadiruha wa-mustaqbaliha." *al-Majallah al-'Arabiyah lil-Ma'lumat* 4, no. 1 (1983): 129-141.

Gives the historical background to and present position of national, public, university, special, and school libraries in Syria.

962 al-Mahasini, Sama' Zaki. "al-Maktabat wa-marakiz al-tawthiq wa-alma'lumat fi al-Jumhuriyah al-'Arabiyah al-Suriyah." *al-Majallah al-'Arabiyah lil-Ma'lumat* 5, no. 1 (1984): 78-86.

ANCIENT LIBRARIES

963 Bradscher, James Gregory. "Ebla's royal archives." *Information Development* 1, no. 4 (October 1985): 238-243.

Archivists, librarians and records and information specialists generally ignore ancient archives as a subject of study, believing it lacks utilitarian value. The 1974 discovery of the clay tablet archive of Ebla (now in Syria), the largest 3rd millennium BC collection thus far uncovered, presents an opportunity to learn something about early archival library records and information practices and a means of gaining greater appreciation of the roots of various professional disciplines and of their common heritage. This paper discusses Ebla, its archives, their creators and custodians, with the aim of providing the reader with an understanding of why and how the clay tablets were created and maintained, as well as an understanding of archival, library and records administration in the 3rd millennium BC primarily as it existed in Ebla.

964 Munthe, Gerhard. "Biblioteker for oss: Verdens eldste bibliotek- biblioteket i Ebla." [Libraries in the past: the world's oldest library- the library in Ebla.] *Synopsis* 21, no. 1 (1990): 9-12. [In Norwegian.]

A library from C. 2600 BC was discovered in Ebla, Syria, 15 years ago. C. 17,000 clay tablets were found, of which 1800 are undamaged. Ebla was a capital of 30,000 inhabitants ruling a population of 300,000, but was destroyed in 1600 BC by the Hittites and later buried in sand. The library contained accounts, legal documents, stock lists, and also literary and historical texts and, important for decoding of the language, bilingual dictionaries. It occupied 2 rooms in the palace. The tablets, with cuneiform text on both sides were arranged standing on shelves. Whilst interpretation of the text has caused controversy, the library gives a clear indication of the cataloging and arrangement used and its role in administration, teaching and research.

965 Wellisch, Hans H. "Ebla: the world's oldest library." *Journal of Library History* 16, no. 3 (Summer 1981): 488-500.

Excavators at Tell Mardikh, Syria (the site of the ancient city-state of Ebla) discovered a number of clay tablets in cuneiform script in 1974 and a vast orderly collection of thousands of tablets dating from 2600-2300 BC in 1975. The collection appears to have comprised archives for the use of government officials and a library. Discusses the arrangement of the tablets, their script and language, and subject coverage. Refers to the controversies arising from the find. Concludes that this discovery of the oldest archives/library hitherto found gives new insights into library practices of 4,500 years ago: transcription of work in foreign languages and scripts, classification, cataloging, and use of incipits and spine titles for easy retrieval.

ARCHIVES

966 al-Hakim, Da'ad. "Mudiriyyat al-Watha'iq al-Tarikhiyyah fi al-Qutr al-'Arabi al-Suri." *Revue d'Histoire Maghrebine* 10 (1983): 161-165.

The Syrian archives were established in 1959 as part of the General Directorate of Museums and Antiquities. They now have about two million documents covering the history of the modern state, the mandate, political parties, and events in Palestine; private papers of Arab personalities, 1915-45; copious legal, administrative, and political documents for the Ottoman period; newspapers and periodicals, 1924-79, and news agency reports; UN material; items on Syria's economic and social history; and mixed court documents from the French period.

CHILDREN'S LITERATURE

967 Syria, Ministry of Culture and National Orientation. "Children's literature in the Syrian Arabic Republic." In *Printed for Children: World Children's Book Exhibition* (pp. 399-404). Munich: K. G. Saur, 1978.

MANUSCRIPTS

968   Jarad, Nuhad Nur al-Din. "al-Makhtutat fi Maktabat al-Asad al-Wataniyah." *Risalat al-Maktabah* 29, no. 4 (December 1994): 4-10.

The article covers the manuscripts at Asad National Library, Damascus, stating the size of the collection. It also describes the efforts made for the conservation and cataloging of the manuscripts.

NATIONAL LIBRARIES

969   al-'Azab, 'Issa. "Dar al-kutub al-Dhahiriyah: dirasat halah." *Risalat al-Maktabah* 32, no. 3 (September 1997): 38-48.

The author describes the establishment of al-Zahiriyyah library in Syria, its location and premises, the sections of the library, the role it has played as the national library, and its present status.

970   Fasheh, Mary Jamil. "Maktabat al-Asad al-Wataniyah." *Risalat al-Maktabah* 26, no. 1 (March 1991): 59-66.

971   Filstrup, E. Christian. "The Syrian National Library." *International Association of Orientalist Librarians Bulletin*, no. 28-29 (1986): 18-19.

Discusses the origins of the Syrian National Library in Damascus. Also describes its premises, collections, preservation and depository function, layout, staffing, the catalogs, and usage.

972   al-Lahham, Ghassan. "The Assad National Library, Syria." In *Information and Libraries in the Arab World*. Compiled and edited by Michael Wise and Anthony Olden, pp. 190-195. London: Library Association Publishing, 1994.

Article included in a collection of papers presenting a comparative review of librarianship and library practices in Arab countries. Details the structure and activities of the Assad National Library in Syria with notes on library use, library staff, and library activities.

973   al-Lahham, Ghassan. "The Assad National Library, Syria." In *National Libraries 3: A Selection of Articles on National Libraries, 1986-1994*. Edited by Maurice B. Line and Joyce Line, pp. 197-200. London: Aslib, 1995.

974   al-Mahasini, Sama' Zaki. "al-Khadamat al-maktabiyah lil-mustafidin min al-maktabat fi al-Jumhuriyah al-'Arabiyah al-Suriyah: Maktabat al-Asad al-Wataniyah." *al-Majallah al-'Arabiyah lil-Ma'lumat* 9, no. 2 (1988): 60-67.

The paper presents a detailed coverage of the functions performed by the Asad National Library.

SERIALS

975 Jond, F. de. "Arabic periodicals published in Syria before 1946: the holdings of the Zahiriyya library in Damascus." *Bibliotheca Orientalis* 36 (September-November 1979): 292-300.

SPECIAL LIBRARIES

976 Lentin, Jerome. "La Bibliotheque de l'Institut Francais d'Etudes Arabes de Damas." [The library of the French Institute of Arab Studies in Damascus.] *L'Arabisant* 18-19 (1981-1982): 2-10.

Describes the organization, content and development of the library of the French Institute founded in 1922 which holds over 40,000 works and 600 periodical titles.

CHAPTER 21

TUNISIA

GENERAL

977 Abdeljaoued, Mohamed. *Les Bibliotheques en Tunisie: introduction a la mise en place d'un reseau de bibliotheques*. Tunis: Institut superieur de documentation, 1988-1989. 2 vols.

978 Abid, Abdelaziz. "Libraries in Tunisia." In *Encyclopedia of Library and Information Science*. Vol. 31 (pp. 204-215). NY: Marcel Dekker, 1981.

Topics discussed include: (1) History (ancient, medieval, modern, and contemporary) and (2) The present library infrastructure (national library, public libraries, school libraries, university libraries, special libraries and information services, and library education).

979 Cooper, Douglas W. "Libraries of Tunisia." *Wilson Library Bulletin* 53, no. 10 (June 1979): 694-699.

Discusses briefly the state of libraries and professional librarianship in Tunisia and the problems involved in acquiring books from overseas. Mentions the collections and activities of the following libraries: the Bibliotheque Nationale; the Bourguiba Institute of Modern Languages; the University of Tunis Faculty of Letters and Humanities and Faculty of Law, Political Science and Economics; the Institute of Arab Belles Lettres; and several embassy-related libraries.

980 Habaili, Hussein. "Tunisia." In *World Encyclopedia of Library and Information Services*. 3rd ed. (pp. 820-821). Chicago: American Library Association, 1993.

Discusses the history of libraries and library education in the country and gives a description of its national, academic, public, school, and special libraries.

981 Houissa, Souheil. "Infrastructure of information and libraries in Tunisia." In *Information and Libraries in the Arab World*. Compiled and edited by Michael Wise and Anthony Olden, pp. 196-213. London: Library Association Publishing, 1994. [Information and libraries in the developing world, vol. 3.]

Article included in a collection of papers presenting a comparative review of librarianship and library practices in Arab countries. Reviews the history and current development of library and information services in Tunisia with particular reference to some of the organizations involved in information technology development and specific bodies comprising the Tunisian information system. Concludes with brief notes on the national library, school libraries; library and information science education and training; university libraries.

982 Krimi, Khemais. "L'informatique en Tunisie: enjeu, limites, et perspectives." *Conjoncture* (March 1985): 12-page section following p. 22.

Outlines the extent of current and projected use of electronic data processing in industry and government, measures encouraging its development, and training and research programs; includes interviews with the head of the Centre national de l'informatique and the director of the Ecole nationale des sciences informatiques.

983 Schubarth Engelschall, Karl. "Bibliothekarische Eindrucke aus Tunisien." [Library impressions from Tunisia.] *Zentralblatt fur Bibliothekswesen* 91, no. 1 (January 1977): 17-21. [In German.]

Account of a two-week visit undertaken at the end of 1975. Three aspects are covered: (1) the Tunisian educational system, with particular reference to its French origins; (2) the Tunisian National Library, founded in 1885 as the Bibliotheque Francaise; (3) the network of Bibliotheques Publiques, containing 565,000 volumes, with around 29,000 registered readers. [LISA]

ARCHIVES

984 Fakhfakh, Moncef. "Conference interregionale sur le developpement des archives." [Interregional conference on the development of archives.] *L'Ecluse* 8, no. 1 (1st Quarter 1996): 9-13.

Presentation given at the conference held in Tunis in May 1995 on the situation in Tunisia. Following independence in 1956, the public archives fell into neglect and general chaos ensued. In 1991-1992 the situation was evaluated and a plan drawn up for a national archive system, implemented in the context of general administrative reform in 1992. Achievements to date by the National Archives include: inventory of accumulated documents, weeding and conservation; treatment of historical collections; building new premises, to open in 1997; and setting up archivist training. Plans are in hand to set up systems for managing future documents from the point of creation at national, regional and local levels.

985 Mechri-Ben Dana, Kmar, and Habib Belaid. "Les archives microfilmees du protectorat: origine, etat du fonds, perspectives." [Microfiche archives from the era of the protectorate: origin, state of the collection, and perspectives.] *Cahiers de Tunisie* 36, no. 1-2 (1988): 33-42.

Details the work of the Commission des Sources de l'Histoire Tunisienne en France (CSHTF), established in 1981 to collect, reproduce, and transfer to Tunis all Tunisian history sources in France to create a microfiche archives. The project has concentrated on documents since the protectorate period that began in 1881.

986 Mechri-Ben Dana, Kmar, Habib Belaid, and Daniele Degez. "Le traitement des sources de l'histoire tunisienne en France." [Management of Tunisian historical sources in France.] *Documentaliste* 26 (November-December 1989): 227-232.

BOOKSELLING

987 Sepehri, Abazar. "A book buyer in Tunisia." *Third World Libraries* 2, no. 1 (Fall 1991): 54-60.

This is part one of a report of a library acquisitions trip made in June and July 1990 by the Middle Eastern Studies Librarian of the University of Texas at Austin. Mr. Sepehri's journey encompassed Tunisia, Algeria and Morocco. It describes various structural obstacles encountered in Tunis along with successes achieved. It offers readers a picture of the publishing bookselling infrastructure in a Third World country.

COMPUTERS IN LIBRARIES AND INFORMATION CENTERS

988 al-Gharbi, Ahmad. "Istikhdam al-hasib al-iliktruni fi marakiz al-tawthiq al-'ilmiyah wa-al-tajribah al-tunisiyah fi al-markaz al-qawmi lil-tawthiq al-fallahi." *al-Majallah al-'Arabiyah lil-Ma'lumat* 3, no. 1 (1982): 92-103.

Discusses the use of computers in documentation centers, including the Agricultural National Documentation Centre. Also, discusses the services rendered to the users of the Center.

INFORMATION CENTERS

989   al-Daly, Abd al-Baqi. "Le centre de documentation nationale. Un pionnier de la documentation en Tunisie." [The national information center. A pioneer of documentation in Tunisia.] *Documentaliste* 17, no. 1 (January-February 1980): 3-11.

The CDN originated in 1957, became an entity in 1966, and commenced automation with UNESCO aid, using MISTRAL software, in 1976. It is a center for general information and communication, empowered to exploit documents relative to all aspects of national and international life. The computer base will be operational in early 1980, and aims include selective dissemination of information, online searching and the formation of a national network. There are growing opportunities for cooperation with national and international institutions, and familiarization with modern technology has been a great asset.

INFORMATION SERVICES

990   Habaili, Hussein. "al-Harakah al-ma'lumatiyah fi Tunis." *al-Majallah al-'Arabiyah lil-Ma'lumat* 5, no. 1 (1984): 54-77.

991   Henda, M. B. "Internet: autoroutes de l'information. Vers une restructuration des systemes documentaires." [Internet: information highways. Towards a restructuring of documentation systems.] *L'Ecluse* 8, no. 2 (2nd Quarter 1996): 12-15.

Article first published in *La Presse de Tunisie* (November 26, 1995). With increasing availability of information services geared to end users, information professionals who do not adopt new technology are being marginalized. Traditional systems must be restructured: developments such as email and the Internet offer viable solutions to developing countries' problems of access to full texts and online research costs. Users now have access to a wide range of flexible information sources, but this goes unrecognized in Tunisian public and university libraries where out-of-date traditional methods persist and no one will take responsibility for initiating modernization.

INFORMATION TECHNOLOGY

992   Hecht, Joy Eliza. *Introducing Information Technology in Third World Cities: The Tunisian Experience*. Ph.D., Massachusetts Institute of Technology, 1988.

993   Seror, Ann, and Sami Rejeb. "Etude de cas de transfert des nouvelles technologies de l'information: l'Institut regional des sciences informatiques et des telecommunications de Tunis, Tunisie." [A case study of the transfer of new information technologies: The Regional Institute of Informatic Sciences and Telecommunications of Tunis, Tunisia.] *Technologies de l' Information et Societe* 8, no. 3 (July 1996): 243-274.

Understandings about the transference of new technologies gained through both lived experience and political science research are compared. The place of innovation networks in the spread of new technologies is explored, starting with the characterization of information and cultural technologies in previous studies. The place of institutional intervention in the transfer of new technologies is discussed, focusing on the collection of data at the Regional Instit of Informatic Sciences and Telecommunications (Tunis, Tunisia); its creation and mission are addressed, along with its organizational structure, transference of new information technologies, and technology transfer interventions. The important role of specialized research centers in the economic, political, and socio-cultural development of nations is emphasized.

LIBRARY COOPERATION

994   Gaiji, M. "The difficulties of organizing a project of resource sharing in a developing country: the case of Tunisia." In *Resource Sharing of Libraries in Developing Countries*. Edited by H. D. L. Vervliet, pp. 158-161. Proceedings of the 1977 IFLA/Unesco Pre session Seminar for Librarians from Developing Countries, Antwerp University, August 30-September 4, 1977. Munich: K. G. Saur, 1979. Resource sharing of libraries in developing countries.

This paper discusses three aspects of Tunisian librarianship: the lack of funds, lack of a clearly defined policy, and lack of qualified personnel. It also describes two attempts at cooperation: the cooperative acquisition and storage of little used serials (run by the National Library and some university libraries) and a program of cooperative cataloging, interlibrary loan and cooperative acquisition proposed by the Tunisian Association of Librarians.

LIBRARY EDUCATION

995   Bouazza, Abdelmajid, and Ribhi Mustafa Elayyan. "Library education in Tunisia and Jordan: a comparative study." *International Library Review* 18, no. 1 (January 1986): 5-14.

Discusses a general assumption that the library does not exist in a vacuum and is affected by cultural, economic and educational background. Briefly describes Jordan and Tunisia, both of which believe in Islam, speak Arabic and have an agricultural economy. Compares the state of the development of library education in Jordan and Tunisia and compares the problems affecting this development.

996 Bouazza, Abdelmajid, and Wahid Gdoura. "Adequation formation/emploi dans le secteur documentaire en Tunisie." [The adequacy of training for employment in the information sector in Tunisia.] *Documentaliste* 28, no. 4-5 (July-October 1991): 193-196.

Analyzes employers' perceptions of recent graduates of Tunisia 's library and information science schools based upon a questionnaire survey of managers of documentation centers and the school of information sciences. Analysis of results reveals that education programs do not adequately meet the needs of the employment market. Suggests recommendations for reforms that would modify information science training programs and make them more relevant to the socioeconomic realities of today.

997 Masliah, Myriam. "L'Institut de Presse et des Sciences de l'Information de Tunis." [The Press and Information Sciences Institute of Tunis.] *Documentaliste* 22 (November-December 1985): 218-220.

NATIONAL LIBRARIES

998 Attia, R. "La Bibliotheque nationale de Tunisie." [The National Library of Tunisia.] *Documentation et Bibliotheques* 39, no. 2 (April-June 1993): 79-82.

Contribution to a thematic issue devoted to national libraries. Describes the history of the Bibliotheque nationale de Tunisie (National Library of Tunis), its building and collections of which many documents date from the colonial era and many in Arabic were acquired in 1950 and after independence. Discusses its legal deposit and national bibliography functions and participation in the International Standard Book Number (ISBN) system. Describes the various library departments, use of the collections and its conservation program in collaboration with other countries.

999 Gardemalm, Jimmy, and Cecilia Falk. "Nationalbiblioteket i Tunis." [The National Library in Tunis.] *Biblioteksbladet* 63, no. 2 (1978): 41-42. [In Swedish.]

Describes the Bibliotheque Nationale de Tunisie. Originally the Bibliotheque Francaise of the College Alloui, it achieved national library status in 1956. It suffers from lack of space in the early 19th century building, which, together with the humidity, puts important North African manuscripts at risk. Despite gifts from Unesco and others, the book fund allows acquisition of only about 7,000 monographs a year, mostly French material. Two volumes of the national bibliography have been published and other bibliographies and catalogs are under preparation. The card catalog is unwieldy, with inadequate classification, and registration of periodicals is neglected. [LISA]

1000 Jeffreys, A. E. *L'Automatisation des catalogues de la Bibliotheque Nationale*. [The automation of cataloguing at the National Library of Tunisia.] Paris: Unesco, 1977, 42 p.

Report instigated by the Government of Tunisia through Unesco. The author worked as an adviser in Jan-Mar 77 to study the practicability of automated cataloging for the National Library of Tunisia as a measure towards Universal Bibliographic Control (UBC). Chapters are as follows: The National Library of Tunisia; Proposed automated system for cataloging and classification; Creation of an automated service; Production of a computerized union catalog for periodicals; Phase 1: Pilot project: Production of a national bibliography; and Pilot project: Production of a list of periodical articles; Phase 2: Retrospective conversion of the catalog to the Roman alphabet; and Extension of the mechanized treatment of periodicals and serials; Mechanized treatment of Arabic texts; Legal deposit bulletin; Library of Congress American Libraries Book Processing Center, Cairo; and Education and training.

PERSONNEL

1001 Gdoura, Wahid, and Abdelmajid Bouazza. "Les besoins en personnel dans le secteur documentaire en Tunisie." [Personnel needs in the information sector in Tunisia.] *Documentaliste* 30, no. 1 (January-February 1993): 42-43, 45-47.

Describes a survey conducted to measure recent developments in employment in the information sector in Tunisia and to study the nature and structure of employed staff, to outline needs through 1994 and to identify recruitment problems met by employers. Suggests remedies to problems caused by an imbalance between professional and non-professionals working together in a library or information center and between the supply of information specialists and the demands of the employment market.

CHAPTER 22

UNITED ARAB EMIRATES

GENERAL

1002 Boumarafi, Behdja Mekki. "Libraries and information services in the United Arab Emirates (UAE): an overview." *International Information & Library Review* 28, no. 4 (December 1996): 331-343.

Paper written following a three-week visit to major libraries in UAE at the end of 1995. Surveys library and information services there. Covers: academic libraries, public libraries, school libraries, and special libraries. Examines factors dictating the need for information services and provision in the UAE and problems affecting its provision. A local library education program is necessary for to ensure adequate library provision.

1003 el-Hadi, Mohamed M. "United Arab Emirates." In *World Encyclopedia of Library and Information Services*. 3rd ed. (pp. 834-835). Chicago: American Library Association, 1993.

Discusses the history of libraries in the country and gives a description of its national, academic, public, school, and special libraries.

1004 Karim, Bakri Musa A. "Economic and social changes in the Emirates: is the information adequate?" In *Information and Libraries in the Arab World*. Compiled and edited by Michael Wise and Anthony Olden, pp. 240-260. London: Library Association Publishing, 1994. [Information and libraries in the developing world, vol. 3.]

Article included in a collection of papers presenting a comparative review of librarianship and library practices in Arab countries. Discusses the economic background and social background to the United Arab Emirates and considers the degree to which the present information services cater for the needs of the country. Describes the public libraries, academic libraries, school libraries, special libraries, and the chambers of commerce as sources of business information. Mentions the Arab Information Bank online database and some of the telecommunications policies affecting information provision in the United Arab Emirates. Concludes with notes on the role of the government in: information technology; printing and publishing; the book trade and the press; censorship; and copyright.

1005 Rasmusson, Jan. "7- ton mobler till Al Ain. 70 tons of furniture for Al Ain." *Biblioteksbladet* 62, no. 14 (1977): 254-257. [In Swedish.]

The Swedish Library Service has just supplied its hitherto largest order of furniture to the proposed University Library of the United Arab Emirates in Al Ain. Two existing schools are to be converted to language and technical laboratories with mini-libraries of 3,000 volumes each, and a third school into a library and administrative building with room for 45,000 volumes. Describes the arrival and fitting of the furniture into the building. [LISA]

ACADEMIC LIBRARIES

1006 Hirsch, D. "United Arab Emirates University Libraries, Al-Ain, United Arab Emirates, September-December, 1993 and February-May 1994." *MELA Notes*, no. 62 (1995): 5-14.

INFORMATION SERVICES

1007 Jones, A. M. E. "The United Arab Emirates and the Internet: cultural and social implications for higher education." *Information Development* 12, no. 1 (March 1996): 16-19.

Electronic media such as the Internet promise to have a major impact on educational institutions and information centers in the United Arab Emirates (UAE). While cost has not been a factor in the implementation of such networks in the Gulf region, social and cultural implications are likely to be profound. The utilization of such information technology needs to be closely allied with appropriate curriculum developments which incorporate cultural perspectives, language needs and the diverse skill levels of likely users in the newly emerging tertiary education sector in the UAE. [A]

SPECIAL LIBRARIES

1008 Jaffer, Mohamed Sadiq. "Medical libraries and their services to the health sector in the United Arab Emirates (1971-1993). In *Information and*

Libraries in the Arab World. Compiled and edited by Michael Wise and Anthony Olden, pp. 214-239. London: Library Association Publishing, 1994. [Information and libraries in the developing world, vol. 3.]

Article included in a collection of papers presenting a comparative review of librarianship and library practices in Arab countries. Presents a state of the art review of medical libraries and medical information services in the United Arab Emirates in the period, 1971 to 1993. Pays particular attention to the faculty of Medicine and Health Sciences of the United Arab Emirates University, the National Medical Library, the Female Private Medical College Library, Dubai, and the Ministry of Health hospital libraries. Concludes with some brief notes of other medical libraries in the country.

1009 Thomas, Philip. "Exploring the Emirates: a visit to the National Medical Library, al-Ain, Abu Dhabi Emirates." *Focus on International & Comparative Librarianship* 23, no. 1 (May 10, 1992): 4-5.

This article describes the building, the collections, online database facilities, funding, segregation of male and female students, and interlibrary loans of the National Medical Library of the University of the United Arab Emirates.

CHAPTER 23

YEMEN

GENERAL

1010 Croken, Barbara, Lealan N. Swanson, and Manfred W. Wenner. *Libraries and Scholarly Resources in the Yemen Arab Republic*. DeKalb, Ill.: American Institute for Yemeni Studies, Northern Illinois University, 1983-1988. 22, [25] leaves.

1011 el-Hadi, Mohamed M. "Yemen." In *World Encyclopedia of Library and Information Services*. 3rd ed. (p. 871). Chicago: American Library Association, 1993.

Discusses the history of libraries in the country and gives a description of its national, academic, public, school, and special libraries.

AUTHOR INDEX

The Arabic letter (') is ignored when it appears at the beginning of a name. The Arabic article (al-) is put at the end of its respective entry

Abbadi, Mostafa el-, **441**
Abbas, Hisham Abdullah, **900-903**
Abd al-Hadi, Zaynuddin Muhammad, **348**
Abd al-Hamid, Khalid Rashid, **349**
Abd al-Jalil, Muhammad al-Fayturi, **74**
Abd al-Latif, Salih 'Abd al-'Aziz, **813**
Abd al-Majid, Ghassan Hamid, **539**
Abd al-Razzaq, Amirah Haqqi, **539**
Abd al-Samad, Nasib, **667**
Abdel Bassit, Ahmed, **477**, **479**, **487**
Abdelgadir, Hamad Abdalla, **952**
Abdel-Hadi, Muhammad Fathi, **67-68**, **83-84**, **231**, **283-284**, **345-347**, **378**
Abdeljaoued, Mohamed, **977**
Abdel-Motey, Yaser Y., **637**, **647**
Abdel-Shafi, Hasan Muhammad, **85**, **480**
Abdo, Mekhag B., **382**
Abdul-Rahman, As'ad, **578**

Abdul-Reheim, Olfat, **500**
Abdulla, Ali D., **928-929**
Abdullah, Muhammad al-Ghazali, **820**, **940**
Abdullah, Yusrah 'Abd al-Ghani, **261**
Abid, Abdelaziz, **86**, **719**, **978**
Abidi, S. A. H., **934**
Abu 'Ajamiyah, Yusra, **586**, **612**, **620**
Abu al-Nasr, Julinda, **136**
Abu al-Nur, 'Abd al-Wahhab, **164**
Abu al-Ruz, Mohammad, **563**, **570**, **625**
Abu Dayeh, K., **606**
Abu-Ghush, 'Asma', **731**
Abu-Haybah, 'Izzat Yasin, **306**
Abu-'Izza, 'Abdullah, **163**
Abu-Laban, 'Abd al-Hakim, **87**
Abu Laban, Nawzat, **624**
Abu-Layl, Amin Sa'id, **744**
Abul-Haj, Ghaleb, **750**
Agrawal, J. C., **843**
Ahmad, Alaa-Aldin A., **626**

Ahmad, Nazir, **39, 88**
Ahmed, Munir D., **285**
Ajlan, Ajlan Mohammad, **777**
Ajlouni, Tha'ir al-, **442**
Akel, Adeeb, **569**
Akhras, Mahmud el-, **1, 89-90, 142, 286, 313, 364, 566, 573, 611**
Akroush, Anwar, **591, 607-608**
Alak, Safa M., **531**
Alami, Ahmad, **2**
Alawady, Sana M., **473**
Albin, Michael W., **69, 81-82, 139, 331, 472, 497, 549**
Albrecht, Lisa, **736**
Alghamidi, Falih Abdullah, **778, 814**
Ali, Abdulrazzaq Hussain, **654**
Ali, Muhammad Sa'id al-Shaykh, **613**
Ali, Rubak Muhammad, **536**
Ali, Sabah A., **531**
Ali, Syed Iftekar, **189**
Ali, Syed Nazim, **201, 361, 383, 391, 425, 427-430, 668**
Alian, R. M., **432**
Aliprand, Joan M., **47**
Aliwi, Muhammad 'Awdah, **280, 336, 368, 526, 528, 542, 550**
Alogla, Sulaiman Ibn Saleh, **834, 914**
Alqudsi-Ghabra, Taghreed, **3, 338, 475, 636**
Alsereihy, Hassan Awad, **877**
Amad, Hani al-,**91, 609**
Aman, Mohammed M., **4-6, 48-49, 93, 143-144, 232, 257, 287-288, 317, 380, 435, 443-446, 638, 935**
American Library Association, **433**
Amin, Abdul-Karim, **551**
Amlah, Ismail al, **498**
Anani, Sarah Yunis al-, **343**
Anani, Shukri al-, **304, 857**
Andrzejewski, B. W., **933**
Anees, Munawar Ahmad, **362**
Ansari, Husain A. al-, **651-652**

Anwar, Mumtaz A., **60, 202**
Anzi, Khalid al-, **249**
Arab League, **308**
Arab League Educational, Cultural and Scientific Organization (ALECSO), **190**
Arab Syposium on Information, **7**
Arfaj, Khaled Abdullatif al-, **824**
Arfaoui, Hassan, **8**
Arif, Mohammad, **835, 867**
Arini, Muhsin (Mohsen el-Arini) al-, **436, 494-495, 513**
Asali, Kamil Jamil al-, **732, 745-746, 751**
Ashfaq, Ahmad, **767**
Ashoor, Mohammad Saleh, **94, 250, 403-404, 779-780, 789-791, 795, 802, 815, 837, 882, 906, 923-925**
Askar, Fahd Ibrahim al-, **174, 225, 836**
Atiyeh, George N., **9, 140, 672**
Atmah, Walid, **122**
Atram, Mohammed A., **911**
Attia, R., **998**
Awf, Zahidah Izzat, **567**
Ayidi, Muhammad 'Awad al-, **117**
Ayyub, Aminah, **614**
Azab, 'Issa al-, **587, 969**
Azu, Majidah Hamid, **687**
Azzawi, Salim Husayn al-, **543**

Bachir, Imad, **176-177**
Badr, 'Adil Fahmi, **10**
Badr, Ahmad Mahmud, **11-13, 40, 259, 365**
Badrah, Ahmad Anwar, **289**
Badran, Udit Marun, **251**
Badri, M. A., **398**
Bahelli, Y., **412**
Bakhit, Bakhit Sulayman al-, **95-96, 583**
Bakhsh, Khuda, **262**
Balkhayyat, Nazhah, **704**
Baridi, Saleh A. al-, **781**
Barnawi, Muhammad 'Ali, **309**

AUTHOR INDEX

Barudi, 'Abd Allah 'Umar, **151**
Basager, M. A., **829**
Bashity, Intisar Muhammad al-, 307
Baydas, Rasha Barghuthi, **178**
Bekkari, O., **718**
Belaid, Habib, **985-986**
Benhawy, Mohamed Amin, **14, 152**
Benjelloun, Mohamed, **719**
Benjelloun-Laroui, Latifa, **694**
Bennani, A., **717**
Berman, Sanford, **737**
Berry, D., **52**
Bezirgan, Basima, **15**
Bhatti, A. M., **729**
Bin 'Isa, 'Abdullah Salih, **337**
Bin Khamis, al-Hadi, **272**
Bin Naser, Sabika A., **645-646**
Binebine, Ahmed-Chouqui, **695**
Blucker, Daniel, **858, 873**
Blum, Rudolf, **447**
Bojanczyk, M. T., **643**
Borovansky, Vladimir T., **65**
Botros, Salib, **339**
Bouazza, Abdelmajid, **86, 399, 995-996, 1001**
Bouderbane, Azzedine, **422**
Boukris, Salima, **8**
Boumarafi, Behdja B. (Buma'rafi), **407-408, 410, 415**
Boumarafi, Behdja Mekki, **1002**
Bouri, Elizabeth Nicolas, **504-505**
Bradscher, James Gregory, **963**
Branca, Paolo, **50**
Brennen, Patrick W., **659**
Brown, Patricia L., **858, 873**
Brum, I. M., **763**
Bu-'Anjah, Kamal, **413**
Bu-'Ayyad, Mahmud, **281, 314, 411**
Buchanan, Elizabeth Anne, **16**
Bukhari, A. A., **400, 850**
Bulliet, Richard W., **332**
Burkard, Gunter, **448**
Burkhart, G., **393**
Buxton, Andrew, **176-177**

Calhoun, Craig, **949**
Camarero, C. G., **17**
Canfora, Luciano, **449-450**
Celli, John P., **915**
Chait, R., **409**
Chammou, Eliezer, **97**
Chandler, George, **203**
Chaudhry, Abdus Sattar
  see Sattar Chaudhry, Abdus
Chaudhry, M. R., **922**
Chelbi, K., **98**
Chen, Ching-chih, **451**
Chen, Pah I, **65**
Chepesiuk, Ronald J., **452, 733**
Choudhury, M. H., **643**
Clark, J. G., **705**
Clavel, Jean-Pierre, **453**
Clews, John, **66**
Coakley, J. F., **975**
Collier, Mel, **249**
Colvin, Peter, **675**
Conaway, Charles William, **652**
Cooper, Douglas W., **979**
Cory, E. S. B., **941**
Croken, Barbara, **1010**

Dahbur, Sidqi, **99, 179, 204**
Daly, Abd al-Baqi, **205, 273, 290, 707, 989**
Damdom, Abdalla, **562**
Dawe, M. P. St. J., **434**
Dawi, 'Ali 'Abd al-Rahman, **684**
Debbas, Isma'il, **615**
Deemer, Selden S., **851, 894**
Degez, Daniele, **986**
Dessouky, Ibtesam A., **657**
Dewachi, Abdulilah, **395**
Dhohayan, Abdulrahman Ibrahim, **889**
Dibs, Mohammad, **291**
Dimitroff, Alexandra, **511**
Diodato, Virgil P., **219**
Diouwara, Oumar, **691**
Diyab, Hamid Shafi'I, **61**
Dobaian, Saad A. al-, **907**
Dosary, Fahad M. al-, **792**

Drummond, William, **949**
Dukaly, Ali Mohammed, **681**
Dyab, Miftah Muhammad, **41**, **153-154**, **350**, **685**
Dziri, Radhie, **8**

Ebeid, Nora, **499**
Ede, Stuart, **454**
Ekere, F. C., **260**
Ekrish, Abdurrahman H., **792**
Elayyan, Ribhi Mustafa, **263**, **558**, **588**, **612**, **627**, **630**, **996**
Ellis, Larry M., **233**
El Rayyes, Nizar, **635**
Estanbouli, M. Nidal, **957**
Evens, Martha W., **182**, **239**

Faduli, Fa'iq, **155**
Fakhfakh, Moncef, **55**, **984**
Falk, Cecilia, **999**
Fannoush, Mohammed Omar, **676**
Farhan, Hamad Hasan, **758**
Farhan, Layla al-, **251**, **543**
Faris, Basim Muhammad, **18**
Farsuni, Fu'ad Hamad, **274**, **377**, **621**
Fasheh, Mary Jamil, **616**, **970**
Fa'ur, 'Ali, **157**
Feiler, Gil, **226**
Fihri, Ahmad Fasi, **702**, **708**, **710**
Filstrup, E. Christian, **971**
Forbes, Lesley E., **941-942**
Frame, J. D., **75**
Francis, Simon, **19-20**, **516**
Freih, Ferial al-, **631**
Freudenthal, Juan R., **512**
Frayhat, Maryam, **617**
Fustukjian, Samuel, **664**

Gaiji, M., **994**
Gallal, Ahmed Mohammed, **677**
Gamal, S. S. el-, **489**
Gandon, Francis, **421**
Gardemalm, Jimmy, **999**
Gardner, Stanley A., **726**
Gdoura, Wahid, **292**, **1001**

Geh, Hans-Peter, **455**
Geshekter, Charles Lee, **931-932**
Ghani, Abdul, **180**, **689-690**
Gharbi, Ahmad al-, **318**, **988**
Gomaa, Nabila, **100**
Gowda, G. Thimme, **930**
Grabler, Susan, **943**
Green, Arnold H., **21**
Grolier, Eric de, **600**

Haarala, A-R., **456**
Habaili, Hussein, **101**, **181**, **369-370**, **980**, **990**
Habib, 'Abd al-Halim, **191**
Haddad, Tarek el-, **244**
Hadi, Mohamed M. el-, **481**, **632**, **1003**, **1011**
Hadidy, Bahaa el-, **131**, **488**, **514**
Hafez, Abdulrasheed Abdulaziz, **890**
Hague, Howard, **648**
Haj Bakry, Saad, **319**
Hajji, M., **696**
Hajrasi, Sa'd Muhammad al-, **22-26**, **234**, **351**
Hakim, Da'ad, **966**
Haluji, 'Abd al-Sattar 'Abd al-Haq al-, **148**
Halwagy, A. S., **496**
Hamade, Samir N., **76**, **878**
Hamadneh, 'Umar M., **352**, **564**, **598**
Hamouda, Ali, **8**
Hamshari, 'Umar Ahmad, **102-103**, **353**, **559**, **571**, **572**, **601**
Hanif, M., **803**
Harb, 'Afaf Ghassan, **743**, **756**
Hasabullah, Sayyid, **26**, **159**
Hashim, Hashim 'Abdu, **909**
Hashim, Mud Ustfan, **235**, **661**, **669**
Hashmi, Syed Ali, **547**
Hashwah, Butrus, **173**
Hassan, S. al-, **653**
Hasu, Ahmad 'Abdullah al-, **236**
Hawash, Abu-Bakr Mahmud al-, **27**
Haythornthwaite, J., **415**

AUTHOR INDEX

Hecht, Joy Eliza, **992**
Heffening, W., **28**
Helal, Ahmed H., **446**
Henda, M. B., **991**
Heymowski, Adam, **693**
Hirsch, D., **1006**
Hmeidi, Ismail, **182**
Hmood, Nahla A., **637**
Hodnebo, Kjell, **944**
Horton, Weldon H., **793**
Houissa, Ali, **104**
Houissa, Souheil, **981**
Hubayl, 'Abd al-Qadir Muhammad al-, **394**
Husam al-Din, Mustafa, **62, 105**
Husayni, 'Abd al-Hasan al-, **156**
Hush, Abu Bakr Mahmood el-, **678-679, 688**
Husib, Margarit B., **544**
Huzaymi, Sa'ud 'Abdullah al-, **798**

Ibn Dohaish, Abdul Latif Abdullah, **868-871**
Ibn Fath Allah, Muhsin, **157**
Ibn al-Khayat, Nazha, **697**
Ibrahim, Abu al-Sa'ud, **70**
Ibrahim, Baha al-, **396**
Ibrahim, Farid Mohammed Selim, **237**
Ibrahim, Ferhad, **457**
Ibrahim, Yahya Muhammad, **264**
Idruj, al-Akhdar, **413**
Imam, Ibrahim, **198**
Imamuddin, S. M., **265-266**
Inayat, Fatin, **145**
Isa, Abdulla Saleh, **783**
Isa, Zuha, **157**
Isaac, Jacob M., **810**
Iskanderani, A. I., **811**
Islam, Manzurul, **908**
Isma'il, Fu'ad Ahmad, **782**
Ismail, M. I., **645-646, 660**
Ismail, Mahmoud Saleh, **525**
Ismail, Noha, **738**
Ismail, Saad Ahmed, **522, 525**
Istasi, Cecile Wesley, **199, 936-937, 947-948, 953**
Itayem, Mahmoud A., **29, 106-114, 137, 146, 165, 183-184, 206-207, 293, 315-316, 320, 371-373, 375, 568**
Ittihad al-'Arabi lil-Maktabat wa-al-Ma'lumat, **42**

Jabr, Kamal, **958**
Jabri, Ibrahim M. al-, **826**
Jackson, Sidney L., **458**
Jacso, Peter, **534**
Jaffer, Mohamed Sadiq, **1008**
Jajawi, Hayfa' Ayyub, **138**
Jajko, Edward A., **115**
Jam'iyyat al-Maktabat al-Lubnaniyah, **670**
Janafawi, Ahmad Mustafa, **683**
Janini, George, **635**
Jarad, Nuhad Nur al-Din, **968**
Jawadah, Kamal Mas'ud, **116**
Jeffreys, A. E., **1000**
Jifri, Sharaf, **844**
Jirjis, Jasim Muhammad, **63, 185, 321, 527**
Johnson, Ian M., **294**
Johnson, Peggy, **706**
Johnston, Colin S., **724-725**
Jond, F. de, **975**
Jones, A. M. E., **1007**
Jordanian Library Association, **592**

Kabesh, Ahmad, **477**
Kahtani, Abdullah Salem Mossa, **768**
Kamaruddin, Abdul Rahman, **322**
Kamel, S., **478**
Kanaan, Ghassan, **182**
Kanamugire, Athanase B., **132, 845-846, 859, 879, 924**
Kan'an, Nawwaf **149**
Karam al-Din, Layla Ahmad, **354**
Karim, Bakri Musa A., **720, 938, 1004**
Kaufmann, Ita, **439, 501**
Kelly Brewin, C., **633**

Kerouani, Odile, **8**
Khabbaz, Ali Fakher al-, **649**
Khafagi, Muhammad Tawfiq, **166, 192-193, 208, 258**
Khafaji, Muhammad Hasan Qasim al-, **63, 185, 532**
Khalaf, Nadim, **665**
Khaldi, Muhammad A. al-, **826**
Khaled, Maged, **515**
Khalid, Farooq A., **389, 405, 634**
Khalid, H. M., **804**
Khalifa, Sha'ban 'Abd al-'Aziz, **6, 30, 117, 167, 759, 765, 935**
Khalil, Jurj, **157**
Kharafi, Faiza al-, **635**
Kharashi, Ibrahim A. al-, **238-239**
Kharuf, Yunis Isma'il al-, **118, 186, 593, 735**
Khawli, Jamal al-, **150**
Kholy, Aziz el-, **482**
Khulaifi, M. al-, **891**
Khurshid, Anis, **31, 43**
Khurshid, Zahiruddin, **51, 385, 390, 769-771, 794, 805-807, 812, 816, 892, 895, 896, 912, 925**
Kindilchie, 'Amir Ibrahim al-, **77, 119, 240, 295, 310, 323, 517-520, 535, 538, 574**
King, Elizabeth J., **784**
Klib, Fadl, **38**
Klunder, Frederick, **431**
Koenig, Marulli, **703**
Koenig, Michael E. D., **703**
Krek, Miroslav, **267**
Krimi, Khemais, **982**
Kusa, Vira, **739**

Lahham, 'Abd al-Jawad al-, **38**
Lahham, Ghassan al-, **959-960, 972-973**
Lai, V. S., **705**
Lajeunesse, Marcel, **416, 420**
Lammers, W., **388**
Lang, L., **764**
Lazzari, Giovanni, **459**

Lees, Nigel, **437**
Lentin, Jerome, **976**
Leroy, J., **366**
Lind, P., **686**
Line, Maurice B., **785**
Loewe, Heinrich, **754**
Lombard, Francois, **453**
Loughridge, Brendan, **711-712**

Machaly, Horeya Ibrahim, **490**
MacKee, Monique, **71**
MacMillan, S., **757**
Macmillen, Sandy, **440**
Madkour, M. A. K., **241**
Mahasini, Sama' Zaki al-, **330, 961-962, 974**
Mahdi, Muhsin, **333**
Mahmood, K., **804**
Mahmoud, U. E., **497**
Majarha, Muhammad al-, **355**
Majid, Shaheen, **133**
Makdisi, John, **72**
Makkawi, Ahmad Hasan al-, **324**
Maktab Juzif Mughayzil, **666**
Maliha, Nuhad, **367**
Maliki, Majbal Lazim Musallam al-, **78, 147, 336, 368**
Mallah, Issam el-, **723**
Mandil, Salah, **482**
Mannuni, M. al-, **699, 715-716**
Mansfield, Jerry W., **913**
Mansour, Farouq, **552, 594**
Manzoor, Suhail, **523-524, 545, 830, 917**
Marghalani, Mohammed Amin, **832, 910**
Markaz al-Imarat lil-Dirasat wa-al-Buhuth al-Istiratijiyah, **209**
Mashali, Huriyyah Ibrahim, **187**
Masliah, Myriam, **997**
Mathami, S. al-, **843**
Mawlawi, Radwan, **340**
Maxin, Jacqueline A., **219**
McIlwaine, John, **56**
McMurdo, George, **808, 916**
McRoberts, Milton R., **831**

AUTHOR INDEX

Meadows, A. Jack, **653, 827, 835, 844, 850**
Mechri-Ben Dana, Kmar, **985-986**
Meherik, Mebrooka Omer, **296, 356, 678-679**
Meissner, Jan, **453**
Menant, J., **423**
Merlet, Shukrieh R., **268**
Midhat, Muhammad Mahmud, **586**
Mirza, Mohammad I., **852, 856**
Misfer, Abdulaziz Mohammad al-, **904**
Miski, Abdelhamid, **713**
Mohajir, A. R., **210**
Mohamed, Mahmoud Girgis, **525**
Mohamed, Yunis Aziz, **679**
Mohammed, Amal, **560**
Mokhtari, M., **714**
Momeni, Mahvash Keshmiri, **120-121**
Monastra, Yahya, **32**
Moran, M. L., **809**
Mufaraji, Moosa N. al-, **727**
Muhadat, Mohammed M., **460**
Muhammad, Yunis 'Aziz, **211**
Muhammed, Abdulbasit Abduljaleel, **639**
Muhyiddin, Hassanah, **671**
Muhsin, Sabah Rahmah, **532**
Mumani, Hasan Ahmad al-, **44**
Munajjid, Salah al-Din al-, **747**
Munshi, Zaki, **831**
Munthe, Gerhard, **964**
Musa, F. A., **252**
Musalam, Muna Abdullah al-, **655**
Musnad, Ibrahim Abdullah al-, **853**
Musned, Saleh Mohammed al-, **854**
Mustafa, 'Adnan, **325**
Mustafa, Alhaj Salim, **945**
Mustafa, 'Awdah Mahmud, **122**
Mustafa, Hind, **325**
Mustafa, Mohammad Hassan, **618**
Mustafa, Suleiman Hussein, **602-603, 628**
Mustafa, Usamah, **275**
Mutahhari, Murtaza, **461**

Mutwalli, Nariman Isma'il, **483**
Myers-Hayer, P., **880**

Naaman, Aida Salman, **662**
Naguib, Ahmad, **476**
Nahari, Abdulaziz Mohamed al-, **45, 886-888**
Najdawi, Amin al-, **213**
Naji, Sarah Yusuf, **426**
Namlah, Ali Ibrahim, **297, 772-773, 898**
Naser, S. B., **660**
Nassr, Mohammad Hamad al-, **760, 766**
Natour, Nahla al-, **575, 610**
Nicholls, Paul, **133**
Nimer, Ribhi Mustafa Elayyan *see* Elayyan, Ribhi Mustafa
Nimr, Najib al-, **157**
Nofal, Adil Mohammed, **926**
Nour, J. S., **479, 487**
Nurcombe, Valerie J., **175**

Obiagwu, Marcel C., **786**
O'Connor, Brigid, **954-955**
Odeh, Abdul-Rahman Mahmoud al-, **585**
Osman, Fawzia Mostafa, **493**
Ouazani, H. E., **701**

Palmer, R. P., **497**
Pantelidis, Veronica S., **73**
Partington, David H., **334**
Pedersen, Olof, **57-58**
Pedersen, R. C., **227**
Plumbe, Wilfred John, **269**

Qaddurah, Layla Ghandur, **168**
Qadi, Wadad al-, **158**
Qaisi, M. al-, **430**
Qandil, Yusuf, **278, 553, 580, 595**
Qarahghawli, 'Afaf Sami, **529**
Qari, Abdulghafoor A., **401**
Qasim, Hishmat Muhammad 'Ali, **33, 188**
Qasim, Nizar Muhammad 'Ali, **123, 242, 548**

Qawasimah, Muhammad 'Abdullah al-, **243, 312, 554, 561**
Qudsi, Taghrid al
see Alqudsi-Gharba, Taghrid Mohammad
Qureshy, A. A., **847**
Qutub, S. al-, **581**

Rahan, G. I., **540**
Rashid, Haseeb F., **761**
Rasmusson, Jan, **1005**
Razzaq, Faik Abdul S., **534**
Razzuqi, Nu'ayma Hasan, **169, 253, 536**
Refaat, Nahed, **499**
Regnier, Jean-Jacques, **170**
Rehman, Sajjadur (Sajjad Ur), **214, 218, 326, 882**
Rejeb, Sami, **993**
Rijan, Safar, **704**
Rizk, Nadia A., **506**
Rodenbeck, John, **507**
Romerio, G. F., **462, 491**
Roper, Geoffrey, **335, 374**
Rosenberg, Diana, **955**
Rosenthal, Franz, **341**
Rubeiz, John, **665**
Ruby, Carmela M., **463**
Ruk, Valiri, **739**
Rumayhi, Fu'ad 'Abd al-Latif al-, **426**

Sa'ati, Yahya Mahmud, **124, 874**
Sabbagh, 'Imad 'Abd al-Wahhab al-, **298, 402, 544**
Sadiq, Umniyah Mustafa, **484**
Safadi, M. Hassan al-, **46**
Sakai, Yasushi, **254**
Salah, T. M., **629**
Saleh, Fathi, **499**
Saleh, Mohammed, **499**
Salem, Shawky, **34-35, 93, 134, 194, 228, 244, 255, 279, 375, 464-465, 640-642, 644, 658**
Salih, G. Khamas, **125, 533**
Salih, 'Izzat Yasin, **502**
Salih, Muhammad Amin, **171**
Salih, Muhannad Muhammad, **521**
Salim, Salim Muhammad al-, **855, 905**
Samadi, Nasim Hasan al-, **245, 387, 392**
Samahah, Imil, **376**
Samarkandi, Abdullatif Abdulhakeem, **800**
Samarrai, Hafidh S. al-, **46**
Samirra'i, Iman Fadil al-, **77, 216-217, 541**
Samoeil, Simon, **767**
Sardar, Ziauddin, **256, 774, 918**
Sari', Sari' Muhammad al-, **342, 881**
Sattar Chaudhry, Abdus, **218, 229-230, 474, 795, 802, 825, 837, 882**
Sayyid, Muhammad Kamal al-, **276**
Schidorsky, Dov B., **752-754**
Schroeter, Daniel, **700**
Schubarth Engelschall, Karl, **983**
Semra, Halima, **417-418**
Sene, Henri, **420**
Sepehri, Abazar, **987**
Seror, Ann, **993**
Sever, Shmuel, **755**
Sewell, Philip Hooper, **948**
Shaer, Abdul Fattah el-, **161**
Shah, M. A., **643**
Shahin, Baha', **327**
Shahin, Sharif Kamil, **141**
Shahla Yaghmai, Nargess, **219**
Sha'lan, Jamal 'Abd al-Hamid, **85, 480**
Shami, Ahmad Muhammad al-, **159**
Shanbari, H. al-, **827**
Sharaf al-Din, 'Abd al-Tawwab, **160-161**
Sharif, 'Abdullah M. al-, **162, 195, 299-301, 680, 682, 883**
Sharif, Mufid al-, **731**
Shatir, Ibrahim, **939, 946**
Shaykh, Muna Muhammad 'Ali al-, **357**
Shbib, Samih, **740-741**
Shearer, Kenneth D., **381**

AUTHOR INDEX

Shehadeh, Lilly, **728**, **762**
Sherwani, Malahat Kaleem, **31**
Shields, Avril, **175**
Shimi, Husni 'Abd al-Rahman al-, **884**
Shishiny, Nadia el-, **479**, **487**
Shniour, Farouk, **562**
Shorbaji, Najeeb al-, **135**, **220-221**, **555**, **582-583**, **589**, **596**, **599**, **622**
Shraim, Omaima, **623**
Shu'ayb, Bakr Muhammad Ahmad, **311**
Shubbar, Mayy Makki, **358-359**
Shubert, Steven Blake, **466**
Sibai, Mohamed Makki, **270**
Siddiqui, Moid A., **397**, **787**, **796**, **817**, **838-842**, **853**, **856**, **860-866**, **872**, **885**
Siewert, Peter, **467**
Simons, Ian, **721**
Skreslet, Paula Youngman, **200**
Slamecka, Vladimir, **485**, **492**
Sliney, Marjory, **36**, **875**
Soltani, P., **126**
Souad, Lola, **698**
Soufan, Hani'a Jarallah, **579**, **604**
Squalli, Hassan, **709**
Srouji, J., **52**
Stockham, Kenneth A., **650**
Sudani, 'Abdullah 'Abd al-Rahim al-, **530**
Sufi, 'Abdullah al-, **619**
Sullivan, Marilyn Gorman, **659**
Sutari, 'Ali al-, **584**
Suwayna', 'Ali al-Sulayman al-, **127**, **246**, **919**
Swanson, Lealan N., **1010**
Swaydan, Nasser M., **128**, **302-303**, **775**, **821-823**, **876**
Syria, Ministry of Culture and National Orientation, **967**

Tadmuri, 'Umar, **196**
Taher, Mohamed, **271**
Tahir, A., **388**
Takemoto, Koho, **254**

Takruri, Sana' al-, **277**
Tamari, Salim, **742**
Tameem, Jamal Abbas, **788**, **801**, **920-921**, **927**
Tamimi, 'Abd al-Jalil, **59**
Tamraz, Ahmad Ali, **222**, **828**
Tasan, Mohammed Ali al-, **833**
Tashkandi, Abbas Saleh, **776**, **799**, **899**
Tay, Ja'far Ibrahim al-, **64**
Tayyeb, Muhammad Ali al-, **848**
Tedd, Lucy A., **406**, **438**
Te'eni, Dov, **486**
Tekfi, Chaffai, **414**
Terashita, Yoichi, **254**
Thabit, Hassan J., **849**
Thiam, Amadou Khoudiedji, **692**
Thiem, Jon, **468**
Thomas, Philip, **1009**
Thoumy, Aimee Salim, **673-674**
Tocatlian, Jacques Jean Marie, **446**, **468-470**
Tornudd, E., **456**
Tovell, Joyce Pressey, **509**
Tunisi, Hammadi Ali al-, **893**
Tuqan, 'Ali Muhammad Wasif, **360**, **748-749**
Turkait, Adla A. al-, **645-646**, **660**

UNESCO, **197**, **223-224**
Uthman, Samir, **247**
Uzun, A., **79**

Varnet, Harvey, **722**
Vassie, Roderic, **129**
Veenhof, Klaas R, **37**
Vernon, Elizabeth, **53-54**, **663**

Wardi, Zaki Husayn al-, **526**
Wellisch, Hans H., **965**
Wenner, Manfred W., **1010**
Weyers, Richard W., **951**
Weyers, Yousif, **950**
White, Linda, **956**
Whittington, Dale, **949**
Wien, Charlotte, **503**

Williams, Peter Havard, **407**
Woodward, A. M., **730**

Xirsi, Cali Cabdiraxmaan, **932**

Yacine, Badiaa, **419**
Yakoubi, Bechir, **424**
Yamauchi, Edwin M., **510**
Yasin, M. **797**
Yavas, U., **797**
Yitzhaki, Moshe, **80**
Young, Harold C., **427, 429**
Younis, Abdul Razeq Mustafa, **38, 329, 556, 565, 576-577, 590, 597, 605**

Yusuf, Qasim, **130**

Zado, Victoria Yousip, **537**
Zahhawi, Fari'ah al-, **172**
Zahran, Mohsen, **471**
Zash, Amal Muhammad, **248, 344, 557**
Zayid, Yusriyah, **363, 508**
Zehery, Mohamed H., **384, 656**
Zidan, Ahmed E., **46**
Zink, Steven D., **626**
Zoltai, S., **328**
Zubaydi, Majid Tuhan al-, **305**
Zubaydi, Muhammad 'Abbud al-, **546**

TITLE INDEX

Arabic letters such as (') and (al-) are ignored when they appear at the beginning of a title. Similarly, "the" is also ignored.

7- ton mobler till Al Ain. 70 tons of furniture for Al Ain, **1005**

A'mal Mu'tamar min ajl Tawhid Fahrasat al-Kitab al-'Arabi Maghriban wa-Mashriqan, Tunis, 28 November-1 December 1984, **92**
A'mal Nadwat Mas'uli Marakiz al-Tawthiq al-Tarbawi li-Dirasat Tanmiyat Nuzum al-Ma'lumat al-Tarbawiyah fi Duwal al-Khalij al-'Arabiyah wa-Taqniniha min ajl Ta'awun Mushtarak; al-Riyad, 15-17 Jumada al-Ula 1401 H, 21-23 Mars, Adhar 1981 M., **379**
Abdul-Hameed Shoman Public Library, **610**
Academic libraries and their services in the Arabian Gulf, **383**
Academic libraries in Iraq, **524**
Academic libraries in Saudi Arabia: a survey report, **787**
Academic libraries in the Kingdom of Saudi Arabia, **788**
Academic Library in the Electronic Age: The Case of Six Arabian Peninsula Countries, **382**
Academic library resources of the Muslim Asia, **43**
Acquisition of conference proceedings from the Arab world, **139**
Acquisition of scientific literature in developing countries: Arab Gulf countries, **391**
Acquisitions from the Middle East, **140**
Adaptations of DDC in the Middle East, **121**
Adawat al-bahth wa-al-istirja' al-bibliyughrafi fi al-'ulum al-ijtima'iyah wa ba'd qadaya al-dabt al- bibliyughrafi al-murtabit biha fi al-Watan al-'Arabi, **231**
Adawat dabt al-intaj al-fikri al-filastini 1876-1986: dirasah wa-tahlil, **735**

Adequation formation/emploi dans le secteur documentaire en Tunisie, **996**
Agricultural information in the Arab world—prospects for regional cooperation, **229**
Ahammiyyat al-'inwan fi fahrasat al-mawad al-thaqafiyah lil-maktabah al-'Arabiyah, **125**
Ahammiyyat al-tawthiq, **168**
Ajdaduna fi Thara Bayt al-Maqdis, **732**
Ajz fi al-qiwah al-'amilah wa-ta'thirahu 'ala khidmat al-kitab, **898**
Akhlaqiyyat al-mihnah lil-maktabiyyin, **173**
Akhta' al-nashirin al-'Arab wa-in'ikasatiha 'ala al-fahrasah, **128**
Alam al-Kutub wa-al-Qira'ah wa-al-Maktabat, **14**
ALECSO and its activities in the field of information, **193**
ALECSO and special library collections in the Arab countries, **364**
Alexandrian Library rises again, **444**
Alexandriana Library: a new opportunity in international cooperation, **454**
Al-Fahrast', la premiere bibliographie et classification ancienne connue, **98**
Algeria, **409**
Algerian Scientific Abstracts, an information system to heighten awareness of Algerian scientific research, **412**
Amaliyyat al-fanniyah fi marakiz al-tawthiq wa-al-ma'lumat, **84**
American librarian in Kuwait, **633**
American University of Beirut, **664**
Amilun bi al-maktabat wa-marakiz al-ma'lumat wa-al-ta'lim al-mustamir, **296**
An al-khizanah al-malakiyah bi al-Maghrib, **699**
Analysis of UK MARC exchange tape variable data field subfield lengths, 1950-1980, **808**
Anasir al-asasiyah lil-siyasah al-wataniyah li-nuzum al-ma'lumat wa-khadamatiha fi al-jumhuriyah al-'iraqiyah, **521**
Anasir al-asasiyah li-najah al-khidmah al-maktabiyah fi al-maktabat al-'ammah, **336**
Antiquity's most famous library to be re-born, **462**
Application of ISBD(M) to Arabic works, **100**
Application of modern technologies in Arab libraries, **771**
Aproximacion a la situation de los paises arabes en materia de informacion y documentacion, **17**
Aqsam al-maktabat fi al-bilad al-'Arabiyah: tahlil manhaji li mutatallibat al-insha' wa-al-tatwir (1), **22**
Aqsam al-maktabat fi al-bilad al-'Arabiyah: tahlil manhaji li mutatallibat al-insha' wa-al-tatwir (2), **23**
Arab Center for Medical Literature, **658**
Arab children's literature in the Republic of Egypt, **476**
Arab countries, **4**
Arab-Islamic cultures and online bibliographical systems, **219**
Arab League Educational, Cultural and Scientific Organization, **193**
Arab League Educational, Cultural and Scientific Organization and its contribution to Middle Eastern libraries, **189**
Arab library in Israel, **755**

TITLE INDEX 301

Arab medical journals: a review, **913**
Arab Republic of Egypt: A Teledocumentation System for the National Information and Documentation Centre, **491**
Arab scientific journalism: achievements and aspirations, **340**
Arab World Libraries and Librarianship 1960-1976: A Bibliography, **73**
Arabia Deserta: the development of libraries in the Middle East, **36**
Arabian Gulf plans its library future, **381**
Arabic formatting with Ditroff/ffortid, **52**
Arabic literature of library and information science, **34**
Arabic literature: uniterm indexing system for storage and retrieval, **180**
Arabic Online Catalog, **896**
Arabic periodical indexing, **668**
Arabic periodicals published in Syria before 1946: the holdings of the Zahiriyya library in Damascus, **975**
Arabic Personal Names: Their Components and Rendering in Catalog Entries, **104**
Arabic printing, **334**
Arabic script on RLIN, **47**
Arabic Writing and Arab Libraries, **266**
Arabisation of automated library systems in the Arab world: need for compatibility and standardisation, **250**
Arabisation of library and information systems, **249**
ARABMARC: a long way to go, **51**
Archival sources concerning modern Somali history: an introduction, **931**
Archives and Libraries in the Ancient Near East, 1500-300 B.C., **58**
Archives and Libraries in the City of Assur: A Survey of the Material from the German Excavations, **57**
Archives microfilmees du protectorat: origine, etat du fonds, perspectives, **985**
Archives: the Arab states, **55**
Archiving at the Oman Centre for Traditional Music, Muscat, **723**
Art library scene in Egypt, **512**
Asalib al-mukhtalifah li taqyim al-muqtanayat fi al-maktabat wa-marakiz al-ma'lumat ma' dirasah li-manhaj al-nazrah al-shamilah (conspectus) wa-istikhdamatihah al-mukhtalifah, **141**
Assad National Library, Syria, **972, 973**
Assessment of the Undergraduate Library and Information Science Program in the College of Basic Education in the State of Kuwait Through the Development and Application of Global Standards: A Case Study, **649**
At the threshold of a library network, **405**
Athar al-maktabah 'ala muyul al-tifl al-qira'iyah, **358**
Athar al-maktabah al-madrasiyah fi tathqif al-nasha' wa-al-shabab, **353**
Athar al-Quds wa-makhtutatiha, **746**
Ausbildung von bibliothekaren, dokumentaren und archivaren im vorderen orient, **285**
Automated bilingual circulation system using PC local area networks, **811**
Automated information system for academic Islamic institutions, **46**

Automated serials control at the University of Petroleum and Minerals using DOBIS/LIBIS periodicals module, **912**
Automation in a special library in Kuwait, **634**
Automatisation des catalogues de la Bibliotheque Nationale, **1000**
Availability of Periodicals in Major Saudi Arabian Libraries: A Descriptive Study of Factors Contributing to Availability within the Framework of National Librarianship, **911**
Awraq al-Rabi' fi al-Maktabat wa-al-Ma'lumat, **167**
Azhar Library: state of the art, **495**
Azhar University library, **494**

Bahrain, **425**
Bahth al-'ilmi al-'Arabi: al-mu'tayat wa-al-tatallu'at, **344**
Bahth al-tajribi fi al-maktabat wa-al-ma'lumat, **13**
Baramij al-hasibat al-saghirah (al-mikruwiyah) al-mustakhdamah fi al-maktabat wa marakiz al-ma'lumat (2), **144**
Baramijiyyat al-jahizah wa-al-musammamah mahalliyyan fi al-maktabat wa-marakiz al-ma'lumat fi al-'Iraq, **541**
Barmajiyyat al-ta'limiyah al-tarfihiyah fi maktabat al-madaris: li-mashah min sihir, **349**
Basic concepts, objectives and scope of online search services in Saudi Arabia, **831**
Bath al-intiqa'i lil-ma'lumat: wasilah taswiqiyah hadariyah, **248**
Bedeutende Bibliotheken der Welt (XXIX): die NB in Kairo; ein Koran 1000 Kilogramm, **501**
Bedeutended Bibliotheken der Welt (XXXIX): Zentralbibliothek der Uni Kairo, **439**
Besoins en personnel dans le secteur documentaire en Tunisie, **1001**
Biblioghrafia al-Filastiniyah al-Urduniyah, 1978, **566**
Bibliographic Control and Services in Egypt: A Survey and Study with Emphasis on the Role of the Egyptian National Library, **473**
Bibliographic control of academic dissertations, **60**
Bibliographic networking in the Arabian Gulf Region: prospects and problems, **404**
Bibliographic networking in the Gulf region, **403**
Bibliographic system for solar energy information on the Middle East, **65**
Bibliographic systems and Arabisation: an overview, **66**
Bibliographical Control in Saudi Arabia: An Inquiry into the Printing and Distribution of Government Publications, with Recommendations for Improvement, **799**
Bibliography: Jewish/ Palestinian Middle East peace perspectives, **736**
Bibliometric analysis of physics publications from Middle Eastern countries, **79**
Bibliometric aspects of medical librarianship in Arab countries, **228**
Biblioteca Alexandrina, **456**
Biblioteker for oss: Verdens eldste bibliotek- biblioteket i Ebla, **964**
Biblioteker i Qatar, **762**
Bibliotheca Alexandrina, **443**

TITLE INDEX 303

Bibliotheca Alexandrina comes to life again after 2,000 years: is there a place for new information technology, **451**
Bibliotheca Alexandrina (Modern), **445**
Bibliotheca Alexandrina: programme architectural et reglement du concours, **453**
Bibliotheca Alexandrina: revival of the Ancient Library of Alexandria Project, **471**
Bibliotheca Alexandrina—reviving a legacy of the past for a brighter common future, **470**
Bibliotheca Alexandrina: the world community helps to build a new library, **463**
Bibliotheca Alexandrina. Une bibliotheque pour le troisieme millenaire nait des cendres de l'antiquite, **469**
Bibliothekarische Eindrucke aus Tunisien, **983**
Bibliotheken in alten Agypten, **448**
Bibliotheque d'Alexandrie et l'histoire des textes, **450**
Bibliotheque dans le camps de refugies sahraouis?, **423**
Bibliotheque de l'Institut Francais d'Etudes Arabes de Damas, **976**
Bibliotheque nationale de Tunisie, **998**
Bibliotheques au Maroc, **694**
Bibliotheques en Tunisie: introduction a la mise en place d'un reseau de bibliotheques, **977**
Bi-lingual bibliographic software for processing library materials in the Arabic language, **802**
Bilingual medical terminology database: design, programing and online servic, **244**
Bina' al-Makaniz wa-Tatwiriha, **372**
Bina' shabakat maktabat jami'iyah 'Arabiyah 'ibra al-qamar al-sina'i al-'Arabi, **323**
Biographical dictionaries: inner structure and cultural significance, **158**
Book buyer in Tunisia, **987**
Book in the Islamic World: a selective bibliography, **69**
Book in the Islamic World: The Written Word and Communication in the Middle East, **9**
Book in the modern Arab world: the cases of Lebanon and Egypt, **672**
Book publishing, **82**
Book-publishing industry in Egypt, **506**
Books for children in Palestine, **757**
Breakeven point for using CD-ROM versus online: a case-study for database access in a developing-country, **131**
Building Information Systems in the Islamic World, **256**
Bunuk al-Ma'lumat, **232**
Bunuk al-ma'lumat fi al-Urdun: mulahazat wa-istintajat, **580**
Bunuk al-Ma'lumat wa-Atharuha 'ala al-Tanmiyah al-Shamilah, **10**
Bunuk al-ma'lumat wa-khadamatiha: tajribat al-Jamahiriyah, **683**
Bunyah al-asasiyah li-marakiz al-tawthiq wa-al-ma'lumat, **195**
Burning of Libraries in Iran and Alexandria, **461**

Cataloging of Middle Eastern materials (Arabic, Persian, and Turkish), **115**
Cataloging with a computer: Dobis/Libis adapted by the University of Petroleum and Minerals, Dhahran, Saudi Arabia, **803**
Cataloguing of audiovisual materials, **807**
Cataloguing operations in Arab university libraries, **88**
Cataloguing practice in university libraries: a comparison of three developing countries (Pakistan, Malaysia, Saudi Arabia), **804**
Cataloguing practices in university libraries of Saudi Arabia, **805**
CD-ROM bibliographic database searching at the KFUPM library: a use analysis, **852**
CD-ROM database quality: some observations based on experience at Sultan Qaboos University library, **725**
CD-ROM databases as an alternate means to online information: the experience of a university library in developing country **428**
CD-ROM searching in an academic library in a developing country, **840**
Censorship and librarianship in Oman, **726**
Centre de documentation nationale. Un pionnier de la documentation en Tunisie, **989**
Characteristics of the literature used by Arab authors in library and information science: a bibliometric study, **76**
Children's books in the Hashemite Kingdom of Jordan, **573**
Children's library services in Algeria, **422**
Children's literature in the Syrian Arabic Republic, **967**
Combined Public/School Library System for the Educational District of Riyadh, Saudi Arabia: A Model for Planning, **904**
Compact disk indexes effect on interlibrary loan at a university library, **865**
Comparative Study of Interlibrary Loan Functions and the Development of a Model Interlibrary Loan Network among Academic Libraries in Saudi Arabia (Resource Sharing, Document Delivery), **864**
Comparative Study of the Perceptions of the School Library Media Specialist's Role as Perceived by Principals, Teachers, and School Library Media Specialists in Public Schools in the State of Kuwait, **654**
Comparing words, stems, and roots as index terms in an Arabic Information Retrieval System, **239**
Components of a Proposed Resource Sharing and Information Network for Academic and Special Libraries in Jordan, **590**
Comprehensive materials availability studies in academic libraries, **837**
Computer services in libraries and information centres of Saudi Arabia, **878**
Computer-based clinical information system, **489**
Computer-based industrial information systems for the Arabian Gulf region, **395**
Computerised information services of ENSTINET: an Egyptian perspective, **479**
Computerized bilingual thesauri: problems of thesauri construction and development in Arabic languages—case studies, **375**
Computerizing information services in Iraq, **534**
Computing environment in an Arabian Gulf country: an organizational perspective, **797**

TITLE INDEX 305

Conference interregionale sur le developpement des archives, **984**
Continuing Library Education: Practices and Preferences of the University and Major Research Library Personnel in Saudi Arabia with Special Emphasis on Technical Services Staff (University Library Personnel, Library Education), **877**
Contributions of Islam to the spread of literacy and development of libraries in the Middle-East, North Africa and the West African Sudan, **260**
Coordination of information resources and services in developing countries with particular emphasis on the Arab world, **317**
Coverage of Islamic literature in selected indexing services, **218**
Creation d'une bibliotheque a l'Assemblee nationale de Djibouti, **434**
Creswell Library in Islamic Art and Architecture at the American University in Cairo. Part one: in the presence of the original owner, 1956-73, **509**
Critical issues in information systems management: an international perspective, **398**
Cultural heritage, social values, and information in the Arab world, **16**
Current library manpower situation in Jordan and projection of demand: a case study for a developing country, **602**
Current library manpower situation in Jordan: factors affecting demand for manpower, **603**
Cyclopaedic Glossary of Library, Documentation, and Information Sciences: English, Arabic, **161**

Dabt al-bibliyughrafi al-qawmi lil-intaj al-fikri al-'Arabi, **62**
Dabt al-bibliyughrafi fi al-Mamlakah al-'Arabiyah al-Sa'udiyah, **798**
Dabt al-bibliyughrafi li muhtawayat al-dawriyyat: al-nash'ah wa-al-tatawwur, **363**
Dabt al-bibliyughrafi lil-dawriyyat fi al-Khalij al-'Arabi: al-istirja' al-kulli, **387**
Dabt al-bibliyughrafi lil-intaj al-fikri fi majal al-tufulah, **61**
al-Dabt al-bibliughrafi lil-khara'it al-jiulujiyah wa-al-wad' fi al-Urdun, **599**
Dabt al-Bibliyughraphi lil-Matbu'at al-Hukumiyah fi al-Sa'udiyah, **822**
Dabt al-bibliyughrafi lil-rasa'il al-jami'iyah fi al-'alam al-'Arabi, **64**
Dabt muhtawa al-suhuf al-lubnaniyah: tajribat markaz al-tawthiq wa-al-buhuth al-lubnani, **669**
Dalil al-'Amali li-Bina' al-Malaf al-Ustaz (Asma' al-Ashkhas, Asma' al-Hay'at, al-Asma' al- Jughurafiyah), **110**
Dalil al-'Amali li-I'dad al-Tasjilat al-Bibliyugrafiyah li-Nizam al-Ma'lumat, **109**
Dalil al-'Amali lil-Musaghghirat al-Filmiyah, **308**
Dalil al-'Amali lil-Tahlil al-Mawdu'i wa-al-Takshif, **183**
Dalil al-'Amali li-Tasnif al-Malaffat al-Suhufiyah wa-al-Mawad al-Mukammilah Laha, **137**
Dalil al-Bibliyughrafi lil-Intaj al-Fikri al-'Arabi fi Majal al-Ma'lumat, 1976-1980, **67**
Dalil al-Maktabat wa-al-Maktabiyin fi al-Urdun, 1984, **586**
Dalil al-Maktabat wa-Marakiz al-Ma'lumat fi Lubnan, **670**
Dalil al-Muwaththiqin wa-al-Maktabiyin fi al-Watan al-'Arabi, **272**

Dalil al-Takshif wa-al-Istikhlas, **178**
Dalil istikhdam jihaz al-maykrofish fi al-Munazmah al-'Arabiyah lil-'Ulum al-Idariyah, **498**
Dalil Khidmat al-tawthiq fi al-Watan al-'Arabi, **192**
Dalil Madaris 'Ilm al-Maktabat wa-al-Ma'lumat fi al-Watan al-'Arabi, **293**
Dalil Marakiz al-Buhuth wa-al-Tawthiq fi al-'Ulum al-Ijtima'iyah bi-al-Mintaqah al-'Arabiyah, **197**
Dalil Marakiz al-Tawthiq wa-al-ma'lumat fi al-Watan al-'Arabi, **190**
Damage to Kuwait's information and library services: report of October 1991 visit, **638**
Dar al-'Ilm fi al-Qarn al-Khamis al-Hijri, **196**
Dar al-kutub al-Dhahiriyah: dirasat halah, **969**
Dar al-kutub al-Misriyah wa-al-maktabat al-mulhakah biha, **502**
Dawr al-ajhizah al-hukumiyah fi mu'alajat mahfuzatiha ghayr al-nashitah, **820**
Dawr al-arshiv al-watani fi-istratijiyyat al-tawthiq wa-al-ma'lumat fi al-Watan al-'Arabi, **163**
Dawr al-hasub fi al-anzima al-mutakamilah lil-maktabat wa-marakiz alma'alumat (al-janib al-fanni wa-altatbiq al-'amali), **581**
Dawr al-maktabah fi khidmat wa-ri'ayat al-atfal dhawi al-hajat al-khassah, **354**
Dawr al-maktabat fi al-nuzum al-qutriyah lil-Ma'lumat wa makaniha fi al-buna al-asasiyah, **208**
Dawr al-marakiz al-thaqafiyah wa-al-maktabat al-'ammah bi baladiyyat Tarablus fi taqdim al-thaqafah lil-tifl: dirasah midaniyah, **687**
Dawr al-Munazzamah al-'Arabiyah lil-Tarbiyah wa-al-Thaqafah wa-al-'Ulum fi istikhdam al-hasib al-iliktruni fi al-maktabat wa marakiz al-ma'lumat fi al-Watan al-'Arabi, **142**
Dawr Khadamat al-Ma'lumat fi Tahqiq al-Tanmiyah al-Idtisadiyah wa-al-Ijtima'iyah fi Misr, **484**
Dawr marakiz al-ma'lumat wa tatbiqatiha al-muqaranah: 'ard wa-talkhis, **191**
Dawr maktabat Ikarda wa khadamat ma'lumatiha fi da'm tatawwur al-zira'ah fi mantaqat al-Sharq al-Awsat wa-Shamal Afriqiyah, **367**
Decision-Making for Automation: Hebrew and Arabic Script Materials in the Automated Library, **54**
Delayed online search: an alternative access mode for developing countries, **488**
Department of Librarianship and Archival Studies and University of Cairo Libraries: Fact Resource Paper and Evaluation and Recommendations, **497**
Design and implementation of automatic indexing for information retrieval with Arabic documents, **182**
Design of a Computer Information System for the Algerian National Archives, **414**
Design of a microfilm information system for a petroleum well file, **644**
Designing micrographics systems in Bahrain, **431**
Determining the mutual dependence between two related disciplines by means of citation analysis: the case of biblical studies and ancient Near-East studies, **80**
Developing a CD-ROM service in Saudi Arabia: some lessons for developing

countries, **846**
Development and Decline of Public Libraries in Egypt: A Shift in National Development Priorities (UNESCO), **504**
Development and implementation of an in-house continuing education program in an academic library, **882**
Development of a national information system in Egypt, **492**
Development of Agricultural Library and Documentation Services in the Sultanate of Oman, **730**
Development of CD-ROM provision at the Sultan Qaboos University in the Sultanate of Oman, **724**
Development of Documentation and Academic Library Services, Iraq, **516**
Development of information system in the cultural context of Muslim Ummah, **210**
Development of library and information services in the Republic of Sudan in relation to international developments, **948**
Development of professional library education in the Arab countries, **300**
Development of the National Documentation Centre, Hashemite Kingdom of Jordan, **600**
Dictionary of Library and Information Science Terminology: (English-Arabic), **162**
Dictionary of Library Terms, English-Arabic, **152**
Difficulties of organizing a project of resource sharing in a developing country: the case of Tunisia, **994**
Dirasah hawla asbab ikhtiyar al-talabah al-Urduniyyin li-takhassus al-maktabat wa-al-tawthiw wa-al-ma'lumat, **596**
Dirasah Hawla Awda' al-Maktabat al-'Ammah wa-Maktabat al-Atfal fi al-Diffah al- Gharbiyah wa Qita' Ghazzah, **756**
Dirasah tarikhiyah lil-dawriyat al-Urduniyah, 1920-1980, **623**
Dirasat 'ilm al-maktabat wa-al-ma'lumat fi al-watan al-'arabi : al-waqi' wa-al-tumuh, **295**
Dirasat al-arshiviyah fi al-'Iraq, **527**
Dirasat fi 'Ulum al-Maktabat wa-al-Tawthiq wa-al-Bibliyughrafiya, **164**
Distribution of Middle Eastern periodicals in the UK libraries: a statistical analysis, **362**
Djibouti, **433**
DOBIS/LIBIS acquisitions subsystem in operation at King Fahd University of Petroleum and Minerals, **816**
DOBIS/LIBIS circulation control system, **812**
DOBIS/LIBIS network of university libraries in Saudi Arabia, **892**
Document delivery and interlibrary lending in the Arab countries, **257**
Documentary Materials in Northern Somali Repositories: A Preliminary Listing, **932**
Dur al-kutub fi al-Quds, **745**

Ebla: the world's oldest library, **965**
Ebla's royal archives, **963**

Economic and social changes in the Emirates: is the information adequate?, **1004**
Economics of American University of Beirut Library, **665**
Education and training in the Arab States, **294**
Education and training of information specialists in French-speaking countries: a comparative study, **416**
Education and training of librarians in Algeria, **417**
Education and training of librarians in the Maghreb (Algeria, Morocco, Tunisia), **418**
Education for Librarianship in the Arab Countries: Present Practices, Problems, and Possible Solutions, **883**
Effectiveness of Two Academic Libraries in Saudi Arabia: An Enquiry into the Main Factors Affecting their Services, **777**
Effects of user characteristics on computer attitudes among undergraduate business students, **826**
Egypt, **435**
Egypt (Ancient), **458**
Egyptian libraries, **436**
Egyptian museum registration project: the challenge and the implementation, **499**
Egyptian university libraries, **440**
Egyptiske nationalbibliotek: eller noget om arabisk informationsstruktur, **503**
Eighth wonder reborn: the new Alexandrian Library, **452**
Electronic information services and bibliographic retrieval education programs at King Fahd University of Petroleum and Minerals Library in Saudi Arabia, **879**
Electronic information services in the libraries of the Kingdom of Saudi Arabia, **829**
Electronic library and library and information science departments in the Arabian Gulf region, **401**
Emergence of Jewish public libraries in nineteenth century Palestine, **752**
Emergence of libraries in the Sultanate of Oman, **720**
Employees' attitudes regarding library services and facilities at the Ministry of Foreign Affairs Library in Saudi Arabia, **927**
Enseignement des nouvelles technologies de l'information dans les ecoles arabes de bibliotheconomie, **292**
Enseignement theorique et pratique de la bibliotheconomie a l'Institut de Bibliotheconomie et Sciences Documentaires d'Oran, **419**
Establishment of a Two-Years Course in Library and Information Studies: A Report to the Ministry of Education in Kuwait, **650**
Etude de cas de transfert des nouvelles technologies de l'information: l'Institut regional des sciences informatiques et des telecommunications de Tunis, Tunisie, **993**
Evaluation of Secondary School Library Media Collections in Khartoum Province, Sudan, **952**

Evaluation of the collections of Saudi university libraries based on the ACRL Standards, **815**
Experience de gestion documentaire integree, l'IREMAN, **170**
Experimental system for creating and managing Arabic Bibliographic Database- a step toward effective international information exchange, **254**
Exploring the Emirates: a visit to the National Medical Library, al-Ain, Abu Dhabi Emirates, **1009**

Factors which effect the development of librarianship and library education in the Arab countries, **299**
Faharis al-mushtarakah lil-dawriyyat: manhajiyyat rasd al-ma'lumat: dirasat halah al-fahras al-jaza'iri lil- dawriyyat, **413**
Faharis maktabatina wa-al-lughah al-'Arabiyah: qadiyyah lil-munaqashah, **105**
Fahrasah al-Mawdu'iyah: Dirasah fi Ru'us al-Mawdu'at al-'Arabiyah, **83**
Fahrasah athna' al-nashr wa-al-bibliughrafia al-wataniyah al-Urduniyah, **571**
Fahrasah wa-al-faharis fi al-maktabat al-Islamiyah: al-dawr, wa-al-ahamiyah, **261**
Fahrasat al-kitab al-'Arabi: mashakil wa-hulul muqtaraha, **103**
Fahrasat al-kitab al-'Arabi: mashakil wa-hulul muqtaraha, **572**
Fahrasat al-matbu'at fi al-maktabat al-madrasiyah, **352**
Faris al-Shidyaq and the transition from scribal to print culture in the Middle East, **335**
Feasibility and Support for an Interlibrary Loan Network among the West Bank and Gaza Academic Libraries (Jordan), **585**
Feasibility of Establishing a National Information Network System for Saudi Arabia: An Analysis, **893**
Fi al-Maktabah al-'Arabiyah wa-al-Ma'ajim, **2**
FID/NANE adopts AID program for libraries and information centres in its region, **194**
Field trip to Palestinian libraries yields audience with Arafat, **733**
First conference of Saudi librarians, **767**
Formation des specialistes de l'information au Maghreb et au Senegal, **719**
Formation of Muslim names, **94**
Friend or foe? The microcomputer in developing countries, **950**
From the manuscript age to the age of printed books, **333**
Further considerations on romanization: Saudi Arabia, **809**

General Information Programme (PGI) and Developing Countries: A Case Study of Iraq, **537**
Geographic Information Systems and Remote Sensing Methods for Assessing and Monitoring Land Degradation in the Sahel Region: The Case of Southern Mauritania, **692**
Geschichte Alexandrias und seiner antiken Bibliothek, **467**
Glimpse of library education in Kuwait, **647**
GOAL network design for the Bibliotheca Alexandrina, **464**
Government archives in northern Sudan, **943**

Gulf War and its effect on information and library services in the Arabian Gulf with particular reference to the State of Bahrain, **427**
Gulfnet in Saudi Arabia: an overview, **891**

Hajah ila markaz bibliyughrafi 'Arabi, **70**
Hal nahnu bi-hajah ila tab'ah 'Arabiyah thaniyah li-qawa'id al-fahrasah al-anglu-amirkiyah al-mu'arrabah?, **111**
Halqah al-Dirasiyah 'an Nuzum al-Ma'lumat wa-al-Tawthiq li-Mustakhdimi al-Ma'lumat fi Majal al-'Ulum al-Ijtima'iyah; 24/11-3/12/1980, Tanjah, al-Maghrib, **224**
Hamasat wa-Nida'at fi Afaq al-Qira'ah wa-al-Kutub wa-al-Maktabat, **25**
Handbook of Comparative Librarianship, **71**
Handicapped in Kuwait and the role of the Internet, **645**
Haq al-mu'allif fi al-'Iraq, **530**
Haq al-mu'allif fi al-ittifaqyiyyat al-duwaliyah, **149**
Haq al-mu'allif fi al-qawanin al-'Arabiyah, **148**
Harakah al-ma'lumatiyah fi Tunis, **990**
Harakat al-ta'lif wa-al-tarjamah wa-al-nashr fi al-Urdun 1967-1976, **611**
Hariq maktabat al-Iskandariyah, **460**
Hasib al-saghir wa-istikhdamatuhu fi al-maktabat wa-marakiz al-ma'lumat (1), **143**
Hasr al-matbu'at al-dawriyah al-Urduniyah: waqfah 'ind hazihi al-qadiyah wa-mu'alajat al-tashri'at al-Urduniyah laha, **621**
Hasub fi al-Maktabah: Dirasah 'an Idkhal al-Hasub fi al-Maktabah al-Madrasiyah, **348**
Hawla ab'ad wa-masafat al-bitaqah al-'Arabiyah fi al-maktabat, **116**
Hawla al-Maktabah wa-al-Kitab: Maqalat wa-Dirasat, **678**
Hawla al-Maktabat fi Qatar, **758**
Hawla tadris 'Ilm al-maktabat, **591**
Hawla taqyim fa'iliyyat al-maktabah al-madrasiyah, **356**
Haykaliyyat al-takhassus fi 'ilm al-ma'lumat fi Lubnan: waqi' wa-afaq, **671**
Hazmat barmajiyyat CDS/ISIS ma hiya, **582**
Health system and medical information services in the Sultanate of Oman, **729**
Hebrew and Arabic scripts materials in the automated library: the United States scene, **53**
Heinrich Loewe's conception of the role of public libraries in Palestine, **754**
Higher education libraries in Sudan: an overview, **938**
Histoire des bibliotheques au Maroc, **695**
Historical Investigation of Mosque Libraries in Islamic Life and Culture, **270**
History of libraries in the Arab world: a diffusionist model, **21**
History of Published Arabic Children's Literature as Reflected in the Collections of Three Publishers in Egypt, 1912-1986, **475**
History of the Arabic-Islamic libraries: 7th to 14th centuries, **263**
Hulul 'Arabiyah li-mushkilat al-istirja' al-khati' lil-ma'lumat, **242**
Human resources for Information Development in Sudan, **953**
Huquq al-ta'lif fi-al-Jaza'ir, **411**

I'adat tarqim al-tasjilat fi qawa'id al-bayanat al-mabniyah bi-istikhdam hazmat barmajiyyat CDS/ISIS li-isdar qawa'im biblughrafiyah, **96**

I'arah al-mutabadalah bayna al-maktabat al-jami'iyah ma' dirasah li waqi' hadha al-nashat bayna al-maktabat al-jami'iyah fi al-Mamlakah al-'Arabiyah al-Sa'udiyah, **857**

I'dad al-makaniz wa-tatwiriha, **371**

IAP Library at King Abdulaziz International Airport, **916**

Ida' al-qanuni wa-tashri'atuhu, **304**

Ida' al-qanuni: nash'atuhu wa-ta'rifuhu, ahdafuhu wa-mazayah, ahammiyyatuhu wa-fawa'idahu, **305**

Idarah al-'ilmiyah al-hadithah fi al-maktabat al-jami'iyah ma' dirasah lil-waqi' al-idari li maktabat jami'at al-Basrah, **542**

Idarah al-hadithah lil-a'mal al-maktabiyah ka madkhal li idarat nuzum al-ma'lumat, **276**

Idarah al-hadithah wa ta'thiraha fi idarat al-nuzum al-maktabiyah, **275**

Idarat al-maktabah al-madrasiyah, **355**

Ihsa' al-bibliyughrafi (al-bibliyumatriks) wa-istikhdamatuhu fi al-dirasat al-'Arabiyah, **77**

Ikhtiyar al-mustalahat lil-maknaz, **376**

Ilaqat al-'amah: qadayah hadithah fi al-maktabat, **338**

Ilm al-bibliyughrafiyah: al-nash'ah wa-al-tatawwur, **187**

Ilm al-Ma'lumat wa-al-Maktabat: Dirasah fi al-Nazariyah wa-al-Irtibatat al-Mawdu'iyah, **289**

Imkaniyyat istikhdam al-hasib al-iliktruni fi al-khadamat al-bibliyughrafiyah, **146**

Impact of CD-ROM database searching on interlibrary loans: the experience of a scientific and technological library in a developing country, **859**

Impact of CD-ROM searching on reference and information services in a university library, **856**

Impact of the Gulf crisis on business information, **642**

Implementing information technology projects in developing countries, **845**

Improving library personnel management, **653**

Improvisations in cataloging of theses and dissertations, **806**

Information access in a developing country: special libraries in Egypt, **511**

Information access through CD-ROM and its impact upon faculty research output: a case of a university in Third World countries—University of Bahrain, **429**

Information content of titles of Arabic periodicals, **176**

Information control in Kuwait: dialectic to democracy, **636**

Information exchange in agriculture, **230**

Information for development: a model for the delivery of information in developing countries, **706**

Information Industry in Saudi Arabia: An Analytical Study Defining Information Industry Policy Issues and Options Through Cooperative Interaction, **824**

Information infrastructure in the Arab countries: an analysis, **35**

Information manpower development program in Egypt, **515**

Information network project in Libyan industry: a critical review, **686**

Information on current research in the Sudan, **947**
Information policies in Saudi Arabia and Malaysia, **825**
Information processing and retrieval in Arab countries: traditional approaches and modern potentials, **241**
Information Revolution and the Arab World: Its Impact on State and Society, **209**
Information Services in Muslim Countries: An Annotated Bibliography of Expert Studies and Reports on Library, Information and Archive Services, **202**
Information technology adoption in Jordanian public sector organization, **626**
Information Technology Transfer to Saudi Arabia, **848**
Information Transfer: The Diffusion of Microcomputers in Saudi Arabian Universities, **849**
Information transmission and the translation of medieval Islamic science, **328**
Information Unit of the Hajj Research Centre, **918**
Informatique en Tunisie: enjeu, limites, et perspectives, **982**
Infrastructure of information and libraries in Tunisia, **981**
Infrastructure of Information Needs and Resources in the Country of Saudi Arabia: An Assessment, **772, 773**
Inside the Gulf crisis: destruction and looting in Kuwait, **640**
Insights into automation training at a Saudi Women's College Library, **880**
Installing a CD-ROM local area network in a science and engineering library, **796**
Institut de Presse et des Sciences de l'Information de Tunis, **997**
Institut du Monde Arabe, **366**
Institute of Diplomatic Studies (IDS) library at the Ministry of Foreign Affairs in Saudi Arabia, **920**
Instruction in the use of academic library, **545**
Intaj al-fikri al-'Arabi fi majal al-maktabat bayna al-kamm wa-al-kayf, **68**
Intellectual content, collection development, and services of the Bibliotheca Alexandrina. A report on the International Symposium hld on November 1-7, 1994 at the Alexandria Conference Center, Alexandria, Egypt, **445**
Interlending in a university library: the KFUPM Library experience, **860**
Interlibrary cooperation in the Kingdom of Saudi Arabia: the holder-of-record system, **858**
Interlibrary loan network among academic libraries of Saudi Arabia, **866**
Interlibrary loan policy and procedures of the King Fahd University of Petroleum and Minerals Library, **861**
Interlibrary loan services of the King Fahd University of Petroleum & Minerals Library, **863**
Interlibrary loans in Morocco, **710**
Interlibrary loans in the Arabian Gulf: issues and requisites, **396**
INTERLOAN: a microcomputer-based interlibrary loan system, **862**
Internet training and utilization by young researchers and creative students in Kuwait, **660**
Internet: autoroutes de l'information. Vers une restructuration des systemes documentaires, **991**
Internet comes to Morocco, **705**

TITLE INDEX 313

Internet gains acceptance in the Persian Gulf, **393**
Intirnit wa-al-maktabah, **221**
Intirnit wa-al-maktabah al-madrasiyah, **357**
Intisakh, **377**
Introducing Information Technology in Third World Cities: The Tunisian Experience, **992**
Investigation into the Use of Sources of Medical Information by the Practicing Jordanian Physicians of Selected Hospitals in Jordan, **630**
Iraq, **519**
Iraq and its National Library, **547**
Iraq's first printed book, **549**
Irshadat li-Tatwir Khadamat al-Maktabat wa-al-Ma'lumat fi Dawlat Qatar: Taqrir min al-Majlis al-Majlis al-Thaqafi al-Baritani ila Wizarat al-Tarbiyah wa-al-Ta'lim, Qatar, **763**
Isham al-khaliji fi majal al-maktabat wa-al-ma'lumat: dirasah tahliliyah wa qa'imah bibliyughrafiyah, **378**
Isharat al-bibliyughrafiyah allazimah lil-bahith, **112**
Islam-Net: the development of an Islamic information network, **322**
Islam wa-mafahim 'ilm al-ma'lumat, **259**
Islamic law bibliography, **72**
Islamic libraries, **262**
Islamic libraries of the Middle East, **268**
Islamic libraries: 7th to 17th centuries, **267**
Islamic Resource Sharing Network: A Feasibility Study for its Establishment among University Libraries of Saudi Arabia and the Republic of Turkey as Representative Islamic Nations, **889**
Israeli censorship in the Occupied Territories, **738**
Israeli censorship, Palestinian rights, and antisemitism, **737**
Istikhdam al-hasib al-ali fi tanzim al-qisasat al-suhufiyah, **138**
Istikhdam al-hasib al-iliktruni fi marakiz al-tawthiq al-'ilmiyah wa-al-tajribah al-Tunisiyah fi al-markaz al-qawmi lil-tawthiq al-fallahi, **988**
Istikhdam al-hasibat al-iliktruniyah fi a'mal al-maktabat wa-al-tawthiq bi al-Watan al-'Arabi, **145**
Istikhdam al-hasub fi al-maktabat al-jami'iyah al-Filastiniyah li-iqamat shabakat ma'lumat bibliyughrafiyah wataniyah bi-istikhdam CDS/ISIS, **743**
Istikhdam al-hawasib fi khadamat al-ma'lumat: malamih 'an al-tajribah al-'iraqiyah, **535**
Istikhdam al-kumpiotar fi maktabat wizarat al-takhtit—al-majlis al-qawmi lil-takhtit sabiqan, **575**
Istikhdam al-lughah al-tabi'iyah fi-istirja' al-ma'lumat wa-mushkilat dhalika fi al-lughah al-'Arabiyah, **243**
Istikhdam al-muwazzafin lil-maktabat al-hukumiyah, **919**
Istikhdam al-tarbawi wa-al-ta'limi lil-maktabah al-madrasiyah, **346**
Istikhdam barnamij CDS/ISIS: al-mustafidun wa-wasa'il al-aman, **95**
Istikhdam nizam CDS/ISIS fi bina' qawa'id bayanat al-qasasat al-suhufiyah wa-al-shakhsiyyat: tajribat markaz al-riyadah lil-Ma'lumat wa-al-dirasat/'Amman, **574**

Istiqrar al-wazifi 'ind al-maktabiyyin, **604**
Istirja' al-Ma'lumat fi al-Lughah al-'Arabiyah, **246**
Istittla' 'an ba'd marakiz al-mu'aqin fi 'Amman, **629**
Istittla' hawla khidmat al-taswir fi maktabat al-Jami'ah al-Urduniyah, **562**
IT diffusion and socio economic change in Egypt, **478**
Itahat al-ma'lumat al-'ilmiyah fi al-Watan al-'Arabi, **207**
Ithbat al-Mulkiyah fi al-Watha'iq al-'Arabiyah, **150**
Ittijahat al-'Amilin fi al-maktabat al-'ammah fi Filastin nahwa hawafiz al-'amal wa-ta'thiriha fi kafa'at al-ida', **749**
Ittijahat al-hadithah fi al-khadamat al-marja'iyah/khadamat al-ma'lumat fi al-maktabat wa-marakiz al-ma'lumat, **217**
Ittijahat al-mawdu'iyah li rasa'il al-majistir fi 'ulum al-maktabat wa-al-ma'lumat fi al-jami'ah al-Mustansariyah: 'ard wa tahlil, **543**

Jadid fi 'alam al-tiqaniyyat al-duwaliyah lil-wasf al-bibliyughrafi, **90**
Jam'iyyat al-maktabat al-urduniyah: dirasat halah, **587**
Jam'iyyat al-maktabat fi Bilad al-Sham: waqi'uha wa subul taf', **278**
Jawlah fi maktabat al-Sahra' al-Maghribiyah, **696**
Job Satisfaction of Professional Librarians: A Comparative Study of Technical and Public Service Departments in Academic Libraries in Jordan, **559**
Jordan, **552, 616**
Jordan Libraries, **556**
Jordan Library Association, **588, 589**
Jordanian National Bibliography, **567**

Kallimachos: The Alexandrian Library and the Origins of Bibliography, **447**
Kashshaf al-kalimat al-muftahiyah fi al-siyaq wa-ihtimalatihi fi al-lughah al-'Arabiyah, **188**
Kashshafat al-dawriyyat al-'Arabiyah: dirasah hasriyah taqyimiyah, **185**
Kayfa 'alajat ba'd duwal al-'alam al-mahfuzat al-muntahiyah, **940**
Khadamat al-bath al-intiqa'i: dirasat ijra'atiha wa mutatallibatiha wa taqyim mukhrajatiha, **536**
Khadamat al-istishariyah fi al-maktabat wa-marakiz al-ma'lumat, **147**
Khadamat al-ma'lumat, **211**
Khadamat al-Ma'lumat bi-Qita' al-Ta'lim fi Misr: Waqai'iha wa Mustaqbaliha, **480**
Khadamat al-maktabiyah: dirasah li-khadama al-qurra' fi maktabat al-Jami'ah al-Urduniyah, **558**
Khadamat al-maktabiyah lil-atfal ma' dirasah li maktabat al-atfal fi al-'Iraq, **550**
Khadamat al-maktabiyah lil-mustafidin min al-maktabat fi al-Jumhuriyah al-'Arabiyah al-Suriyah: Maktabat al-Asad al-Wataniyah, **974**
Khadamat al-Marja'iyah wa-al-Irshadiyah fi Maktabat al-Malik 'Abd al-'Aziz al-'Ammah bi al-Riyad: Dirasah Taqwimiyah, **905**
Khara'it wa-al-wad' fi maktabatina, **598**
Khidmah al-maktabiyah wa-al-atfal al-'Arab, **350**
Khidmah al-marja'iyah wa-qism al-maraji' ... wa-maktabatina, **579**
Kutub al-nadirah: ta'rifiha, masadiriha, hifziha wa-istirja'iha, **342**

Kuwait, **632**

Lebanon, **662**
Lecture publique en Algerie: l'exemple d'Oran, **421**
Lessons from the design and implementation of a computer system for the Sudanese Planning Ministry, **949**
Librarianship in Kuwait after the Gulf War, **637**
Librarianship in Lebanon in the post-civil war period, **663**
Librarianship in the Arab world, **3**
Librarianship in the Muslim World 1984: Volume-2, **31**
Libraries, **32**
Libraries and archives, **37**
Libraries and information centers in Saudi Arabia, **770**
Libraries and information in, Algeria: past, present and future prospects, **408**
Libraries and Information in the Middle East, **19**
Libraries and Information in the Near East and Central Asia, **20**
Libraries and information infrastructure in Syria, **959**
Libraries and information services in the United Arab Emirates (UAE): an overview, **1002**
Libraries and information systems in the Arab Gulf States: after the war, **380**
Libraries and librarianship in Qatar, **759**
Libraries & Librarianship in Saudi Arabia, **769**
Libraries and library education in Oman, **727**
Libraries and library services in the Socialist People's Libyan Arab Jamahiriya, **679**
Libraries and Scholarly Resources in the Yemen Arab Republic, **1010**
Libraries at Makkah al-Mukarramah, **871**
Libraries in Iraq: a short report, **520**
Libraries in Iraq and Egypt: a comparative study, **517**
Libraries in Kuwaiti financial institutions: their functions and potentials, **657**
Libraries in Republic of Libya, **676**
Libraries in Saudi Arabia, **776**
Libraries in Saudi Arabia: some reflections, **785**
Libraries in Sudan, **936**
Libraries in Syria, **957**
Libraries in the Middle East: an overview, **5**
Libraries in Tunisia, **978**
Libraries of Madina-al-Munawwarah (during the Ottoman period), **869**
Libraries of Tunisia, **979**
Libraries of two women's colleges in Saudi Arabia, **784**
Libraries: the Arab states, **29**
Library abuse in academic institutions: a comparative study, **786**
Library and information science education in Morocco: curriculum development and adaptation to change, **714**
Library and information science education in Morocco: notes on a recent visit, **712**

Library and information science education in Morocco: observations on a recent visit to the 'Ecole des Sciences de l'information' and the 'Center National de Documentation' in Rabat, **711**
Library and information science education in Saudi Arabia, **885**
Library and information services at the King Faisal Centre for Research and Islamic Studies at Riyadh, **917**
Library and information services in Arab countries, **6**
Library and information services in Egypt, 1979, **481**
Library and information services in Jordan, **555**
Library and information services in the Sudan, **937**
Library and information work in Egypt: perspective of a volunteer working in Assiut, **437**
Library automation in Jordan, **565**
Library buildings in the 1980s: The Middle East and North Africa, **279**
Library co-operation in the military hospitals of Saudi Arabia, **873**
Library education in Libya, **685**
Library education in Qatar, **765**
Library education in Tunisia and Jordan: a comparative study, **995**
Library information education in Algeria, **415**
Library science programs in the State of Bahrain, **432**
Library services and political uprising in Eastern Jerusalem, **750**
Library training programs in East Africa: an evaluation, **934**
Libya, **677**
Life and Fate of the Ancient Library of Alexandria, **441**
Linguistic obstructions to scientific information in high technology areas, **843**
LIS consultancy in the Arab world: the Sudanese experience, **945**
Longitudinal profile of a national database search service, **485**

Ma ba'da al-mantiq al-bulini: al-tatawwurat al-akhirah fi asalib istirja' al-ma'lumat, wa-subul istifadat al-tawthiq al-'Arabi minha, **235**
Ma huwa hatha al CD/ROM, **135**
Ma'ahid al-'Ilm fi Bayt al-Maqdis, **751**
Ma'ayir al-muwahhadah lil-dawriyyat al-Misriyah, **508**
Ma'lumat min ajl al-Tanmiyah fi al-Watan al-'Arabi: Mabniyah 'ala al-Awraq allati Quddimat ila al-Multaqa al-Awwal Hawla al-Shabakah al-'Arabiyah lil-Ma'lumat, Tunis, 1987/6/12-8, **206**
Madakhil al-hay'at al-'Arabiyah wa-muqtarahat li-hululiha, **123**
Makaniz fi al-Watan al-'Arabi, **373**
Makaniz muta'addidat al-lughat wa-manhajiyyat i'dadiha, **369**
Makaniz muta'addidat al-lughat: min al-nazariyah ila al-tatbiq: al-waqi' wa-al-tumuh, **370**
Makhtut al-'Arabi wa-malamihihi al-madiyah, **307**
Makhtutat al-'Arabiyah fi Filastin, **747**
Makhtutat al-'Arabiyah: Faharisaha wa-Fahrasatiha, **306**
al-Makhtutat al-Maghribiyah, **716**
Makhtutat fi Maktabat al-Asad al-Wataniyah, **968**
Maktaba, **28**

TITLE INDEX

Makkah al-Mukarramak Library, **870**
Maktabah al-'ammah li baladiyyat al-Zarqa': fir' al-atfal: dirasat halah, **614**
Maktabah al-'Arabiyah al-wataniyah, **313**
Maktabah al-akadimiyah fi al-'Iraq bayna al-waqi' wa-'am 2000, **525**
Maktabah al-Jami'iyah Da'amah lil-Bahth al-'Ilmi: A'mal al-Nadwah al-'Arabiyah al-Thalithah lil-Ma'lumat lil-Ittihad al-'Arabi lil-Maktabat wa-al-Ma'lumat, **42**
Maktabah al-madrasiyah qalb al-barnamij al-tarbawi, **359**
Maktabah al-madrasiyah wa-dawruha fi tashji' 'adat al-qira'ah wa-ta'ziz al-minhaj al-madrasi, **360**
Maktabah al-mutanaqqilah, **312**
Maktabah al-wataniyah al-'Arabiyah limadha? wa-kayfa?, **314**
Maktabah al-wataniyah fi al-Mamlakah al-'Arabiyah al-Sa'udiyah, **888**
Maktabah al-wataniyah: waqi' wa-ru'ya mustaqbaliyah, **601**
Maktabah wa-al-Bahth, **33**
Maktabat wa-al-Ma'lumat bi al-Madaris wa-al-Kulliyyat, **351**
Maktabah wa-al-tilifizyun wa dawrihima al-i'lami fi al-'alam al-'Arabi, **18**
Maktabat al-'ammah fi khitat al-tanmiyah bi al-Mamlakah al-'Arabiyah al-Sa'udiyah, **903**
Maktabat al-adyirah fi mantaqatay al-Quds wa Bayt Lahm: dirasat halah, **739**
Maktabat al-Asad al-Wataniyah, **970**
Maktabat al-Atfal, **347**
Maktabat al-Iskandariya al-jadidah: markaz thaqafi hadari yahya min jadid, **442**
Maktabat al-Islamiyah fi Bayt al-Maqdis, **744**
Maktabat al-jami'iyah wa-tahaddiyat tiknulujyah al-ma'lumat, **44**
Maktabat al-Lubnaniyah: waqi' marir wa afaq mahdudah, **661**
Maktabat al-madaris al-thanawiyah fi liwa' 'Ajlun, **617**
Maktabat al-madrasiyah fi al-Mamlakah al-'Arabiyah al-Sa'udiyah, **909**
Maktabat al-madrasiyah fi al-Salt, **615**
Maktabat al-madrasiyah fi al-Urdun, **619**
Maktabat al-munazamat al-'Arabiyah wa-al-duwaliyah wa-al-marakiz al-thaqafiyah fi al-Urdun, **625**
Maktabat al-mustashfayat: ahammiyatiha, ahdafiha wa-khadamatiha, **368**
Maktabat al-mutakhassisah: tarikhuha, ta'rifuha, ahdafuha wa-tahawwuliha al-mu'asir ila marakiz al-ma'lumat, **365**
Maktabat al-wataniyah al-jami'iyah: dirasah tahliliyah, **45**
Maktabat baladiyat Tulkarm—'al-maktaba al-'amma', **606**
Maktabat fi al-Urdun, **554**
Maktabat fi al-Urdun: Waqi' wa-Tumuhat, **557**
Maktabat fi Filastin: Dirasah Mashiyah hawla Waqi' al-Maktabat wa-al-Maktabiyyin fi Filastin, **734**
Maktabat fi-Suriyah: hadiruha wa-mustaqbaliha, **961**
Maktabat jami'at al-Malik Sa'ud fi al-mizan, **782**
Maktabat jami'at al-Nilayn: taqrir wa-khuttat 'amal, **939**

Maktabat Jami'at Mu'tah: rafid thaqafi mumayyaz fi janub Urdunina al-'aziz: istitla' musawwar, **560**
Maktabat ka-munazzamah maftuhah: nahwa tatbiq li mafhum al-nizam al-maftuh fi idarat al-maktabat, **274**
Maktabat ma'had al-bulitiknik, **628**
Maktabat wa-al-harakah al-maktabiyah fi al-Urdun, **553**
Maktabat wa-marakiz al-ma'lumat bi dawlat al-Bahrayn: al-waqi' wa-al-tatallu'at al-mustaqbaliyah, **426**
Maktabat wa-marakiz al-tawthiq fi al-'Iraq, **518**
Maktabat wa-marakiz al-tawthiq wa-al-ma'lumat fi al-Jumhuriyah al-'Arabiyah al-Suriyah, **962**
Maktabatuna al-'Amma wa-al-haja al-massa lil-tatwir, **607**
Malamih al-jadidah fi al-tab'ah al-jadidah min tasnif diwi al-'ishri, **118**
Management of libraries in Saudi Arabia: practices and constraints, **872**
Managing a library automation project, **794**
Manahij wa-al-baramij al-dirasiyah fi 'ilm al-maktabat wa-al-ma'lumat fi al-Watan al-'Arabi, **301**
Manhajiyat al-Bahth al-Qanuni: Turuq I'dad al-Rasa'il al-Jami'iyah fi al-Qanun wa-al-Ta'liq 'ala al-Ahkam wa-Kitabat al-Istisharat wa-Istikhdam al-Maktabah al-Qanuniyah, **684**
Manhajiyyat nizam al-ma'lumat: tatbiq fi al-tawthiq, **171**
Manpower deficiency in Saudi Arabia: its effect on the library and information profession, **897**
Manpower shortage and education for librarianship in Jordan, **605**
Maqalat fi 'Ulum al-Maktabat wa-al-Tawthiq wa-al-Ma'lumat, **1**
Marakiz al-makhtutat wa adillatuha di al-Maghrib al-Aqsa, **715**
Marakiz al-ta'lim bayna al-nazariyah wa-al-tatbiq fi jami'at al-Khalij al-'Arabi, ma' isharah khassah li-markaz al-ta'allum fi jami'at al-Musil, **522**
Masadir al-ma'lumat al-iliktruniyah wa-ta'thiriha 'ala al-maktabat, **216**
Masadir al-Ma'lumat fi Duwal al-Khalij al-'Arabi, **394**
Masadit al-ma'lumat: al-suwar, **564**
Mashakil tatbiqat al-hasibat al-iliktruniyafi al-maktabat wa-marakiz al-ma'lumat fi al-aqtar al-'Arabiyah, **213**
Mashru' al-bahth wa masadir al-ma'lumat fi 'alam al-maktabat wa-al-ma'lumat, **11**
Matbu'at al-hukumiyah al-sa'udiyah: nash'atiha wa-numuwwiha, **821**
Matbu'at al-hukumiyah fi al-Mamlakah al-'Arabiyah al-Sa'udiyah: dirasah bibliyughrafiyah, **823**
Mauritania, **691**
Mawad al-sama'iyah wa-al-basariyah fi al-maktabat wa-'ilaqatiha bi al-maktabah al-'Arabiyah, **204**
Mawad al-sama'iyah wa-al-basariyah: ahamiyyataha wa-mutatalibatiha, **563**
Mawsu'ah al-'Arabiyah fi al-Watha'iq wa-al-Maktabat, **160**
Measuring scientific activity in lesser developed countries, **75**
Medical information in the Kingdom of Saudi Arabia: the case for library co-operation, **875**
Medical librarianship course, Kuwait, March-April 1984, **648**

TITLE INDEX 319

Medical libraries and their services to the health sector in the United Arab Emirates (1971-1993), **1008**
Medical library services in Kuwait: history and future prospects, **659**
Message of the Library, **622**
Micro-Airs: A Microcomputer-Based Arabic Information Retrieval System Comparing Words, Stems, and Roots as Index Terms, **238**
Microcomputer based database management system in a university library, **817**
Microcomputer Training Guidelines for the College of Education of King Saud University: A Pilot Study Based on the Concerns-Based Adoption Model, **854**
Microcomputer workstations as complements to a fully automated library system, **793**
Middle East, **30, 175**
Middle East information: the Arab Information Bank, **233**
Milkiyah al-adabiyah wa-al-faniyah fi Lubnan, **666**
Min adawat al bahth al-'ilmi: al-muqabalah, **343**
Min ajl al-Takhtit li-Tatwir al-Arshiv bi al-Bilad al-'Arabiyah, **59**
Modernization and continuity in library development in Palestine under the British Mandate (1920-1948), **753**
Morocco, **698**
Mosque libraries: a bibliographic essay, **271**
Mu'alajah al-Fanniyah lil-Ma'lumat: al-Fahrasah, al-Tasnif, al-Tawthiq, al-Takshif, al-Arshiv, **91**
Mu'alajah al-lughawiyah lil-ma'lumat, **181**
Mu'jam al-Hadith fi 'Ilm al-Maktabat wa-al-Ma'lumat: Injilizi, 'Arabi, **153**
Mu'jam al-Mawsu'i li-Mustalahat al-Maktabat wa-al-Ma'lumat: Inkilizi-'Arabi, **159**
Mu'jam al-Mu'arrab lil-Mustalahat al-Maktabiyah: Inkilizi-'Arabi, **151**
Mu'jam al-Mustalahat al-Maktabiyah: 'Arabi-Inkilizi, Inkilizi-'Arabi, **155**
Mu'jam Mustalahat 'Ilm al-Ma'lumat: Mu'jam Mashruh: Injilizi-'Arabi, **154**
Mu'assasat wa-madaris 'ilm al-maktabat wa-al-mal'lumat fi al-Watan al-'Arabi, **290**
Mudiriyyat al-Watha'iq al-Tarikhiyyah fi al-Qutr al-'Arabi al-Suri, **966**
Muhawalah li-taqrib al-mafahim bayna al-fahrasah wa-al-istirja' (al-bibliyughrafi), **247**
Mujamma' al-malaki li-buhuth al-hadarah al-Islamiyah (Mu'assasat al-Bayt) wa maktabatihi, **624**
Mumarasah al-midaniyah khilal al-baramij al-ta'limiyah li-'ilm al-maktabat, **298**
Munazzamat al-mutakhassissah wa dawruha fi haql al-maktabat wa-al-ma'lumat, **303**
Muqaddimah fi al-Fahrasah wa-al-Tasnif, **85**
Muqawwimat al-Dawr al-Tarbawi lil-Maktabat al-Madrasiyah: Dirasah Tatbiqiyah, **884**
Musaghghirat al-filmiyah fi al-maktabat wa-marakiz al-ma'lumat, **309**
Musaghghirat al-filmiyah: mazayaha wa-istikhdamatiha al-mukhtalifah, **311**
Mustafidun min al-maktabat al-akadimiyah: dirasah li-manhajiyyat bahth mushkilat ta'limihim wa-ittijahatihim wa-naw'iyyatihim, **40**

Mustaqbal mihnat al-maktabat wa-al-ma'lumat bayna al-nazariyah wa-al-tatbiq, **27**
Mustaqbal yaqtarin bi al-hadir, **702**
Mutatallibat al-nuhud bi-qita' al-ma'lumat, **205**
Muwasafah al-'Arabiyah: al-ma'lumat wa-al-tawthiq–dalil 'anasir al-bayanat al-bibliyughrafiyah: tatbiqat al-Tazwid, **165**
Myths of the universal library: from Alexandria to the postmodern age, **468**

Nadwah al-Iqlimiyyah Hawl al-Siyasat al-Wataniyyah li-Nuzum al-Ma'lumat wa Khadamatiha fi al-Buldan al-'Arabiyah, Amman, al-Mamlakah al-Urduniyah al-Hashimiyah, June 17-20, 1989, **212**
Nadwat al-Tiqniyah al-Hadithah fi Tanzim wa-Idarat al-Ma'lumat: al-Mun'aqidah bi-Ma'had al-Idarah al-'Ammah fi al-Fatrah min 5-6 Rabi' al-Akhir 1407 H., **819**
Nadwat Tawthiq al-Ma'lumat al-Idariyah (1989: Ma'had al-Idarah al-'ammah, Riyadh, Saudi Arabia), **818**
Nag Hammadi Library: a collection of Coptic works discovered in Upper (southern) Egypt in 1945, **510**
Nahwa al-shabakah al-wataniyah lil-Ma'lumat fi al-'Iraq, **548**
Nahwa istratijiyah wataniya li-nuzum al-ma'lumat wa-khadamatiha fi al-Urdun, **577**
Nahwa qa'idat ma'lumat lil-watha'iq wa-al-khattiyyat al-'Arabiyah, **236**
Nahwa tatwir maktabat al-atfal, **345**
Namat al-qiyadi li-mudiri wa-mudirat al-maktabat al-'ammah wa-al-jami'iyah fi al-Diffah al-Gharbiyah kama yatasawwaruhu al-'amilun fi hathihi al-maktabat, **748**
Nas al-mutarabit (al-haybirtixt): mahiyyatuhu wa-tatbiqatuhu, **251**
Nash'at al-maktabat al-Islamiyah, **264**
Nashat al-bibliyughrafi fi al-Watan al-'Arabi, **179**
Nashat al-tawthiq wa-al-ma'lumat fi Jami'at al-Duwal al-'Arabiyah, **172**
Nata'ij al-murtabata bi-'amaliyat i'adat al-fahrasah, **102**
National Archives of Egypt, **472**
National Bibliography in Saudi Arabia, Egypt and Tunisia: Analytical and Comparative Study with a View to Planning a Saudi Arabian National Bibliography, **800**
National information policies and networks in Morocco, Tunisia, Egypt and Sudan: a comparative study, **199**
National infrastructure of library and information services in Arab countries, **214, 326**
National libraries in the Arab World, **315, 316**
National Library of Egypt, **500**
National Library: An Analysis of the Critical Factors in Promoting Library and Information Services in Developing Countries: The Case of Saudi Arabia, **886**
Nationalbiblioteket i Tunis, **999**
Nazrah 'ala al-awda' al-rahinah lil-maktabat fi al-Mamlakah al-Maghribiyah, **697**

Nazrah shamilah 'ala khadamat al-tawthiq fi al Watan al-'Arabi, **166**
Near East since 1920, **15**
Near or Middle East? Choice of name, **97**
Networked resources on politics in the Middle East, **227**
New Biblioteca Alexandrina, **446**
Newspaper journalism in Libyan Jamahiriya: a review, **689**
Nizam al-duwali li-sijil bayanat al-musalsalat (ISDS), **87**
Nizam al-ma'lumat al-ali fi maktabat jami'at al-Yarmuk, **584**
Nizam al-ma'lumat wa-dawruha fi khidmat al-mustafidin, **240**
al-Nizam al-Maghribi lil-ma'lumat "Maghribnet": mahattah mumayyazah lil-ta'awun al-'Arabi al-Urubbi, **707**
Nizam bank ma'lumat al-watha'iq: tajribat ma'had al-idarah al-'ammah bi al-Riyad, **836**
Nizam ma'lumat idari lil-markaz al-watani lil-watha'iq fi al-'Iraq: muqtarah khittat tasmim, **532**
Nizam maktabah mumaknan bi-istikhdam al-hasibah al-maykruwiyah "al-Warka', **539**
Nuova biblioteca di Alessandria d'Egitto, **459**
Nuzum al-aqras al-basariyah al-muktanazah wa-ta'thiriha 'ala nuzum al-istirja' al-mubashar lil-ma'lumat, **245**
Nuzum al-Ma'lumat fi al-'Ulum al-Ijtima'iyah: al-Halqah al-Dirasiyah al-Thalithah al-Mun'aqidah bi-al-Markaz, fi al-Muddah min 10-28 Nuvimbir, 1979, **223**
Nuzum al-Ma'lumat wa-al-Hasib al-Iliktruni: Mabadi' Tahlil al-Nuzum, Tasmim al-Nuzum, Tanfiz al-Nuzum, Taqyim al Ada', **255**

Of making many books there is no end': the classical Muslim view, **341**
Oman, **721**
Oman er der kun en bibliotekar, **728**
On your MARC, get set, go, **389**
Online and Kuwait, **646**
Online automation at the University of Petroleum and Minerals Library, 1980, **789**
Online in Saudi Arabia, **839, 851**
Online search service at the King Abdulaziz University Library, Jeddah, Saudi Arabia, **832**
Online searching in a university library of a developing country, **838**
Organizing a library in Libya, **675**
Oriental origins of the Alexandrian Library, **466**
Outlook on the new information system of petroleum products distribution in Iraq, **540**
Overview of the impact of the Iraqi aggression on libraries, information and education for librarianship in Kuwait, **637**

Partners in developing CD-ROM services for developing-countries, **132**
PC-based research-oriented clinical information system: a case study of Kuwait, **643**

Peace and information in the Middle East, **226**
People of the book: information policy and practice in the Muslim world, **200**
Periodical literature, **362**
Periodique agricole au Maroc: production, diffusion et accessibilite, **718**
Plan for Public Library System Development in Saudi Arabia, **900**
Planning for an Automated Cooperative Library Network of University Libraries in Saudi Arabia: An Exploratory Study, **778**
Planning for library automation at the University of Petroleum and Minerals, **790**
Plans for Establishing and Developing the Social Research Studies and Information Center Libraries in Saudi Arabia, **768**
Potential for CD-ROM technology in less-developed countries, **133**
Potential of DOBIS/LIBIS and MINISIS for automating library functions: a comparative study, **795**
Pour l'implantation d'un reseau d'information sur l'urbanisme et l'amenagement du territoire, **717**
Preparing catalogers for the electronic environment: an analysis of cataloging and related courses in the Arabian Gulf region, **390**
Prescriptive Model for Planning a National Scientific and Technical Information System for Egypt, **490**
Prescriptive Model for Planning and Implementing a Resource Sharing and Information Networking System among Saudi University Libraries (University Libraries), **890**
Presentation du projet de creation d'une banque maghrebine d'information industrielle, **709**
Principles in planning library education programs in the Muslim world, **297**
Printing in the medieval Islamic underworld, **332**
Private institutions and computer utilization in community service and education: the case of the Abdul-Hamid Shoman Foundation, **578**
Problemes de legislation en matiere d'information dans les pays africains, **420**
Problems affecting the development of libraries in Algeria, **407**
Problems facing public libraries in developing countries, with special reference to Saudi Arabia: a state-of-the-art, **901**
Problems of book development in the Arab world with special reference to Egypt, **339**
Problems of Children's literature in the Kingdom of Saudi Arabia, **810**
Problems of communication and information-handling among scientists and engineers in Saudi universities, **827**
Problems of social science research in Palestine: an overview, **742**
Proceedings of the Symposium on New Technology in Libraries: Prospects and Problems for Libraries in the Gulf States, 26, 27, 28 April 1982, **386**
Professional library development, manpower education and training in Jordan, **597**
Profile of medical research publications from the GCC countries, 1990-1994, **388**

Prognosis of Academic Achievement in Library and Information Science in Morocco: Comparison of Examinatorial and Nonexaminatorial Prediction Models, **713**
Projections of library and information workers in Kuwait in its post-war development, **652**
Proposal for Planning an Interlending System for the Libraries of Cairo City in Egypt, **493**
Proposed computer-based methodology for planning an Arab information network, **319**
Proposed Standards for University Libraries in Saudi Arabia, **783**
Provision of information to industry: a comparative study of Saudi Arabia and the UK, **835**
Public access online catalogue at the University of Petroleum and Minerals Library, **895**
Public access searching through DOBIS, **894**
Public and private libraries in the Hijaz up to 1925, **868**
Public libraries development reconsidered: the case of Egypt, **505**
Public libraries in Saudi Arabia, **902**
Publication patterns of scientists working in Saudi Arabia, **906**

Qa'ima al-muwahada lil-dawriyat al-ajnabiyah fi al-Urdun, **620**
Qa'imat Ru'us al-Mawdu'at al-'Arabiyah al-Kubra, **117**
Qadayah fi Fahrasat al-Matbu' al-'Arabi: al-Qawa'id wa-al-Hulul, **122**
Qaddim kitaban tunshi' maktaba, **608**
Qadiyat al-Ikhtizan wa-al-Istirja' al-Iliktruni lil-Ma'lumat al-Bibliyujrafiyah ma'a Namudhaj Mi'yari li-Ashkal al-Ittisal, **234**
Qadiyat al-Takhtit al-I'lami fi al-Watan al-'Arabi, **198**
Qamus al-Ma'lumatiyah: 'Arabi, Inkilizi, Faransi, **156**
Qamus al-Ma'lumatiyah; Faransi-Inkilizi-'Arabi, **157**
Qanawat al-ittisal fi idarat al-maktabat, **277**
Qatar, **760**
Qatar library services: present problems and future prospects, **761**
Qatar national library, **766**
Qatar's progressive GIS program, **764**
Qawa'id al-bayanat al-bibliyughrafiyah wa-marahil tasmimiha bi-istikhdam maykru CDS/ISIS, **253**
Qawa'id al-fahrasah al-anglu-amirkiyah, al-tab'ah al-thaniyah muraja'at 1988, **113**
Qawa'id al-fahrasah al-anglu-amirkiyah/al-tab'ah al-thaniyah: al-tab'ah al-'Arabiyah al-ula, **107**
Qawa'id al-Shabakah al-'Arabiyah lil-Ma'lumat li Tartib al-Madakhil fi al-Faharis wa-al-Bibliyughrafiyat wa-al-Adillah, **184**
Qiwa al-bashariyah al-'amilah fi al-maktabat wa-marakiz al-ma'lumat fi al-Mamlakah, **899**
Qiyas al-bibliyughrafi wa-tatbiqatihi fi majal al-ma'lumat wa-al-maktabat, **78**
Qiyas wa-al-taqwim lil-majmu'at al-maktabiyah: dirasah fi falsafat al-asalib bayna al-nazariyah wa-al-tatbiq, **222**

Questions sur la production culturelle au Maroc: lecture preliminaire du 'repertoire des ecrivains marocains membres de l'union des Ecrivains du Maroc', **701**

Raqm al-duwali al-mi'yari lil-kitab: al-darurah wa-mustalzamat al-tatbiq, **63**
Rebuilding the Library of Alexandria, **445**
Recent changes in library education in Egypt, **496**
Recent developments in Muslim, Arab and Egyptian library and information services, **203**
Recent studies in Middle Eastern printing history: a review essay, **331**
Recommendations for Somali entries in library cataloguing systems, **933**
Reference books, **374**
Reflection of reality—authority control of Muslim personal names, **129**
Regional interlibrary loan network of Arabian Gulf academic libraries, **397**
Relationship Between Political Alignment and Scientific Communication: A Bibliometric Study of Egyptian Science Publications, **474**
Relevance of microcomputers to health improvement in developing countries, **482**
Repertoire des bibliotheques et des organismes de documentation sur le monde Arabe, **8**
Report on a visit to Egypt, April 1993, **438**
Report on some archives in Equatoria Province, Sudan, **944**
Report on the second annual conference of the Arabian Gulf Chapter of the Special Libraries Association, January 1994, **406**
Research and scientific publishing in Saudi Arabia, **908**
Resource sharing among libraries in developing countries: the Gulf between hope and reality, **399**
Resource sharing in Gulf academic libraries '95, **400**
Resource-sharing networks in developing countries, **329**
Resources for Sudanese studies: the Sudan archive of the University of Durham, **941**
Responding to researchers' and faculty use patterns and perceptions of CD-ROM services, **924**
Revival of the Alexandria Library (Bibliotheca Alexandrina): a unique project of the twenty-first century, **465**
Role of information in science and technology transfer in Arab countries, **215**
Role of information in the information technology trade between the UK and Saudi Arabia, **844**
Role of libraries in Somalia's reformation, **929**
Role of National Libraries in Developing Countries, with Special Reference to Saudi Arabia, **887**
Role of the King Abdulaziz City for Science and Technology in information services in the Kingdom of Saudi Arabia, **833**
Role of training in development: some reflections from Sudan, **954**
Royal Palace archives of Rabat and the Makhzen in the 19th century, **700**
Ru'us al-mawdu'at al- 'Arabiyah al-maqlubah afdal min al-ru'us al-tabi'iyah, **130**

TITLE INDEX 325

Ru'us al-mawdu'at al-'Arabiyah: madkhal li-dirasah, **124**

Samkatalog over Mauretaniens arabiska handskrifter-ett forsta forsok, **693**
Sarkis, Yusuf Ilyan, **81**
Saudi Arabia, **775**
Saudi Arabia: indigenous sources of information, **774**
Saudi Arabian librarianship: an annotated bibliography (1950-1986), **801**
Saudi Arabian National Center for Science and Technology (SANCST) Database, **830**
Saudi Arabian national data bases and use of GULFNET/BITNET at KFUPM Library, Dhahran, **847**
Scholarly publisher in Egypt, **507**
School libraries in Kuwait: before and after the Gulf War, **656**
Science and technology information transfer in developing countries: some problems and suggestions, **201**
Science research in Kuwait--a bibliometric analysis, **635**
Scientific and technical archiving system of ENSTINET: 'STARS', **487**
Scientific and Technical Information Transfer: Promoting Information Acquisition in the Saudi Arabian Industrial Sector (Scientific Information), **834**
Searching CD-ROM databases for non-English-speaking users, **430**
Serials acquisition in the Middle East, **361**
Serials in the Libyan Jamahuriya, past and present, **690**
Shabaka al-'Arabiyah lil-ma'lumat: bayna al-haqiqah wa-al-khayal, **320**
Shabakah al-'Arabiyah lil-ma'lumat: nazrah nahwa mustaqbalin afdal, **318**
Shabakah al-'Arabiyah lil-ma'lumat: tasawwur jadid, **325**
Shabakat al-Intirnit, **327**
Shabakat al-ma'lumat al-sina'iyah al-'Arabiyah: hadiruha wa-mustaqbaliha, **324**
Shabakat al-ma'lumat al-wataniyah al-mutakhassisah fi al-Kuwayt: nash'atiha, tattawuriha, ma'uqat tanmiyatiha, **631**
Shabakat al-ma'lumat fi al-duwal al-namiyah, **321**
Short account of the development of DOBIS/LIBIS Regional Centre at KFUPM, **791**
Siyanat al-kutub wa-al-muhafazah 'alayha, **330**
Siyar wa-al-tarajim fi tasnif *"al-Fihrist"* li Ibn al-Nadim, **119**
Siyasat tabadul al-i'arah bayna al-maktabat 'ala al-mustawa al-qutri wa-al-qawmi, **258**
Socio-Cultural Factors Affecting the Adaptations of the Dewey Decimal Classification in the Middle East, **120**
Somalia, **930**
Somalia's reconstruction: an opportunity to create a responsive information infrastructure, **928**
Some Leading Muslim Libraries of the World, **265**
Special libraries of the Kingdom of Saudi Arabia, **915**
State of automation in selected libraries and information centres in Saudi Arabia, **792**
Statistical study of online searches in an academic library, **842**

Strategic Planning in University Libraries in Saudi Arabia: An Exploratory Study, **781**
Structure and rendering of Arabic proper names for bibliographic purposes, **104**
Study of Availability and Actual Usage of Arabic and English Monographs in Science and Technology in Three Academic Libraries in Saudi Arabia, **828**
Study of hospital and medical libraries in Riyadh, Kingdom of Saudi Arabia, **914**
Study of Supply and Demand of Library and Information Workers in Kuwait: Five-Year Projections and Recommendations for Human Resources Planning (Library Workers, Manpower Shortages), **651**
Study of the effect on online searching of CD index in a science and engineering library, **841**
Study of the Factors Influencing the Adoption of CD-ROM Technology in Libraries in Saudi Arabia, **853**
Study of the Libraries in Girls' Credit Hour Secondary Schools in Kuwait, **655**
Su'ubat allati tuwajih talabat al-dirasat al-'ulyah fi majal al-khidmah al-maktabiyah: dirasat halah li-maktabat jami'at al-Basrah, **526**
Subul al-ta'awun bayna al-maktabat al-jami'iyah al-sa'udiyah fi bina' al-majmu'at, **874**
Sudan, **935**
Sudan Archive of the University of Durham, **942**
Sudan's National Documentation Centre, **951**
Sultan Qaboos University in Oman, **722**
Survey of education for library and information science in Egypt, the Maghreb countries, and Sudan, **284**
Survey of User's Attitudes Toward the Resources and Services of Three University Libraries in Saudi Arabia, **923**
Syntactically-Based Preprocessor for a Limited Experimental Arabic Document Retrieval System, **237**
Syria, **960**
Syrian National Library, **971**
System for processing bilingual Arabic/English text, **252**
System migration: challenges for libraries in the Arabian Gulf region, **385**
Systematic Design of a Proposed Model for School Library Media Center Programs in Saudi Arabia, **910**

Ta'awun bayna al-maktabat al-sa'udiyah fi majal al-ijra'at al-fanniyah, **876**
Ta'awun fi majal al-tazwid bayna al-maktabat al-jami'yah fi al-Mamlakah al-'Arabiyah al-Sa'udiyah, **813**
Ta'lim al-jami'i fi haql al-maktabat wa-al-ma'lumat: muqaranah bayna al-'Iraq wa-al-Sa'udiyah wa-Misr, **544**
Ta'lim al-maktabat fi al-Mamlakah al-'Arabiyah al-Sa'udiyah, **881**
Ta'lim al-mustamir li-ikhsa'i al-ma'lumat fi al-Watan al-'Arabi, **287**
Ta'lim wa-al-ma'lumat fi majal al-arshiv fi al-Watan al-'Arabi, **225**
Ta'thir al-hasub 'ala barnamij ta'lim 'ulum al-maktabat wa-al-ma'lumat, **288**
Tab'ah al-hadiyah wa-al-'ishrun min nizam tasnif diwi al-'ishri, **114**

TITLE INDEX

Tabadul bayna al-maktabat al-'Arabiyah min ajl ittifaqiyah 'Arabiyah li tabadul al-watha'iq, **281**

Tables and photos on the Iraqi aggression to the library and information infrastructure in Kuwait, **641**

Tadaffuq al-bayanat 'ibra al-hudud wa-al-qadayah dhat al-'ilaqah bi-khadamat al-maktabat wa-al-ma'lumat, **220**

Tadrib al-maktabiyyin fi al-Jumhuriyah al-'Iraqiyah, **551**

Tadris 'ilm al-maktabat wa-al-ma'lumat fi kuliyat al-mujtama, **592**

Tadris al-jami'i li-'ilm al-maktabat wa-al-hajah al-urduniyah, **595**

Tadriss 'ilm al-maktabat wa-al-ma'lumat fi al-Watan al-'Arabi, **286**

Tadub ('ayn): al-Taqnin al-Duwali al-'Am lil-Wasf al-Bibliyughrafi, **108**

Tadub (kaf): al-Taqnin al-Duwali lil-Wasf al-Bibliyughrafi lil-Kutub, **106**

Tadub (mim, ghayn, kaf): al-Taqnin al-Duwali lil-Wasf al-Bibliyughrafi lil-Mawad Ghayr al-Kutub, **99**

Tahlil al-bibliyughrafi wa-imkaniyyat al-istifadah minhu fi al-khadamat al-maktabiyah, **74**

Tahlil al-intaj al-fikri fi majal manahij al-bahth fi 'ilm al-maktabat wa-al-ma'lumat, **12**

Tahlil al-mawdu'i wa-al-takshif, **127**

Tajribah al-Maghribiyah li-maknanat al-mu'tayat al-bibliyughrafiyah, **708**

Takhassus al-maktabat wa-al-ma'lumat fi al-kharitah al-akadimiyah, **24**

Takhassus al-Maktabat wa-al-Ma'lumat: Madkhal Manhaji Wi'a'i, **26**

Takhassus al-masadir al-ta'limiyah wa-al-maktabat bi-kulliyyat al-mujtama' al-urduniyah: dirasah naqdiyah, **593, 594**

Takshif, **186**

Takshif al-dawriyyat fi duwal al-Khalij al-'Arabi: al-itar al-nazari, **392**

Tanmiyat adab al-atfal fi al-'alam al-'Arabi, **136**

Tanmiyat Maharat al-'Amilin fi al-Maktabat wa Marakiz al-Ma'lumat bi-Misr: Dirasah Nazariyah Tatbiqiyah, **513**

Tansiq bayna Marakiz al-Buhuth fi al-Duwal al-'Arabiyah—Abhath al-Nadwah al-'Ilmiyah al-Thaniyah: al-Khittah al-Amniyah al-Wiqa'iyah al-'Arabiyah al-Ula, **282**

Tanzim marakiz al-tawthiq wa-tasyiriha, **273**

Taqnin al-duwali lil-wasf al-bibliyughrafi wa-qawa'id al-jam'iyah al-faransiyah lil-taqnin, **101**

Taqnin al-duwali lil-wasf al-bibliyughrafi: tahlil wa taqyim min wijhat nazar 'Arabiyah, **86**

Taqrir 'an al-dawrah al-thaniyah lil-mu'alajah al-faniyah lil-ma'lumat: al-fahrasah wa-al-tasnifat wa-al-arshif, **570**

Taqrir hawla awda' markaz tawzi' al-kitab al-Urduni, **569**

Taqyim al-watha'iq al-rasmiyah, **174**

Tarikh maktabat al-Haram al-Makki, **867**

Tarkibah al-urduniyah al-muwahhadah, **568**

Tarkibat al-bibliyughrafiyah al-mustakhdamah fi al-maktabat wa-marakiz al-ma'lumat al-urduniyah, **583**

Tashri'at al-maktabiyah fi al-'Iraq, **546**

Tasnif al-'ulum al-sihhiyah fi al-maktabat al-tibbiyah: dirasat halah li-maktabat kulliyyat tub Baghdad, **529**
Tasnif wa-anzimatuhu, **89**
Taswiq khadamat nuzum ma'lumat al-tanmiyah fi-Ifriqiyah wa-al-Maghrib al-'Arabi: dirasah muqaranah, **704**
Tatawwur al-Maktabat al-Jami'iyah fi al-Jaza'ir, **410**
Tatawwur al-tarikhi lil-maktabat fi Libya min aqdam al-'usur, **680**
Tatawwur khadamat al-ma'lumat lil-makfufin wa-du'af al-basar, ma' dirasat halah 'an Misr, **483**
Tatbiq al-'amali li tasnif diwi al-'ishri fi maktabat jami'at al-Basrah: dirasah midaniyah, **528**
Tatbiq al-qawa'id al-duwaliyah fi faharis al-maktabat al-jami'iyah fi al-'Iraq: dirasah taqwimiyah, **533**
Tatwir khadamat al-maktabah al-'ammah, **337**
Tatwir majmu'at al-maktabat al-jami'iyah fi al-Sa'udiyah wa-taqyimiha, **814**
Tawthiq al-tarbawi bi al-Sudan, **946**
Tawthiq li-baramij wa-nuzum al-ma'lumat: dirasah li-mustalzamatihi wa-ma'uqatihi, **169**
Tawthiq wa-al-tawthiq al-Filastini, **740**
Tawthiq wa-sultat al-isdar, **741**
Tifl wa-al-qira'ah wa-al-khidmah al-maktabiyah al-'ammah, **688**
Tiknologia al-ta'lim fi al-maktabat: imkaniyat tatbiqiha wa-al-tadarub 'alyha fi al-duwal al-namiyah, **291**
Tiqaniyah al-ma'lumatiyah al-mustakhdamah fi al-maktabat wa marakiz al-ma'lumat al-Sa'udiyah: dirasah lil-mushkilat wa-al-hulul, **855**
Tiqaniyyat al-aqras al-daw'iyah al-madghutah CD-ROM wa-tatbiqatiha al-haliyah wa-al-mustaqbaliyah: dirasah wafiyah li-ihda mazahir sina'at al-ma'lumat al-mutaqaddimah wa-ta'thiratiha 'ala bunyat al-ma'lumat al-'Arabiyah, **134**
Tiqaniyyat al-bahth bi al-ittisal al-mubashar wa-al-aqras al-muktanazah wa-istikhdamatiha fi jami'atay Baghdad wa-al-Musul, **538**
Tiqaniyyat al-hadithah fi al-maktabat, **310**
Towards a national information policy for Egypt, **477**
Towards effective information processing in high office: an analysis of decision support systems in the national governments of Israel and Egypt, **486**
Trade book publishing in Saudi Arabia past and present, **907**
Training at the grassroots: an integrated approach to training library assistants in Southern Sudan, **955**
Training library assistants at the University of Juba, **956**
Training of Egyptian Information Specialists: A Multifaceted System Approach, **514**
Traitement des sources de l'histoire tunisienne en France, **986**
Translation and expansion of classification systems in the Arab countries and Iran, **126**
Trattamento informatico della lingua araba, **50**
Trends of users: a study in Iraqi scene, **523**
Tropical Librarianship, **269**

TITLE INDEX

Tunisia, **980**

United Arab Emirates, **1003**
United Arab Emirates and the Internet: cultural and social implications for higher education, **1007**
United Arab Emirates University Libraries, Al-Ain, United Arab Emirates, September-December, 1993 and February-May 1994, **1006**
University libraries in Arab countries, **41**
University libraries in Socialist People's Libyan Arab Jamahiriya: an introduction to Sebha university library, **681**
University library development in the Arab Gulf region: a survey and analysis of six state university libraries, **384**
University library planning: the experience of the University of Petroleum and Minerals, **780**
University Library Practices in Developing Countries, **39**
University of Petroleum and Minerals: a model for an academic library, **779**
University publishing in Lebanon, **674**
University Publishing in Lebanon: A Historical and Comparative Study of the Publishing Programs of the Five Universities in Lebanon, **673**
Use of Arabic in computerized information interchange, **48**
Use of Arabic script in computerized information systems, **49**
Use of computers in libraries and information centres in Jordan: a survey, **576**
Use of database management systems at the University of Basrah Library, **531**
Use of Information Sources by Faculty in the Physical Sciences and Social Sciences at King Abdulaziz University (Saudi Arabia), **926**
Use of information technology by scientists in British and Saudi Arabian universities: a comparative study, **850**
Use of international documents in developing countries, **703**
Use of the DDC in the Arab world, **93**
Use of topic sentences for evaluating the representativeness of Arabic article titles, **177**
User education at the Oran University of Science and Technology, **424**
User reactions to the online catalog the University of Petroleum and Minerals Library, **925**
User Satisfaction in a Government Library: A Case Study of the Ministry of Foreign Affairs in Saudi Arabia (Library Services), **921**
User services at the KFUPM Library, Dhahran, Saudi Arabia, **922**
The Uses of Mass Communication Under a Crisis Situation: A Comparative Study of Kuwaiti's Utilization of Information Sources Before and During the Iraqi Occupation of Kuwait, **639**
Usus al-'ammah lil-ta'awun bayna al-maktabat, **280**

Vanished Library, **449**

Wad' al-mihani li mudarrisi 'ilm al-ma'lumat wa-al-maktabat fi al-Watan al-'Arabi, **283**

Waqa'i' al-Nadwah al-'Arabiyah al-Sabi'ah lil-Ma'lumat: al-Nashr wa-al-Dabt al-Bibliyughrafi lil-Nitaj al-Fikri al-'Arabi: 'Amman, 20-23 Jumadi al-Akhir 1417 H/2-6 Tishrin al-Thani 1996 M, **7**
Waqi' al-khadamat al-maktabiyah fi maktabat al-mukhayyamat al-filastiniyah fi al-Diffah al-Gharbiyah, **731**
Waqi' al-khidma al-maktabiyah fi madaris Wikalat al-Gawth, **618**
Waqi' al-maktabat al-'ammah fi al-Urdun, **609**
Waqi' al-maktabat al-tibbiyah fi al-Urdun, **627**
Waqi' al-maktabat wa-al-harakah al-maktabiyah fi Suriya, **958**
Waqi' maktabat al atfal fi al-Urdun, **612**
Waqi' Maktabat al-Madaris al-Thanawiyyah fi al-Urdun, **613**
Waqi' maktabat kulliyyat al-mujtama' fi al-Urdun, **561**
Waqi' wa-mustaqbal al-ta'lim al-akadimi fi 'ilm al-ma'lumat wa-al-maktabat fi Duwal al-Khalij al-'Arabi, **402**
Wasa'il wa-asalib tadris 'ilm al-maktabat wa-al-ma'lumat fi al-Watan al-'Arabi, **302**
Wasf al-wazifi lil-'amilin fi al-maktabat aw marakiz al-ma'lumat wa-al-tawthiq, **38**
Watha'iq al-Lubnaniyah bi al-Mikrufilm, **667**
Watha'iq al-tarikhiyah al-libiyah wa-amakin tawajudiha dakhil al-Jamahiriyah al-'Arabiyah al-Libiyah al-Sha'biyah al-Ishtirakiyah, **682**
Wiederaufbau der Bibliothek von Alexandria, **457**
Wiederentstehung der Alexandrina, **455**
Writings on African Archives, **56**

Yemen, **1011**

SUBJECT INDEX

Abbasids
   See Islamic libraries;
Libraries—history
Abdul Hameed Shoman
   Foundation (Jordan), **579**
Abdul Hameed Shoman Public
   Library (Jordan), **610**
Abstracting, **178**, **183**
   See also Indexing
Academic libraries, **29-30**, **39-46**, **351**
   automated information system for, **46**
   bibliographic control of dissertations, **60**
   cataloging, **88**
   conferences, **42**
   databases in, **44**
   library users, **40**
   national, **45**
   networking, **323**
   resources, **43**
   user education, **40**
   user services, **40**
Acquisition(s)
   See Collection development
Administration and management, **273-277**

Agricultural information, services, **367**
Agricultural National Documentation Centre (Tunisia), **988**
Agricultural Sciences and Technology (AGRIS), **48**
AGRIS
   See Agricultural Sciences and Technology (AGRIS)
Ajloun school libraries (Jordan), **617**
ALECSO
   See Arab League Educational, Cultural and Scientific Organization
ALEPH, **54**
Alexandria Library, **441-471**
   architecture, **443**, **453**, **459**, **463**, **469**
   history, **441**, **447-450**, **458**, **460-461**, **466-467**
Algeria, **407-409**
   abstracting, **412**
   academic libraries, **408-410**
   development, **410**
   archives, **414**
   bibliographic systems, **412**
   copyright, **411**

documentation centers, **408**
indexes, **413**
information infrastructure,
408
information services, **241, 412**
information systems, **412-414**
information technology, **408**
intellectual property, **411**
library and information science
education, **284-285**
library development, **407-408**
library history, **408-409**
library legislation, **420**
national libraries, **408-409**
professional education, **408-409, 415-419**
public libraries, **408-409, 421**
publishing industry, **408**
school libraries, **408-409, 422**
serials control system, **413**
special libraries, **408-409, 423**
training for staff **416-418**
user education, **424**
American University in Cairo, **509**
American University of Beirut,
664-665
Amman Polytechnic Library, **628**
Anglo-American cataloging rules,
107, 111, 113, 123
See also Cataloging
Algerian Scientific Abstracts, **412**
Arab Bibliographic Center, **70**
Arab Center for Medical Literature,
658
Arab Information Bank, **233**
Arab Information System Network
(ARIS-NET), **206, 319-320**
Arab League Educational, Cultural
and Scientific Organization
(ALECSO), **142, 189, 193,
318, 364**
Arabian Gulf countries **378-381**
academic libraries, **382-384**
development, **384**
information services, **382**
interlibrary loan, **396-397**
administration and
management, **398**

automation, **385**
bibliographic control, **387**
bibliographic networking,
403-404
bibliometric studies, **388**
cataloging and classification,
389-390, 404
teaching, **390**
CD-ROM services, **388**
collection development, **391**
scientific literature, **391**
computerized bibliographic
records, **389**
conferences, **379, 386**
development of libraries in,
381
indexing, **392**
serials, **392**
industrial information systems,
395
information resources, **394**
information services, **379, 393**
information storage and
retrieval, **387, 395**
information systems, **380,
389, 398**
evaluation, **398**
management, **398**
interlibrary loan, **396-397**
Internet access and use, **393**
library cooperation, **399-400**
literature review, **378**
medical literature,
bibliometric analysis, **388**
networks and networking,
403-405
online catalogs, **389**
online information retrieval,
428
professional education, **379,
401-402**
resource-sharing, **399-400,
404**
serials, **387**
indexing of, **392**
system migration, **386**
Arabic names
See also Personal names

SUBJECT INDEX

cataloging, **103-104**
Arabic script
    See also Technical services
  computerized bibliographic records, and, **47-49, 51, 53-54, 249**
  formatting, **52**
  word processing and, **50, 252**
Arabization of library and information systems, **249-250**
    See also individual library and information systems
ARABMARC, **51**
Aramco, **915**
Archives and archiving, **55-56, 59, 91, 160, 163**
  ancient, **37, 57-58**
  encyclopedias, **160**
  governmental, **174**
  guides, **8**
  information sources, **225**
  legislation, **55**
  study and teaching, **225**,,
ARIS-NET
    See Arab Information System Network
Asad National Library (Syria), **959, 968, 970-974**
Assiut University (Egypt), **437**
Associations
    See Library associations
Assur, **57**
Audiovisual materials
  use in libraries, **291**
Authority control, **54, 94**
    See also Bibliographic control
Authority files, **110**
Automatic indexing, **188**
    See also Indexing
  evaluation, **182**
Automation,
    See also Computerization
  bibliographic records, **53-54**
Azhar Library, al- (Egypt), **494-495**

    See Azhar University Library
Azhar University Library, al- (Egypt), **494-495**
    See also under Egypt—Islamic libraries; Islamic libraries; Mosque libraries
Baghdad University, **528, 538**
Bahrain, **425-426**
    See also Arabian Gulf countries
  academic libraries, **382, 384, 425, 428-430**
    development, **384**
    information services, **382, 393**
  CD-ROM services, **428-430**
    impact on research productivity, **429**
    use studies, **429**
  Gulf War impact on libraries in, **427**
  information services, **426-430**
  information storage and retrieval, **429**
  information systems
    microform materials and services, of, **431**
  Internet access and use, **393**
  library history, **425**
  national libraries, **425**
  professional education, **425, 432**
  public libraries, **425**
  school libraries, **425**
  special libraries, **425**
  use studies, **429**
  user aids, **430**
Basrah University (Iraq), **526, 528, 531, 542**
Biblical studies
  citation analysis, **80**
Bibliographic control, **7, 60-64, 97, 170**
  children's literature, **61**
  conferences, **7**
  dissertations, **60, 64**

ISBN, **63**
national bibliography, **62**
serials, **363**
Bibliographic databases, **66, 254**
Bibliographic description, **86, 100-101**
Bibliographic records, **254**
Bibliographic services, **179**
Bibliographic systems, **65-66**
Bibliographic tools, **231**
Bibliographical citations, **112**
Bibliographies, **2, 67-69, 71-73, 96, 98, 119, 160, 187**
    development, **98**
    need for, **70**
    production of, **170**
Bibliography
    See Documentation
Bibliometric studies, **74-80**
Bibliotheca Alexandrina
    See Alexandria Library
Bibliotheque de l'Institut Francais d'Etudes Arabes de Damas (Syria), **976**
Bibliotheque Nationale de Tunisie, **998**
Bilingual databases, **244**
Biographical dictionaries, **158**
Biographies, **81, 119**
Book publishing, **82, 341**
Books
    importance of, **14**
    preservation, **330**
Books, history
    bibliographies, **69**
    conferences, **9**
Boolean logic, **235**
Bourguiba Institute of Modern Languages (Tunisia), **979**
British Consul (Saudi Arabia), **915**
Buildings
    See Library buildings
Cairo University Library, **439**
Callimachus, **447**
Cataloging and classification, **30, 54, 83-130**
    See also Indexing; Online cataloging

children's literature, of, **347, 352**
handbooks, manuals, etc., **109-110**
non-book materials, **99**
CD-ROMs, **20, 44, 131-135, 388, 428-430, 538, 646, 706, 724-725, 796, 829, 840-842, 845-846, 852-853, 856, 859, 865, 878, 924**
CDS/ISIS, **54, 95-96, 253, 574, 580, 582-583, 597, 743**
Centre de Documentation Nationale (Tunisia), **989**
Centre National de Documentation (Morocco), **711-712**
Children's Literature
    development, **136**
Children's libraries
    See School libraries
Citation analysis, **74, 76, 80**
Civilization, **2**
Classification
    See Cataloging and classification
Clippings, **137-138**
CODAR-UFD, **48**
Collection development, **139-141, 165**
    serials, of, **361**
College libraries
    See Academic libraries
Commission des Sources de l'Histoire Tunisienne en France (CSHTF), **985**
Computer networks and networking, **206**
    See also Networks and networking
    conferences, **206**
Computerization, **5, 145**
Computers in libraries
    use of, **142-146**
Conference proceedings
    acquisition, **139**
Consultancy and consultants, **147**
Continuing education, **29, 287, 296**
Cooperation,

SUBJECT INDEX 335

See Library cooperation
Coordinate subject indexing, **180**
Copyright, **148-150**
Creswell Library of Islamic Art and Architecture (Egypt), **509**
Cultural heritage, **16**
Databases, **96, 232-233, 236, 244**
   effect on development, **10**
Descriptive cataloging, **106, 108, 116, 123, 125, 128**
   rules, **99**
Device Independent Typesetter RunOFF, **52**
Dewey Decimal Classification system, **93, 114, 118, 120-121, 126**
Dictionaries, **2**
   biographical, **158**
   linguistic
      Arabic-English, **155**
      Arabic-English-French, **156**
      English-Arabic, **151-155, 159, 161-162**
      French-English-Arabic, **157**
Diroff/ffortid
   See Device Independent Typesetter RunOFF
Disabled, information services for the, **483, 629**
Dissertations
   bibliographic control, **60, 64**
   indexes, **64**
Djibouti, **433-434**
   academic libraries, **433**
   special libraries, **434**
DOBIS/LIBIS, **51, 54, 88, 250, 404, 771, 779, 790-791, 793-795, 802-803, 807, 811-812, 816, 878, 892, 894-896, 912**
Document delivery
   See Interlibrary loan
Documentation, **1, 91, 163-172, 236**
   encyclopedias, **160**
Documentation centers
   directories, **190, 192, 195**

   management, **273**
Doha Public Library, **762**
Ebla's royal archives, **963**
Ebla's royal libraries, **964-965**
Ecole des Sciences de l'information (Morocco), **711-712**
Education
   See Professional education
Egypt, **4, 435-438, 517**
   academic libraries, **4, 41, 435-437, 439-440, 494-495**
      history, **439-440, 494-495**
   Alexandria Library
      See Alexandria Library
   archives, **472**
   art libraries, **512**
   bibliographic control, **436, 473**
   bibliographic services, **473**
   bibliometric studies, **474**
   children's literature, **475-476**
   clinical information, **489**
   continuing education, **513**
   Creswell Library of Islamic Art and Architecture, **509**
   disabled, information services for the, **483**
   ENSTINET
      See Egyptian National Scientific and Technical Information Network
   foreign libraries, **436**
   government offices, information services in, **486**
   information policy, **477-478**
   information services, **203, 241, 477-486, 491-492, 517**
   information storage and retrieval, **487-488**
   information systems, **489-492**
   interlibrary loan, **493**
   Islamic libraries, **494-495**
   library cooperation, **329**
   library history, **435-436**

microform materials and services, **498**
mosque libraries, **435-436, 494-495**
museums, **499**
Nag Hammadi Library, **510**
national libraries, **4, 435-436, 473, 500-503**
networks and networking, **329**
online information retrieval, **488**
professional education, **284-285, 435-436, 496-497, 513-515, 517, 544**
public libraries, **4, 435-436, 504-505**
  Alexandria Library, **443-446, 451-457, 459, 462, 464-465, 469-471**
  development of, **504-505**
publishers and publishing, **339, 475, 506-507, 672**
research libraries, **443-446, 451-457, 459, 462, 464-465, 469-471**
resource sharing, **329**
school libraries, **4, 435-436**
science literature, bibliometric analysis, **474**
serials, **508**
socio-economic development, role of libraries in, **484**
special collections, **509-510**
special libraries, **4, 435-436, 511-512**
STARS
  See Scientific and Technical Archiving System
training of staff, **513-515, 517**
union lists, **508**
Egyptian Academy of Scientific Research and Technology, **492**
Egyptian National Scientific and Technical Information Network (ENSTINET), **437, 477, 479, 485, 487**
Empirical research, **13**

See also Research methods
Encyclopedias, **160**
Ethics, **173**
Fatimids
  See Islamic libraries; Libraries—history
FID Regional Organization for North Africa and the Middle East (FID/NANE), **194**
Fihrist, al- (Ibn al-Nadim), **119**
Fihrist, al- (Index), **668**
Filing rules, **184**
Finance, **5**
General International Standard Bibliographic Description for Monographic Publications (ISBD/G), **108**
General Organization of the Alexandria Library (GOAL), **464**
Girl's College of Arts (Saudi Arabia), **885**
Government publications, **175**
  evaluation, **174**
Guides
  See also under individual topics
Gulf Cooperation Council
  See Arabian Gulf countries
Gulf Organization for Industrial Consulting (GOIC), **395**
Gulf War, **36**
Gulfnet, **404, 430, 660, 829, 839, 847, 891**
Handicapped
  See Disabled, information services for the
Horizon, **51, 54**
Hospital libraries, **368**
Hypertext systems, **251**
Ibn al-Nadim, **119**
ICARDA library, **367**
IFLA
  See International Federation of Library Associations and Institutions

SUBJECT INDEX 337

Imam Mohammad Ibn Saud
    Unibersity, **802, 885**
Indexes, **261**
    evaluation, **185**
    importance of, **261**
Indexing, **85, 91, 97, 127, 176-188,
    233, 238-239, 244, 261**
    automatic, **182, 238-239**
    evaluation, **176-177, 182**
    importance of, **261**
    information retrieval, and, **247**
Industrial information networks,
    324
Information, **19-20**
Information centers, **29, 189-197,
    303**
    aid to, **194**
    directories, **190, 192**
    management, **273**
    role in professional education,
        303
Information infrastructure, **36**
Information marketing, **29**
Information networks, **206**
    See also Networks and
    networking
Information policy, **5, 16, 198-200**
    conferences, **198**
Information processing language,
    181
Information profession, **27**
    literature review, **27**
Information resources, **11, 33**
Information retrieval
    See Information storage
    and retrieval
Information science, **1, 22-24, 26**
Information service centers, **195**
    See also Information
    centers
    directories, **190, 192**
Information services, **6, 10-12, 17,
    201-224, 241, 248**
    audiovisual materials, **18**
    bibliographies, **202**
    citation analysis, **74**
Information storage and retrieval,
    170-172, 176, 180, 231-248

experimental, **238-239**
evaluation, **182**
socio-cultural aspects, **16**
technical aspects, **48, 53, 86,
    97, 100-101, 103, 129,
    254**
Information systems, **170, 233,
    238-240, 249-256**
    design, **255**
    development, **256**
    evaluation, **255**
    management, **276**
Information technology, **209, 292**
    conferences, **209**
Information transfer/transmission,
    201, 328, 340
Institute of Arab Belles Lettres
    (Tunisia), **979**
Institute of Diplomatic Studies,
    Ministry of Foreign Affairs
    (Saudi Arabia), **920**
Institute of Public Administration
    (Saudi Arabia), **885, 915**
Institute of Research and Study on
    the Arab and Muslim World
    (IREMAN), **170**
Institute of the Arab World
    See Institut du Monde
    Arabe
Intellectual life, **25**
    bibliographies, **68**
    conferences, **9**
Intellectual property
    See Copyright
Interactive multimedia, **251**
Interlibrary loan, **257-258**
INTERLOAN, **862**
International Airports Project,
    Ministry of Defence and
    Aviation, Saudi Arabia, **916**
International Communications
    Agency (US, Saudi Arabia),
    808, 915
International Federation of Library
    Associations and Institutions
    (IFLA)
    conferences, **126, 129**
International organizations, **29**

International Serials Data System (ISDS), **87**
International Standard Bibliographic Description (ISBD), **86-87, 90, 102**
International Standard Bibliographic Description for Monographs (ISBD/M), **100-101, 106**
International Standard Bibliographic Description for Non-Book Materials (ISBD/NBD), **99**
International Standard Book Number (ISBN), **63**
Internet access and use
   school libraries, in, **357**
Iraq, **4, 516-521**
   academic libraries, **4, 41, 516, 519-520, 522-526**
      administration and management, **542**
      indexes and indexing, **533**
      library users, **523**
      user education, **545**
   administration and management, **542**
   archives, **57**
      study and teaching, **527**
   bibliographic description, **533**
   book publishing, **520**
   cataloging and classification, **528-529**
   CD-ROM services, **538**
   computers in libraries, use of, **535**
   copyright, **530**
   database management systems, **531-532**
   development, **521**
   Dewey Decimal Classification, **528**
   documentation, **516**
   documentation centers, **518, 534, 536**
   indexing, **533**
   information policy, **521**
   information services, **241, 393, 516-518, 534-538**
   information storage and retrieval, **532, 538**
   information systems, **531-532, 539-541**
   integrated library systems, **539**
   intellectual property, **530**
   Internet access and use, **393**
   library history, **519-520**
      ancient **57**
   library instruction, **545**
   library legislation, **546**
   medical libraries, **529**
   national, libraries, **4, 519-520, 547**
   networks and networking, **520, 548**
   online information retrieval, **538**
   online information services, **525**
   printing history, **549**
   professional education, **285, 517, 519, 543-544**
   public libraries, **4, 519-520**
   publishers and publishing, **520**
   school libraries, **4, 519-520, 550**
   softwares, **541**
   special libraries, **4, 519-520, 529**
   training of staff, **517, 551**
   user education, **545**
Iraqi Centre for Scientific Documentation, **534, 536**
IREMAN
   See Institute of Research and Study on the Arab and Muslim World
ISBD
   See International Standard Bibliographic Description
ISBD (G)
   See General International Standard Bibliographic Description for Monographic Publications
ISBD (M)

SUBJECT INDEX 339

See International Standard Bibliographic Description for Monographs
ISBD (NBD)
   See International Standard Bibliographic Description for Non-Book Materials
ISBN,
   See International Standard Book Number
ISDS
   See International Serials Data System
Islam and librarianship, **259-260**
   See also Libraries—history
Islam Net, **322**
Islamic Development Bank, **915**
Islamic Foundation for Science, Technology and Development (IFSTAD), **46**
Islamic law
   bibliographies, **72**
Islamic libraries, **203, 261-271, 867-871, 918**
   directories, **265**
Islamic names,
   cataloging, **94**
Job descriptions **38**
Jordan, **4, 552-557**
   academic libraries, **4, 39, 41, 552, 554-556, 558-562**
      automation, **584**
      job satisfaction, **559**
      user services, **562**
   audiovisual materials, **563-564**
   automation, **565, 576**
   bibliographic control, **599**
   bibliographic databases, **568, 583**
   bibliographies, **566**
      national, **567, 571**
   biographical databases, **574**
   book distributors, **569**
   cataloging and classification, **103, 570-572**
      study and teaching, **570**
   cataloging in publication, **571**
   children's literature, **573**
   clippings, **574**
   computers in libraries, use of, **575-576, 580-581**
   conferences, **581**
   directories, **586**
   disabled, information services for the, **629**
   documentation centers, **555, 600**
   employment, **603**
   indexing, **571, 581**
   information needs, **556**
   information policy, **577**
   information services, **241, 555-556, 561, 578-579**
   information storage and retrieval, **571, 580-583**
   information systems, **581, 584**
   information technology, **626**
   institutional libraries, **629**
   integrated library systems, **581**
   interlibrary loan, **585**
   international organizations libraries, **625**
   library associations, **556, 587-589**
   library cooperation, **329, 590**
   library history, **552, 555-556**
   maps, **598-599**
      bibliographic control, **599**
   medical information, **630**
   medical libraries, **627**
   national bibliography, **567, 571**
   national libraries, **4, 552, 554-556, 600-601**
   networks and networking, **329, 556, 590**
   periodicals, **622**
   personnel, **602-605**
   polytechnic library, **628**
   professional education, **552, 555-556, 570, 591-597, 605**
      curricula, **593**

public libraries, **4, 552, 554-556, 606-610, 614**
publishers and publishing, **611, 623**
reference services, **579**
resource sharing, **329, 590**
school libraries, **4, 552, 554-556, 612-619**
serials, **620-623**
   history, **623**
   union catalogue, **620**
serials control, **621**
   legislation, **621**
special libraries, **4, 552, 554-556, 575, 618, 624-629**
staff, **602-605**
technical services, **571, 581**
training of staff, **597**
translation, **611**
use studies, **630**
Jordan Library Association (JLA), **556, 587-589, 591-592, 605, 625**
Journalism, **340**
Keyword indexing, **188**
   See also Indexing
   evaluation, **176-177**
King Abdulaziz City for Science and Technology, **802, 829, 833, 839, 847, 891**
King Abdulaziz University, **811, 832, 885, 915, 920, 926**
King Abdulaziz Women's College, **880**
King Fahd University of Petroleum and Minerals Library (KFUPM), **404, 771, 779-780, 786, 789-791, 793-796, 803, 805-807, 812, 816-817, 829, 837-838, 840-842, 845-846, 852, 856, 859-863, 865, 879, 882, 892, 894-896, 915, 922-925**
King Faisal Centre for Research and Islamic Studies, **917**
King Faisal Specialist Hospital, **915**
King Faisal University, **915**
King Saud University, **782, 843, 854, 885**
Knanazawa Institute of Technology, Japan, **254**
Kuwait,
   See also Arabian Gulf countries
academic libraries, **4, 39, 382, 384, 632-633**
   development, **384**
   information services, **382**
automation, **634**
bank libraries, **657**
bibliometric studies, **635**
business information services, **642**
business libraries, **657**
censorship, **636**
clinical information system, **643**
CD-ROM services, **646**
consultants, **633**
disabled, information services for the, **483**
employment, **651-652**
financial institutions, libraries in, **657**
Gulf War impact on information services, **637-641**
information network, **631**
information resources, **639**
information services, **241, 393, 637-641, 645-646, 654-659**
information storage and retrieval, **643-646**
information systems, **643-644**
Internet access and use, **393, 645**
library history, **632**
medical libraries, **658-659**
microfilm information system, **644**
national libraries, **4, 632**
online information services, **645-646**
personnel, **651-653**

SUBJECT INDEX 341

professional education, **285, 647-650**
  impact of Gulf War, **637**
public libraries, **4, 632**
school libraries, **4, 632, 654-656**
science literature, bibliometric analysis, **635**
special libraries, **4, 631-632, 634, 657-659**
staff, **652-653**
user training, **660**
Kuwait Institute for Scientific Research, **631**
Laws
  See Library laws
League of Arab States, **172**
Lebanese Documentation and Research Center, **669**
Lebanon, **4, 661-663**
  academic libraries, **4, 41, 662-665**
  publishing, **673-674**
  copyright, **666**
  directories, **670**
  government publications, **667**
  indexing, **668-669**
  intellectual property, **666**
  library history, **662**
  national libraries, **4, 662**
  professional education, **285, 662, 671**
  public libraries, **4, 662**
  publishing and publishers, **672-674**
  school libraries, **4, 662**
  special libraries, **4, 662**
Legal deposit, **304-305**
Legislation, **304-305**
Librarians
  directories, **272**
Librarianship, **3, 27, 31**
  See also Information profession
  literature review, **27**
Libraries, **19-20, 28, 31-33**
  ancient, **37, 57-58**
  development of, **22-23, 28, 36-37**
  encyclopedias, **160**
  guides, **8**
  history, **15, 21, 28, 32, 261-271**
  problems of, **29**
Libraries and mass media, **18**
Libraries and television, **18**
Libraries in education
  role of, **14**
Library administration
  See Administration and Management
Library and information science literature, **34**
Library associations, **30, 278**
  history and development, **278**
Library buildings, **279**
Library collections, **33**
Library cooperation, **36, 280-282, 320**
  Arabian Gulf countries, **399-400**
  conferences, **282**
Library education
  See Professional education
Library laws, **5**
  See also Legislation
Library legislation
  See Legislation
Library management
  See Administration and Management
Library networks
  See Networks and networking
Library of Congress Classification, **126, 129**
Library schools, **14, 293**
  directories, **293**
Library science, **1, 22-24, 26**
Library services
  See Information services
Libya, **675-680**
  academic libraries, **41, 676-677, 681**
  archives, **682**
  databases, use of, **683**

information seeking behavior,
    law students, **684**
information services, **679**
law information resources,
    684
library history, **676-677, 680**
national libraries, **676-677**
networks and networking, **686**
professional education, **285,
    676, 685**
public libraries, **676-677, 687**
school libraries, **676-677, 687-
    688**
serials, **689-690**
special libraries, **676-677, 684**
Ma'had al-Idarah al-'ammah
    (Saudi Arabia), **818-819, 836**
Madrasa libraries, **21**
Mansoura University Hospital
    (Egypt), **489**
Manuscripts, **236, 306-307**
    indexes, **306**
    indexing, **306**
    Islamic, **9**
    preservation, **364**
Mauritania, **691**
    academic libraries, **691**
    geographic information
        systems, **692**
    information systems, **692**
    library history, **691**
    manuscripts, **693**
    national libraries, **691**
    networks and networking,
    professional education, **691**
    public libraries, **691**
    school libraries, **691**
    special libraries, **691**
Mecca, **870-871**
Medical journals, **913**
Medical terminology database, **244**
Message of the Library, The
    (Jordan), **622**
Micro-AIRS (Arabic Information
    Retrieval System), **238-239**
Microform materials and services,
    308-311

MINISIS, **51, 54, 109, 250, 580,
    795, 802, 878**
Ministry of Finance and National
    Economy (Saudi Arabia), **915**
Ministry of Foreign Affairs (Saudi
    Arabia), **921, 927**
Ministry of Planning (Saudi
    Arabia), **915**
Mobile libraries, **312**
Morocco, **694-698**
    academic libraries, **41, 698**
    agricultural information, **718**
    archives, **699-700**
    bibliometric studies, **701**
    CD-ROM services, **706**
    documentation, **702**
    industrial information, **709**
    information use, **703**
    information marketing, **704**
    information services, **704-706,
        709**
    information storage and
        retrieval, **707-709**
    information systems, **704**
    interlibrary loan, **710**
    Internet access and use, **705**
    library history, **694-695, 698**
    library legislation, **420**
    manuscripts, **715-716**
    national libraries, **698**
    networks and networking, **717**
    professional education, **284-
        285, 698, 711-714,
        719**
        curriculum development,
            714
    public libraries, **698**
    royal archives, **699-700**
    school libraries, **698**
    serials, **718**
    special libraries, **696, 698-700**
    training of staff, **719**
Mosque libraries, **270-271**
    See also Libraries—
        history; Islamic libraries
Mosul University (Iraq), **522, 538**
Mu'assasat al-Bayt (Jordan), **624**
Mu'tah University (Jordan), **560**

SUBJECT INDEX 343

Muslim libraries,
    See Islamic libraries;
Libraries--history
Muslim names, **94, 103, 129**
    See also Personal names
Mustaniriyah University, al-, **543**
Nag Hammadi Library (Egypt),
    510
National bibliography, **62**
    See also Legal deposit
    need for, **70**
National Committee for
    Documentation in Tunisia,
    199
National Documentation Center of
    Morocco, **199**
National Documentation Center
    (Sudan), **199, 936, 951**
National Information and
    Documentation Center, Egypt
    (NIDOC), **199, 477, 491**
National information policy, **199**
    See also Information
    policy
National libraries, **4, 29-30, 313-316**
    feasibility study, **314**
National Research Council (Egypt),
    477
National Records Office (Sudan),
    943
Networks and networking, **199, 317-328**
    See also Library
    cooperation; Resource-sharing
    evaluation, **326**
News clippings
    See Clippings
Nilayn University (Sudan), **939**
Oman, **720-721, 727**
    See also Arabian Gulf
    countries
    academic libraries, **382, 384, 721-722**
        CD-ROM databases use
        in, **724**
        development, **384**
        information services, **382**
    agricultural information, **730**
    archives, **723**
    CD-ROM databases
        evaluation, **725**
        use, **724**
    censorship, **726**
    collection development, **726**
    health information services,
        729
    information services, **393, 729**
    Internet access and use, **393**
    library history, **720-721**
    medical information services,
        729
    national libraries, **721**
    online information retrieval,
        724
    online information services,
        724
    professional education, **721, 727**
    public libraries, **721, 728**
    school libraries, **721**
    special libraries, **721, 729-730**
Oman Centre for Traditional
    Music, **723**
Online catalog, **53**
Online cataloging, **51, 53-54**
Online information retrieval, **131, 133, 170, 219, 237, 323, 326**
    See also Information
    storage and retrieval
Online information services, **216, 244**
Oran (Algeria)
    public libraries in, **421**
Oran University
    See Universite d'Oran
Palestine, **731-734**
    academic libraries, **743**
    bibliographic control, **735**
    bibliographies, **736**
        national, **735**
    camp libraries, **731**
    censorship, Israeli, **737-738**
    church libraries, **739**
    documentation, **740-741**
    information services, **731,**

742, 750
  problems of, 742
 information systems, 743
 interlibrary loan, 585
 Islamic libraries, 744-745
 Jewish libraries in, 752
 library history, 732, 752-753, 755
 manuscripts, 746-747
 networks and networking, 743
 personnel, 734, 748-749
 private libraries, 751
 public libraries, 750-755
   employees, 748-749
 school libraries, 756-757
   conditions, 756
   information services, 757
 staff, 734, 748-749
Periodical literature, 362
Personal names, 94, 103-104, 129
Physically handicapped
  See Disabled, information services for the
Physics and Physicists, bibliometric analysis, 79
Preservation, 5, 269, 330, 342, 364
  See also Conservation
Printing history, 331-335
 conferences, 9
Professional education, 5, 27, 29-30, 283-303
  See also Information science; Library science; Professional training
  See also under individual countries
 curricula, 292, 295, 301
 development, 299-300
 impact of technology on, 288, 292
 planning, 297
 teaching methods, 302
Professional training, 294
Professional ethics
  See Ethics
Professional publications, 30
Public libraries, 4, 29-30, 336-337
Public relations, 338

Publishers and publishing, 7, 14, 339-341
Qatar, 758-762
  See also Arabian Gulf countries
 academic libraries, 39, 382, 384
   development, 384
   information services, 382
 geographic information systems, 764
 information services, 393, 758-763
 information systems, 764
 Internet access and use, 393
 library history, 758-760
 national libraries, 760-761, 766
 professional education, 765
 public libraries, 760, 762
 school libraries, 760
 special libraries, 760
Qatar National Library, 761
Qatar Public Library, 762
Qatar University, 765
Qatar University Library, 761
Rare books, 342
Readers and readership, 5, 25
Reference materials, 2, 374
 bibliography, 2
Reference services
  See Information services
Refugee libraries, 423, 618
Regional Institute of Informatic Sciences and Telecommunications of Tunis, 993
Research
 libraries and, 33, 42
Research centers
 guides, 8
Research Libraries Information Network (RLIN), 47
Research methods, 12-13, 343-344
 interviewing, 343
Resource sharing, 320, 329
 Arabian Gulf countries, 399-400, 404

SUBJECT INDEX 345

RLIN
   See Research Libraries Information Network
Salt school libraries (Jordan), **615**
Sarkis, Yusuf Ilyan, **81**
Saudi Arabia, **4, 767-776**
   See also Arabian Gulf countries
   academic libraries, **4, 39, 382, 384, 771, 775-791, 793-796**
      abuse of materials in, **786**
      automation, **778, 789-791, 793-796**
      collection development, **813-816**
      continuing education, **877, 882**
      cooperation among, **864, 866, 874**
      development, **384**
      effectiveness, **777**
      information needs, **784**
      information services, **382, 777, 784, 837, 922**
         employees' attitudes regarding, **927**
         impact of CD-ROM on, **856**
         user's attitudes towards, **923**
      information use, **828**
      interlibrary loan, **857, 859-866**
      networks and networking, **778, 892**
      personnel, **877**
      planning, **780-781**
      resource sharing, **813, 864, 866, 889-890**
      serials in, **911**
         automated control of, **912**
      staff, **877**
      standards, **783**
      training of staff, **877**
   administration and management, **819, 872**
   archives, **820**
   automation, **778, 789-797**
   bibliographic control, **798-799, 822-823**
   bibliographies, **801**
      national, **800**
   cataloging and classification, **802-809**
      audiovisual materials, of, **807**
      romanization of Arabic characters, **809**
      softwares, **802-803**
      theses and dissertations, of, **806**
   CD-ROM services, **796, 829, 840-842, 845-846, 852-853, 856, 859, 865, 878, 924**
   children's literature, **810**
   circulation, **811-812**
   collection development, **813-816**
   conferences, **767, 818-819**
   continuing education, **877, 882**
   database management systems, **817**
   documentation, **818-819**
   employment, **897**
   government libraries, **919-921**
   government publications, **799, 820-823**
      bibliographic control, **822-823**
      bibliographies, **823**
   hospital libraries, **858, 914**
   industrial information, **835**
   information centers, **768, 770, 878**
      automation, **792**
      computer use in, **797, 878**
   information industry, **824**
   information infrastructure, **773**
   information needs, **772-773**
   information policy, **824-825**
   information resources, **772,**

774, 837
   scientists' use of, **850**
information seeking behavior, **826-828**
   engineers, **827-828**
   scientists, **827-828**
   students, **826**
information services, **393, 774, 829-833, 837, 878-879, 886, 922**
   employees' attitudes regarding, **927**
   impact of CD-ROM on, **856**
   industrial, **835**
   medical, **875**
   science and technology, **834**
   user's attitudes towards, **923**
information storage and retrieval, **831-832, 836-842, 855**
information technology in, **771, 844-845, 848-850, 853**
information transfer, **844-845, 848-849**
interlibrary loan, **857-866**
   impact of CD-ROMs on, **865**
interlibrary loan systems, **862**
Internet access and use, **393**
Islamic libraries, **867-871, 918**
library cooperation, **858, 864, 866, 873-876**
library history, **775**
local area network installation, **796**
medical information services, **875**
medical journals, **913**
medical libraries, **914**
military libraries, **873**
national libraries, **4, 775, 886-888**
   role in socioeconomic development, **887**

networks and networking, **778, 889-893**
   interlibrary loans, **864, 866**
online catalog, **894-896**
online information retrieval, **771, 793, 838-842, 845, 853, 856, 878-879, 894-896**
online information services, **831-833, 851, 878-879**
personnel, **877, 897-899**
private libraries
   history, **868**
professional education, **285, 544, 775, 877-885**
public libraries, **4, 775-776, 867-871, 900-905**
   history, **868-869**
   information services, **905**
   planning, **903**
   problems, **901**
   reference services, **905**
   staff, **898**
publishing and publishers, **906-908**
   patterns, **906**
resource sharing, **813, 858, 864, 866, 889-890**
science and technology information, **834**
school libraries, **4, 775-776, 904, 909-910**
   role in education, **884**
serials, **911-913**
   medical journals, **913**
special libraries, **4, 775-776, 796, 858, 867-871, 873, 914-921**
staff, **877, 897-899**
training of staff, **776, 879-880**
user education, **854**
user studies, **923-927**
   CD-ROM services, and, **924**
   information sources, and, **926**
   online catalog, and, **925**

SUBJECT INDEX 347

women's colleges, **784**
Saudi Airlines, **915**
Saudi Arabian Consulting House, **915**
Saudi Arabian Industries Corporation, **915**
Saudi Arabia Monetary Agency, **915**
Saudi Arabian National Center for Science and Technology (SANCST) Database, **830**
School libraries, **4, 29-30, 345-360**
  administration and management, **355**
  automation, **348**
  cataloging and classification, **85**
  computers in, use of, **348**
  development, **345**
  Evaluation of services in, **356**
  impact on children, **354, 358, 360**
  indexing of library materials, **85, 352**
  information services, **350**
  Internet access and use in, **357**
  role in education, **346, 349, 359**
Scientific activity, **75**
Scientific and Technical Archiving System, Egypt (STARS), **487**
Sebha University Library (Libya), **681**
Serials, **361-363**
  acquisition, **361**
  bibliographic control, **363**
Shidyaq, Faris al-, **335**
Social Research Studies and Information Center (Saudi Arabia), **768**
Solar energy information, **65**
Somalia, **928-930**
  academic libraries, **930**
  archives, **931-932**
  cataloging and classification, **933**
  information infrastructure, **928**

information policy, **928**
information services, **929**
library history, **930**
national libraries, **930**
professional education, **930, 934**
public libraries, **930**
role of libraries in socioeconomic development, **929**
school libraries **930**
special libraries, **930**
training of staff, **934**
Spain, Islamic libraries in
  See Islamic libraries; Libraries—history
Special collections, **364**
Special libraries, **4, 29-30, 365-368, 406**
  conferences, **406**
STAIRS, **51, 250**
Statistical surveys, **35**
Subject cataloging
  See Cataloging and classification
Subject headings
  See Thesauri
Subject indexing
  See Indexing
Sudan, **935-937**
  academic libraries, **39, 935-936, 938-939**
  archives, **940-944**
  bibliographic control, **936**
  consultants and consultancy, **945**
  documentation, **946**
  documentation centers, **936, 951**
  information management, **949**
  information services, **937, 947-948, 950, 953**
  information systems, **936**
  information technology
    impact on development, **949-950**
  international assistance, **936**
  library associations, **936**

library cooperation, **329**
library history, **935-936**
library legislation, **936**
national libraries, **935-936, 951**
networks and networking, **329**
professional education, **284-285, 935-936, 953-956**
public libraries, **935-936**
resource sharing, **329**
school libraries, **935-936, 952**
special libraries, **935-936**
training of staff, **953-956**
Sudan Library Association, **936**
Sultan Qaboos University (Oman), **722, 724-726**
Syria, **957-962**
    academic libraries, **41, 957, 959-961**
        international organizations, influence of, **957**
    ancient libraries, **963-965**
    archives (ancient), **963-965**
    archives (modern), **966**
    automation, **959**
        impact of, **959**
    bibliographies
        national, **957**
    cataloging and classification, **957**
    children's literature, **966**
    documentation centers, **957, 962**
    information services, **959, 962**
    library associations, **957**
    library development, **959**
    library history, **957, 959-961**
    library legislation, **957**
    manuscripts, **968**
    national libraries, **957, 959-961, 968-974**
    personnel, **959**
    professional education, **285, 959-961**
    public libraries, **957, 959-961**
    school libraries, **957, 959-961**
    serials, **975**
    special libraries, **957, 959-961, 976**
    staff, **959**
    training of staff, **957**
Syrian Library Association, **957**
Technical services, **47, 53, 84, 86, 97, 100-101, 103-104, 129, 254**
    See also Cataloging and classification
Telecommunication, **209, 319**
    conferences, **209**
    policy, **209**
Thesauri, **117, 369-376**
    computerized, **375**
    construction of, **369, 371-375**
    problems of developing, **371**
    terminology selection for, **376**
Training
    See Professional training
Translation, **328**
Transliteration, **54, 115, 377**
Tulkarm Public Library (Jordan), **606**
Tunisia, **977-983**
    academic libraries, **41, 978, 980-981**
    archives, **984-986**
        conferences, **984**
    bookselling, **987**
    computers in libraries, use of, **988**
    documentation centers, **988-989**
    information centers, **989**
    information processing system, **982**
    information services, **978, 981, 989-991**
    information storage and retrieval, **988**
    information technology, **992-993**
    Internet access and use, **991**
    library cooperation, **993**
    library history, **978, 980-981**
        ancient, **978**
    library legislation, **420**

national libraries, **978, 980-981, 983, 998-1000**
    automation, **1000**
networks and networking, **983, 994**
personnel, **1001**
professional education, **284-285, 978, 980-981, 995-997**
public libraries, **978, 980-981, 983**
resource sharing, **993**
school libraries, **978, 980-981**
special libraries, **978-980-981**
staff, **1001**
training of staff, **996**
Tunisian National Library, **979, 983**
Umayyads
    See Islamic libraries; Libraries—history
Umm al-Qura University, **885**
United Arab Emirates, **1002-1005**
    See also Arabian Gulf countries
academic libraries, **382, 384, 1002-1004, 1006**
    development, **384**
    equipment, **1005**
    information services, **382**
health information services, **1008-1009**
information services, **393, 1002, 1004, 1007-1009**
Internet access and use, **393, 1007**
library history, **1003-1004**
medical libraries, **1008-1009**
public libraries, **1002-1004**
school libraries, **1002-1004**
special libraries, **1002-1004, 1008-1009**
United Arab Emirates University Libraries, Al-Ain, **1005-1006**
Uniterm subject indexing, **180**
Uniterms, **180**
Universite d'Oran (Algeria), **419, 424**
University libraries
    See Academic libraries
University of Bahrain, **428-430**
University of Jordan, **558, 562**
University of Juba (Sudan), **956**
University of Tunis, **979**
University of Yarmouk (Jordan), **584**
Use studies, **76, 80**
User services
    See Information services
Users, **33**
VTLS, **51**
Warka', al-, **539**
Yemen, **1010-1011**
    academic libraries, **1011**
    directories, **1010**
    information services, **393**
    Internet access and use, **393**
    library history, **1011**
    national libraries, **1011**
    public libraries, **1011**
    school libraries, **1011**
    special libraries, **1011**
Zahiriyyh Library, al- (Syria), **969**
Zarqa' Municipal Library (Jordan), **614**

About the Compilers

LOKMAN I. MEHO is a Ph.D. candidate at the School of Information and Library Science, University of North Carolina, Chapel Hill.

MONA A. NSOULI is Head Librarian, Institute for Palestine Studies, Beirut, Lebanon.

ISBN 0-313-31098-X

HARDCOVER BAR CODE